A Union of Peoples

A Union of Peoples

Europe as a Community of Principle

PAVLOS ELEFTHERIADIS

OXFORD
UNIVERSITY PRESS

OXFORD
UNIVERSITY PRESS

Great Clarendon Street, Oxford, OX2 6DP,
United Kingdom

Oxford University Press is a department of the University of Oxford.
It furthers the University's objective of excellence in research, scholarship,
and education by publishing worldwide. Oxford is a registered trade mark of
Oxford University Press in the UK and in certain other countries

First Edition published in 2020
Impression: 1

Published in the United States of America by Oxford University Press
198 Madison Avenue, New York, NY 10016, United States of America

British Library Cataloguing in Publication Data
Data available

Library of Congress Control Number: 2019955611

ISBN 978–0–19–885417–3

Printed and bound by
CPI Group (UK) Ltd, Croydon, CR0 4YY

To Leonidas, Iris & Pericles

Preface

This book offers a general theory of European Union law. It proposes a theory of European Union law that I shall call progressive internationalism. I believe that the best political and legal philosophy of the European Union sees the EU as a global model of ambitious international cooperation based on sharing power, while at the same time recognizing the equal sovereignty of its members.

This reading is controversial. Most scholars tend to view the European Union as a federation in the making. They interpret its doctrines as matters of constitutional law. They say that not only power but also sovereignty is being shared among the member states. I cannot agree with these views. As I will argue, the key to understanding European Union law is the important distinction we make in law and in politics between the principles that apply to a state and those that apply to a union of states.

This distinction gives rise to two distinct domains of legal doctrine: that of constitutional law and that of public international law. These are taught as separate subjects at university and are normally practised by specialist practitioners. But the distinction is based on substantive differences. The principles and assumptions of constitutional law do not apply to public international law and vice versa. I argue that this distinction is important for European Union law. If one reads more carefully the Treaties and the case law of the Court of Justice of the European Union the picture that emerges is of an area of law that approximates international law, not constitutional law. This is a view explicitly taken by the Court of Justice of the European Union, which has said that 'the EU is, under international law, precluded by its very nature from being considered a State'.[1] The European Union is not a state in the making but an international union of self-governing states, a creation of public international law, or the law of nations, in its most progressive form.

It must follow, in my view, that the fundamental principles of the European Union are principles of the law of nations. Just like any other international or domestic institution, the EU does not have a fundamental or basic law in the form of a constitution. Its basic laws are the treaties among the member states. The body of legal principles establishing the EU's main institutions, their powers, and their limits are to be found exclusively in these international treaties. The substance of these principles is international, not constitutional. International law provides a somewhat different framework of principle, which applies primarily to the relations between states, not to state institutions and their relations to citizens.

[1] Opinion 2/13 on accession to the ECHR, 18 December 2014, par. 156, ECLI:EU:C:2014:2454

Of course, this does not mean that the substantive obligations created by EU law are weak or optional. On the contrary, they are serious limitations on the powers of the member states. Yet the way in which they bind is international, not constitutional. Or so I will argue in the pages that follow.

A second aim of this book is to illustrate the analytical power of a distinct approach to law, which I defended a few years ago, which I call constructivism or the practical theory.[2] I take issue with the dominant 'legal positivist' theory of law and mode of legal scholarship. My view, which follows arguments made by Ronald Dworkin and Nigel Simmonds, is that legal doctrine and legal practice are manifestations of our ordinary moral judgment.[3] Law is not a hierarchical order of rules that has a foundation in a set of facts. It is not based on a 'rule of recognition' or a 'basic norm' as Kelsen, Hart, and other theorists who endorse legal positivism have claimed. As I will argue, the positivist view invites a certain confusion in the legal interpretation of the European Union, because under the legal positivist analysis EU law has to have an empirical foundation in some kind of disposition or conduct. It is only when we see law with the lenses of this theory, that EU law appears destined to compete and conflict with national constitutional law. This is because the positivist theory cannot distinguish between domestic and international law, since all law has, supposedly, the same empirical foundation.

Because the competition between domestic law and EU law is inevitable under the legal positivist framework, anyone who supports EU law and European integration must be willing to say that the European Union's 'rule of recognition' ought to be superior to the national 'rule of recognition'. Yet, this dilemma is as false as legal positivism itself. The law does not have this empirical foundation.

I proceed instead on the different assumption that a legal order is a construction of practical reason, based on historical decisions and available legal materials. My own view is that the best practical argument for law is formal. It constructs a theory of law from the materials of the equality of persons as free and equal citizens. Such a theory gives us a comprehensive theory of the distinction between as well as the relations between domestic and international law. A constitution is the manifestation of moral judgments about political legitimacy and constitutional justice.[4] Similarly, international law emerges as a moral judgment about the relation of states.

[2] Pavlos Eleftheriadis, *Legal Rights* (Oxford: Oxford University Press, 2008).

[3] See Ronald Dworkin, *Law's Empire* (London: Fontana, 1986); NigelSimmonds, *Law as a Moral Idea* (Oxford: Oxford University Press, 2007).

[4] I make this argument in Pavlos Eleftheriadis, 'Legality and Reciprocity' 10 *Jerusalem Review of Legal Studies* (2014) 1–17; Pavlos Eleftheriadis, 'Power and Principle in Constitutional Law' 45 *Netherlands Journal of Legal Philosophy* (2016) 37–56; Pavlos Eleftheriadis, 'Hart on Sovereignty' in Andrea Dolcetti, Luís Duarte d'Almeida, and James Edwards (eds), *Reading HLA Hart's 'The Concept of Law'* (Oxford: Hart Publishing, 2013) 59–80. I hope to be able to offer an extensive defence of this view in a forthcoming book, which I tentatively call *The Deliberative Constitution*.

Since they are judgments concerning different things, constitutional law and international law do not compete. Strengthening European integration does not undermine the constitutional integrity of states. In this sense, international law and constitutional law are mutually supportive. By obscuring this fact, legal positivism is the cause of many erroneous theories of EU law.

I use a relatively new term to describe the European Union. I call it a 'union of peoples', a term that I have been using for some time.[5] I derive it from John Rawls's discussion of international justice. I am particularly attracted by Rawls's suggestion that liberal societies must see each other as 'peoples', by which he meant 'agents of international society with moral character'.[6] Rawls outlined accordingly a set of moral principles of international law that applies specifically to such liberal societies (and does not apply in the same way to 'decent hierarchical societies', although it may be extended to them).[7] The rules of liberal 'peoples' are meant to recognize each other's commitment to constitutional government and lead to the idea of a 'Society of Peoples' as a 'realistic utopia'.[8] I believe that something similar should apply to our analysis of the European Union. We cannot see it merely as a project of independent states that face each other as partners in some economic transaction. Their mutual relations are moral in character. The European Union is an ethical project of democracies that recognize the moral standing of each other. Hence, what they are trying to achieve must be understood as a progressive form of internationalism, appropriate to liberal democracies. It should not be seen as the building of a new 'constitution' for a new state.

The same term 'union of peoples' has also been used by scholars who endorse a rather different theory, that of 'demoicracy'. My good friend and colleague at Oxford, Kalypso Nicolaïdis, a professor of international relations, speaks of a 'union of peoples who govern together, but not as one' in her powerful defence of a theory of 'demoicracy'.[9] These theorists believe that a doctrine of democracy can be applied to an international project of different democracies, without a single 'demos'. As I explain in Chapter 10, I disagree with this statement. But our ideas are very similar in almost every other way, and in the case of Kalypso Nicolaïdis

[5] See Pavlos Eleftheriadis, 'The Structure of European Law' 12 *Cambridge Yearbook of European Legal Studies* (2009–2010) 121, at 144; Pavlos Eleftheriadis, 'The Moral Distinctiveness of the European Union' 9 *International Journal of Constitutional Law* (2011) 695–713, at 710 and 713.

[6] John Rawls, *The Law of Peoples* (Cambridge, Mass.: Harvard University Press, 1999) 27.

[7] ibid 70.

[8] ibid 3–6.

[9] Kalypso Nicolaïdis, 'European Demoicracy and its Crisis' 51 *Journal or Common Market Studies* (2013) 351–69, at 353. See also Francis Cheneval and Kalypso Nicolaïdis, 'The Social Construction of Demoicracy in the European Union' 16 *European Journal of Political Theory* (2017) 235–60, at 240. Nicolaïdis said that the European Union was a 'union of states and peoples' in Kalypso Nicolaïdis, 'We the Peoples of Europe' 83 *Foreign Affairs* (2004) November/December Issue, 97–110, at 101. She uses the term 'union of peoples' in Kalypso Nicolaïdis and Janie Pelabay, 'One Union, One Story? In Praise of Europe's Narrative Diversity' in Alex Warleigh-Lack (ed.), *Reflections on European Integration* (London: Palgrave, 2008).

our ideas were perhaps formed together as we taught an inter-disciplinary seminar with Philippe van Parijs and David Miller a few years ago. Nevertheless, my argument is not that of 'demoicracy'. As I hope to make clear in the chapters that follow, I do not believe that we should see the European Union as a political body that should be compared to a state. I do not think that the language of 'demoicracy' is appropriate in the case of the EU. Even though the Union has legal personality in international law, it acts always as a body of the law of nations, always subject to the conditions and modalities of the law of international organizations. The distinction between a constitutional framework and an international framework remain, in my view, still fundamental. This is what my first chapter, on borders and authority, is meant to explain in particular. I return to the same theme in Chapter 10, the last chapter.

The arguments offered here are legal but also highly theoretical. They do not relate, at least not directly, to the current crisis of legitimacy of the European Union or the difficulties of Brexit,[10] or the existential crisis of the Eurozone, or of the deep economic and political crisis of the Eurozone periphery.[11] Although these questions are very significant and bring the abstract theories into context, the discussion offered here is intentionally removed from them. The questions faced by the European Union are questions of political principle and will last even when the current troubles fade away. The questions we ask are both legal and philosophical, because they are connected to our deepest assumptions about the state. We need to approach these questions as abstract questions of general principle. Whatever happens to the European project in the next few years, these abstract questions will remain relevant.

I hope that this book will contribute to this general theoretical debate, as well as assist current debates about the future of Europe. I approach these questions both from the point of view of abstract scholarship, and also from the point of view of the practising lawyer. Much of our most practical doctrines in EU law have theoretical depth, which is worth exploring both for its own sake and also for guiding courts and practitioners. These are our questions. How are we to understand international justice and justice within the European Union? What are our duties as citizens of member states as well as of the European Union? How far can a member state share its authority without losing its self-government? Does the European Union impede domestic democracy? These are some the questions that this book seeks to answer.

Athens, 20 December 2019

[10] For my views on Brexit see Pavlos Eleftheriadis, 'Constitutional Illegitimacy over Brexit' 88 *Political Quarterly* (2017) 182–8.

[11] I have written extensively about Greece and its particular problems. See for example Pavlos Eleftheriadis, 'The Misrule of the Few: How the Oligarchs Ruined Greece' *Foreign Affairs*, November/December, 2014; Pavlos Eleftheriadis, 'Only a New Political Order Will Rescue Greece', *Financial Times*, 27 May 2012.

Acknowledgements

I am grateful to the Faculty of Law at the University of Oxford for granting me research leave in Michaelmas Term 2012, Trinity Term 2014, and Michaelmas Term 2017 in order to work on this book. I am also grateful to the Principal and Fellows of Mansfield College for providing research leave at the same time as well as moral and material support at all times.

Some chapters were presented over the years at various places including at Boston College, the European University Institute, New York University, University College London, King's College London, Cambridge University, the British Institute of International and Comparative Law in London, the Free University of Amsterdam, the University of Athens, and Tallinn University. I am grateful to all the participants for their suggestions and criticism. I benefited in particular from conversations with Tony Arnull, Richard Bellamy, Francis Cheneval, Dimitris Chrysochoou, Gareth Davies, George Gerapetritis, Christos Hadjiemmanuil, Mattias Kumm, George Letsas, Massimo La Torre, Vlad Perju, Andrea Sangiovanni, Robert Schutze, Takis Tridimas, Neil Walker, Steve Weatherill, Joseph Weiler, Lorenzo Zucca, as well as the late Neil MacCormick.

Some of the ideas presented here were first tried out in seminar I jointly taught in Oxford in Trinity Term 2012 and 2013 with Kalypso Nicolaïdes, David Miller, Cecile Fabre, and Philippe van Parijs, who enriched these ideas without necessarily agreeing with them. Other colleagues at Oxford have been generous with their comments and discussion. I am grateful in particular to Nick Barber, Paul Craig, Julie Dickson, Timothy Endicott, Stephan Enchelmaier, Michael Freeden, John Gardner, Grant Lamond, Dorota Leczykiewicz, Adam Perry, Sionaidh Douglas Scott, Alison Young, Paul Yowell, Jeremy Waldron, Derrick Wyatt, and Steve Weatherill.

I am also grateful to my various students over the years, especially those in my seminars for 'Constitutional Principles of the European Union', which I teach almost every year to the postgraduate students at the Faculty of Law at Oxford.

For many discussions on the financial markets, the EMU, banking, and monetary policy I am especially grateful to Hugo Dixon, Christos Hadjiemmanuil, Yannis Kassimatis, Andreas Koutras, Yannis Manuelides, Dimitris Vayanos, and Jamie Whyte. My research visit to the Bank of Greece in 2017–2018 was invaluable for me in order to understand how little I knew, and still know, about banking. I am grateful to Heather Gibson, Christina Tsochatzi, Olga Stamatopoulou, Yannis Stournaras, and Yannis Mourmouras.

If it wasn't for all these people and institutions and many others, this book would not have been possible. I am very grateful to all of them.

Table of Contents

Table of Cases

INTERNATIONAL COURT OF JUSTICE

COURT OF JUSTICE OF THE EUROPEAN UNION

CZECH REPUBLIC

DENMARK

GERMANY

FRANCE

ITALY

UNITED KINGDOM

UNITED STATES

SPAIN

POLAND

1
The Jurisprudence of Integration

One of the most pressing and difficult questions raised by the European Union is the relationship between the founding Treaties of the European Union and the constitutions of the member states. European Union law is supposed to apply to the domestic legal order immediately and without any need for domestic incorporation. This entails an important adjustment of the domestic law-making process.

This adjustment is of constitutional significance for the legal order of the member states. This is because the member states of the European Union law have changed the method by which they normally make law in order to accommodate legal instruments made by the European Union. This was true even in the United Kingdom, as its Supreme Court explicitly acknowledged in the *Miller* judgment.[1] This internal constitutional adjustment raises not only questions of constitutional law but also important questions of political philosophy. How is this adjustment made? Is it a matter of European Union law alone? Or is it an internal process of the states? This is important because it tells us whether the member states remain independent or sovereign states. As many critics of the European Union have observed, the states' independence is challenged when their laws are made in cooperation with other states and outside their borders, or when a state may be outvoted in the Council of Ministers of the EU.

These questions are unique to the European Union. It is the only international organization that makes its own laws that entail direct effect and primacy. In the case of other treaties, for example that of the World Trade Organization or the North American Free Trade Agreement, these questions do not arise because these treaties do not create mechanisms of further law-making by their own institutions, nor do they provide for majority voting in that process. In addition, they are not supposed to operate in domestic law nor are they expected to displace domestic law.

It is different, however, with the European Union. It provides for powerful secondary legislation and enjoys both direct effect and supremacy in relation to domestic law. So every member state must have an answer to this question: 'how exactly and on what basis does the law of the European Union apply with direct effect within our legal order?' Each member state must have a constitutional theory of the European Union. The answer given by the Court of Justice of the European

[1] *R (on the application of Miller and another) v Secretary of State for Exiting the European Union* [2017] UKSC 5; [2017] 2 WLR 583, par. 81. I offered a detailed commentary on the case in Pavlos Eleftheriadis, 'Two Doctrines of the Unwritten Constitution' 13 *European Constitutional Law Review* (2017) 525.

A Union of Peoples. Pavlos Eleftheriadis. Oxford University Press (2020). © Oxford University Press.
DOI: 10.1093/oso/9780198854173.001.0001

Union (CJEU) in its early judgments was that European law not only has direct effect in the domestic jurisdictions but that it also has primacy. It prevails over any conflicting domestic laws because it was its own 'legal system' or a 'new legal order'.

In *Costa v ENEL* the Court said:

> By contrast with ordinary international treaties, the EEC Treaty has created its own legal system which, on the entry into force of the Treaty, became an integral part of the legal systems of the Member States and which their courts are bound to apply ... By creating a Community of unlimited duration, having its own institutions, its own personality, its own legal capacity and capacity of representation on the international plane and, more particularly, real powers stemming from a limitation of sovereignty or a transfer of powers from the states to the Community, the Member States have limited their sovereign rights, albeit within limited fields, and have thus created a body of law which binds both their nationals and themselves.[2]

These paragraphs have become the canonical statement of the place of European law in the member states. The Court of Justice is not simply saying that European Union law is another area of law. It says that it is its own 'legal system'. Since this legal system is regulated by its own principles, it must be taken to be 'autonomous'. The Court did not state this syllogism explicitly in *Costa* but made it apparent in later cases.[3] Stephen Weatherill has summarized this ambitious doctrine by saying that on the basis of these pronouncements: 'the Court's early judgments deliberately avoid the conventional discourse of international Treaties in order to create a founding myth of juristic novelty within the EU'.[4] It follows from this reasoning that the EU 'legal system' must, on account of its novelty, be 'autonomous' from the law of the member states as well as from international law.

[2] Case 6/64 *Flaminio Costa v ENEL* [1964] ECR 585.

[3] See for example Opinion 1/91, *Draft Agreement on the European Free Trade Association and the EEA*, [1991] ECR I-06079, ECLI:EU:C:1991:490, paras 30, 35, and 47. The autonomy of EU law has been mentioned in many other cases, most notably in Case C-459/03, *Commission of the European Communities v Ireland (MOXPlant)* [2006] ECR I—04635, ECLI:EU:C:2006:345, Joined Cases C-402/05 P and C-415/05P, *Yassin Abdullah Kadi and Al Barakaat International Foundation v Council of the European Union and Commission of the European Communities* [2008] ECR I-06351, ECLI:EU:C:2008:461, par. 282, Opinion 2/13 of the Court, *Accession of the European Union to the European Convention for the Protection of Human Rights*, 18 December 2014, ECLI:EU:C:2014:2454, par. 166 and in Case C-284/16 *Slovak Republic v Achmea BV* ECLI:EU:C:2018:158, Grand Chamber, 06 March 2018, paras 33–7. For many interesting essays on the idea of autonomy of EU law from international law see R. A. Wesseland and S. Blockmans (eds), *Between Autonomy and Dependence: The EU Legal Order Under The Influence of International Organisations* (The Hague: T.M.C. Asser Press/Springer, 2013).

[4] Stephen Weatherill, *Law and Values in the European Union* (Oxford: Oxford University Press, 2016) 224.

1.1 The 'Autonomy' of European Union Law

What does the 'autonomy' of EU law mean? The Treaties do not say anything about it. The Court of Justice of the EU created the principle partly on the basis of a provision of the Treaties that requires member states not to submit a dispute concerning the interpretation or application of the treaty to any method of settlement other than those provided for in the Treaty. The Court concluded that this provision gave the Court of Justice exclusive jurisdiction to hear all disputes arising among the member states.[5] This has been the standard theory of European Union law offered by the Court of Justice and has been stated in numerous judgments of the Court but also in scholarly commentary.[6]

Recently, this theory led the Court to hold that the proposed accession of the European Union to the European Convention of Human Rights (ECHR), may be contrary to the Treaties (even though accession to the ECHR is being envisaged by the Treaty of Lisbon, so that it is a dispute settlement 'provided for in the Treaties').[7] The most recent mention of autonomy came with the higher authority of the full court of the Court of Justice in its judgment on the revocability of the United Kingdom's Article 50 TEU notification of its intention to withdraw in *Wightman*, which arose as a preliminary reference from the Scottish courts:

> According to settled case-law of the Court, that autonomy of EU law with respect both to the law of the Member States and to international law is justified by the essential characteristics of the European Union and its law, relating in particular to the constitutional structure of the European Union and the very nature of that law. EU law is characterised by the fact that it stems from an independent source of law, namely the Treaties, by its primacy over the laws of the Member States, and by the direct effect of a whole series of provisions, which are applicable to their nationals and to the Member States themselves. Those characteristics have given rise to a structured network of principles, rules and mutually interdependent legal relations binding the European Union and its Member States reciprocally as well as binding its Member States to each other.[8]

[5] Opinion 1/91, *Draft Agreement on the European Free Trade Association and the EEA*, [1991] ECR I-06079, ECLI:EU:C:1991:490, par. 35.

[6] See for example J. H. H. Weiler and U. R. Haltern, 'Autonomy of the Community Legal Order—Through the Looking Glass' 37 *Harvard International Law Journal* (1996) 411.

[7] Opinion 2/13 of the Court, *Accession of the European Union to the European Convention for the Protection of Human Rights*, 18 December 2014, ECLI:EU:C:2014:2454. For discussion see Turkuler Isiksel, 'European Exceptionalism and the EU's Accession to the ECHR' 27 *European Journal of International Law* (2016) 565–89; E. Spaventa, 'A Very Fearful Court? The Protection of Fundamental Rights in the European Union after Opinion 2/13' 22 *Maastricht Journal of European and Comparative Law* (2015) 35–56.

[8] Case C-621/18, *Wightman et al. v Secretary of State for Exiting the European Union*, Court of Justice of the European Union (Full Court), 10 December 2018, ECLI:EU:C:2018:999, par. 45.

This is a standard account of the autonomy of EU law as set out in the case law of the court over the years. But what does it mean?

The clearest and most complete theoretical defence of the doctrine of the autonomy of EU law in legal theory was offered by René Barents, a scholar of European Union law who now sits as a judge at the General Court.[9] Offering a detailed and sophisticated analysis of the Court of Justice's case law Barents noticed that the Court's position entailed that 'in every respect this law exercises its legal effects in an independent manner' so that it was independent from any other 'legal system'.[10] For Barents, autonomy meant that Community law was valid and applicable in the territory of the member states exclusively by virtue of itself.[11] But why is EU law autonomous? Barents argues that: 'The indivisible nature of Community law follows from the concept of internal market which represents the foundation and therefore the *raison d'être* of this law, since only through the establishment and functioning of a single market can the objectives set out in Article 2 EC be attained.'[12] The Community was set up to create a single economy among the member states. This entails 'autonomy' as an inherent characteristic of EU law that requires the uniformity of its laws: 'Any attempt to explain Community law in terms of law derived from national legal orders inevitably results in a denial of its Community character and, as a consequence, in a denial of its *raison d'être*: to provide a common framework for the regulation of the single economy of the Member States.'[13] Barents' argument is that the autonomy of Community law is the result of its contents. It is not derived from a 'first constitution', is not the result of some constitutional 'revolution', or the actions of a supposed '*pouvoir constituent*'. Instead, it is a matter of what the Treaties *say*. Since Community law constitutes a self-referential system, its autonomous interpretation does not add to Community law an element which is not already present in its nature.[14]

Some scholars have made parallel arguments defending the idea of autonomy of EU law or similar principles of independence. Armin von Bogdandy has argued, for example, that the EU Treaties have a constitutional character such that they 'organize' the positive legal material, supply arguments for a creative application

[9] René Barents, *The Autonomy of Community Law* (The Hague, Kluwer Law International, 2004). See also René Barents, 'The Precedence of EU Law from the Perspective of Constitutional Pluralism' (2009) 5 *European Constitutional Law Review* 421. In his latest article Barents endorsed pluralism as the proper framework within which 'autonomy' was to be understood.

[10] ibid 253.

[11] ibid 253.

[12] ibid 217.

[13] ibid 271.

[14] ibid 314. Grainne de Burca also concluded that the case law of the court necessarily makes a connection between 'supremacy' and 'sovereignty' so that the Court derives the principle of supremacy from some kind 'of claim to sovereignty on behalf of the EC'; see Grainne de Burca 'Sovereignty and the Supremacy Doctrine of the European Court of Justice' in Neil Walker, *Sovereignty in Transition: Essays in European Law* (Oxford: Hart, 2003) 449, at 460.

of the law, and maintain law as 'social infrastructure'.[15] The basic treaty rules are norms of primary law having a 'normative founding function for the whole of the Union's legal order; they determine the relevant legitimatory (*sic*) foundations in view of the need to justify the exercise of public authority. "Founding" principles express an overarching normative frame of reference for all primary law, indeed for the whole of the Union's legal order.'[16]

Similarly, Robert Schütze has suggested that the 'normative force' of European law does not derive from public international law, but from the European Union Treaties themselves. He therefore concludes that the ultimate normative base within Europe—its 'originality hypothesis' or '*Grundnorm*'—are 'the European Treaties as such'.[17] Schütze is one of the few theorists to make claims clearly in relation to Kelsen's ideas about the hierarchy of legal norms.

In a similar way Koen Lenaerts, who is now the President of the Court of Justice, has spoken of the Union as an 'autonomous political authority'.[18] In a detailed study of the role of EU law in domestic legal systems, Lenaerts has drawn an analogy between the way in which EU law treats international law under a doctrine of 'monism' and the way in which it treats domestic law. He thus argued that the relationship between an 'autonomous' EU law and the law of the member states should follow a similar 'monist' theory. He said that 'it would appear odd if an ever closer Union, which as we know since *Van Gend en Loos* is an autonomous legal order going beyond the demands of ordinary international law, in practice gave less effect to its legal norms internally than it accords to norms of international law'.[19]

Nevertheless, the argument for the autonomy of EU law and for a 'monist' theory faces important obstacles. The first is that the European Treaties are treaties of public international law, as the CJEU often reminds us. They are already part of a legal arrangement that presupposes that the European Union is a creation of the

[15] Armin von Bogdandy, 'Constitutional Principles' in Armin von Bogdandy and Jürgen Bast (eds), *Principles of European Constitutional Law* (Oxford: Hart Publishing, 2007) 14–17. In the second edition of the work, the author speaks of 'founding principles' and does not use the title 'constitutional principles'. See Armin von Bogdandy, 'Founding Principles' in Armin von Bogdandy and JürgenBast (eds), *Principles of European Constitutional Law* (Oxford: Hart Publishing; Munich, Beck Publishing, 2010) 11. A shorter version of the 2010 essay has been published as Armin von Bogdandy, 'Founding Principles of EU Law: A Theoretical and Doctrinal Sketch' 16 *European Law Journal* (2010) 95.

[16] von Bogdandy, 'Constitutional Principles' 21.

[17] Robert Schütze, *European Constitutional Law*, 2nd edn (Cambridge: Cambridge University Press, 2016) 58.

[18] See Koen Lenaerts and D. Gerard, 'The Structure of the Union According to the Constitution for Europe: The Emperor Is Getting Dressed' 29 *European Law Review* (2004) 289.

[19] Case 26/62 *N V Algemene Transporten Expeditie Onderneming van Gend en Loos v Nederlandse Administratie der Belastingen* [1963] ECR 1. See Koen Lenaerts and Tim Corthaut, 'Of Birds and Hedges: The Role of Primacy in Invoking Norms of EU Law' 31 *European Law Review* (2006) 287–315, at 292. See further Koen Lenaerts and Marlies Desomer, 'Bricks for a Constitutional Treaty of the European Union: Values, Objectives and Means' 27 *European Law Review* (2002) 377–407; Koen Lenaerts, 'Constitutionalism and the Many Faces of Federalism' 38 *American Journal of Comparative Law* (1990) 205. For an illuminating summary of the position he calls 'European monism' see Mattias Kumm, 'Beyond Golf Clubs and the Judicialization of Politics: Why Europe Has a Constitution Properly so Called' 54 *The American Journal of Comparative Law* (2006) 505, at 513–15.

member states under international law. In what sense can EU law be 'autonomous' from the law that creates its founding documents?

Neil MacCormick, who in addition to being a leading philosopher of law also participated in the drafting of a new European Constitution as a Member of the European Parliament, observed that the idea of the autonomy of EU law does not fit at all well with the Treaties. He noticed that the effective legislature for the Community is the Council of Ministers, 'whose members are identifiable only by reference to the place they hold according to state-systems of law'. MacCormick also observed that 'the process of constitutional amendment for both Union and Community remains a process of treaty-making among member states'.[20] MacCormick concluded that the position that the legal orders of the member states are intended to 'retain validity' only through the mediation of EU law was questionable.[21]

Indeed, this is something that has now been confirmed by the Court of Justice of the EU. In *Wightman* the Court ruled that by explicitly providing a process for the unilateral withdrawal of a member state from the European Union, the treaties recognized the 'sovereign' right of a member state to withdraw.[22] The Court concluded that: 'The revocation by a Member State of the notification of its intention to withdraw, ... reflects a sovereign decision by that State to retain its status as a Member State of the European Union, a status which is not suspended or altered by that notification (...), subject only to the provisions of Article 50(4) TEU'.[23] It follows that member states remain sovereign while they are members of the European Union. But if they are sovereign, then their relations with one another must be matters for public international law, which is based on the idea of state sovereignty. The court further said that the independence of the member states follows from the values of liberty and democracy which are common values in the EU.

These values require the independence and reciprocity of the members as states as follows:

> As is apparent from Article 49 TEU, which provides the possibility for any European State to apply to become a member of the European Union and to which Article 50 TEU, on the right of withdrawal, is the counterpart, the European Union is composed of States which have freely and voluntarily committed themselves to those values, and EU law is thus based on the fundamental premise that each Member State shares with all the other Member States, and recognises that those Member States share with it, those same values ...[24]

[20] Neil MacCormick, *Questioning Sovereignty* (Oxford: Oxford University Press, 1999) 117.
[21] ibid.
[22] Case C-621/18, *Wightman et al. v Secretary of State for Exiting the European Union*, Court of Justice of the European Union (Full Court), 10 December 2018, ECLI:EU:C:2018:999, par. 56.
[23] ibid par. 59.
[24] ibid par. 63.

The court concludes that on the basis of these general values, it would not be lawful to prevent a member state to change its mind after giving notification, so that 'given that a State cannot be forced to accede to the European Union against its will, neither can it be forced to withdraw from the European Union against its will'.[25] If there was any doubt on that point, it must have been dispelled by the Court's explicit reference to the Vienna Convention on the Law of Treaties (VCLT), which confirms beyond any doubt that the EU treaties rely on the independence of the member states on the same basis as ordinary public international law.[26]

The second hurdle to the idea of autonomy of European Union law is that the treaties themselves say nothing about it. It is possible to read the provisions on the single market without any reference to absolute primacy and without the EU law's 'autonomy'. Bruno de Witte has, thus, criticized the apparent 'circularity' of the doctrine of supremacy of EU law.[27] He observed that: 'the view that supremacy does not set EC law completely apart from the general body of international law finds additional support in the continuing two-dimensional character of supremacy: it is a legal reality only to the extent that national courts accept their "mandate", and the practice shows that this acceptance, so far, is selective and generally based on the national courts' own constitutional terms'.[28] De Witte also noted that the arguments of the Court of Justice about the 'special nature of the European Community' may have been 'overstated', and that its arguments were 'needed more to convince the national judicial interlocutors of the Court than to justify the formulation of the principles themselves'. [29] So Barents' argument that the substance of the treaties leads to autonomy is difficult to accept, especially since the treaties provide for the heavy dependence of EU law on domestic political, judicial, and administrative processes, something which Barents accepts but dismisses as immaterial.

Many other theorists reject the doctrine of autonomy, on similar grounds.[30] It was therefore not a surprise that when the CJEU invited academics to reflect on the

[25] ibid par. 65. At the same time the court affirmed the doctrine of the 'autonomy' of EU law, at par. 45.

[26] ibid paras 70–1. A detailed analysis of the Vienna Convention was also offered by the Advocate General's Opinion in the case, ECLI:EU:C:2018:978. At paras 77–85, Advocate General Campos Sanchez-Bordona noted the EU was not party to the VCLT nor were all of the member states, but argued that since the 'Treaty on European Union is an international treaty between States and, at the same time, the constituent instrument of an international organisation (the European Union)' it could be subject to the VCLT. He concluded that in order to fill the lacunae in Article 50 TEU, 'there is nothing to preclude recourse being had to Article 68 of the VCLT, even though it does not reflect, *stricto sensu*, a rule of customary international law'.

[27] Bruno De Witte, 'The Nature of the Legal Order' in Paul Craig and Grainne de Búrca (eds), *The Evolution of EU Law* (Oxford, Oxford University Press, 1999) 177.

[28] ibid 209.

[29] ibid 208. For some of the more recent complexities, see Anthony Gerard, 'Me and My Shadow: The European Court of Justice and the Disintegration of European Union Law' 31 *Fordham International Law Journal* (2008) 1174; Paolisa Nebbia, 'The Double Life of Effectiveness' 10 *Cambridge Yearbook of European Legal Studies* (2007–2008) 287.

[30] See for example T. Schilling, 'The Autonomy of the Community Legal Order: An Analysis of Possible Foundations' 37 *Harvard International Law Journal* (1996) 389, Bruno de Witte, 'European Union Law: How Autonomous Is its Order?' 65 *Zeitschrift für Öffentliches Recht* (2010) 141; Piet

fifty years of the judgment in *Van Gen den Loos*, which first set out the doctrine of a 'new legal order', a distinguished expert in EU law expressed scepticism towards the 'autonomy 'of EU law. On that occasion Ingolf Pernice spoke of EU law's 'embedded autonomy', politely rejecting the most direct consequences of the doctrine as it had been originally set out by the Court.[31]

More importantly perhaps than any scholarly rejection, no national court has accepted the idea of the 'autonomy' of EU law as set out by the Court of Justice. As we shall see in greater detail in Chapter 3, all national courts have taken an entirely different view. They say that European Union law exists because of domestic law and through each state's constitutional process.[32] The most famous rejection of the Court's theory of 'autonomy' of EU law was given by the German Federal Constitutional Court in its judgment on the Maastricht Treaty, the treaty that moved the European Economic Community into the further integration of the 'European Union' and created the architecture of the common currency.[33] The case was a challenge by a Mr Brunner of the Federal law amending the German constitution so as to enable the Federal Republic to accede to the Maastricht Treaty. The judgment is highly abstract and technical, because it concerns the possible compatibility of the new treaty with the 'unamendable' core articles of the German Constitution. But in the course of its long judgment the Court makes it clear that EU law operates both politically and legally by virtue of national law and is in no sense 'autonomous': 'It is the law approving accession to a community of States which provides democratic legitimation, both of the existence of the community of states itself and of its powers to take majority decisions which bind the member States.'[34]

The German Constitutional Court also said that neither citizenship nor the European Parliament make the EU itself democratically legitimate. And in one of most controversial parts of the judgment, the Court concluded that for democracy 'not to remain merely a formal principle' it requires that 'the citizen who is entitled to vote must be able to communicate in his own language with the sovereign authority to which he is subject'.[35] As we will see later, these doubts are also echoed in

Eeckhout, 'Human Rights and the Autonomy of EU Law—Pluralism or Integration?' 66 *Current Legal Problems* (2013) 169–202.

[31] Ingolf Pernice, 'The Autonomy of the EU Legal Order–Fifty Years After Van Gend', in A. Tizzano, J. Kokott, and S. Prechal (eds), *50ème Anniversaire de l'arrêt Van Gend en Loos, 1963–2013* (Luxembourg: Office des publications de l 'Union européenne, 2013) 55–80, at p. 66.

[32] For the reaction of the national courts in summary see Stephen Weatherill, *Law and Values in the European Union* (Oxford: Oxford University Press, 2016) 228–47. For the interesting argument that the process creates a 'coordinate' constitutional order see Charles Sabel and Oliver Gerstenberg, 'Constitutionalising an Overlapping Consensus: The ECJ and the Emergence of a Coordinate Constitutional Order' 16 *European Law Journal* (2010) 511.

[33] *Brunner*, 89 BVerfGE 155; published in English in [1994] 1 CMLR 57.

[34] ibid 37.

[35] ibid par. 41. Some of the most extreme aspects of this judgment have been moderated in the much more nuanced later judgment of the German Constitutional Court in *Honeywell*, BVerfG, 2BvR 2661/06.

other national courts, although not perhaps in precisely those terms. But the Court raises here the question of the political nature of the EU and its ability to inspire trust or provide adequate institutions of participation.

In their own incremental way the English courts have also reached the view that European Union law applies domestically only through the national legislation that incorporates it. They have accepted the primacy of EU law, but only on the basis that domestic law requires it. In order to make this work they created the novel idea of 'constitutional statutes', or statutes that have constitutional significance and can only be repealed explicitly by parliament, but cannot be ignored—or 'impliedly repealed'—by later acts of parliament, as Dicey's original doctrine had assumed.[36] The United Kingdom Supreme Court held in the landmark *Buckinghamshire* (or '*HS2*') decision of 2014 that EU law becomes law in the United Kingdom through the operation of and subject to the United Kingdom constitution.[37] The Court rejected the submission that EU law applied autonomously in the United Kingdom and explained that EU law was dependent on domestic law:

> Contrary to the submission made on behalf of the appellants, that question cannot be resolved simply by applying the doctrine developed by the Court of Justice of the supremacy of EU law, since the application of that doctrine in our law itself depends upon the 1972 Act. If there is a conflict between a constitutional principle, such as that embodied in article 9 of the Bill of Rights, and EU law, that conflict has to be resolved by our courts as an issue arising under the constitutional law of the United Kingdom.[38]

There is nothing surprising in this doctrine. All other national courts have ruled that the effect of EU law depends on national constitutional law. The national courts and the Court of Justice are therefore caught in some kind of jurisprudential impasse. The Court of Justice believes in 'autonomy'. The national courts do not.

Commentators have long said that this is merely an academic disagreement without real practical application. Recently, however, a real constitutional conflict emerged, with potentially catastrophic consequences for the Union. This was the

[36] For the constitutional dimensions of the role of EU law in the United Kingdom see Pavlos Eleftheriadis, 'Two Doctrines of the Unwritten Constitution' 13 *European Constitutional Law Review* (2018) 525.

[37] *R (Buckinghamshire County Council and others) v Secretary of State for Transport* [2014] UKSC 3, 1 WLR 324, par. 206 (Lord Neuberger and Lord Mance, with whom Lady Hale, Lord Kerr, Lord Sumption, Lord Reed, and Lord Carnwath agreed). For an analysis see Paul Craig, 'Constitutionalizing Constitutional Law: HS2' (2014) *Public Law* 373. The doctrine has been restated and refined in *R (on the application of Miller and another) v Secretary of State for Exiting the European Union* [2017] UKSC 5; [2017] 2 WLR 583; [2018] AC 61.

[38] *R (Buckinghamshire County Council and others) v Secretary of State for Transport*, par. 79. This judgment clarified some things left uncertain by the judgment which for the first time confirmed the primacy of the EU Treaty over UK Acts of Parliament in *R v Secretary of State for Transport, Ex p Factortame Ltd (No* 2) [1991] 1 AC 603.

challenge to the Eurozone's emergency measures, which were challenged before the German Constitutional Court. The Court expressed very strong doubts as to the legality of the Outright Monetary Transactions (OMT) programme of sovereign bond purchases by the European Central Bank (ECB).[39] Yet, the programme of purchases was key to the survival of the Eurozone. The German court put the survival of the Eurozone at risk, by suggesting that the Bank's programme was contrary to German and European law and that German authorities should not participate in it. The Court did not rule immediately on the issue, but made a preliminary reference to the CJEU asking it to provide an interpretation of the ECB's actions.

The case was politically very controversial because the German court seemed to be saying that in its view, Germany, which is the largest economy and greatest beneficiary of the Eurozone, had no responsibility for the Eurozone's deeply flawed architecture. If the ECB's actions were held unlawful, it was likely that the member states of the Eurozone's periphery would suffer grave economic consequences and might have been forced to leave the common currency. Nevertheless, the case was resolved when both the Court of Justice and the German Constitutional Court concluded that the OMT programme as announced did not violate EU or German law, so that the more controversial elements of the German Court's judgment were not put to the test.[40] Yet, the potential for conflicting judgments by the two courts raised a question of great constitutional significance: what happens if the courts cannot agree? What would have happened to the European Union, if on something of this significance the two courts came up with conflicting judgments? The question was not new, but it had never occurred in such a dramatic fashion.[41]

1.2 Legal Interpretations

The issue of the autonomy of EU law is important but also controversial and highly abstract. We need to examine it with the best theoretical tools we have. It is evident

[39] Federal Constitutional Court, *Gauweiler and Others v Deutscher Bundestag*, Case No. 2 BvR 2728/13, Order of 14 January 2014.

[40] Case C-62/14, *Peter Gauweiler and Others v Deutscher Bundestag*, ECLI:EU:C:2015:400 (Grand Chamber) 16 June 2015. For commentary see Federico Fabbrini, 'After the OMT Case: The Supremacy of EU Law as the Guarantee of the Equality of the Member States' 16 *German Law Journal* (2015) 1003. The German Constitutional court accepted the Court of Justice's reading of EU law, in Federal Constitutional Court, *Gauweiler and Others v Deutscher Bundestag*. Case 2 BvR 2728/13, Judgment of 21 June 2016. See Mehrdad Payandeh, 'The OMT Judgment of the German Federal Constitutional Court: Repositioning the Court within the European Constitutional Architecture' 13 *European Constitutional Law Review* (2017) 400–16.

[41] In the Danish *Ajos* case regarding age discrimination, the Danish Supreme Court refused to comply with a ruling of the Court of Justice. See Rass Holdgaard, Daniella Elkan, and Gustav Krohn Schaldemose, 'From Cooperation to Collision: The ECJ's *Ajos* Ruling and the Danish Supreme Court's Refusal to Comply' 55 *Common Market Law Review* (2018) 17–53.

that the ideas of a legal system of transnational law and of a constitutional order will be key to understanding how European Union law takes effect in domestic law. For a long time jurisprudence hesitated to engage with these questions. But in recent years many legal philosophers have sought to understand the Union's legal architecture in a theoretically systematic fashion. I will now turn to three legal theorists who have made substantial and distinctive contributions to this debate: Mattias Kumm, Julie Dickson, and George Letsas.

A standard way of describing the problem is by way of a choice between the primacy of the competing legal orders of national law and European Union law. The term 'legal order' is a term used by the Court of Justice. Although the Court has not made the link itself, the idea of a 'legal order' is often deployed by legal theorists along the standard way of understanding law as a 'system' of norms, as proposed by Kelsen and Hart. Mattias Kumm, for example, although not a friend of Kelsen's theory, has seen the question as one requiring the resolution of a 'constitutional conflict' between the supremacy of the national or the European legal order.

The conflict is constitutional, Kumm believes, because it involves the wholesale adoption of a general framework for the law of the European Union. Kumm has proposed that the question before the national courts was 'to construct an adequate relationship between the national and the European legal order on the basis of the best interpretation of the principles underlying both'.[42] Kumm's argument seems to be that the answer requires that we organize the relationship between two competing legal orders that have rival 'constitutions'. So he adds: 'The relevant question is, therefore: what is the interpretation of the relationship between national constitutions and the EU constitution that *best fits and justifies legal practices in the European Union, seen as a whole*?'[43] If the question is put in this way, as a constitutional conflict, it follows that there can only be three answers to it: either the European order prevails as a whole, or the national order prevails as a whole, or there is a stalemate.

These answers offer a rough and ready account of the three main groups of approaches to EU law, to which I will return in later chapters. The first is a 'federalist' view of EU law which as we have seen is reflected in much of the case law of the

[42] Mattias Kumm, 'The Jurisprudence of Constitutional Conflict: Constitutional Supremacy in Europe before and after the Constitutional Treaty' 11 *European Law Journal* (2005) 262–307, at 286.

[43] ibid. Kumm further says (ibid at p. 287): 'The question is therefore: what is the best understanding of the relationship between national and European constitutions, given the normative commitments underlying legal practice in Europe, seen as a whole? What is the interpretation of the relationship between national constitutions and the EU constitution that *best fits and justifies legal practices in the European Union*? What makes national and European constitutional practices in Europe appear in their best light?' My disagreement with Kumm is not on the pursuit of a justificatory argument. I agree that this is the way of legal reasoning. My disagreement is in his framing of the question. As I will argue below, the question is not one of a 'constitutional conflict', since EU law does not make constitutional claims. EU law is only part of the law of nations, which complements the national constitution and manages the interdependence of states. If there is friction and inconsistencies with national law, this is a matter of substantive law, not a matter of constitutional architecture.

CJEU and the writings of Barents, Lenaerts, and von Bogdandy.[44] The second is the 'constitutional' approach, as we find it in some domestic courts and something Neil MacCormick called 'pluralism under international law'.[45] The third view is that of 'pluralism' or 'radical pluralism', which is close to Kumm's own solution, which he calls 'constitutionalism beyond the state'.[46] Kumm's outline of the problem as one of a choice concerning the primacy of legal orders captures something of these distinctions. But not everyone accepts Kumm's framework of analysis, even if the division into these approximate theories or families of theories of EU law remains largely true.[47]

Julie Dickson offers a rival analysis of the same problem. Dickson's suggestion is that we do not need to choose between rival legal systems, as proposed by Kumm and others.[48] She proposes that the idea of a legal system is fluid, so that the disagreement between 'federalist', 'constitutional', and 'pluralist' theories may concern the construction of different accounts of a legal system and not the relevant primacy of one system among others. There may be political and moral reasons for departing from the standard account of the legal order or legal system that we apply to states.

Dickson suggests that our analysis of 'legal system' must be motivated by an evaluation of what states and transnational organizations are supposed to do. Criticizing Kelsen's idea of a 'Grundnorm' Dickson argues that 'legal systems cannot be studied in isolation from the political and societal organizations of which they are a part', so that 'a legal system is not a self-sufficient free-floating normative entity'.[49] She offers a sophisticated account of the legal system of the European

[44] For another sophisticated federalist reading of EU law see Robert Schütze, *From Dual to Cooperative Federalism: The Changing Structure of EU Law* (Oxford: Oxford University Press, 2009).

[45] The theoretical defence of this view is to be found in Neil MacCormick, *Questioning Sovereignty* (Oxford, Oxford University Press, 1999) and its detailed unfolding as an interpretation of EU law in Stephen Weatherill, *Law and Values in the European Union* (Oxford: Oxford University Press, 2016) 153–256.

[46] Kumm says that his view 'is committed to the rule of law but it does not insist on a clear source based hierarchical ordering of norms with an ultimate legal rule at its apex as suggested by dominant positivist accounts of law. It takes seriously fundamental rights, democracy, and subsidiarity as basic principles guiding legal practices, but it is not voluntaristic. It does not conceptually place the will of "We the People" centre stage. It takes seriously the idea of legal constraints guiding judicial decision-making—it is positivist in this weak sense—but it does emphasise the requirement for national courts to engage in politically aware general practical reasoning and principled judgment.' Kumm, 'The Jurisprudence of Constitutional Conflict' (n. 42) 305. Similar arguments are offered by John Erik Fossum and Agustín José Menéndez, *The Constitution's Gift: A Constitutional Theory for a Democratic European Union* (Lanham: Rowman & Littlefield, 2011); Richard Bellamy, 'Sovereignty, Post-Sovereignty and Pre-Sovereignty: Three Models of the State, Democracy and Rights within the EU' in Neil Walker (ed.), *Sovereignty in Transition: Essays in European Law* (Oxford: Hart, 2003) 167.

[47] Kumm divides up the theories into 'European monism', 'constitutionally tolerant dualism', and 'Common European Constitutionalism' in his 'Beyond Golf Clubs and the Judicialization of Politics: Why Europe Has a Constitution Properly so Called' 54 *The American Journal of Comparative Law* (2006) 505–30.

[48] Julie Dickson, 'Towards a Theory of European Union Legal Systems' in Julie Dickson and Pavlos Eleftheriadis (eds), *Philosophical Foundations of European Union Law* (Oxford: Oxford University Press, 2012)25.

[49] ibid 38.

Union, which is based on the way its courts work together to interpret the law in a spirit of openness and flexibility and not by a 'desire to dominate'.[50] Dickson proposes that the models set up by Kelsen and Hart may not have application to the EU, if the circumstances of transnational law have changed the substance of what we are observing. She proposes that the question of legal system is bound up with issues of political identity and self-determination.[51]

Others go even further. George Letsas believes that the very idea of a legal system as a hierarchical order of rules is mistaken in itself. He therefore takes issue with the description of the problem as a choice between rival 'systems'. If there are no 'legal systems' then there is no choice to be made between them. In Letsas' view the understanding of the problem as a conflict between 'systems' is flawed because it is based on the legal positivist model of law. Letsas refers to Kumm's analysis in particular and concludes that it 'is still hostage to legal positivism' because it assumes that 'law is a system of norms that may conflict and that it is contingent whether the system contains conflict rules'.[52] The theory favoured by Kumm—pluralism—relies on the idea of a 'rule of recognition' which produces the relevant list of enacted rules or norms that jointly make up the legal order, adjusting it simply for the position that rules of recognition conflict. So for a sophisticated positivist view 'when conflict rules contained in multiple rules of recognition do not converge, no legal norm settles how conflicts between legal norms are to be resolved, so we must look somewhere else, at morality'.[53]

Letsas believes that law is not a system of norms but a process of interpretation and deliberation, in the way described by Ronald Dworkin.[54] For this view the project of legal doctrine as well as the task of legal theory is directly moral, in light of relevant institutional practices that are open to interpretation. The idea of an institutional architecture is thus very different from that of a formal 'legal system'. As Dworkin put it: 'We construct a conception of law—an account of the grounds needed to support a claim of right enforceable on demand in that way—by finding a justification of those practices in a larger integrated network of political value.'[55] If we apply this idea to EU law, we will say that our interpretations need to find the

[50] ibid 48–9. She concludes: 'In order to be a legal system, then, I propose that something has to make a claim to normative self-determination. This claim, however, can come in many forms, including granting permission to another normative system to operate within the normative realm of the system making the grant, and even granting a permission for that second system's norms to prevail over the legal norms of the granting system under certain conditions.' ibid 50. Dickson rejects the simple and highly formal account of the legal system offered by Kelsen, Hart, and Raz.

[51] ibid 52.

[52] George Letsas, 'Harmonic Law: The Case Against Pluralism' in Julie Dickson and Pavlos Eleftheriadis (eds), *Philosophical Foundations of European Union Law* (Oxford: Oxford University Press, 2012) 77, at 104.

[53] ibid.

[54] See Ronald Dworkin, *Law's Empire* (London: Fontana, 1986); Ronald Dworkin, *Justice in Robes* (Cambridge, Mass.: Harvard University Press, 2007).

[55] Ronald Dworkin, *Justice for Hedgehogs* (Cambridge, Mass.: Harvard University Press, 2011) 405.

justification of claims of right into the domestic legal order that have some of their grounds in EU law. So Letsas invites us to look at EU law as a set of institutions that need justification in exactly this way, so as to become relevant to legal practice. Letsas argues that we should describe the question of the relation between EU law and constitutional law as one of ordinary interpretation or moral construction. The institutional setting does not suggest that there are two systems claiming their 'independence' of each other. There is only one 'system', or one domain of moral reflection and interpretation.

In Letsas' view 'nobody is to have the ultimate say on the constitutional issues that divide the CJEU and national courts because nobody can decide these issues: they are determined by objective moral principle'.[56] In this view the legal system of the EU is not 'autonomous' because no autonomous legal system exists anywhere in the world. Our legal interpretations are always interdependent.

This discussion between three highly original legal theorists helps perhaps to situate the question of the relations between EU and domestic law within the landscape of general jurisprudence. It is obvious that the questions they address have many dimensions and their disagreements are like equations with many variables. We shall return to these debates and to these alternative theories of EU law in Chapter 3, where I will argue that, with one important qualification, Letsas' approach is the correct one. But from this very brief introduction it becomes obvious that, irrespective of whether one endorses the sophisticated positivist framework seemingly endorsed by Kumm, the pragmatic account of the legal system endorsed by Dickson, or the deliberative and interpretive framework endorsed by Letsas, the relevant questions are multi-layered.

In complex ways all these legal theories turn one way or another on the political nature of the European Union. They all rely on the relevant moral and political principles that apply to its unique institutional structure. Whether one chooses the idea of conflict rules, of a flexible idea of a legal system, or the idea of law as interpretation, the legal architecture itself depends on the question of what the European Union is and what makes it *legitimate*.[57]

1.3 Political Interpretations

What is the political nature of the European Union and what are the values that underpin it? No one can approach these questions without reflecting on Europe's recent crisis of legitimacy. The financial crisis that started in 2008 brought about a deep loss of support for the project of European integration. Many people now

[56] Letsas, 'Harmonic Law' (n. 52) 107.

[57] I argued for this point in greater detail in Pavlos Eleftheriadis, 'The Idea of a European Constitution' 27 *Oxford Journal of Legal Studies* (2007) 1–21.

associate their own misfortunes with the opening up of borders to trade, finance, and immigration, the creation of the Euro, or of the opening up of the European Union to the countries of Easter Europe. This loss of faith has resulted in some remarkable electoral setbacks for those supporting the European Union. Britain voted to leave the European Union in 2016, which was bolstered by the general election result of Decembr 2019. Anti-European populist parties were also elected into government in Hungary, Poland, Greece, and ultimately Italy. Similar parties secured a strong showing in France, the Netherlands, Austria, and Germany, although their progress seems to have stalled in the European elections of 2019.

These concerns are not new. Similar criticisms of the European Union were made in 2005, when electorates rejected the new 'European Constitution' in referenda held in France and the Netherlands. But the most recent loss of faith is deeper. It calls into question the fundamental reasons for having a European Union. The ideals of European integration are at risk. But what are they?

We must start by refining our question. What we are talking about is not a political utopia. We cannot hope to persuade everyone that the European Union is perfect in every way or that it leads to a perfect society. We do not have such a hope for domestic politics either. We aim at some balance between constitutional justice and social justice, even if we disagree both about ends and about means with our fellow citizens. The justification of political decisions works therefore without requiring unanimity in political or social affairs. This is why the relevant questions concern not only outcomes but also processes, where citizens are heard and become party to decision-making, even if ultimately their views are not endorsed. We are interested not just in consequences but also in institutions. This is why when we assess political institutions the most important question we ask is that of political legitimacy. How can the institutions of the European Union be legitimate?

Legitimacy is not popularity or justice or success in other things. But what is it and how does it relate to the European Union? The European Union's founders used to believe that its purpose was to bring about the eventual political union of Europe in a way that Joseph Weiler has called 'messianic'.[58] For the founders like Schumann, the 'ever closer union' was an end in itself. Nothing more was needed to be said, since integration was a noble aim, however long into the future it would have to be imagined. Other social ideals or ideals of justice were secondary to this unifying theme. This federalist dream still survives in some recent theoretical

[58] See J. H. H. Weiler, 'Deciphering the Political and Legal DNA of European Integration: An Exploratory Essay' in Julie Dickson and Pavlos Eleftheriadis (eds), *Philosophical Foundations of European Union Law* (Oxford: Oxford University Press, 2012) 137, at 146–56. Weiler says for example: 'But it is not just the rhetoric. The substance itself is messianic: a compelling vision which has animated generations of European idealists where the 'ever closer union among the peoples of Europe', with peace and prosperity as icing on the cake, constituting the beckoning Promised Land'; ibid at p. 146. The question of the precise self-interested motives of the founding states is, however, very complex. See for example Andrew Moravcsik, *The Choice for Europe: Social Purpose and State Power from Messina to Maastricht* (Ithaca: Cornell University Press, 1998) 86–158.

attempts to account for the European Union, for example in Guy Verhofstadt's arguments—that a united Europe will be much stronger and much more capable of addressing the challenges of our era.[59] Yet, all these arguments still seem to stumble on the unwillingness of leaders, as well as their voters, to contemplate the radical abandonment of existing models of state-centred government. Federalism seems either unattainable or unattractive.

Is there an alternative argument for the European Union in a continent troubled by the challenge of open markets, unpredictable migration flows, and great financial uncertainty? In one of the most widely read recent discussions of these big questions, Loukas Tsoukalis summarizes the loss of faith in the European Union as a problem of 'output legitimacy'.[60] Tsoukalis offers both concrete analysis and pragmatic proposals for addressing the crisis. His general view is that 'unlike nation states, Europe has very few shared myths and symbols and little common identity either to draw from'.[61] Tsoukalis' point is of course true and not new. It was also made a long time before the crisis hit by a leading scholar of nations and nationalism, Anthony D. Smith, who observed that the idea of 'Europe' still 'lacks a premodern past—a 'prehistory' which can provide it with emotional sustenance and historical depth'.[62] Tsoukalis relies on the continuing validity of these observations to conclude that the lack of national myths, symbols, and identity turn the issue of the legitimacy of European institutions into one of policy outcomes. The European project in general depends only on its 'capacity to deliver' he concludes. And as long as this remains true, 'the European project will be fragile' and 'its fragility becomes most obvious in times of crisis'.[63]

One cannot really disagree with this observation. The loss of 'output' legitimacy is certainly at the heart of the current loss of faith in the EU. There are ways in which the European Union has not delivered. But this may not be the core of the problem of the loss of legitimacy. It just makes worse a deeper worry, which was evident in the British referendum campaign. For many of the critics the EU fails not because its policies do not work, but because they exist. These critics say that such policies should not have been there in the first place. The criticism is that it is inappropriate that important social and political matters are decided by a supranational organization and not the states themselves. Some of the most salient arguments in the Brexit debate in the United Kingdom were those that spoke on political principle,

[59] See Guy Verhofstadt, *Europe's Last Chance: Why the European States Must Form a More Perfect Union* (New York: Basic Books, 2017); Daniel Cohn-Bendit and Guy Verhofstadt, *For Europe! Manifesto for a Postnational Revolution in Europe* (Munich: Carl Hanser Verlag, 2012).

[60] Loukas Tsoukalis, *In Defence of Europe: Can the European Project Be Saved?* (Oxford: Oxford University Press, 2016). For the distinction between 'input' and 'output' legitimacy see Fritz W. Scharpf, *Governing in Europe. Effective and Democratic?* (Oxford: Oxford University Press, 1999), ch. 1.

[61] Tsoukalis, *In Defence of Europe* (n. 60) 3.

[62] Anthony D. Smith, 'National Identity and the Idea of European Unity' 68 *International Affairs* (1991) 55–76, at 62.

[63] Tsoukalis, *In Defence of Europe* (n. 60) 3.

not on the attainment of policies. These critics say that the European Union not only lacked the symbols of statehood but that it is, in its nature, *antagonistic* to statehood.

This argument against the European Union, namely that the EU challenges the legal and political authority of states, was made with remarkable clarity as far back as 1991 by the British historian and journalist Noel Malcolm. In a powerful essay, which probably shaped the thoughts of many conservative activists, scholars, and politicians over the years, Malcolm argued that the arguments in support of European unity on account of the already happening increase in international interdependence in trade, finance, and regulation were wide off the mark. What was at issue with the EU, he thought, was not just the sharing of 'power' but the sharing of 'sovereignty', at least as the ultimate aim of the 'federalists'.[64]

Malcolm explained that sovereignty, conceived as political authority, was not 'power', and that whereas power could be shared, sovereignty could not. Whereas a nation may have to share power with its neighbours, it alone will remain sovereign over its decision to do so. He said: 'Sovereignty means constitutional independence, the exercise of plenary and exclusive political authority in a legal order. The idea that constitutional independence can be "pooled" is therefore an evident absurdity. Why do people believe in this idea, or say that they believe in it?'[65]

Malcolm put the argument in terms of 'sovereignty' but it can also be made with reference to the parallel idea of democracy. In his wide-ranging study *Democracy in Europe* the political theorist Larry Siedentop argued that the European Union was not equipped to take over democratic institutions from the states.[66] He wrote that as a result 'democratic legitimacy was at risk'.[67] Siedentop makes a distinct argument about the legitimacy of the EU. His challenge is not that the EU fails to deliver, but that it attempts to deliver in an area in which it should not be involved at all. By trying to intervene, it undermines sovereignty and therefore self-government.

Siedentop's argument seems to be that that without sovereignty there cannot be self-government and without self-government there cannot be democracy, and that without democracy there cannot be justice. In other words, Siedentop suggests that the project of integration does not merely affect delegated power, but it affects democracy itself. It undermines political legitimacy inside the member states. This is a challenge to the European Union's political legitimacy at its core. It suggests that what the EU seeks to do undermines the political institutions of the nation state, that the EU usurps powers that ought to belong strictly to states. This challenge is powerful because it is entirely abstract and principled. It does not depend

64 Noel Malcolm, *Sense on Sovereignty* (London: Centre for Policy Studies, 1991); reprinted in Martin Holmes (ed.), *The Eurosceptical Reader* (London: Palgrave, 1996) 342–67. See also Noel Malcolm, 'The Case Against "Europe"' *Foreign Affairs* (1995) March/April.

65 Malcolm, *Sense on Sovereignty* (n. 64) 25.

66 Larry Siedentop, *Democracy in Europe* (London: Penguin, 2000).

67 ibid 1.

on the success of populist movements—although some populist movements have sought to rely on it. The challenge would have the same validity even if the populist enemies of Europe disappeared tomorrow.[68]

A similar argument has also been used by the German Federal Constitutional Court in outlining the limits of European integration from the point of view of the German Constitution. In its judgment on the legality of the ratification of the Lisbon Treaty, the Court said that the states remain 'the masters of the treaties' and control the transfer of power from them to the European Union.[69] The Court insisted that one of the tests it will apply to the treaty was whether the further transfer of powers to the European Union affected the constitutional 'identity' of Germany according to its own constitution. It approved the Treaty of Lisbon, after it found it was not trying to amend the constitutional principles that are 'essential' to Germany.[70] It was not changing 'the identity of the constitution' or the essential principles of the Basic Law. The court said that, even though the German constitution is open to further European integration, it sets out its own limits to integration, that have to do with a core of self-government that cannot be surrendered to transnational processes. The Court specified that the areas where the constitution required self-government were: (a) the monopoly of force by the police and the army; (b) public revenue and public expenditure; (c) the social welfare state; and (d) decisions relating to culture, family, and education.

This argument concerning constitutional self-government raises a question of philosophical significance: can there be an international institution such as the European Union, which requires the intense sharing of power without causing at the same time the destruction of sovereignty? Is there a choice to be made between the EU and state sovereignty, as Noel Malcolm suggests? And if so, what should the choice be?

There are, I believe, three different ways to respond to Siedentop's 'self-government' question. The first is *federalism*. That is to say that for the good of Europe and its citizens the transition described by the German Constitutional Court ought to take place. A federal state is a goal to be endorsed by progressive peoples. Since sovereignty can only reside in one place, that place must be Europe as a whole. Federalist theories normally ground this argument on the value of European *unity*. They speak, for example, about the merits of an integrated European 'public sphere' or about the great value of renewed European strength in international affairs.[71] A focal point of such federalist proposals is sometimes the

[68] The argument also has a less sceptical variation, namely that the European Union as it is does not challenge democracy but a misguided further integration might do so in the future. This more moderate critique of the European Union appears in Larry Siedentop, *Democracy in Europe* (London: Penguin, 2000).

[69] *Re the Lisbon Treaty*, 2 BvE 2/08 et al., Federal Constitutional Court, 30 June 2009, par. 335. The judgment is available in English translation at http://www.bverfg.de.

[70] ibid par. 218.

[71] See Jürgen Habermas, *The Crisis of the European Union: A Response, trans. by Ciaran Cronin* (Cambridge: Polity Press, 2012).

'Brentano Constitution', which was the original constitution proposed in 1952 by Heinrich von Brentano, which could still serve as a blueprint for a 'United States of Europe', providing for a parliament, a senate, an executive council, and a court of justice.[72] When the CJEU speaks of the 'autonomy' of European Union law and of the nature of its legal order as a 'new legal order' of international law, for the benefit of which the member states have limited their sovereign rights, it appears to prepare the ground for a transformation of this kind.[73]

The second response is *statism*. This answer would agree with the distinctions and the conclusions drawn by Malcolm and the German Constitutional Court. Statists would say that it is too early to think of such a radical transformation. If we wish to respect the goods of self-government and the principle of democracy, we must protect states, national independence, and constitutional identity.[74] Statists are not necessarily hostile to the European Union. Although some of them would want it dismantled (for example, most advocates of Brexit in the United Kingdom would wish it destroyed), some would argue that it cannot proceed any further with integration than it has so far. Statist theories can accept a role for the European Union, while at the same time emphasizing the virtues of community, memory, and cohesion as essential ingredients of democratic self-government. Statism has often at its core an ideal of a single political community with a high degree of cultural and moral coherence.

What the federalist and the statist response have in common is that they share the democracy dilemma as described by Larry Siedentop and the German Court. One has to *choose* between conventional democracy and integration. The first model—the federalist—chooses integration. The second model—the statist—chooses conventional democracy. Both federalists and statists can rely on the philosophical point that political authority must be single, comprehensive, and supreme. This fundamental presupposition of constitutional law—shared by authors as diverse as Hobbes, Rousseau, and Max Weber—points to something like an impossibility theorem for the European Union: if states are to retain their authority, they must impose their primacy over the Union. For their authority to survive, the idea of the supremacy of EU law must be false. In the course of his discussion on sovereignty and power Noel Malcolm wrote: 'Each time we delegate the exercise of important areas of our authority to "Europe", we do not lose sovereignty or become less sovereign; we merely become more likely to lose our sovereignty. We become closer, that is, to the moment when our constitution will be remodelled into a subordinate part of a federal constitution.'[75]

[72] See Guy Verhofstadt, *Europe's Last Chance: Why the European States Must Form a More Perfect Union* (New York: Basic Books, 2017) 259–68.

[73] Case 26/62 *N V Algemene Transporten Expeditie Onderneming van Gend en Loos v Nederlandse Administratie der Belastingen* [1963] ECR 1.

[74] For a discussion of 'statism' see Brian Barry, 'Statism and Nationalism: A Cosmopolitan Critique' in Ian Shapiro and Lea Brilmayer (eds), *Global Justice* (New York: New York University Press, 1999) 12–66.

[75] Noel Malcolm, 'Sense on Sovereignty' (n. 64) 27.

It must be obvious by now that the questions of the most appropriate legal theory of the European Union and the question of the most appropriate political theory are closely connected. The two domains go hand in hand: legal theories derive from political assumptions and political theories look to legal structures as they do in the arguments made by Noel Malcolm, Larry Siedentop, and the German Constitutional Court. It is possible, however, to articulate a third answer.

I will argue in the chapters that follow that we can indeed reject the sovereignty dilemma. The stark dilemma between sovereignty and integration is false. The European Union is not yet a federal state, nor is it on the way to becoming one. But we can have deeper integration, including in fiscal and social matters as well as consequent obligations of solidarity, without threatening the self-government of states or by transferring their sovereignty to a new political community. International law has the means of separating clearly the two projects of promoting European integration and, at the same time, of protecting self-government. This can happen without compromise or confusion. This is a new legal and political view of the EU which I call 'internationalism'. This is the view I defend in this book.

1.4 Internationalism

The 'internationalist' account of the European Union is a relatively recent argument. It is also a complex argument, because it relies on a distinction between issues of power and issues of sovereignty. The first step in setting out an internationalist theory of the European Union would be to show that an institutional structure is conceivable that combines the unity of the European Union with the unity of the member state.[76] This is not a middle ground between federalism and statism, because it rejects what both theories believe to be a 'sovereignty dilemma'. For the internationalist view Noel Malcolm's stark contrast between sovereignty and integration is false. The internationalist view advocates a different ideal, namely that of an 'internationalist state', or a state that retains its sovereignty while recognizing its deep commitments and duties to those outside it in a spirit of reciprocity and cosmopolitanism. Such a state retains sovereignty, while sharing power.

An important challenge for this argument is to show how constitutional law and the law of nations can co-exist without incoherence.[77] This is the task of this book.

[76] This idea is often put in terms of 'pluralism', but in my view the term 'internationalism' is more successful. See for example Neil Walker, 'The Idea of Constitutional Pluralism' 65 *Modern Law Review* (2002) 317, where both 'radical pluralism' and 'hierarchical constitutionalism' are rejected. See also Neil Walker, *Intimations of Global Law* (Cambridge: Cambridge University Press, 2017) p. 203. I discuss pluralism in detail in Chapter 3.

[77] For a thorough analysis of the European Union as an international legal 'experiment' see Bruno de Witte, 'The European Union as an International Legal Experiment' in Grainne de Burca and J. H. H. Weiler (eds), *The Worlds of European Constitutionalism* (Cambridge: Cambridge University Press, 2012) 19–56. I defended a similar view in Pavlos Eleftheriadis, 'The Idea of a European Constitution'

It is to show that the European Union can be a community of principle combining democratic sovereignty with transnational integration without compromising constitutional principle. The European Union does so by being internationalist both within itself and in what it expects from the member states to do. I shall argue that the European Union is a union of peoples and a community of principle, whose legal architecture is that of the law of nations and whose justifying principles are international principles addressing the proper relations among states.

In the fertile phrase used by Stephen Weatherill, the Union's basic purpose is the 'management of the interdependence' of states.[78] Properly conceived, the EU is a project of states that come to share powers for certain purposes as a union of democratic peoples, without committing themselves to a future federal union or constitutional unity and without compromising the institutions or the integrity of their democratic self-government. The starting point of internationalism is the recognition of the moral value of democracy in the context of the institutions of free political communities or states. This must be in my view the point of departure for any theory of the political legitimacy of the European Union.

27 *Oxford Journal of Legal Studies* (2007) 1; Pavlos Eleftheriadis, 'Pluralism and Integrity' 23 *Ratio Juris* (2010) 365.

[78] Stephen Weatherill, *Law and Values in the European Union* (Oxford: Oxford University Press, 2016) 3. Anand Menon has made the same point: 'Far from being some kind of state in the making, the Union is a tool of existing states.' See Anand Menon, Europe: *The State of the Union* (London: Atlantic Books, 2008) 213.

2
Borders and Legitimacy

Larry Siedentop's critical argument about democracy in Europe relies on some important assumptions about the nature of democracy that need further scrutiny. Siedentop identifies a political and moral risk for democracy in the fact that the European Union is eroding the member states' traditional powers.[1] He argues that transferring these powers weakens democracy. But why is this so?

The argument presupposes that the state and at least some of its democratic institutions have inherent moral value that cannot be replicated at the level of the European Union. Siedentop's argument appears to be that only states can meet the social and cultural presuppositions that make self-government possible. This means that borders matter for democracy. If states are to be independent and self-governing, they must have borders that set them apart from other states and from international institutions.

Many philosophers take the precisely opposite view on the moral value of sovereignty. They say that the supposed dilemma between self-government and integration is not a real one. The scope of our moral concern must be universal. Borders do not matter, they say, at least not in that way. All our moral values are realizable in a multiplicity of ways, including by way of transnational actions and institutions that leave borders fluid. This is what 'globalist' or 'cosmopolitan' philosophers say: all persons in the world are equal in claiming equal concern and respect, irrespective of where they happen to be. The same values apply to all irrespective of borders. It follows that there is nothing special about the state and the relations of citizenship. Larry Siedentop, Noel Malcolm, and the German Constitutional Court must be wrong to say otherwise, these views suggest.

These arguments are not always favourable to the European Union. If borders are irrelevant, then we must see the European Union with some scepticism, since it does not remove borders. It merely joins some states together to remove internal borders in order to create new external ones. This is why many have spoken of a 'fortress Europe'.[2] But some globalists believe that ultimately the European Union may be a good thing towards a cosmopolitan distribution of resources, since it is a welcome step in the right direction of dismantling borders among states. The EU for them means that more people can assist other people within a larger framework

[1] Larry Siedentop, *Democracy in Europe* (London: Penguin, 2000).
[2] See Simon Caney, *Justice Beyond Borders: Global Political Theory* (Oxford: Oxford University Press, 2005) 264.

A Union of Peoples. Pavlos Eleftheriadis. Oxford University Press (2020). © Oxford University Press.
DOI: 10.1093/oso/9780198854173.001.0001

of institutions.[3] Others believe that the overcoming of borders is a good thing, because it creates new 'checks and balances' between insiders and outsiders.[4]

Some theorists believe that the relevant values can also—and at the same time—be pursued by European institutions without conflict. Miguel Maduro has argued, for example, that it is 'artificial to assume the national polity as the natural jurisdiction for full representation and participation'.[5] He argues in favour of an alternative conception of constitutionalism for which 'constitutional ideals are not dependent on nor legitimized by the borders of national polities'.[6]

In Mattias Kumm's version of the same argument, member states and the European Union are capable of promoting the same 'republican' constitutional principles, so that they can both 'promise to respect, protect and promote the realization of the republican principles of human rights, democracy and the rule of law, while respecting national identities'.[7] Kumm's pluralism proceeds from the assumption that the breaking down of conventional state understandings is a good means for achieving republican ends. The European Union may be seen as a better vehicle for achieving justice. Rather than defend statism and borders, a genuine concern for justice and moral values defends European—and if possible, global—unity. Or so this argument goes.

Is this a good argument? It is a complicated one, touching on both legal theory and political ideals. But these issues are fundamental to any theory of the European Union, even if they take us far afield from European Union law. Federalist and statist theories rely on some version of these arguments about the ethical standing of states and the relevance of borders to legitimacy. This is the necessary prologue to any theory of the European Union or any other transnational political organization. We need to resolve now this fundamental theoretical question: how exactly are borders related to political legitimacy?

2.1 Borders and Authority

Some philosophers take the view that borders are, in principle, morally irrelevant. They believe that all persons in the world have a moral duty to assist others, as long as they have the economic means of doing so. I shall call this the 'global view' of

[3] This is the view, for example, of Helder de Schutter, 'The Solidarity Argument for the European Union' in Frank Vandenbroucke, Catherine Barnard, and Geert de Baere (eds), *A European Social Union After the Crisis* (Cambridge: Cambridge University Press, 2017) 68–91.

[4] Nico Krisch, *Beyond Constitutionalism: The Pluralist Structure of Postnational Law* (Oxford: Oxford University Press, 2010) 86.

[5] Miguel Poiares Maduro, 'Europe and the Constitution: What if this Is as Good as it Gets?' in J. H. H. Weiler and Marlene Wind (eds), *European Constitutionalism Beyond the State* (Cambridge: Cambridge University Press, 2003) 74–102, at 101.

[6] ibid 74.

[7] Mattias Kumm, 'Beyond Golf Clubs and the Judicialization of Politics: Why Europe Has a Constitution Properly so Called' 54 *The American Journal of Comparative Law* (2006) 505, at 528.

justice. For this view borders do not change moral responsibility.[8] The global view of justice supports the attitude that the European Union is just another agent in our collective effort to bring about the good or to achieve justice. So it is close to a view implied by the observations of Loukas Tsoukalis, namely, that if European Union's policies solved more of people's problems then the legitimacy of the EU would be improved or even restored.

The global view of justice goes further. It takes borders to be irrelevant anywhere in the world, not just within the European Union. The difference is this. In the European Union member states have willingly removed some of the effects of borders in their mutual relations by way of the founding treaties. In some respects borders are invisible and the movement of persons and goods across borders is 'frictionless', in the language recently used in the United Kingdom. The global view is therefore quite a different position, because it suggests that the tests of justice apply irrespective of intentionally hard borders.

Examining this more ambitious view will assist us in understanding the European Union in the following way. If borders are irrelevant anywhere in the world, even against the fact that states have not lifted some of the restrictions they entail, then they must also be irrelevant in the European Union, where the states agreed to set up a single market. If the background global view of justice is right, then our attitude towards the European Union should be globalist in the same way.

Other philosophers reject the 'global view' and draw a distinction between global and domestic justice. They believe that state borders and political institutions create a morally significant distinction between fellow citizens and others. They say that a duty of social justice is only owed to citizens and to those who are in a similar position to citizens, e.g. long-term residents, but not outsiders. Those outsiders are not morally indifferent of course. They do have equal moral standing as persons. But duties to them are not a matter of the same claim of distributive justice that fellow citizens have. Outsiders only have a distinct duty of humanitarian assistance, which requires action not whenever there is significant surplus or inequality, but only when what is at stake is something much more important, such as survival itself. This is the view taken by John Rawls in his *Law of Peoples*.[9] I shall call this the 'political view'.

[8] See for example Simon Caney, *Justice Beyond Borders: A Global Political Theory* (Oxford: Oxford University Press, 2005); Charles Beitz, *Political Theory and International Relations*, rev edn (Princeton: Princeton University Press, 1999); Peter Singer, *The Life you Can Save: How to Do your Part to End World Poverty* (New York: Random House, 2010), Peter Singer, 'Famine, Affluence and Morality' 1 *Philosophy and Public Affairs* (1972) 229–43. The literature is now vast and includes very many other important contributions by leading political and legal philosophers.

[9] See for example John Rawls, *The Law of Peoples* (Cambridge, Mass.: Harvard University Press, 1999); Michael Blake, 'Distributive Justice, State Coercion, and Autonomy,' 30 *Philosophy and Public Affairs* (2001) 257–96; Thomas Nagel, 'The Problem of Global Justice' 33 *Philosophy and Public Affairs* (2005) 113–47; Onora O'Neill, *Bounds of Justice* (Cambridge: Cambridge University Press, 2000); Samuel Freeman, 'The Law of Peoples, Social Cooperation, Human Rights, and Distributive Justice' 23 *Social Philosophy and Policy* (2006) 29–68; Francis Cheneval, *The Government of the Peoples: On*

The political view believes that borders matter for justice. It needs to explain what appears to be an inconsistency in its position. Although both views start from similar universalist premises about moral responsibility that extends in principle over the fate of all other human beings, the political view insists that distributive justice applies narrowly within a political society. But why should this be the case? Why does moral concern not entail a claim for a fairer distribution for everyone, as the globalist view suggests? The political view is thus criticized for this apparent contradiction, which could be due to an unwarranted bias towards people of a common background, i.e. people 'like us'. We need to properly expand our thinking, the globalists say, in order to see that the scope of social justice is global. If persons are to enjoy equal moral status, they should enjoy it everywhere in the same way. Or so the global view believes.

The most powerful defence of the political view focuses on the nature of the political relationship that ties citizens together. The political view relies fundamentally on the idea that the duties of social justice are not global but arise from the bond of citizenship. Because we act together in creating public laws that one way or another determine our lives in common and produce the fruits the cooperation, we have an equal claim over the profits of our cooperation. It is, in effect, a citizenship 'dividend'. Distributive justice arises, thus, from the circle of law-making and cooperation. This is the main thrust, for example, in the arguments of Thomas Nagel in support of Rawls' distinction between insiders and outsiders.[10] For Nagel the fact that we are joint creators of coercive public laws determines the scope of social justice.

In response to this argument a vibrant debate has arisen among political philosophers on the question of whether background institutions of coercion are necessary for distributive justice or not.[11] Who is ultimately responsible for bringing about global justice, whatever its requirements? Is it the international community as a whole or are the individual states to act on their own? Is the same duty binding on each individual separately as well in addition to any institution?

These questions are very important in practice, because the international community has, in fact, very few political institutions with which to deliver global

the Idea and Principles of Multilateral Democracy (New York: Palgrave Macmillan, 2011). The political view is shared by Thomas Pogge, whose distinct arguments are based on the causal link between domestic and global institutions and extreme poverty. See Thomas Pogge, *Politics as Usual: What Lies behind the Pro-Poor Rhetoric* (Cambridge: Polity Press, 2010); Thomas Pogge, *World Poverty and Human Rights: Cosmopolitan Responsibilities and Reforms*, 2nd edn (Cambridge: Polity Press, 2008). This list is highly selective.

[10] See Nagel, 'The Problem of Global Justice' (n. 9).

[11] See e.g. Michael Blake, 'Distributive Justice, State Coercion, and Autonomy' 30 *Philosophy and Public Affairs* (2001) 257–96; Anthony Julius, 'Nagel's Atlas' 34 *Philosophy and Public Affairs* (2006) 176–92; Andrea Sangiovanni, 'The Irrelevance of Coercion, Imposition, and Framing to Distributive Justice' 40 *Philosophy and Public Affairs* (2012) 79–110.

justice with any assurance of success.[12] Such institutions include the multilateral organizations, such as the United Nations, the World Trade Organization, and the World Health Organization, but does not include institutions with any presence in individual countries. International organizations do not have an executive arm, so to speak. They rely for almost everything on states. So even if we knew what the requirements of global social justice were, we would still be incapable of complying with them, if an executive arm of social justice was missing. Does this mean we would then have a separate duty to set up institutions with global reach?

As soon as we ask these questions, we are aware of their further political dimensions. If the duty of global justice shifts from the delivery of a just distribution as its ultimate *end*, to the duty of setting up institutions that are capable in principle to deliver those ends as the necessary *means*, what further safeguards do we need in order to set up just global institutions? Global political institutions must be fair and legitimate in principle, in exactly the same sense that domestic political institutions must be fair and legitimate. But what does this mean in a global context? Does the creation of the executive arm of global justice not itself raise questions of accountability, representation, and democracy? Are we now speaking of a 'global state' that would take over the functions of individual states, with a common legislature, judiciary, and executive? Shouldn't the availability or unavailability of institutions of global justice have an effect on the content of any duties of global justice in turn?

Here is an illustration of some of the associated problems with a purely international attempt to bring about the same ends, where states take it upon themselves to bring about the desired result. The constraints of legitimacy are here put differently but they are as demanding. If a certain international distribution were to be delivered through a manifestly unjust process of imposition, for example through colonial conquest, would not that distribution be, for that reason alone, unacceptable?[13]

The conclusion is inescapable. But if colonialism is always illegitimate and cannot be justified even if it hypothetically leads (against historical experience) to a better distribution of resources, why not consider other institutional arrangements as potentially illegitimate? Other forms of violation of the independence of self-governing states might also have the same effect of rendering otherwise desirable distributive outcomes morally unacceptable. Colonialism may be the most extreme case of a common wrong of *paternalism*. We could think of less serious violations along similar lines. For example, a government may bribe the officials of another country in order to achieve a good end (think of the scandals in the award of the football World Cup or of the Olympic Games to a developing nation,

[12] For the discussion of the problem of 'assurance' in international law and especially in the context of international trade, see Aaron James, *Fairness in Practice: A Social Contract for a Global Economy* (Oxford: Oxford University Press, 2012) 103–27.

[13] Some such examples are discussed in the excellent essay by Arthur Isak Applbaum, 'Forcing a People to Be Free' 35 *Philosophy and Public Affairs* (2007) 359.

for example). Or a foreign agent may infiltrate a government in order to bring about the right decision (think about the secret services of a democratic country secretly intervening in the political processes of an authoritarian country with misinformation and lies in order to bring about a fairer distribution of resources). The stain of illegitimacy would blight any distribution of wealth that resulted from such actions. And even a more benevolent enforcement of distributive pattern might also be illegitimate.

For example, a European Union initiative might be illegitimate if it happened through an unwarranted decision of the Court of Justice of the European Union, if it manifestly violated the EU's founding treaties.[14] All these political violations create problems for legitimacy, even if the substantive distribution they achieve were perfectly just from the narrow point of view of a distribution of resources as the output (assuming that the principle of justice tell us what the output should be). An *illegitimate* distribution is wrong, whatever its substantive content. *Institutional legitimacy* must therefore be an important component of global justice, just as it is an important component of domestic justice. Just like in the domestic case, institutional legitimacy may be prior to social justice. But what does legitimacy require? How does this idea apply to international institutions and distributions?

2.2 Examples of Benevolence

I shall outline three different scenarios of social justice-seeking actions. Assume that motivated by a desire to be the best moral person he can be, Karl, a postgraduate student of philosophy, sets out to act on global inequality.[15] He raises money and provisions through donations from affluent well-wishers and sets off on a cargo ship for Freetown in Sierra Leone. He chooses Freetown because he has heard stories of great suffering due to war, disease, and poor institutions.

Here are three possible ways Karl's venture may end up:

(i) **Benevolent Harm**: When Karl arrives in Freetown, he sees a large group of women and children. They look desperate, so he gives them money and

[14] That this is a condition for the application of a decision of the Court of Justice in Germany has been set out by the German Constitutional Court in *Honeywell BVerfG*, 2 BvR 2661/06, of 06.07.2010.

[15] I shall assume that Karl is motivated by something like Peter Singer's argument in 'Famine, Affluence and Morality' (n. 8) for direct individual action, although nothing turns on this fact. The examples are intentionally simplistic and do not correspond to the way modern sophisticated aid organizations deliver aid. This chapter is not making the claim that these simplifications reflect how aid works in practice. It is merely using these crude simplifications to clarify a point of principle. The point has escaped some philosophers but it seems to me that it has been immediately clear to practitioners on the ground. An earlier version of this section was published as Pavlos Eleftheriadis, 'Cosmopolitan Legitimacy' in Jorge Luis Fabra-Zamora (ed.), *Jurisprudence in a Globalized World* (Cheltenham: Edward Elgar, 2020) 196–221.

provisions. He sets out to return to the port. When he arrives back he hears that the people he has helped were part of a rebel group that is terrorizing the countryside by recruiting child soldiers and forcing them to commit atrocities. Karl has unintentionally assisted this group.

(ii) **Helpless Delegation**: Karl chooses to delegate the task of distributing the aid to Ernest, a local politician who seems powerful and knowledgeable. Ernest knows about the local needs and could—potentially—bring about a fair distribution in the town, if he wanted to. He is educated and sounds serious. But Karl has no way of holding Ernest accountable. He cannot guarantee that Ernest's decisions will be the right ones, or that his actions will be overseen by an independent judge. Ernest could, conceivably, use the money and provisions for his own ends, for example to favour his clan and allies. Karl has no mechanism at his disposal for preventing this. He cannot realistically claim back any donations he has made.

(iii) **Benevolent Good**: Before he ventures out on the field Karl sends representatives with the task of establishing patterns of a desired distribution according to an acceptable social model for Sierra Leone. When he arrives in Freetown, he has already identified those in need on account of reliable social and demographic data. He gives the required provisions only to those charities working in the relevant areas so that the highest possible number of people will benefit. He cannot monitor the charities but he is optimistic that they will do what he asked them to.

These are three cases of benevolence. Has Karl achieved the aims of social justice in each one of these cases?

In the case of 'benevolent harm' it is clear that he has not. His motives were good, but the outcome was disastrous: he has assisted the outlaws that are destroying the country. They will use his generosity in order to fund their military campaign. The benevolence of the intention is surely cancelled out by the ghastliness of the result. Karl has a lot of explaining to do.

The case of 'helpless delegation' is different. It is impossible to know its precise outcome. We do not have the information. There is no guarantee that the donations will end up in the right hands. We could end up with a scenario similar to the first case. Or we end up with the provisions reaching the truly needy. We do not know. This surely cannot make Karl's actions wrong in themselves. No intentional action is ever free of the risk of failure. But a question arises over Karl's preparations. Does he not have a duty, both to his donors and to his intended recipients to have a plan of action that minimizes risks in light of well-known facts about the county he wishes to assist? Given the context of his concern for social justice, not merely with the alleviation of pain, does he not need institutional 'assurance' of some kind? In our example, he has left everything to chance. Karl's actions seem irresponsible.

The problems raised by these two cases have been well documented by development economists. William Easterly, for example, has spoken of the general unintended consequences of aid. He has argued that aid has been ineffective through lack of local knowledge by assisting corruption, creating the wrong incentives, and other complications.[16] These are not new objections, of course. Peter Singer explicitly acknowledges these difficulties in the process of giving, without changing his view that giving is a moral duty nevertheless.[17] He responded to the challenge by saying that 'in the past, a lot of official aid has been misconceived and misdirected and has done little good'. He still is able to conclude, however, that if more money were available, it would have been spent more wisely: 'But it scarcely seems possible that, if we truly set out to reduce poverty, and put resources into doing so that match the size of the problem—including resources to evaluate past failures and learn from our mistakes—we will be unable to find ways of making a positive impact.'[18] This is not an adequate response. The question here is not about making a 'positive impact' on some people. We are setting out to bring about social *justice*, not to make a one-off charitable donation. When we set out to achieve justice our responsibility is to act justly not to make 'a positive impact'.

What about the case of 'benevolent good'? We may say that Karl has done good. He has delivered provisions to people in need. Is this enough to meet the tests of social justice? It seems it meets Peter Singer's test of making a 'positive impact'. But the problem is that in this case too Karl has no overall idea of the likelihood that the pattern of distribution he hopes to achieve will meet the tests of social justice. As we said above, distributive justice is about a *pattern* of distribution. It seems that Karl does not have an overview of the distribution of resources he is bringing about among the relevant groups.

This problem has two dimensions: first, he does not have a pattern of desired distribution *internally*, i.e. among the people of Sierra Leone and their relative levels of destitution or need. Second, he does not have a target as to the desired distribution *externally*, i.e. between this people and all the other peoples of the world who are also needy.

A further problem is that his involvement, we have assumed, is time limited. Since he is not being assisted by established institutions and acts on his own, out of a sense of personal duty, his involvement cannot be indefinite. So he cannot correct

[16] William Easterly, *The White Man's Burden: Why the West's Efforts to Aid the Rest Have Done so Much Ill and so Little Good* (Oxford: Oxford University Press, 2006), which argues that ambitious plans for development aid often fail for lack of local knowledge or because they create the wrong incentives.

[17] Singer responds in *The Life you Can Save* (n. 8) 105, where he notes Easterly's arguments and responds that aid has been ineffective because it is normally politically motivated in order serve the interests of the giving power (ibid 106–10).

[18] ibid 110–11.

his mistakes. He may not be able to bring a second or third shipment of aid, if his first shipment goes wrong. The effects of his actions are not within his power to address over time.

I believe that in this case Karl has violated at least some of the requirements of distributive justice. This is so irrespective of the particular details of the outcomes he has brought about. This may sound counterintuitive, but it follows, I believe, from distinguishing between three different rationales: *charity, alleviating destitution*, and *achieving distributive justice*.

Some global theorists, including in my view Peter Singer, fail to distinguish between the three rationales. The first rationale is that of charity or benevolence, the simple desire to assist someone in need not out of justice but out of charity. The second rationale is that of corrective justice. It addresses a very specific wrong, namely the reality of absolute destitution and follows from a moral duty to rescue. The third rationale is focused on inequality as such and is addressing the unjust difference in distributive shares among persons. This rationale works irrespective of whether one of them is destitute. What matters is the difference between the parties, not the state of the loser. It is clear that the same act of assistance may satisfy all three rationales: my giving may be charitable, prevent destitution, and redress inequality at the same time.

Yet the claim that global justice theorists make is that there is a distinct duty of social justice to act from the third type of rationale. Their concern is with global distributive justice. Hence, in order for global justice to function as a reason for giving to those in need, it must be supported by an overall account of what is being achieved in addressing *distributive shares*. It is not enough to say that we are alleviating destitution for some somewhere in the world.

The distinction between the three rationales of benevolence is made clear in Rawls' *Law of Peoples*. Destitution is, for Rawls, the subject of a 'duty of assistance' in favour of 'burdened societies'.[19] It is a true moral duty but it is something that is very different from social justice. The duty to alleviate destitution has a cut-off point, namely the point where a society becomes 'well ordered', at which point other nations do not have a duty to assist. This is not a principle of 'distributive justice' because it is not about the *inequality* between the weaker and the stronger societies. The aim of the duty of assistance is not to address inequality in distributive shares, but to provide essential relief in order to alleviate the pains and humiliations of destitution.

Similarly, when Thomas Nagel discusses global justice he is concerned with differences of wealth, not absolute levels of poverty that call for a humanitarian response. Nagel says that humanitarian duties 'hold in virtue of the absolute rather than the relative level of need of the people we are in a position to help'.[20] He

[19] Rawls, *The Law of Peoples* (n. 9) 106.
[20] Nagel, 'The Problem of Global Justice' (n. 9) 119.

contrasts these duties to the duties of social justice, which are 'concerned with the relations between the conditions of different classes of people, and the causes of inequality between them'.[21] Destitution and distribution are two different grounds for claims of justice. By mixing the two questions together, Karl has failed to pursue his aim to bring about justice. By having no plan or strategy to respond to inequality, Karl does not seem to take distributive justice seriously.

2.3 Forced Justice

What if Karl had a plan about distributive shares? Let us assume that, having read Rawls and Nagel, Karl comes up with a plan to address relative poverty levels based on a detailed report on social justice in Sierra Leone and the world. So now we have a fourth scenario as follows:

(iv) **The Forced Plan**: Karl's representatives on the ground provide him with an up-to-date report on social trends and patterns of distribution, internally and externally. He thus designs a full, global, pattern of social justice and sets out to hand out assistance with as much accuracy as possible according to the plan. His charities are only to give provisions in areas where there is need, in such a way that Rawls' second principle of justice will be satisfied in accordance with a relevant map of need. His contributions are enough to lift everyone according to the general plan, and he hopes that residents will be grateful for having a chance to live under Rawlsian principles.

This example, too, exhibits a distinct moral failure even though it is carefully focused on a plan for social justice. In fact, all four cases are examples of the same moral failure. In each case Karl's actions were illegitimate. This is so even though in the last two cases, he may have caused no harm.

Karl has acted unjustly because he has ignored the self-governing institutions of the recipients of his aid. He has treated the local institutions as if they did not exist. In all four scenarios Karl is seeking to impose solutions of justice on a people ignoring the fact that a people has collectively organized itself by creating self-government. By treating the national institutions as non-existent and by seeking in each case to impose his own social ideal on Sierra Leone, Karl has treated its people as mere recipients of his actions not as persons worthy of equal respect.

Irrespective of whether he had good intentions, which he did, and irrespective of whether he produced any good results, which he also did in some scenarios, Karl's actions did not promote the cause of justice. This example derives any power

[21] ibid.

it may have from the fact that while the institutions of Sierra Leone may not be perfect, they are delivering a multi-party democracy with free and fair elections. For example, until recently the President was Ernest Bai Koroma, a former insurance executive, who won the presidential election of 2007, was re-elected in 2012. He left office peacefully in 2018 on the election of Julius Maada Bio. The fact that democratic institutions are more or less successful in Sierra Leone suggests, as Arthur Isak Applbaum has very helpfully argued, that the citizens of Sierra Leone 'are free enough to count as authors' so that their collective body can be held to 'constitute a shared agent'.[22]

The key to the argument is that shared political agency can exist on the basis of functioning institutions such that ignoring collective agency is unacceptable paternalism towards all those who jointly create such a collective agent. Applbaum's own proposal is that political legitimacy exists if there is 'an adequate connection between the governors and the governed (the procedural prong)' as well as 'adequate protection of at least basic human rights (the substantive prong)'.[23] If the two tests are met then the state that is thereby created is worthy of moral respect in that it is the 'locus of respect and responsibility'.[24] It is a 'normative people' in Applbaum's suggestive phrase, which has moral standing, which entails moral duties of respect on both insiders and outsiders. If we accept this argument, we can say that Karl fails because he did not ask if a 'normative people' exists. He never considered the moral duties he owes to a 'normative people'.

One way of looking at this is as another aspect of moral *equality*. Justice in political matters requires respect for the equality of persons as free and equal citizens. This equality of persons is the most important principle of any political community and it is only possible through the creation of political institutions. This is true both for the domestic case but also for the international case.

The fact that others have exercised their natural duty of justice, owed to one another but not to a colonial power, to constitute themselves as a self-governing state, gives them a claim to equal recognition as a collective agent. They are due this recognition because they are a 'normative' people, or simply a 'people', in the proper sense of the term—as a legitimate collective agent worthy of respect in a world of peoples. That a people has set up institutions of self-government is not a formality or a detail. If one undermines the institutions of a foreign nation, one undermines equality everywhere. Our duties to respect the fundamental equality of persons as citizens, is fundamental. It is even prior to any claim of social justice. This is the point I wish to develop in the next three sections.

[22] Arthur Isak Applbaum, 'Forcing a People to Be Free' 35 *Philosophy and Public Affairs* (2007) 359–400, at 386.
[23] ibid 388.
[24] ibid 391.

2.4 Illegitimacy as Injustice

The four cases help us contrast the substantive differences between the 'political view' and the 'global view' of global justice. For the 'political view' only those citizens sharing in the institutional structure of a self-governing state are subject to the requirements of social justice. Nagel argues that when we share a state with others we are subject to coercive rules and involuntary terms of association. Such terms are imposed on all of us 'in the name' of each member, so that we are all considered 'joint authors' because our will is actively 'engaged' in their production.[25]

These facts create a certain social relation with other citizens, Nagel claims, which creates on us an obligation that our relations with all others are guided by the principles of egalitarian social justice. When the underlying social relation is absent, the duties are absent too. Nagel's conclusion is that states are not merely instruments for realizing the value of justice. Instead, 'their existence is precisely what gives the value of justice its application, by putting the fellow citizens of a sovereign state into a relation that they do not have with the rest of humanity, an institutional relation which must then be evaluated by the special standards of fairness and equality that fill out the content of justice'.[26]

It follows that in the global domain we are only bound by weaker ties of humanitarian moral concern to persons outside our own political community. Efectively Nagel makes first a point of principle, that the relation of citizenship is morally distinct and then a point of fact, namely that outside of a state there does not exist a similar underlying social relation of citizenship.

Critics of Nagel have attacked both premises. One group of Nagel's critics have criticized the general principle. They challenge the idea that social justice requires a 'political relationship' at all. They argue that membership in a political society has no serious moral implications. Simon Caney, for example, argues that for what he calls the 'cosmopolitan' outlook there is no fundamental difference between the domestic and global realms 'such that the values that are appropriate in the former realm are inappropriate in the latter' and that the principles to be applied in the global realm should be 'continuous' with those we think appropriate in the domestic realm.[27] For cosmopolitan arguments of this type, borders make little difference. This is the familiar 'global view of social justice' we encountered above.

A second group of critics, however, challenges Nagel's minor premise only, namely the factual observation that modern international institutions and transactions have not created a sufficiently robust relationship among distant strangers. Cohen and Sabel argue that in contemporary global politics 'we have a mix of precisely the conditions of interdependence, cooperation and institutions that have

[25] Nagel, 'The Problem of Global Justice' (n. 9) 128–9.
[26] ibid 120.
[27] Caney, *Justice Beyond Borders* (n. 8) 265.

the justice-generating implications' that feature in Nagel's theory.[28] In their view international regimes and institutions entail justice-generating conditions of collective normative engagement, similar to that which exists in the domestic case. The appropriate response to these interactions is not a world republic, but institutions of rule-making that ought to be flexible and creative under what they call a 'pluralist' view. For their position, these new forms of international interrelations should create novel institutional moral responses. These, however, are a matter of social justice, not a matter of mere humanitarian concern. I shall call this view 'institutional globalism' and will contrast it to the 'global view' of Caney and Singer.

How do these positions respond to the four scenarios of direct aid I outlined above? I start with the 'political view'. The facts of Karl's expedition concern a strictly bilateral relationship. They link a citizen of one state with the citizens of another. It follows that under Nagel's political conception no issue of social justice has arisen between them. Since givers and recipients are not fellow citizens of the same political community, their relations lie outside the framework of social justice. They are bound by ordinary ties of justice which includes all forms of corrective justice (i.e. avoiding harm, some duty to rescue etc.). Karl was under no duty of distributive justice to give up his own resources in order to adjust existing inequalities that he did not cause. He only has a duty of humanitarian assistance if and when it arises.

The second view we have identified, 'global institutionalism', starts with the facts of international cooperation relevant to the case. Let us assume for the purposes of this argument that the relations between the United Kingdom (Karl's origin) and Sierra Leone are remote. There is no institutional framework similar to that described by Cohen and Sabel and sufficient to create moral relations of shared agency. For example, they are not members of the same 'trade union' such as the European Union or NAFTA. Let us assume this to be true even though the UK and Sierra Leone have strong connections and interactions via the United Nations, the Commonwealth of Nations, the IMF, the WHO, and other international institutions. If this is the case, then duties of justice may arise in principle between the two states under public international law. They will not arise between the citizens of one directly to the citizens of the other. There is no shared domain of social justice between them. Just like the 'political conception' the 'institutional globalist' will interpret Karl's expedition as a private event among unconnected persons. In that reading no issues of social justice arise between them. What Karl did was, at most, an act of supererogation.

[28] Joshua Cohen and Charles Sabel, '*Extra Rempublicam Nulla Justitia*?' 34 *Philosophy and Public Affairs* (2006) 147, at 166. See also Thomas Pogge, 'Severe Poverty as a Human Rights Violation' in Pogge (ed.), *Freedom from Poverty as a Human Right: Who Owes What to the Very Poor?* (Oxford: Oxford University Press, 2007) 11–53. Pogge's view is distinct in that it sketches an argument concerning a duty not to cause social injustice through our own institutions, which is not strictly speaking an argument for 'distributive justice' but an argument for corrective justice which seeks to remedy a direct moral wrong.

It is also possible, however, that this institutional view may reach a different interpretation of the underlying facts. Sierra Leone and the United Kingdom may be connected with sufficient links of trade, immigration, and aid so that they do constitute a common domain of shared agency and therefore justice. If so, the 'institutional globalists' will on this particular case, and because of the facts on the ground, take the same view as the 'global justice' view, namely that because of institutional integration the citizens of the two countries stand towards each other in a relation of citizenship or in a relationship of social justice.

What would this mean? The 'global justice' view argues that a moral relationship always exists between Karl and the citizens of Sierra Leone. Such a relationship exists, this view says, irrespective of national borders and membership and connects Karl to the residents of Freetown unconditionally, creating duties of social justice for him and anyone like him. His actions of assistance were attempts to do the right thing under common moral duties of global justice. We may say that the duty was well performed in the last two cases, but not in the first two. Something like it should follow from adopting the global view.

Nevertheless, whichever of the three positions one takes on Karl's actions from the point of view of social justice, the question of legitimacy remains open. It operates in exactly the same way. If the people of Sierra Leone are a 'normative people', whose decisions matter morally, then all Karl's actions were *illegitimate* in all four scenarios. While they may or may not have promoted a just distribution of resources, according to the preferred theory of global distributive justice, they are unacceptable from the point of view of the separate moral duty to respect political institutions.

We may thus say that Karl's actions are violations of the principles of 'international' or, more accurately since we are dealing here with a private person acting towards a forcing political community, *'cosmopolitan' legitimacy*. Whatever their character from the point of view of distributive justice, our hero's actions are illegitimate from the point of view of the justice of institutions or from the point of view of constitutional justice.

Principles of cosmopolitan legitimacy tell us that whenever a state meets the elementary tests of legitimacy by having taken steps in its political history to set up legitimate constitutional institutions, it can be taken by others to be a *people* in a normative sense. Such a state has won the capacity to be a collective agent, whose decisions matter morally. A people has a distinct claim to moral status and respect. If, like Karl, we come to ignore its decisions and seek to force upon it our own decisions or views on a pattern of social justice, we act unjustly because we violate the principle of political legitimacy as it applies to international institutions. The illegitimacy of Karl's actions lies not in their outcome but in what they attempted to do. Karl acted wrongly by ignoring in principle the institutions of Sierra Leone. Merely by setting out to achieve his benevolent aims without regard to the way local institutions address the same aims he disregarded a people's moral standing and acted without authority.

He did so, first, by ignoring Sierra Leone's institutions. He bypassed all domestic authorities, local or national, as if they did not exist. Second, he acted unilaterally in seeking to impose a social ideal with the force of the money he had at his disposal. In the examples we considered, the recipients of his aid had no opportunity to contribute to the ideal as a public political project. By setting out to impose his own social ideals, Karl *usurped* the legitimate political functions of legislation and policy-making. By doing this he failed to show equal respect to the citizens of Sierra Leone. These citizens made their country's institutions possible, for example, by voting in elections and holding office. He treated them as if their actions did not matter.

If he had not ignored them he would have had available to him also the means to pursue his aims without uncertainty. We may assume that local institutions could have provided both accountability and co-ordination, through a national civil service and court system. A democratic legislature, a process of scrutiny, a mechanism of administration through an effective government, and the oversight of courts through a fair judicial process would have all been put to use in the service of social justice. These are not just matters of instrumental value. They are matters of political legitimacy.

It is important to see that the question of legitimacy is independent and indeed prior to the question of social justice. One does not need to settle on a view regarding the 'political view', the global view or the 'global institutional view', or that of 'global justice' to see that legitimacy has priority.

One of our most basic moral duties, one that is a universal, general, and comprehensive moral duty, is the duty to respect the legitimate political institutions that were set up by our fellow human beings. This duty exists whenever these institutions meet the basic tests of legitimacy for political institutions.[29] Karl was misled by his failure to take into account that domestic legitimacy entails a cosmopolitan duty of respect for other people's institutions.

2.5 International Legitimacy

The distinction between legitimacy and full justice is generally accepted for the domestic case.[30] Legitimacy works as a preliminary to justice. A state cannot be

[29] This is what Rawls calls a 'reasonably just constitutional democratic society' in *The Law of Peoples* (n. 9) 49–51.

[30] See for example Philip Pettit, 'Legitimacy and Justice in Republican Perspective' 65 *Current Legal Problems* (2012) 59–82; Allen Buchanan, 'Political Legitimacy and Democracy' 112 *Ethics* (2002) 689–719; Thomas Nagel, 'Moral Conflict and Political Legitimacy' 16 *Philosophy and Public Affairs* (1987) 215–40; Pierre Rosanvallon, *Democratic Legitimacy: Impartiality, Reflexivity, Proximity* trans. by Arthur Goldhammer (Princeton: Princeton University Press, 2011).

just—whatever the distribution of resources it achieves—if it does not have a sound constitutional structure guaranteeing the equal moral standing of all. In that sense legitimacy is *prior* to justice. Legitimacy is the test that grants political authority. In the domestic case the aims of social justice can only be appropriately pursued through the means of political authority, which means the proper constitutional means provided for each political society. If this is true for the domestic case then it must also be true for the international case. Is it?

Principles of legitimacy outline the proper exercise of political authority. The way, however, that the idea of legitimacy applies to the international context is a relatively new and unexplored question.[31] Colonialism, as we saw above, is perhaps the starkest case of international *illegitimacy*—of always acting without authority. The motives of conquest and the outlook of racial or other superiority are surely enough to render any outcome unjust.[32] But the wrongness of colonialism as we know it historically may cloud our thinking. What if the motives of the enforcers were entirely good ones? What if Karl was the leader of well-meaning colonizers? What if his aims were to colonize only in order to alleviate human suffering?

By setting aside issues of aggression and violence we can have a clearer view of the ways in which institutions and their legitimacy are relevant to justice. And we shall see that unilateral aid is always illegitimate. The wrongness of aid that ignores domestic institutions lies in its paternalism. Those taking the initiative are telling the members of the society being assisted what they should do. They say to the assisted that their attempts at setting up a moral community—or of becoming a 'normative people' in Applbaum's terminology—failed. It is an act of usurpation of responsibility.

Actions of this kind treat the whole people with lack of appropriate respect. This is why I believe Rawls argues that it would be unfair to seek to equalize conditions among two societies, where one of them had chosen to industrialize and the other had not.[33] Rawls assumed that it would be unfair to seek to reverse decisions a society has taken freely. Denying the effects of one's decision is the same thing as denying them the power to decide in the first place.

[31] For some relevant discussions of legitimacy and global justice see Allen Buchanan and Robert O. Keohane, 'The Legitimacy of Global Governance Institutions' 20 *Ethics and International Affairs* (2006) 405–37; Jon Mandle, *Global Justice* (Cambridge: Polity Press, 2006) 78–101; Mattias Kumm, 'The Legitimacy of International Law: A Constitutionalist Framework of Analysis' (2004) 15 *European Journal of International Law* 907, John Tasioulas, 'The Legitimacy of International Law', in Samantha Besson and John Tasioulas, *The Philosophy of International Law* (Oxford: Oxford University Press, 2010) 97–116; Allen Buchanan, 'The Legitimacy of International Law' in Besson and Tasioulas (eds) 79–96; Allen Buchanan, *Justice, Legitimacy and Self-Determination: Moral Foundations for International Law* (Oxford: Oxford University Press, 2004); Ronald Dworkin, 'A New Philosophy of International Law' 41 *Philosophy and Public Affairs* (2013) 1. I shall return to these issues in section 7 below.

[32] For these types of racist and hateful motives in the nineteenth century see Peter Gay, *The Cultivation of Hatred* (New York: Norton, 1994).

[33] Rawls, *The Law of Peoples* (n. 9) 117–18. Rawls also believed that it would be wrong in principle to intervene in the affairs of a 'decent society'(ibid 83–4).

Some people say that this does not matter. Simon Caney dismisses Rawls' argument and considers it 'extremely unjust toward individuals'.[34] He asks: 'Why should a member of a Third World country be economically disadvantaged because of a decision that the political elite in that country made and with which they disagreed?'[35] However, Caney mistakenly thinks that Rawls' argument derives its force from the consent of those disadvantaged.

Rawls' argument is different. It derives its force not from consent but from the value of institutions as a whole and from the need for legitimate constitutional institutions. Institutions may be legitimate and bind us even when we have not consented to them. Constitutional institutions need not be accepted by everyone over whom they rightfully claim legitimacy. And just like a constitution may be the legitimate constitutional framework for a single state, public international law is the legitimate framework for the world beyond each state.

This is the particular role of international law: to create a legitimate framework through which states come together in order to communicate, to provide facilities to each other's citizens, and to cooperate. In the absence of a world state, Rawls argues, all legitimate states must work together to create a 'democratic peace' between them built on the basis of international law.[36] From constitutional law we move to international law. Without such institutions, there can be no global justice.

Caney rejects this argument by adopting, in effect, an instrumental way of thinking about the state. He sees all institutions as the means to a higher end, namely, the satisfaction of people's interests. He derives, for example, a 'human right' not to suffer from poverty from the fact that 'persons have an interest in having the opportunity not to suffer from poverty'.[37] But this leaves no room for legitimacy. It takes us back to the tests of 'output'. Actions and institutions are to be assessed only on the basis of their outcomes. Caney dismisses arguments from the legitimacy of institutions or the self-government of states by claiming that such arguments 'penalize' those born into an impoverished system and 'depriving them of the very means to live, simply because of their "place of birth"'.[38] On this basis Caney concludes that there is an overwhelming duty of justice to 'eradicate poverty'.[39] Yet, the arguments of Rawls and Nagel were very different. They were not 'penalizing' the poor by respecting their legitimate institutions. Poverty is not caused by our response to it. As Karl's examples show, no individual person has the power to alleviate poverty around the world single-handedly. We should, of course,

[34] Caney, *Justice Beyond Borders* (n. 8) 130.

[35] ibid.

[36] Rawls, *The Law of Peoples* (n. 9) 44–54. For the basic principles of international law see ibid 37.

[37] Simon Caney, 'Global Poverty and Human Rights: The Case for Positive Duties' in Pogge (ed.), *Freedom from Poverty as a Human Right*(n. 28) 275, at 277.

[38] ibid 283. See also Caney, *Justice Beyond Borders* (n. 8) 111–12.

[39] Caney, 'Global Poverty and Human Rights: The Case for Positive Duties' (n. 37) 288.

alleviate suffering whenever we can. But this is not a demand of social justice, it is a demand of charity.

A similar but more sustained argument for the relative insignificance of institutions is made by John Tasioulas on the basis that institutions national or international make little difference to our moral position. Tasioulas postulates that an authority is legitimate when its outcomes are likely to be correct, or 'when its putative subjects would likely better conform with the reasons that apply to them by treating the putative authority's directives as content-independent and exclusionary reasons for action than if they adopted some other guide'.[40] Tasioulas adopts here Joseph Raz's view of authority and adapts it to the international domain. He concludes that what matters for legitimacy is 'enhanced conformity with reason', even if it is not 'perfect conformity'.[41]

Nevertheless, this is no theory of legitimacy. Under such a theory the structures of law have no priority. It is a theory of outcomes, not processes. But this comes at a cost. This instrumental view would perhaps see nothing wrong in Karl's usurpation of state authority if it would produce some of the desired outcomes. For if global poverty could be addressed through a new colonialism then colonialism becomes a duty of justice. Caney and Tasioulas provide little argument to deflect this unattractive conclusion which I am sure they would wish to reject.[42]

Most philosophers would wish to retain legitimacy as a standard feature of all international law and politics. They would wish to maintain just *processes*. But how? One attempt to show that appropriate process is prior to outcomes is offered by Allen Buchanan, who specifies, contrary to Tasioulas, that 'the rules of a legitimate institution have a privileged status vis a vis our reasons for acting' and that 'their having this privileged status is not dependent on their content'.[43] In Buchanan's view legitimacy is less demanding than justice and it is for that reason easier to reach.[44]

Buchanan argues that for what he considers the 'dominant' philosophical view legitimacy justifies a 'right to rule' and requires six elements: (a) the institution's agents are morally justified in engaging in governance functions; (b) use morally justified coercion; (c) are exclusively justified in exercising coercion; (d) are justified in excluding others from exercising governance activities; (e) those whom the institution attempts to govern have a content-independent moral obligation

[40] Tasioulas, 'The Legitimacy of International Law' (n. 30) 100.

[41] ibid 102.

[42] This problem also makes less persuasive Samantha Besson's argument that 'individual autonomy' is the legitimating ground of international law because she too fails to explain the distinct moral standing of state institutions. See Samantha Besson, 'The Authority of International Law—Lifting the State Veil' 31 *Sydney Law Review* (2009) 343, 374.

[43] Buchanan, 'The Legitimacy of International Law' (n. 31) 83. Buchanan contrasts legitimacy to 'authority' which entails the 'right to be obeyed' as well; see for example Buchanan, 'Political Legitimacy and Democracy' (n. 30) 691 and Buchanan, *Justice, Legitimacy and Self-Determination* (n. 31) 237.

[44] Buchanan, 'The Legitimacy of International Law' (n. 31) 81.

to comply with all the rules the institution impose; and (f) citizens have a duty not to interfere with the institution's effort to secure compliance. Buchanan considers these requirements to be too strong to apply to anything except states. A different set of requirements should apply, he thinks, to international institutions which would not include, for example, the exercise of coercion.

Buchanan argument is that in the international context political power is legitimate if it does a credible job of protecting at least the most basic human rights of those over whom it wields power, as long as it provides this protection through processes, policies, and actions that themselves respect the most basic human rights and is not a usurper.[45] On the basis of these premises Buchanan postulates a 'robust natural duty of justice', which is related to a 'moral equality' principle.[46] Buchanan's overall argument is very rich in detail and highly original. However, it lacks clarity in one important respect.

Why should anyone be concerned with the *most basic* human rights only and not with the *full range* of human rights? Why not consider that an institution is only legitimate if it protects all of justice or people's welfare interests in the fullest sense? Why draw a distinction between basic and non-basic rights? The problem here is that if legitimacy is something less than full justice, then it cannot prevail over full justice. We face a paradox. Why should we prefer less justice than more? I don't think Buchanan's effort to elevate legitimacy on the basis of 'basic rights' can succeed.

2.6 Constitutional Justice

To understand political legitimacy at home and abroad we need to draw a distinction between matters concerning constitutional institutions and other matters of justice. If, like Buchanan, Caney, and Raz we seek to ground our moral decisions on personal welfare or the occasional 'interests' that are served by our actions or institutions, it will be hard to draw any such distinction. Since all actions affect all interests in complex ways, each decision is to be assessed on its own on the basis of its consequences. How our interests are affected by our actions requires a detailed assessment one case at a time. Actions may have the same effect as institutions. Consequential or welfarist theories cannot properly account for the role of institutions. Yet institutions matter for legitimacy irrespective of the detailed outcome of the decisions taken by them. How can this be?

[45] Buchanan, *Justice, Legitimacy and Self-Determination* (n. 31) 247; Buchanan, 'Political Legitimacy and Democracy' (n. 30) at 703.

[46] Buchanan, *Justice, Legitimacy and Self-Determination* (n. 31) 85–97; Buchanan, 'Political Legitimacy and Democracy' (n. 30) at 704.

'Welfare' theorists draw the distinction by identifying some interests as fundamental. Allen Buchanan, for example, argues that basic human rights are personal *interests* with a particular priority. Such theories, however, have great trouble explaining how or why some interests are indeed prior. The argument sounds dogmatic and unconvincing.[47] A much better way, which I have supported in greater detail in the past,[48] is an argument originating with Kant and renewed by John Rawls. For this argument the priority of institutions over consequences is a matter of *a priori* moral principle.

Kant tells us that our moral questions are to be answered without reference to any of our empirical aims. This is a condition which he terms an '*a priori*' argument. For Kant, our thinking about how we ought to treat each other starts from premises that are independent of any of our aims. We should ask what is the right thing to do, not what is good for us to do.[49]

Rawls makes the same argument on the basis of a more circuitous philosophical argument. Rather than refer to *a priori* moral premises Rawls pursues a constructivist argument according to which our moral principles must be in 'reflective equilibrium' with our considered moral judgments. Kant's conclusions are not of course closed to interest theorists. Some of the interest theorists reach very similar conclusions via a different route. I will therefore concentrate on these conclusions on the role of institutions without much attention to the underlying philosophical justifications.

Kant's argument begins from the assumption that pluralism about the good is an inescapable fact of the human condition. A supposed realm of self-evident moral ideals, a 'natural good', as assumed by some natural law thinkers, does not exist. We must therefore start with the formal or *a priori* thought that human beings are self-governing agents thinking for themselves. If we are not to fall into obvious contradiction we owe those other agents that share the world with us equal moral standing. At the heart of Kant's argument is an ideal of dignity of all human beings as follows:

> Every human being has a legitimate claim to respect from his fellow human beings and is turn bound to respect every other. Humanity itself is a dignity; for a human being cannot be used merely as a means by any human being (either by others or even by himself) but must always be used at the same time as an end. It is just in this that his dignity (personality) consists, by which he raises himself above

[47] I have argued to this effect against the arguments of Joseph Raz in Pavlos Eleftheriadis, 'Human Rights as Legal Rights' 1 *Transnational Legal Theory* (2010) 371–92 and against Jim Griffin in Pavlos Eleftheriadis, 'Human Rights for Liberals' 3 *Global Justice* (2010) 42–8.

[48] Pavlos Eleftheriadis, *Legal Rights* (Oxford: Oxford University Press, 2008).

[49] For modern defences and manifestations of Kant's arguments about law see Arthur Ripstein, *Force and Freedom* (Cambridge, Mass.: Harvard University Press, 2009); Onora O'Neill, *Constructing Authorities: Reason, Politics and Interpretation in Kant's Philosophy* (Cambridge: Cambridge University Press, 2015).

> all other beings in the world that are not human beings and yet can be used, and so over all things.[50]

Kant's starting point is thus the equality of free agents. He does not rely on a dogmatically asserted list of values, goods, or ends.

But what kind of social arrangements should there be for a community of equal and autonomous agents, as bearers of equal moral claims on the basis of equality reciprocity? The idea of equal agents sharing the world leads to one obligation of reciprocity which Kant calls 'innate' right, namely, the following formal principle of freedom: 'Freedom (independence from being constrained by another's choice), insofar as it can coexist with the freedom of every other in accordance with a universal law, is the only original right belonging to every man by virtue of his humanity.'[51]

Of course, what this principle means depends on what we enter into the ambiguous term *universal law*. Freedom is not to be an *ad hoc* arrangement but a matter of institutions that apply equally to all. From the idea of reciprocity we are thus led to the idea of a legitimate constitution. A system of constitutional law is the response to the requirement that we respect the 'innate right to freedom' of everyone in a shared world.

This argument shows that purely *private* and therefore voluntary relations among people cannot possibly guarantee that they will respect each other's innate equality. A man who acts with respect towards all others has no guarantee that others will do the same towards him. He may be tempted to accept inequality out of some kind of virtuous self-sacrifice. But he has then violated the very terms of equal moral standing because he has accepted that he can be the instrument of others.

Kant's basic argument for creating law or a public mechanism of law-making and law-enforcement is that in a state of purely private monitoring and enforcement there would be no way of respecting equality. The public mechanism—or 'public right'—is the key to the 'civil condition'. This argument is not saying that some interests deserve priority. It only says that if we wish to respect others as agents we must live with them under the terms of public law or the terms of constitutional justice.

This is a *constructivist* argument, because its starting point is merely the statement of the problem of how to live side by side with other moral agents while respecting everyone's *equal* moral standing. The argument is also *formal* in the limited sense that it constructs an answer through the careful elaboration of the

[50] MM, 6:462. Kant's argument identifies innate equalityas independence from being bound by others to more than one can turn bind them, the idea of being one's own master (*sui iuris*), as well as the idea of being beyond reproach.

[51] MM, 6:238.

question. Kant's answer to the question of how to make possible the equal standing of persons in a shared world is that it can only happen through public institutions of law that recognize rights and duties on the basis of universality and reciprocity.[52] The point here is that without legality there is no equal citizenship. If equal citizenship has priority then so does the constitution.

Reflection about law starts with the statement of this problem of practical life, namely, of how to live together as equals. Constitutional law is its detailed solution. Kant writes that the 'civil condition' is not simply a union for some common end or the pursuit of some interests in welfare, but a union which is 'in itself an end' and which is the 'unconditional and first duty in any external relation of people in general, who cannot help mutually affecting one another'.[53]

Setting up a constitutional order that complies with the principles of equality and reciprocity is thus the 'supreme formal condition' (*conditio sine qua non*) of all other external duties, without which no external duty is possible. The principle is necessary and formal because no empirical end can be the focus of a similar agreement: 'for, since people differ in their thinking about happiness and how each would have it constituted, their wills with respect to it cannot be brought under any common principle and so under any external law harmonizing with everyone's freedom'.[54] Kant makes a simple point about the priority of legitimate institutions: an effective and egalitarian legal order is a *pre-condition* for any other form of social justice.

Rawls makes a similar point. He tells us that the natural duty of justice to support legitimate institutions is distinct but on a par with other natural duties such as the duty of mutual aid, i.e. 'the duty of helping another when he is in need or jeopardy, provided that one can do so without excessive risk or loss to oneself'; the duty 'not to harm or injure another'; and 'the duty not to cause unnecessary suffering'.[55] These are horizontal relations to other persons with whom we come into contact without having any special relationship with them. These natural duties are moral duties that apply irrespective of one's relationship to a given state. In that sense they are 'natural':

> A further feature of natural duties is that they hold between persons irrespective of their institutional relationships; they obtain between all as equal moral persons. In this sense the natural duties are owed not only to definite individuals,

[52] Kant assumes that equality leads us to the 'universal principle of Right', which requires reciprocity under a *universal law*: 'Any action is *right* if it can coexist with everyone's freedom in accordance with a universal law, or if on its maxim the freedom of choice of each can coexist with everyone's freedom in accordance with a universal law.' MM, 6:230.

[53] Kant, 'On the Common Saying: That May Be Correct in Theory, but Is of no Use in Practice' in Kant, *Practical Philosophy*, trans. and edited by Mary J. Gregor (Cambridge: Cambridge University Press, 1996) 8:289, p. 290.

[54] ibid 8:290, p. 291.

[55] Rawls, *A Theory of Justice*, rev edn (Oxford: Oxford University Press, 1999) 98.

say to those cooperating together in a particular social arrangement, but to persons generally.[56]

These duties, Rawls tells us, are owed from every person to every other. One of the natural duties of justice is to set up institutions of government. The duty is entirely independent and indeed prior to any objectives of social justice or the satisfaction of welfare interests. This is the key to the value of legitimate states.

2.7 Jurisdiction

The argument we have just examined for constitutional justice has direct consequences for the understanding of the international community—and of the European Union as one element of it. If we owe a duty of justice to respect institutions of our own state, when it meets the test of legitimacy, we shall then have entirely similar duties to other states who do the same for their people and territory. These duties are from the start international or cosmopolitan. Whenever state institutions are appropriately organized and constitutionally legitimate, the people that brought them about have responsibility for them.

A legitimate constitutional structure is something of value because it recognizes our creative and moral potential as agents. A legitimate state is thus not a set of ephemeral encounters. Its value lies not in the goodness of the results it secures but in the fact that it is an attempt at securing equal respect for everyone through institutions of justice. As Rawls and Kant explain, this kind of human excellence derives from justice and not from goodness and it is a matter of our actions themselves—not dependent on achieving any particular end through them.[57]

Everyone can understand the difficulties and challenges of creating and sustaining legitimate institutions. Michael Walzer, for example, has explained that the moral standing of states depends on the political communities that underpin them and on some idea of a 'communal integrity' which 'derives its moral and political force from the rights of contemporary men and women to live as members of a historic community and to express their inherited culture through political forms worked out among themselves'.[58] We do not need to accept this picture in its entirety. Stability may be more important than cultural homogeneity. The moral standing of political communities has been explained by Kant somewhat more austerely with the metaphor of a tree with its own trunk and roots:

[56] ibid 99.

[57] We could perhaps say that they have 'adverbial' value, as explained by Dworkin in *Justice for Hedgehogs* (Cambridge, Mass.: Harvard University Press, 2011) 216–17, 419.

[58] Michael Walzer, 'The Moral Standing of States: A Response to Four Critics' 9 *Philosophy & Public Affairs* (1980) 209–29, at 211.

> for a state is not (like the land on which it resides) a belonging (*patrimonium*). It is a society of human beings that no one other than itself can command or dispose of. Like a trunk, it has its own roots; and to annex it to another state as a graft is to do away with its existence as a moral person and to make a moral person into a thing, and so to contradict the idea for the original contract, apart from which no right over a people can be thought.[59]

The value of a state is brought about both by its ethical excellence in seeking—although not always achieving—justice for its citizens, but also from the forms of civic friendship that it establishes. Justice as well as civic friendship make a state politically legitimate.[60]

Whenever constitutional justice has been achieved the state institutions are legitimate and they constitute a 'jurisdiction'. The personal duty of respect to any legitimate state that exists beyond the borders of our own state I shall call 'the duty of jurisdiction'. The duty of jurisdiction requires us to respect appointed officers in the host state and recognize in them the moral standing of all the co-legislating citizens and their success in setting up just or nearly just institutions. It is a natural duty that binds everyone in a way parallel to the natural duty of justice to respect the institutions of our own state. The moral basis of jurisdiction, however, has a reciprocal effect. Jurisdiction entails the recognition of reciprocal duties owed by all states to all persons: citizens or non-citizens. The Kantian view of international justice is therefore based on reciprocity.

Rawls takes a very similar view of reciprocity regarding the foundations of international law, or what he calls the 'law of peoples': 'As reasonable citizens in domestic society offer to cooperate on fair terms with other citizens, so (reasonable) liberal (or decent) peoples offer fair terms of cooperation to other peoples. Part of the background terms of cooperation is a set of distributive principles that require assistance to "burdened" nations, but not a general "difference principle" reducing inequalities.'[61] A people 'will honor these terms when assured that other peoples will do so as well'.[62]

This interpretation of international law was also defended by Ronald Dworkin, who searched for the grounds of international law not in any kind of rule of recognition with global reach but in arguments of political morality that give meaning to global institutions.[63] Dworkin argued for an interpretation of international law in terms of the aims of 'democratic peace'. Dworkin argued that the basis of international law is the idea of mutual respect and of peaceful coexistence of sovereign states on the basis of reciprocity. He wrote: 'Each traditional state therefore has a

[59] Kant, Towards Perpetual Peace, 8:344, in Kant, *Practical Philosophy* (n. 53) p. 318.

[60] For a similar argument that historical ties bind morally see Anna Stilz, 'Why does the State Matter Morally? Political Obligation and Particularity' in Sigal R. Ben-Porath and Rogers M. Smith (eds.), *Varieties of Sovereignty and Citizenship* (Philadelphia: University of Pennsylvania Press, 2012) 244–64.

[61] Rawls, *The Law of Peoples* (n. 9) 113–17.

[62] ibid 25.

[63] See Ronald Dworkin, 'A New Philosophy of International Law' 41 *Philosophy and Public Affairs* (2013) 2–30.

duty to pursue available means to mitigate the failures and risks of the sovereign-state system. That duty of mitigation provides the most general structural principle and interpretive background of international law.'[64] This argument then leads to a moral account of public international law, which explains its moral distinctness from constitutional law.

Our argument therefore requires us to reject Mattias Kumm's suggestion that constitutional law and international law can merge under a common framework of constitutionalism. We cannot accept Kumm's suggestion that: 'Constitutional law properly so called extends beyond the nation and beyond the state in Europe.'[65] Constitutional law and international law remain *structurally* distinct. I believe instead that if we are to respect other peoples as in principle our equals, we must provide for a framework under which the various peoples can deal with each other on the basis of reciprocity and equality. This is what the law of nations is meant to achieve. It falls on us, as citizens of a particular state to respect jurisdiction wherever we find it. This is one of our cosmopolitan duties.

So this long argument about legitimacy and international institutions takes us back to arguments about the constitutional or other political aims of the European Union. At the start of this chapter we examined Mattias Kumm's argument that the 'republican principles' that inform modern democracies apply in exactly the same way to the European Union. In Kumm's view, the European Union 'is founded on principles that are a common heritage of the European tradition as it has emerged in the second half of the twentieth century'.[66] For this argument state institutions and the European Union are expected to promote the same 'republican' constitutional principles of a democratic state so that 'whether or not the EU does in fact establish legitimate constitutional authority is a question that allows for qualified answers'.[67] We have now outlined a full argument rejecting Kumm's suggestion. We have argued that states do not ground their moral standing on instrumental arguments because they are not merely vehicles for the satisfaction of interests or the achievement of welfare goods which could also be satisfied by other structures.

States and their borders play a unique role for political legitimacy: they create stable relations of reciprocity and equal citizenship that can only exist within the framework of a political community organized under the rule of a lawful jurisdiction. A jurisdiction may be very large or very small, but it must be organized in a coherent, coercive, and permanent way on the basis of the rule of law. This is the only way we have of respecting others as equals. As we have seen, international

[64] ibid 19.

[65] Kumm, 'Beyond Golf Clubs and the Judicialization of Politics' (n. 7) 505, at 513, at 528. In my view constitutional law is the law of a jurisdiction, whereas EU law is the law of a union of peoples. The view that the European institutional arrangements are a particular type of constitution is also defended by J. H. H. Weiler, 'In Defence of the Status Quo: Europe's Constitutional *Sonderweg*' in J. H. H. Weiler and Marlene Wind (eds.), *European Constitutionalism Beyond the State* (Cambridge: Cambridge University Press, 2003) 7.

[66] Kumm, 'Beyond Golf Clubs and the Judicialization of Politics' (n. 7) 505, at 517.

[67] ibid 523.

law and its institutions do not compete with jurisdictions but complement them. International law creates lawful relations between states without setting up a global jurisdiction imitating the institutions of the state. We argued that equal citizenship can only be protected by a single jurisdiction organized according to geographical domains. Following Kant's argument, we said that this is the only way we have of respecting each other as equal citizens under a *universal* law of freedom.

The argument does not entail anything in particular about the required size of self-governing communities. A political community can be very large or it can be very small; it can be the United States or it can be Malta. The argument, therefore, does not rule out the future emergence of a European superstate, if history allowed something like that to happen. But the creation of such a state must take place through an appropriate political process, which cannot be a matter of duty or other moral requirement to complete. In any event, the European Union treaties do not set in motion such a process. Hence the EU is not a jurisdiction, at least not yet, although it may become one in the future. Once a jurisdiction emerges it will then have value as an independent political community. Whether a new jurisdiction exists is, inevitably, both a matter of law and a matter of fact.

In the chapters that follow I will now argue that as things stand today the European Union is not a jurisdiction. It is a creation of international justice. Its law requires that each state respects all others and respects the treaties that they have entered into. States are responsible for keeping their word under international law, but also for upholding solidarity and assistance whenever the principles of fairness require. Sovereignty thus entails institutions of reciprocity both at the international and the cosmopolitan level. This argument explains why state consent and treaty-making are at the heart of international law but do not fully determine its content.[68] International law is guided by the equality of states, not as an arbitrary arrangement on the basis of unlimited state consent, but as a moral fundamental.[69] There is nothing artificial to the division of the world into independent political communities or states.[70] As is the case of all law, the law among peoples is part of our ethical horizon.

[68] For a similar argument see Eyal Benvenisti, 'Sovereigns as Trustees of Humanity: On the Accountability of States to Foreign Stakeholders' 107 *American Journal of International Law* (2013) 295–333.

[69] I endorse the arguments made by Ronald Dworkin, 'A New Philosophy of International Law' 41 *Philosophy and Public Affairs* (2013) 2–30.

[70] The term 'artificial' was used by Miguel Poiares Maduro to criticize a conception of constitutional law that is focused on independent political communities in Maduro, 'Europe and the Constitution' (n. 5) 74–5. Maduro argued that states are organized on the basis of some 'idealized construction of the common good' which hides the 'true nature of constitutionalism: the balancing of diverse and often conflicting interests and fears' (ibid p. 75). I disagree with this instrumental view of the constitution. I defend above the alternative view that constitutions derive their ideal content from our ethical duty to respect others as equals. For further development of this point see Pavlos Eleftheriadis, 'Power and Principle in Constitutional Law' 45 *Netherlands Journal of Legal Philosophy* (2016) 37–56 and Chapter 10 below.

3
Dualism

If we take the idea of political legitimacy seriously, then borders matter morally. In the last chapter we rejected instrumental theories of authority and defended an ethical argument about the justification of institutions of equal citizenship. Pursuing this thought further, we can say that a constitution is key to domestic political legitimacy, because it sets out how legal and political authority can be exercised under the principles of equal citizenship. When a constitution works well it sets up stable institutions of jurisdiction that can respect reciprocity among persons under the rule of law, or under what Kant calls 'a universal law of freedom'. This argument also leads to an egalitarian view of international law because it explains how a community that meets the tests of political legitimacy even by the smallest of margins wins its rightful place in a global community of self-governing peoples. The set of common rules that binds states to one another we therefore call 'public international law' or 'the law of nations'. This law is not the law of any particular state nor is it purely the creation of states. It is to be contrasted to constitutional law, as the law of a jurisdiction. International law is in effect the law uniting the separate jurisdictions in a legal order that does not seek itself to be a jurisdiction. In all these senses public international law is unique.

Constitutional law and public international law do not overlap. They pursue different ends by different means. International law allows states to enter into agreements with other states and provides a specific law of treaties setting out how this can work in practice. If such rules are followed, states are bound by the words of their representatives. Of course domestic law and international law may end up covering the same subject matter as they do, for example, when they protect human rights or set environmental standards. But even when they overlap in subject matter, they do not overlap in legal content. International law is in principle a matter for state responsibility and only indirectly a matter for the domestic courts. Domestic constitutional protection, by contrast, is an immediate concern of domestic courts: it creates claimable rights and direct remedies. An international environmental standard creates state responsibility that applies among states. A domestic environmental standard creates claimable remedies for private parties. For international rules to create domestic remedies, there has to be a process of domestic incorporation.[1]

[1] This process of incorporation can be either statutory, as in the case of the United Kingdom, or constitutional, as in the case of the Netherlands. In both cases, however, the domestic constitution provides for the recognition of international standards in domestic law. In that sense, both countries are effectively dualist.

A Union of Peoples. Pavlos Eleftheriadis. Oxford University Press (2020). © Oxford University Press.
DOI: 10.1093/oso/9780198854173.001.0001

I now wish to argue that the distinction between constitutional law as the law of a jurisdiction and international law as the law of nations lies at the centre of the European Union's legal structure. It is not enough for this argument to accept that the founding documents of the EU are treaties of public international law. Nobody denies that they were treaties, when first concluded. Some say, however, that these treaties have acquired new legal meaning, having evolved into something more significant. The fact that the foundational documents of the European Union were once drafted as international treaties does not answer the question of their current role. It may have been just an accident of history, now fully overcome by subsequent events. The transformation of the treaties to a virtual constitution for Europe has happened, the argument goes, partly through political practice and partly through the case law of the Court of Justice of the European Union and the law of the member states. The argument is that that the law has moved on: the treaties have become a constitution in all but name.

I wish to reject this argument. I do not believe that the treaties have evolved into something other than treaties of public international law. What has changed, however, is our understanding of international law. We accept today, in a way that we perhaps did not in the 1950s, that international law creates significant obligations on sovereign states about how to conduct their domestic affairs. But this change does not change the nature of international law, it merely changes its content. International law is now far more progressive than it was fifty years ago. The European Union is one element of this significant general development.

My argument is that even after closer integration and the numerous decisions of the Court of Justice mentioning the 'autonomy' of EU law, the logic of the law of nations or of public international law continues to permeate the treaties and informs their best interpretation. An *internationalist* reading of European Union law is both the best *political* theory of the Union and also the best *legal* interpretation of the practice pursued by the Court of Justice and the domestic courts. From the first treaty of the Coal and Steel Community to the latest Treaty of Lisbon, the basic mechanism of European law-making is that of a treaty of public international law. This is what I will try to establish in this chapter.

3.1 The Puzzle of European Union Law

The member states did not create the European Union in order to replace the existing states. The European Union, whatever else it may be, is a creation of international agreements connecting states to one another under standard rules of public international law. So the Union can only continue to exist in its present form as long as the states that entered into these treaties continue to exist.[2] The treaties confirm the statehood of all the member states in the most public way, by pronouncing it explicitly. The most recent EU Treaty, the Treaty of Lisbon of 2009 provided such explicit recognition. Article 4(2) of the Treaty on the European Union (TEU), as amended by the Treaty of Lisbon, states: 'The Union shall respect the equality of Member States before the Treaties as well as their national identities, inherent in their fundamental structures, political and constitutional, inclusive of regional and local self-government.' The treaty specifies further that the Union shall respect the member states' 'essential State functions, including ensuring the territorial integrity of the State, maintaining law and order and safeguarding national security'. Moreover, Article 50 TEU also provides for a process of withdrawal from the EU, a process that was initiated by the United Kingdom in March 2017 and completed in January 2020. But even the earlier treaties always started by stating the obvious fact that these were agreements among states. So the model of EU as a union of self-governing states has always been recognized in the Treaties.[3]

At the same time the European Union is very different from any other international organization. The Treaties have created entirely novel international mechanisms of shared legislation and adjudication. The integration they have brought about is so deep that lawyers routinely call it a 'constitution'.[4] These mechanisms empower Union institutions with unconditional law-making and adjudicative powers with immediate or 'direct' effect and 'primacy' over any contrary domestic law. This means that EU law affects the lives of ordinary citizens immediately, both by virtue of the treaties themselves and on the basis of secondary legislation made by the EU's institutions. Moreover, as is well known, the Court of Justice of the European Union has broad powers to interpret and apply the law. The Court of Justice believes that these features of EU law are true on the basis of internal features of the Treaties and EU law in general, not because of international or constitutional law. As we saw in Chapter 1, the Court has consistently held that EU law is not an order of public international law but is a 'new legal order' which is 'autonomous' from other legal orders.[5]

[2] See Article 54(1) TEU (ex 52 TEU): 'This Treaty shall be ratified by the High Contracting Parties in accordance with their respective constitutional requirements. The instruments of ratification shall be deposited with the Government of the Italian Republic.'

[3] See also Case C-621/18, *Wightman and Others v Secretary of State for Exiting the European Union*, ECLI: EU:C:2018:999, where the court affirmed the sovereign right of the United Kingdom to revoke its notification of its intention to withdraw. A view of the EU as a creation of international law was outlined in Bruno de Witte, 'European Union Law: How Autonomous Is its Order?' 65 *Zeitschrift für Öffentliches Recht* (2010) 141, at 146.

[4] See for example J. H. H. Weiler, *The Constitution for Europe: 'Do the New Clothes Have an Emperor' and other Essays on European Integration* (Cambridge: Cambridge University Press, 1999); Allan Rosas and Lorna Armati, *EU Constitutional Law*, 2nd edn (Oxford: Hart, 2012); Robert Schütze, *European Constitutional Law*, 2nd edn (Cambridge: Cambridge University Press, 2015).

[5] See for example the classic constitutional cases: Case 26/62 *Van Gend en Loos* [1963] ECR 1, Case 6/64 *Costa v ENEL* [1964] ECR 585, Case 11/70 *Internationale Handelsgesellschaft* [1970] ECR 1125, Case 106/77 *Simmenthal* [1978] ECR 629, Case 314/85 *Firma Foto Frost v HZA Lubeck Ost* [1987] ECR I-4199.

This position was restated to great effect in the Opinion of the Court on the Accession of the EU to the European Convention on Human Rights, where the Court halted the accession of the European Union to the European Convention. The Court of Justice held that one of the special characteristic of the EU legal order is its 'autonomy' from the law of the member state and from international law, stressing in particular that: 'EU law is characterised by the fact that it stems from an independent source of law, the Treaties, by its primacy over the laws of the Member States'.[6] The Court said that the autonomy enjoyed by EU law in relation to the laws of the member states and in relation to international law requires that the interpretation and application of a doctrine of fundamental rights should take place within the institutions of the EU, and not with reference to the European Court of Human Rights as a quasi-appeal court for the Union. The Court offered the following general outline of the European Union:

> The pursuit of the EU's objectives, as set out in Article 3 TEU, is entrusted to a series of fundamental provisions, such as those providing for the free movement of goods, services, capital and persons, citizenship of the Union, the area of freedom, security and justice, and competition policy. Those provisions, which are part of the framework of a system that is specific to the EU, are structured in such a way as to contribute—each within its specific field and with its own particular characteristics—to the implementation of the process of integration that is the *raison d'être* of the EU itself.[7]

The Court then drew the conclusion that the 'specific characteristics' and the 'autonomy' of the EU legal order entail that its judicial system should remain independent in order to ensure consistency and uniformity in the interpretation of the law:

> In particular, the judicial system as thus conceived has as its keystone the preliminary ruling procedure provided for in Article 267 TFEU, which, by setting up a dialogue between one court and another, specifically between the Court of Justice and the courts and tribunals of the Member States, has the object of securing uniform interpretation of EU law (…), thereby serving to ensure its consistency, its full effect and its autonomy as well as, ultimately, the particular nature of the law established by the Treaties (…).[8]

[6] Opinion 2/13 of the Court, *Accession of the European Union to the European Convention for the Protection of Human Rights*, 18 December 2014, ECLI:EU:C:2014:2454, par. 166.

[7] Opinion 2/13, par. 172.

[8] Opinion 2/13, par. 176.

The Court concluded that accession to the European Court of Human Rights would be contrary to the required 'autonomy' of EU law. It would create an unacceptable dependence onto the Strasbourg Court: 'since the ECHR would form an integral part of EU law, the mechanism established by [accession] could—notably where the issue concerns rights guaranteed by the Charter corresponding to those secured by the ECHR—affect the autonomy and effectiveness of the preliminary ruling procedure provided for in Article 267 TFEU'.[9] The Court therefore, controversially, concluded that accession to the ECHR would undermine the 'specific characteristics of EU law and its autonomy'.

This interpretation of EU law, has created a significant theoretical puzzle. How can states be subject to the European Convention on Human Rights while the European Union itself cannot be? What are the distinct features of EU law that make it 'autonomous' from international treaties? How does the 'new legal order' of the EU relate to the orders of the member states? These questions are both theoretically difficult and practically important.

3.2 The Plurality of Legal Orders

Philosophers and lawyers do not normally think that the existence of many legal orders in the world is a problem or a puzzle, as long as these orders do not make conflicting claims over the same territory.[10] Indeed, the plurality of legal orders was a standard feature of European history in pre-modern times. Throughout the middle ages a person could be under the jurisdiction of many legal orders at the same time, for example, of the ecclesiastical courts, feudal courts, commercial courts, or urban or guild courts.[11] Montesquieu, for example, describes the variety of laws that he observed in his own lifetime as a natural development of historical factors applying to each place. He arrives at a general principle as follows: 'the government most in conformity with nature is the one whose particular arrangement best relates to the disposition of the people for whom it is established'. He then adds: 'Laws should be so appropriate to the people for whom they are made that it

[9] Opinion 2/13, par. 197.

[10] The next several paragraphs derive from Pavlos Eleftheriadis, 'The Law of Laws' 1 *Transnational Legal Theory* (2010) 597.

[11] See Harold J. Berman, *Law and Revolution: The Formation of the Western Legal Tradition* (Cambridge, Mass.: Harvard University Press, 1983) 273–94. Berman writes (at p. 274): 'Developing partly in emulation of and partly in rivalry with the canon law, each of the various types of secular law eventually came to be treated—though in widely varying degrees—as a legal system, that is as an integrated and organically developing body of legal institutions and concepts ... Feudal law and manorial law, to a somewhat lesser extent mercantile and urban law, and to a still lesser extent royal law were more rooted in custom and therefore merged more gradually, than the cannon law of the church ... Indeed, the first systems of secular law did not *need* to be portrayed in textbooks or taught in university courses in order to be accepted as integrated, ongoing, autonomous bodies of law.'

is very unlikely that the laws of one nation can suit another'.[12] Since Montesquieu, philosophers routinely accept that a legal system operates under its own terms and is shaped by its own participants. Any problems created by the plurality of legal orders in the world can be dealt with by each legal order on its own. Any private persons that are caught in disputes that are subject to two or more jurisdictions, have recourse to private international law, which is always part of domestic law, i.e. the law where the case happens to arise.

This analysis does not capture the role of public international law, however. International law is, or appears to be, a legal order that deals with the relations among states and for a long time it was known as 'the law of nations'. It is certainly not the law of a single people. International law aspires to cover the whole of the world without being the law of any particular place and covers governments and officials without being the law of any particular legislator. Whereas private international law is part of the law of a single people, public international law is taken to be another legal order of its own. This distinctness of international law is, however, a matter of heated disagreement. The precise relationship between domestic law and international law has been a source of puzzlement and theoretical speculation for a long time.

Hans Kelsen believed that international law was the effective foundation of municipal law. He considered that any 'pluralistic' view, according to which international and national law were two different and mutually independent systems of norms was 'untenable', since both systems were to be considered 'as simultaneously valid legal norms'.[13] In Kelsen's view the only way of avoiding logical contradiction was to subsume one to the other, so his theory has been called 'monism'.[14] Kelsen argued that the most consistent position would be to say that the validity of a national legal order 'must be found in international law'.[15] H.L.A. Hart, whose view of law was largely sympathetic to that of Kelsen, took the precisely opposite view. He thought that international law was law in a weaker sense compared to its domestic counterparts. It was a 'set' of rules, but not a legal system' since it lacks a legislature and a judiciary with 'compulsory jurisdiction'.[16] Hart concluded that international law was not a legal 'system', but a 'set of separate primary rules of obligation which are not united' with the help of a 'rule of recognition' that could create a 'single system'.[17] For Hart, international law is a set of rules without a single master rule creating rules of validity. Strictly speaking, therefore, for Hart international legal

[12] Montesquieu, *The Spirit of the Laws*, translated and edited by Ann M. Cohler, Basia Carolyn Miller, and Harold Samuel Stone (Cambridge: Cambridge University Press, 1989) 8.

[13] Hans Kelsen, *Pure Theory of Law*, trans. by Max Knight (Berkeley: University of California Press, 1967) 328.

[14] For Kelsen's monism, see Lars Vinx, *Hans Kelsen's Pure Theory of Law: Legality and Legitimacy* (Oxford: Oxford University Press, 2007) 176–80.

[15] Kelsen, *Pure Theory of Law* (n. 13) 336.

[16] H.L.A. Hart, *The Concept of Law*, 2nd edn (Oxford: Oxford University Press, 1993) 232–3.

[17] ibid 233.

rules are not legally 'valid', at least not in the strict technical sense he reserves for domestic law.[18]

Ronald Dworkin rejected both these accounts. He considered international law to be law in the proper interpretive and moral sense that applies to all legal orders.[19] International law is to be understood through the perspective of political morality with particular adjustments for the international case. For Dworkin the interpretation of international rules should advance the purpose of mitigating the flaws and dangers of the Westphalian system. It follows that international rules must be interpreted in a way 'that makes the best sense of the text, given the underlying aim of international law, which is taken to be the creation of an international order that protects political communities from external aggression, protects citizens of those communities from domestic barbarism, facilitates coordination when it is essential, and provides some measure of participation by people in their own governance across the world'.[20] So for Dworkin the subject matter of international law is distinct because it regulates, in principle, the relations between states, not the relations between states and their citizens. Nevertheless, their method is common in that it seeks to provide the best interpretation in light of the most appropriate principles of morality. Other 'substantive' views of international law have been offered, among others, by John Rawls, Allen Buchanan, and Eyal Benvenisti.[21]

Many theorists of international law are still attracted by the positivist theories of Kelsen and Hart, however. Such theorists often say that international law is a positive order of rules, just like any other system of law.[22] The distinction between domestic and international law is for them only one of content, not one of form. The substantive difference is simple: domestic law is about individuals whereas international law is about states. The formal similarity is also very clear. If law is just a conventional and 'positive' creation of each political community, according to its own political processes, then the variety of laws just matches the variety of communities and that is all there is to it. By extension, however, international law is also a conventional creation which took place through the actions of officials or other

[18] ibid 234. As a result, international rules are binding not when they are 'valid' by reference to a master rule, but when they are 'binding if they are accepted and function as such' (ibid 235).

[19] See Ronald Dworkin, 'A New Theory of International Law' 42 *Philosophy and Public Affairs* (2013) 2–30.

[20] ibid 22.

[21] See John Rawls, *The Law of Peoples* (Cambridge, Mass.: Harvard University Press, 1999) 35–7; Allen Buchanan, *Justice, Legitimacy, and Self-Determination: Moral Foundations for International Law* (Oxford: Oxford University Press, 2004) 14–70; Eyal Benvenisti, 'Sovereigns as Trustees of Humanity: On the Accountability of States to Foreign Stakeholders' 107 *American Journal of International Law* (2013) 295–333.

[22] See for example the essays by Samantha Besson, John Tasioulas, and Liam Murphy in Samantha Besson and John Tasioulas (eds), *The Philosophy of International Law* (Oxford: Oxford University Press, 2010). See also Liam Murphy, 'Law Beyond the State: Some Philosophical Questions' 28 *European Journal of International Law* (2017) 203–32.

relevant institutions or other state action. The form of a legal system is the same in both cases, according to the legal positivist view.

It is very hard to defend this view in light of the very many differences between the origins of domestic and international law. The traditional positivist tools, such as Hart's 'rule of recognition' are clearly absent in the international context.[23] Who 'makes' international law? Who are its 'officials'? What is its constitutional framework? Which government is it the instrument of? These questions have very elusive answers in the international context. For that reason, many international legal theorists are abandoning the positivist story.[24]

Nevertheless, international law is routinely taken to be law. Scholarly studies freely compare international and national law and explore the ways in which these separate legal orders—separate but both 'legal'—interact. Such studies show that, whatever its historical character, international law is clearly becoming more and more relevant to domestic law-makers and adjudicators on account of its content. They offer many important examples of overlapping legal regulation and jurisdiction. In fact, more and more practising lawyers observe that international law and national law do not have entirely different content any more. They note that there are now very important overlaps in both their immediate subject matter and overall purpose.

Lord Bingham, one of the most distinguished judges in the United Kingdom, made precisely this observation about international law:

> I used to be much attracted by the description of public international law as 'The Law of Nations'. It seemed to reflect the lustre of Gentili and Grotius, to invest the subject with a grandeur and dignity separating it from the mundane concerns of everyday life, to conjure up a vision of proud and equal sovereigns, declining to bow the knee to one another but condescending to parley through the medium of their immune envoys. I now think ... that the expression, if not actually pernicious, is better avoided. For although international law comprises a distinct and recognizable body of law with its own rules and institutions, it is a body of law complementary to the national laws of individual states, and in no way antagonistic of them; it is not a thing apart; it rests on similar principles and pursues similar ends; and observance of the rule of law is quite as important on the international plane as on the national, perhaps even more so.[25]

The key to the changes observed by Lord Bingham is the fact that international law now engages very strongly with the fate of individuals, either as business

[23] As Hart himself discussed in *The Concept of Law* (n. 16) 232–7.

[24] See for example Benvenisti, 'Sovereigns as Trustees of Humanity: On the Accountability of States to Foreign Stakeholders' (n. 21).

[25] Tom Bingham, *The Rule of Law* (London: Penguin, 2010) 110.

players or as victims of state action. In his discussion of the idea of the 'rule of law' Lord Bingham gave several examples touching on the relevance of the principle of international rule of law on the life of individuals, e.g. war detainees or terror suspects. International lawyers give many other examples. In an influential account, Anne Marie Slaughter wrote of the global economy creating 'global litigation' and described a process by which we see the emergence of an 'integrated system of law', in which courts go beyond 'the comity of nations' in engaging in dialogue with one another in transnational disputes.[26] The nature of these disputes is such that courts of different legal systems may well come to face them at the same time. Many other scholars make similar observations.[27]

This takes us back to the views of Montesquieu because, even though he did not live to see the flourishing of public international law, he considered the law of nations and the law of a political society manifestations of the same idea, that of law. Law for Montesquieu was not just an instrument of government. Montesquieu was part of tradition of political thought that had not heard of legal positivism and for which law was one element of the realization of our moral life. He reserved for this ideal the term '*droit*' as opposed to the simpler '*loi*' (translated in the recent Cambridge edition into 'Right' as opposed to 'law'). So he writes:

> Considered as inhabitants of a planet so large that different peoples are necessary, they have laws bearing on the relations that these peoples have with one another, and this is the RIGHT OF NATIONS. Considered as living in a society that must be maintained they have laws concerning the relation between those who govern and those who are governed, and this is the POLITICAL RIGHT. Further, they have laws concerning the relations that all citizens have with one another, and this is the CIVIL RIGHT.'[28]

Montesquieu gives us the intimations—although nothing more—of a different account of international law as something parallel to national law through a substantive account of the content and purpose of law as '*droit*'—and not merely as '*loi*'.[29] This is now a view defended by Dworkin and other justice-based theories of law. It is the view I too will defend in this chapter.

[26] Anne Marie Slaughter, 'A Global Community of Courts' 44 *Harvard International Law Journal* (2003) 191, at 205.

[27] See also Jenny Martinez, 'Towards an International Judicial System' 56 *Stanford Law Review* (2003) 430 and the various examples in Benvenisti, 'Sovereigns as Trustees of Humanity: On the Accountability of States to Foreign Stakeholders' (n. 21).

[28] Montesquieu, *The Spirit of the Laws* (n. 12) 7.

[29] A more sophisticated such view of international institutions is developed by Rousseau and, most clearly, Kant. For an excellent overview and discussion see Amanda Perreau-Saussine, 'Immanuel Kant on International Law' in Tasioulas and Besson (eds), *The Philosophy of International Law* (n. 22) 53–78.

3.3 Law and Legal System

We are now able to return to the theoretical debate concerning the European Union's legal system that we examined in the first chapter. We have examined in some detail the theoretical models of Kelsen and Hart, the models of legal positivism. They present domestic and international law as rival 'legal systems'. What makes them into systems is a pre-existing framework of formal rules made under a master rule, either a 'basic norm' or a 'rule of recognition'.

We can now see that Mattias Kumm's search for a rule of priority between legal systems follows directly from the legal positivist model of law.[30] If law is a system of rules, we need to find out which system applies to us.[31] By contrast, Julie Dickson and George Letsas follow different models. Dickson proposes that the idea of a legal system is not formal but fluid, on the basis of social and political circumstances. Letsas, following Dworkin's view of law as a practice of moral judgment, goes even further. He believes that the idea of a system is entirely unnecessary.

The question of the relationship between domestic and international law is also a current question of practice. In their daily practice judges and lawyers encounter very regularly the refugee conventions, environmental conventions, and of course human rights conventions that create domestic obligations. These are all manifestations of international law, creations of what we could call the 'international legal order'. What happens when domestic law and international law cover the same subject matter in different ways? An instructive example of this problem, unique in its directness, is the case of *Medellin v Dretke*.[32] In this case the US Supreme Court had to deal with the issue of the fate of a Mexican national who had been sentenced to death in the United States for the rape and murder of two teenage girls. As it turns out the criminal process of Arizona had failed to respect the defendant's rights as a foreign national, under the Vienna Convention on Consular Relations.

The International Court of Justice had already ruled in *Avena*[33] that the United States had failed to respect its obligations as to consular notification and required the United States to take—unspecified—remedial action. Importantly, the

[30] See for example Mattias Kumm, 'The Jurisprudence of Constitutional Conflict: Constitutional Supremacy in Europe before and after the Constitutional Treaty' 11 *European Law Journal* (2005) 262–307.

[31] In effect, if I understand his views correctly, Kumm is a moral globalist and a legal pluralist. He believes that states and international institutions pursue the same welfare ends or 'values', and that the legal arrangements of states and the EU are entirely parallel, so that they can both have a 'legal system'. Pluralism emerges when the European Union as a whole fails to make a categorical choice on which legal system has primacy. See Mattias Kumm, 'Beyond Golf Clubs and the Judicialization of Politics: Why Europe Has a Constitution Properly so Called' 54 *The American Journal of Comparative Law* (2006) 505–30.

[32] *Medellin v Dretke*, 128 S Ct 1346 (2008). 552 US 491 (2008). For commentary see Yuval Shany, *Regulating Jurisdictional Relations Between National and International Courts* (Oxford: Oxford University Press, 2009).

[33] *Avena and other Mexican Nationals (Mexico v United States)*, 2004 ICJ 12.

International Court of Justice did not require the annulment of any of the convictions. There was no suggestion that the failure to notify had affected the trial in any way or made the conviction any less secure. On the other hand, the defendant might have had a better chance at defending himself, had the Mexican consulate been alerted to his case. The International Court required the United States to respond through its own courts to the failure to respect the consular arrangements. The US Supreme Court ruled, in a majority judgment, that the International Court of Justice judgment does not of its own force constitute binding federal law. The court refused to accept any challenge to the conviction and sentence of the Mexican national, who was duly executed soon after the judgment was handed down.

The conflict generated here was direct and dramatic. Either the capital punishment was secure or it was not. In the end, the Supreme Court held that it was lawful and secure. But the international court's ruling had sought to have a direct bearing on a subject matter traditionally associated with the national criminal process, namely the rights of the accused in a criminal trial, an attempt that, seemingly, failed. The proliferation of international courts and tribunals over the last twenty years suggests that such dramatic choices may become more frequent. But how are we to resolve these potential conflicts and overlaps in judicial powers and judgments? The obvious answer, obvious at least to legal scholars, is that we ought to resolve them by way of law, namely a 'law of laws' which sets out the relations between different legal orders. But how can this be possible without paradox?

The traditional answer is given by the theories of law that look at a legal order as a system of rules in the manner of Kelsen and Hart, created positively by a certain political community. For these views laws become laws because of the existence of a legal system. What is exactly the relation between law and legal system?

H.L.A. Hart argued that a legal system is set up when persons see themselves as operating under the 'union' of primary and secondary norms.[34] Hart said that the legal system marks the development from a pre-legal to a legal world, when rules of recognition, adjudication, and change, create a public method of holding legal rules valid or invalid. Such rules 'together are enough to convert the regime of primary rules into what is indisputably a legal system'.[35] The central elements of Hart's idea of law, namely the idea of legal validity and of the 'union' of primary and secondary rules makes sense only in the context of a legal system. But what kind of rule of recognition exists for public international law? And would not such a rule conflict with the rules for domestic law, since it seems to overlap with it over the geographical area it covers? This determined Hart's view of international law as follows: 'Different interpretations of the phenomena to be observed are of course possible; but it is submitted that there is no basic rule providing general criteria of validity for the rules of international law, and that the rules which are in fact

[34] H.L.A. Hart, *The Concept of Law*, 2nd edn (Oxford: Oxford University Press, 1994).
[35] ibid 94.

operative constitute not a system but a set of rules, among which are the rules providing for the binding force of treaties.'[36] So Hart's view was that international law was not a proper legal system, although it could be said to be a 'set of rules' deriving their force from practice and not from the 'union of primary and secondary rules'.

A similar position, although less explicit about international law, is offered by Joseph Raz. His view is, very broadly, that laws are created by the legal system, but that the legal system itself is not a pure legal creation: 'Every state—by which is meant a form of political system and not a juristic person—has one legal system that constitutes the law of that state, and every municipal legal system is the law of one state. Since, then, the identity of a legal system is bound up with that of the state the law of which it is, the relation between law and state necessarily affects the problem of scope.'[37] In his discussion of the institutional nature of law Raz left it open that international law may be a proper legal system.[38] But in the end, he agreed with Hart that only states could have legal systems, because his account of legal system requires a strong rule of recognition and consistent practices of officials, features that are absent from international relations.[39]

This is also the view taken by a self-conscious application of Raz's ideas onto the law of the European Union by Keith Culver and Michael Giudice.[40] Their analysis proposes, however, that 'supra-state' law, should not be conceived on the basis of the conventional theory of the legal system, but on the basis of a new theory according to which 'supra-state' law exists due to the 'interactions, or what we will call relations of mutual reference, between EU institutions and Member state institutions which share and exchange norms and normative powers to create, apply, and enforce norms'.[41] Their description of the European Union is not therefore as a legal 'system' but as a '*sui generis* form of legal order qua variegation of legal institutions, whose origins in overlapping and intersecting institutions might over time be gradually displaced by pan-European legal norms and legal institutions, much as in common law systems, customary law has been gradually displaced by statute and precedent'.[42] In other words, EU law is not a legal system, but has the institutional potential of becoming more like a state legal system.

[36] ibid 236.

[37] Joseph Raz, *The Authority of Law* (Oxford: Clarendon Press, 1979) 98–9.

[38] ibid 105. See also Joseph Raz, 'Human Rights Without Foundations' in John Tasioulas and Samantha Besson (eds), *The Philosophy of International Law* (Oxford: Oxford University Press, 2010) 321, where Raz recognizes that human rights are valid reasons for the limitation of state sovereignty but leaves it open whether the limitation is also legally valid, as well as morally so.

[39] Raz writes for example: 'Nothing is part of a legal system unless either it is a rule of recognition of the system, or the courts ought to recognize and apply it' ('The Identity of Legal System' 97). On Raz's views see Keith Culver and Michael Giudice, *Legality's Borders: An Essay in General Jurisprudence* (Oxford: Oxford University Press, 2010) 41–78.

[40] Keith Culver and Michael Giudice, 'Not a System but an Order: An Inter-Institutional View of European Union Law' in Julie Dickson and Pavlos Eleftheriadis (eds), *Philosophical Foundations of European Union Law* (Oxford: Oxford University Press, 2012) 54–76.

[41] ibid 68.

[42] ibid 75.

This view, however, is not really different from that of Hart, because Hart too believed that only state law was subject to criteria of validity set out in a rule of recognition, whereas international norms emerge through practice. Culver and Giudice provide a sophisticated description of the 'inter-institutional' practices that give rise to international norms, but fail—like Hart—to explain why this alternative theory of law applies only to international law and not to state law.

One way of understanding the position taken by Culver and Giudice is by saying that Hart's view of the legal system should not be taken to be the only available theory of law because the circumstances of law have changed. In a way, Hart is out of date. In their view a more sociologically informed theory of law should be open to the possibility of 'inter-institutional' practices that make law among states.[43] But holding Hart's theory to be one of sociological observation, which should be updated from time to time, risks robbing it entirely of any content. If Hart was merely trying to describe our practices, then his theory would only be true for the time and place of his observations.

The focus of Kelsen and Hart's theories of law is entirely different, however. They were trying to offer a *philosophical*, not a sociological account of law. Their arguments suggested a general and abstract theoretical framework for the idea of law, which could be deployed in legal interpretations in any context, domestic or international. This was not a sociological ambition. A sociologist of law can tell us, for example, that law is 'whatever people identify and treat through their social practices as "law"'.[44] In this sense anything at all can count as law and a legal system. Contradictory ideas and systems could end up being law and legal systems. Although there is nothing wrong with this view as a tool for the study of societies, this account is pointless for legal scholarship itself. If we accepted this view of law, then no criterion or set of criteria would be in a position to guide us in identifying and discussing 'law' and 'legal system'. We would be free to call several things 'international law' or 'domestic law' without consistency or principle. The sociological answer is no answer at all, but merely a restatement of the problem.

A different approach to the Hart and Raz framework on international legal systems has been proposed by Julie Dickson.[45] Dickson departs from Raz in adjusting the theory of legal systems on account of the political nature of the institutions they involve. She argues that political considerations are relevant in the construction of the basic idea of a legal system. In the case of the European Union she believes that the relevant conception of legal system does not entail a claim to constant

[43] At one point Culver and Giudice say that 'the legal order of the EU embodies a remarkable transformation in the nature of law-state's borders', ibid at 73.

[44] Brian Tamanaha, *A General Jurisprudence of Law and Society* (Oxford: Oxford University Press, 2001) 166.

[45] Julie Dickson, 'Towards a Theory of European Union Legal Systems' in Julie Dickson and Pavlos Eleftheriadis (eds), *Philosophical Foundations of European Union Law* (Oxford: Oxford University Press, 2012) 25–53.

supremacy. So she argues that 'claims to normative self-determination can be claims that it lies with within the grant of a given legal system to permit the operation of other legal systems within their normative domain, and can have as their content that the norms of those other systems prevail over the norms of the system granting the permission in cases of conflict'.[46]

Legal systems exist when they make a claim to 'normative self-determination', and in the case of the EU such claims are made both by the EU and the member states. Dickson's solution, although potentially more flexible, is not in the end that different to Hart and Raz. This is evident when she says that a system can recognize and 'permit'—and therefore subsume—the supremacy claim of another system for some reason. She says: 'so long as the permissions so granted remain within the normative determination of the granting system, which hence still 'calls the shots' as regards the relations between itself and other normative systems, then this remains a claim to normative self-determination, and the system claiming it remains a distinct legal system'.[47] But if one system 'calls the shots', it then enjoys the primacy that Kumm had in mind. In Dickson's analysis of the European Union, there are rival legal systems and only one of them ends up 'calling the shots'.

We need thus to return to the theoretical questions posed by EU law as a legal system which makes a claim to supremacy. This is our challenge: we are asking if it is possible to reconcile two views that seem irreconcilable. On the one hand we have the view that law exists in a legal system with certain features (this is the view of Kelsen, Hart, and Raz). On the other, we have the example of EU law or international law that is held to be a legal system without meeting those standards. Most courts say that EU law and international are really 'law'. Either the philosophers or the courts must be wrong. We cannot hold both statements to be true at the same time.

Tthe legal positivist theories take the first proposition to be true. They say that legality is defined in terms of a hierarchical relation to a 'basic norm' or a 'rule of recognition'. In Hart's explicit account, since the status of international legal norms does not depend on a 'rule of recognition' but on social practices, international law is therefore entirely secondary or, more correctly, a different category altogether. The world of international legal norms will thus not truly engage or much less conflict with national law. Domestic institutions may help themselves to some of it by occasionally giving international rules some kind of domestic 'legality', but this confirms the position that international law is not truly law—and therefore EU law is not 'law'. Indeed, this was more or less the position on EU law defended by John Finnis in his discussion of the *Miller* litigation in the Supreme Court, where he drew a very sharp distinction between proper 'statutory rights' made according to UK constitutional law and those rights created by European institutions and

46 ibid 49.
47 ibid 50.

taking effect only in the 'international plane' and having no impact in the law of the United Kingdom except as recognized by executive action that keeps the United Kingdom in the European Union.[48]

What, thus, emerges from the Hart and Raz view of law is a theoretical position that could be called 'national monism': only national law is proper law. In other words, if the law is exhaustively determined by the national sources, then there cannot be a conflict with another system. This way, however, the law of nations becomes entirely subsumed to the law of states. This view, may be logically possible, but it contradicts the established practice of states and courts. It fails to explain a case like *Medellin*. The problem faced by the Supreme Court there was the existence of a direct judgment of the International Court of Justice requiring domestic authorities to respect the rules of consular protection. It is logically conceivable to speak of the ICJ's judgment merely as a political event to be taken account of, in the sense that all political events are to be taken account of. One could say that it is not the ground of any legal rights and obligations, since the only possible such ground is the only relevant legal system, namely the legal system of the United States.

Nevertheless, no national court accepts such a position. All national courts treat international law with at least a modicum of respect as law. Even the Supreme Court rejected this extreme view in its own judgment. Chief Justice Roberts reasoned as follows:

> No one disputes that the *Avena* decision—a decision that flows from the treaties through which the United States submitted to ICJ jurisdiction with respect to Vienna Convention disputes—constitutes an *international* law obligation on the part of the United States. But not all international law obligations automatically constitute binding federal law enforceable in United States courts. The question we confront here is whether the *Avena* judgment has automatic *domestic* legal effect such that the judgment of its own force applies in state and federal courts.[49]

In its judgment the US Supreme Court recognized that international law is *law*. It creates legal obligations on the United States. Such obligations do not derive from the domestic legal system—so, in a way, the domestic legal system does not 'call the shots' in Julie Dickson's terminology.

I believe that the US Supreme Court's position that international law is law, even though it is independent of domestic law, is not really compatible with the views of the legal system put forward by Kelsen, Hart, and Raz. If the international legal

[48] John Finnis, 'Terminating Treaty-based UK Rights', *U.K. Constitutional Law Blog* (26 Oct 2016) (available at https://ukconstitutionallaw.org/). Some such view was accepted only by the minority of Supreme Court in *R (Miller) v Secretary of State* [2017]UKSC 5, [2018] AC 61.

[49] *Medellin v Dretke*, p. 8. Indeed Chief Justice Roberts' whole judgment proceeds from the interpretation of the international legal materials as legal materials, precisely in order to determine if the relevant international treaty is 'self-executing' in US law (as well as a source of international law obligations).

order cannot be a legal system, then there cannot be international legal obligations at all and the US is not bound by any such law. If Chief Justice Roberts saw law in the way suggested by the theories of legal system offered by Kelsen, Hart, and Raz he would have said that the International Court of Justice was outside the relevant legal system and could not, therefore, be creating any legal obligations at all.

But he did not say that. He said that international law is law, which has true legal effects but which may not have 'automatic' effects in domestic law, by which he meant that it can create no remedies there. So for Chief Justice Roberts international law is law in the proper sense of the word. But it is law about a different thing, the relations between states.

Mindful of these kinds of problems Hans Kelsen argued in exactly the opposite way from Hart and Raz. He said the best understanding of international law is by way of a 'monist' view, according to which we are to understand the whole of law, domestic and international, as a single legal system.[50] In Kelsen's view, all national legal orders are validated by public international law. So here we have the complete reversal of the Hart and Raz argument. Rather than start from the domestic case and cast our net outwards, so to speak, Kelsen tells us to think of the international as primary and as a condition for the validity of the national.[51]

Kelsen's theory, however, is too radical. It too fails to explain the *Medellin* judgment. This is because under a monist perspective, the Supreme Court ought to have followed the dictates of international law *in preference* to domestic law. This is what monism requires. Yet, it is a practice that no state follows anywhere in the world. Even the Netherlands, which is generally considered a 'monist' state, allows international law to have effects domestically only to the extent that its constitution permits, which it does in a series of Articles discussing the effect of international law.[52] So the Netherlands is not a 'monist' state in Kelsen's sense, but a state which, much

[50] Hans Kelsen, *Pure Theory of Law*, trans. by Max Knight (University of California Press, 1967) 328–44.

[51] For a recent defence of Kelsen's monism see Paul Gragl, *Legal Monism* (Oxford: Oxford University Press, 2018). Gragl summarizes the argument (p. 338) for the unity of law as follows: 'Applied to the relationship between international and national law, this entails that these two bodies of law either find themselves in a hierarchical connection with one another in a unitary body of law, or that they are created by a third superimposed legal order. However, since there is no third legal order creating international and national law, it must necessarily be the case that they are part of the same monist legal order through the principle of effectiveness. Furthermore, by exposing the concept of sovereignty as a mere legal concept and equating the state with its own legal order, Kelsen succeeds in demystifying the last political arguments against monism and the legal nature of international law.'

[52] These are Articles 91 and 94 of the Dutch Constitution, among others. Article 91(3) provides that the preference for Treaties is conditional on ratification having been approved by two thirds of Parliament. Article 94 provides that 'Statutory regulations in force within the Kingdom shall not be applicable if such application is in conflict with provisions of treaties or of resolutions by international institutions that are binding on all persons.' For a recent discussion see Leonard Besselink, 'The Proliferation of Constitutional Law and Constitutional Adjudication, or How American Judicial Review Came to Europe After All' 9 *Utrecht Law Review* (2013) 19–35. cf Bruno De Witte, 'Do Not Mention the Word: Sovereignty in Two Europhile Countries: Belgium and the Netherlands' in Neil Walker (ed.), *Sovereignty in Transition* (Oxford: Hart, 2003), at 351.

like the United States Supreme Court did in *Medellin*, recognizes the effect and role of international law as *law*, but gives it effect only to the extent that its own constitution permits it. Kelsen's monism is not how the Netherlands views international law. Indeed, Kelsen's reduction of international law to a 'system of rules' leaves no room for looking at it from a substantive point of view, as the law of nations, nor does it sufficiently distinguish it from the law of a jurisdiction that is appropriate for a political community. Kelsen's theory does not tell us how public international law could possibly have a distinct structure as the law of nations.

3.4 From Plurality to Pluralism

How do these problems help us understand European Union law? Most theorists avoid an explicit engagement with the theoretical puzzles identified by Kelsen and Hart. As far as I know there is only one theorist who explicitly argues that the treaties are a 'Grundnorm' for the member states, as suggested in Kelsen's model. The EU law scholar Robert Schütze has written that the EU treaties have now become the 'Grundnorm' of the European legal order.[53] Such defences of European monism, however, are rare. Most theories are happy to note the different position of European Union law in relation to domestic law. The *Medellin* decision of the United States Supreme Court gives to international law a role that is, in principle, not dissimilar to the role of EU law identified by the member states courts. Just like international law, European Union law is recognized as law, but its effects are structurally distinct to those of ordinary constitutional or other domestic law. For this reason most EU legal scholars do not seek to understand European Union law through the lenses of Hartian 'statism' or Kelsenian monism.

Many of them are speaking of the EU as a unique legal order whose main feature is that it is a 'pluralist' legal order. Over the past two decades, pluralism has emerged as perhaps the dominant theoretical approach to EU law.[54] Yet, as I will

[53] See Robert Schütze, *European Constitutional Law*, 2nd edn (Cambridge: Cambridge University Press, 2016) 43–76. I discuss Schütze views in detail in Chapter 5.

[54] See for example Mattias Kumm, 'Who is the Final Arbiter of Constitutionality in Europe?: Three Conceptions of the Relationship Between the German Federal Constitutional Court and the European Court of Justice' 36 *Common Market Law Review* (1999) 351; Mattias Kumm, 'The Jurisprudence of Constitutional Conflict: Constitutional Supremacy in Europe before and after the Constitutional Treaty' 11 *European Law Journal* (2005) 262–307; Mattias Kumm, 'The Moral Point of Constitutional Pluralism: Defining the Domain of Legitimate Institutional Civil Disobedience and Conscientious Objection' in Pavlos Eleftheriadis and Julie Dickson (eds), *Philosophical Foundations of European Union Law* (Oxford: Oxford University Press, 2012) 216–46; S. Besson, 'From European Integration to European Integrity: Should European Law Speak with Just One Voice?' (2004) 10 *European Law Journal* 257; Massimo La Torre, 'Legal Pluralism as an Evolutionary Achievement of Community Law' (1999) 12 *Ratio Juris* 182; Nicholas W. Barber, 'Legal Pluralism and the European Union' 12 *European Law Journal* (2006) 306; Miguel Poiares Maduro, 'Contrapunctual Law: Europe's Constitutional Pluralism in Action' in Neil Walker (ed.), *Sovereignty in Transition: Essays in European Law* (Oxford: Hart, 2003) 501. See also the collections of essays Matej Avbelj and Jan Komárek (eds),

show, pluralism is a response to the paradoxes created by the formalism of the legal positivists—and becomes unnecessary when one views EU law under a substantive interpretation.

The first defence of a theory of pluralism was that proposed by the late Sir Neil MacCormick. In his book *Questioning Sovereignty*, MacCormick offered an analysis of the legal structure of the European Union in terms that sought to tame and explain what he identified as the 'juridical pluralism' between the national courts and the European Court of Justice.[55] MacCormick's conclusion was that we could describe that set of legal relations as a 'plurality of institutional normative orders', where 'constitutional pluralism prevails'.[56] The main theme is that European Union law challenges traditional legal theory and constitutional doctrine, because EU law and the law of the states interact in an entirely new way.

MacCormick started his analysis of EU law from the complexity of the Union's institutional machinery of law-making. He observed that the legislature for the European Community was—at the time—the Council of Ministers 'whose members were identifiable only by reference to the place they hold according to state-systems of law'. So the legislator for the European Union was defined, partly, through national laws and processes. He also noticed that 'the process of constitutional amendment for both Union and Community remains a process of treaty-making among member states'.[57] Here too, the most important power of law-making belonged to institutions and processes fully determined by the constitutional law of the member states. MacCormick concluded that it is questionable if the legal orders of the member states intended to 'retain validity' only through the mediation of EU law.[58] We are thus left with little support for the proposition that EU law was autonomous and therefore primary. For this reason McCormick rejected the monist analysis more or less offered by the Court of Justice. He concluded that there was 'no hierarchical relationship in the rank-order international law-community law-Member State law'. He concluded that 'these are interacting systems, one of which constitutes in its own context and over the relevant range of topics a source of valid law superior to other sources recognized in each of the member state systems'.[59] It was for each court to determine the law according to each own rules.

Constitutional Pluralism in the European Union and Beyond (Oxford: Hart, 2012); and Matej Avbelj and Gareth Davies (eds) *Research Handbook on Legal Pluralism and EU Law* (London: Edward Elgar, 2018).

[55] Neil MacCormick, *Questioning Sovereignty: Law, State and Nation in the European Commonwealth* (Oxford: Oxford University Press, 1999).

[56] ibid 104.

[57] ibid 117.

[58] ibid 117.

[59] ibid 117.

MacCormick concluded that these relations could not be hierarchical. He said:

> For each state, the internal validity of Community law in the sense mandated by the 'supremacy' doctrine results from the state's amendment of constitutional and sub-constitutional law to the extent required to give direct effect and applicability to Community law. On the other hand, the Community's legal order is neither conditional upon the validity of any particular state's constitution, nor upon the sum of the conditions that the states might impose, for that would be no Community at all ... so relations between states *inter se* and between states and Community are interactive rather than hierarchical.[60]

What does this mean, however, for the constitutional law of the member states? If there is no hierarchy between national and EU law, how do we decide possible conflicts between them? The fact that the Court of Justice is to interpret EU law according to its own principles and that national courts are to determine the relations between EU law and national law according to their own principles does not rule out differences of interpretation over competence or delegation. Here is MacCormick's surprising answer about their interaction:

> It follows also that the interpretive power of the highest decision-making authorities of the different systems must be, as to each system, ultimate. It is for the ECJ to interpret in the last resort and in a finally authoritative way the norms of Community law. But equally, it must be for the highest constitutional tribunal of each member state to interpret its constitutional and other norms, and hence to interpret the interaction of the validity of EC law with higher level norms of validity in the given state system.[61]

The answer is surprising because it denies the premise on which it was based. The premise was that there was no hierarchy between the EU and national law. But if there is no hierarchy, the national court ought to accommodate EU law as if it were equal to national law. Lack of hierarchy means equality. Instead, MacCormick's pluralism advises the courts to maintain two inconsistent monisms: EU monism and national monism. But this affirms the hierarchy and does not deny it. MacCormick's suggestion that each court is finally authoritative in its own domain affirms both hierarchies at the same time. MacCormick then adds that there is no reason to regret the incoherence. This is what MacCormick has called 'radical pluralism'. It is the view that 'it is possible that the European Court interprets Community law so as to assert some right or obligation as binding in favour of a person within the jurisdiction of the highest court of a member state, while that court in turn denies that such a right or obligation is valid in terms of the national

[60] ibid 117–18.
[61] ibid.

constitution'. Such conflicts are 'not logically embarrassing' because 'strictly, the answers are from the point of view of different systems'.[62] Yet, this analysis seems to be going beyond the affirmation of primacy. It also assumes that the two systems are not actually communicating. It weakens the premise that they are 'interacting'.

We need to break down MacCormick's construction of radical pluralism to its two constituent components. Its first component is the presupposition that constitutional authority relies on a hierarchy of rules. The national legal order takes the constitution to be the highest rule while the European legal order takes the treaties to be the highest rule, under a determinate 'rule of recognition' or 'basic norm'. The second component concerns the scope of the relevant legal system, or its subject matter. MacCormick does not specify if the European legal order includes the member states, or if each member state has its own legal system. His position remains ambivalent on which one is the relevant territorial or substantive domain. This explains, I think, MacCormick's claim that 'strictly' the conflicting answers derive from different legal systems but are also overlapping. European Union law does claim to cover the domains covered by the national systems, although the national systems may deny it.

Pluralism, as we noted above, refuses to adjudicate these conflicting claims. This version of pluralism is *radical* because it leaves both questions open: which rule is the highest rule and which system is the relevant system. Pluralism is not, therefore, a view taken by public international law. Public international law makes a certain claim to primacy for its own subject matter: the law regarding relations between states. This is a limited claim, defined by its content. International law makes its claim to primacy precisely because it does so within a framework of dualism. Dualism from the point of view of public international law does not say that there are two *parallel* orders, but that there are two *different* orders, so that state law and public international law have distinct tasks. There is no hierarchy between them. Since the orders are different, they do not overlap and the question of a hierarchy does not arise. Strictly speaking, therefore, international law applies not because it enjoys 'primacy' over another set of rules that competes with it, but because nothing else takes its place in the domain of the law of states.[63]

Article 27 of the Vienna Convention on the Law of Treaties, for example, requires as follows: 'A party may not invoke the provisions of its internal law as justification for its failure to perform a treaty.' This provision refers to obligations arising under treaties, i.e. obligations of a state towards another state. In one sense Article 27 gives precedence to Treaties over domestic law because it says that domestic law

[62] ibid 119.

[63] For dualism in international law—and the misuses of the term 'monism'—see the extremely clear and valuable discussion in Mario Mendez, *The Legal Effects of EU Agreements: Maximalist Treaty Enforcement and Judicial Avoidance Techniques* (Oxford: Oxford University Press, 2013) 37–47. See also the extensive discussion of dualism in Arangio-Ruiz Gaetano, 'Dualism Revisited: International Law and Interindividual Law' 86 *Rivista Di Diritto Internazionale* (2003) 909–99.

cannot be an excuse for a failure to respect a treaty. But a more accurate reading is that domestic law has no place in relations between states. If it has no place, it is wrong to say that it has an *inferior* place. Read in this way, Article 27 does not entail monism and does not create the conflict that MacCormick describes above.

A dualist account of international law, which is implicit in Article 27, gives full recognition to international law as the law of nations, without compromising the authority of national law, as the law of a jurisdiction. This reading of dualism in a way accepts the insight of Dickson, because it says that legal orders come in different shapes and forms. The international legal order is something very different from the domestic one :it does not claim to be a jurisdiction. But this reading also accepts the suggestions made by Letsas, that the idea of legal systems is unhelpful, because it says that what matters is the *subject matter* of the two legal frameworks, not their form as a supposed hierarchy of rules. Rather than look for a fundamental 'rule of recognition', those who wish to apply international law must focus on its substantive content as the law of nations, in order to understand its proper effect in a domestic legal order.

This substantive and interpretive approach to the question of the effect of international law is routinely taken by English courts. These courts never speak in terms of 'rival' legal systems. It is a well-established doctrine of English law that international relations is not something appropriate for national judicial determination from the point of view of its substance. Conversely, the making of a treaty does not alter domestic law. The leading case outlining this dualist position in the United Kingdom is the decision of the Judicial Committee of the House of Lords in the *International Tin Council* case.[64] Lord Oliver identified two principles of '*non-justiciability*' that courts in England and Wales should observe in respect of international treaties. The first principle is that 'it is axiomatic that municipal courts have not and cannot have the competence to adjudicate upon or enforce the rights arising out of transactions entered into by independent sovereign states between themselves on the plane of international law'.[65] The second principle is that:

> as a matter of the constitutional law of the United Kingdom, the Royal Prerogative, whilst it embraces the making of treaties, does not extend to altering the law or conferring rights upon individuals or depriving individuals of rights which they enjoy in domestic law without the intervention of Parliament. Treaties, as it is sometimes expressed, are not self-executing. Quite simply, a treaty is not part of English law unless and until it has been incorporated into the law by legislation.[66]

The two principles show how in practice international law has a structurally different position in the domestic legal order. Although it binds the United Kingdom

[64] *J H Rayner (Mincing Lane) ltd v Department of Trade and Industry* [1990] 2 AC 418.
[65] ibid 499.
[66] ibid 500.

as a subject of international law, it does not create new rights and duties for its citizens.

There are some exceptions to this general rule. In a case concerning the issue of when and how the substantive provisions of the United Nations Convention on the Rights of the Child (UNCRC) were directly enforceable in English Law, Lord Kerr left it open that some international treaties on human rights, having been 'the product of extensive and enlightened consideration', might be thought to be relevant in the recognition of rights of UK citizens, even if they have not been incorporated.[67] Customary international law is also treated differently. Since the decision of the Court of Appeal in *Trendtex Trading Corp v Central Bank of Nigeria*[68] it has occasionally been assumed by English courts that if a rule of customary international law is shown to exist, it is automatically received into domestic law. But these exceptional statements do not change the fundamental structural point about the role of international law. If anything, they confirm it.

So dualism is not a doctrine about two distinct legal orders as formal hierarchies of 'norms' that sit side by side and occasionally conflict. It is a substantive doctrine about the appropriate content of national and international law and their institutions in light of their distinct subject matters. Dualism makes the substantive assumption that international law has a distinct role to play from that of the domestic legal order. Under a dualist framework, a national court can recognize the effectiveness and validity of the legal relations arising between states under international law, although at the same time withholding judgment on them. Such matters are not justiciable before national courts. So dualism is not national monism. It is not a doctrine that denies—as H.L.A. Hart did—the character of international law as law.[69]

Radical pluralism takes a different view. It appears to reject the reading of European Union law as a substantively different legal order. Radical pluralism assumes that European Union law and domestic law occupy the same domain of social or legal life so that their conflict is real, because the rules of each legal order collide. When such conflict occurs, it cannot be lawfully resolved, because there is no hierarchical relation between them. As MacCormick put it: 'relations between states *inter se* and between states and Community are interactive rather than hierarchical'.[70] Radical pluralism suggests, in effect, that in the case of EU law we are faced with two *overlapping monisms*. These two monisms are in competition because they overlap, at least in the areas that fall under the scope of EU law. MacCormick says that under 'radical' pluralism there is no need to choose. We can

[67] *R (on the application of SG) v Secretary of State for Work and Pensions* [2015] UKSC 16, par. 256.

[68] *Trendtex Trading Corp v Central Bank of Nigeria* [1977] QB 529 (CA), at 533 (Lord Denning).

[69] For the distinction between statist monism, international monism, and dualism see Massimo La Torre, 'Legal Pluralism as an Evolutionary Achievement of Community Law' 12 *Ratio Juris* (1999) 182–95, at 183–4.

[70] MacCormick, *Questioning Sovereignty* 117–18.

accommodate them both. This is a 'radical' position because it suggests that there is no legal resolution to the conflict. MacCormick says: 'that is all that is to be said as a matter of law'.[71]

This is a very odd position. What if a national court openly defied a doctrine of the European Court of Justice? How should the Court of Justice respond? Does European Union law remain silent on this most fundamental of challenges? This is not a theoretical possibility any more. In 2014 the German Constitutional Court threatened to bring down the 'Outright Monetary Transactions' programme of the European Central Bank, which had been crucial to the survival of the Eurozone, on the basis that it was beyond the Bank's jurisdiction and violated the German Constitution.[72] The German court made a preliminary reference to the Court of Justice making its views perfectly clear that the actions of the European Central Bank were manifestly unlawful. The Court of Justice returned a judgment that for the most part vindicated the Bank. In its second OMT judgment the German Constitutional Court accepted the European Court's interpretation of EU law and a constitutional crisis was averted.

If this was a close call, a judgment of the Danish Supreme Court of December 2016 was an act of open defiance. The Court ruled that it was not bound by the Court of Justice's judicial doctrine of a principle of 'age discrimination', since this was not an explicit principle of the EU Treaties.[73] The Danish Court's interpretation of EU law clashes directly with that of the Court of Justice in rejecting the possibility of deriving unwritten principles from the Treaty. According to radical pluralism, such disagreements pose no legal problem at all. The two courts can continue pursuing their own constitutional visions. The reality, of course is very different. The disagreement between the two courts must be possible to resolve in law. Otherwise the ideal of the rule of law is defeated, both in the domestic constitutional order and in the legal order of the European Union. The courts that will deal with this problem need to reach a determinate answer.

We could imagine a more threatening but equally destructive conflict between, say, Viktor Orban's courts and the Court of Justice of the European Union, over the

[71] MacCormick, *Questioning Sovereignty* 119. A very similar view is put by N.W. Barber, who argues that there may be many inconsistent 'rules of recognition' in a single system, so that none of them would enjoy primacy in N.W. Barber, 'Legal Pluralism and the European Union' 12 *European Law Journal* (2006) 306–29. See also N.W. Barber, *The Constitutional State* (Oxford: Oxford University Press, 2010) 145–71.

[72] Case 2 BvR 2728/13 et al. Order of 14 January 2014. For an informative account of this episode see Dariusz Adamski, 'Economic Constitution of the Euro Area after the *Gauweiler* Preliminary Ruling' 52 *Common Market Law Review* (2015) 1451–90.

[73] Case no. 15/2014 *Dansk Industri (DI) acting for Ajos A/S v The estate left by A.*, Supreme Court of Denmark. The case arose after a preliminary reference to the Court of Justice in Case C-441/14 *Dansk Industri v Rasmussen*, ECLI:EU:C:2016:278. For an informative account see Mikael Rask Madsen, Henrik Palmer Olsen, and Urška Šadl, 'Competing Supremacies and Clashing Institutional Rationalities: The Danish Supreme Court's Decision in the *Ajos* Case and the National Limits of Judicial Cooperation' 23 *European Law Journal* (2017) 140–50.

fate of the Central European University, which the Orban government is actively undermining for political reasons. Radical pluralism seems not to understand the basic function and role of a legal order. It sees law merely as a technical order of rules, not as a set of principles protecting the rule of law for moral purposes. This is not accidental.

Radical pluralism is intimately connected to Hart's 'positivist' and largely technical view of law. MacCormick himself was one of Hart's most distinguished students. If we believe, with Hart, that a legal order is just a system of prevailing rules organized hierarchically with a 'rule of recognition' at the top, then the existence of EU law as a 'new legal order' must imply a new rule of recognition. If there are two such rules, they will conflict, but their conflict will not be possible to resolve in law, since the disagreement will concern the very presuppositions of validity.[74] Those who follow Hart's view of law generally conclude that EU law has upset the unity or order or rules assumed by legal positivism and has created radical uncertainty of precisely this kind. But if you believe that the law is the creation of a master rule, you will also have to accept that no legal resolution is possible. Thus some theorists welcome this constitutional uncertainty as something normal or indeed positive.

Nico Krisch, for example, relying explicitly on Hart's theory, sees recent developments towards the strengthening of international and transnational legal structures as having resulted in a deep challenge to law's unity or 'anchor'.[75] He advocates an alternative 'pluralist' theory which explicitly 'eschews the hope of building one common, overarching legal framework that would integrate postnational governance, distribute powers, and provide for means of solving disputes between the various layers of law and politics'.[76] Krisch believes that the division of labour between the different domains of domestic and transnational law should be set by each domain by itself, without a 'common legal point of reference to appeal to for resolving disagreement'.[77] Krisch is happy to accept the ensuing confusion. These arguments entail, for example, that a stronger state could lawfully force a constitutional position on another state or a stronger court on a weaker court, without any legal redress. But without a coherent institutional structure to speak of, every argument about the merits of any institutions will be futile. Even the debate on

[74] This is well explained by Neil MacCormick who speaks of a risk of 'constitutional conflict' in Neil MacCormick, *Questioning Sovereignty: Law, State, and Nation in the European Commonwealth* (Oxford: Oxford University Press, 1999) 102–21. I made the same point in Pavlos Eleftheriadis, 'Aspects of European Constitutionalism' 21 *European Law Review* (1996) 32–42; and Pavlos Eleftheriadis, 'Begging the Constitutional Question' 36 *Journal of Common Market Studies* (1998) 255–72.

[75] Nico Krisch, *Beyond Constitutionalism: The Pluralist Structure of Postnational Law* (Oxford: Oxford University Press, 2010) 11.

[76] ibid 69.

[77] ibid 69. Nick Barber similarly welcomes this kind of incoherence suggesting that it is sustainable if the resulting conflicts remain unresolved indefinitely: '[I]inconsistent laws need not demand inconsistent action; the constitutional dilemma can remain unresolved, provided that each side exercises restraint'; Barber, *The Constitutional State* (n. 71) 170.

global justice would become impossible, because no institutional structure would available to guide us.

Krisch, following Hart, endorses the austere view of law as a hierarchy of rules. He thus sees only two options for post-national or transnational law. One is the appropriation of constitutional architecture for the whole globe, in effect a new global legal order. The other is abandonment of any attempt at coherence. These are the two sets of theories that Krisch discusses in his book as respectively the 'constitutional' view and the 'pluralist' view.[78] This mistaken reading of transnational law is forced by the theoretical framework Krisch adopts from Hart and Kelsen. If you believe that a legal system is a formal hierarchy of 'rules' which exists by virtue of a rule of recognition or a 'basic norm', then you must make up your mind about which rule of recognition is true for each geographical domain, before you say that there exists a legal system. It also follows, as Kelsen saw, that only one legal system can exist for each part of the world. Hart's inflexible theory makes radical pluralism the only alternative to Kelsen's monism. In my view both theories are equally false.

3.5 Constitutional Dualism

We have observed that the legal positivist account of law has produced two paradoxical accounts of EU law. The first paradoxical account is the theory of European 'monism'. It supposes that the EU is the foundation of all law in the member states, even though it is derivative from their constitutional processes and the European Union Treaties. The second paradoxical account is 'radical pluralism'. It says that there are no legal rules applying to the relations between EU law and domestic law because both EU and domestic legal rules apply to that relationship. Both of them are based on a picture of law as a hierarchy or 'system' of rules created by a formal doctrine of legal validity as outlined by Kelsen and Hart. But this a very inadequate theory of law, which leads to paradoxical accounts not only of international law, but also of constitutional law.[79]

It is time to leave behind the positivist account. I will now return to Kant's theory of law and the idea of states as lawful jurisdictions, which I sketched in Chapter 2. If law is a moral judgment concerning lawful jurisdiction, then any theoretical account of law must start from a theory of political legitimacy.[80] We take as our

[78] See Krisch, *Beyond Constitutionalism* (n. 75) 23–4.

[79] See Pavlos Eleftheriadis, 'Power and Principle in Constitutional Law' 45 *Netherlands Journal of Legal Philosophy* (2016) 37–56; and Pavlos Eleftheriadis, 'In Defence of Constitutional Law' 81 *Modern Law Review* (2018) 154–78.

[80] For an excellent account of Kant's view that law and ethics are two parts of moral philosophy see B. Sharon Byrd and Joachim Hruschka, *Kant's Doctrine of Right: A Commentary* (Cambridge: Cambridge University Press, 2010) 3–5. This is the view of law that I defended in Pavlos Eleftheriadis, *Legal Rights* (Oxford: Oxford University Press, 2008).

starting point, following Kant and Rawls, the premise that persons have a duty of justice to set up and maintain a civil condition and a constitutional order, where social life as a whole can be organized on the basis of general rules and principles that make possible equal citizenship on the basis of reciprocity. This moral account of law ascribes law a certain purpose which Dworkin has identified as the justification of the comprehensive and coercive powers of the state.[81] This moral account identifies a constitution not just on its history but on the basis of its content. The process is a 'self-reflective' one, on the basis of which the constitution exists not on the basis of some prior causal event, but as a practical judgment.[82]

For this moral account of the legal order, a constitution is not a formal order of rules, the way Kelsen presents it, but a set of institutions whose aim is to achieve equal citizenship for all. The constitution encompasses powers of law-making, law-enforcement, and adjudication under a common framework of public laws. In Chapter 2 I called this framework 'jurisdiction'. I need now explain in greater detail what I mean by the term.

Locke used the word 'jurisdiction' to mean 'being subjected to the will or authority of any other man' and I think this captures very clearly the idea of the authoritative claims of a legitimate state. Locke contrasted the civil condition to the state of nature, where all men are equal 'in respect of jurisdiction or dominion over one another'.[83] He meant that in a state of nature all men had neither jurisdiction, nor dominion over one another. By contrast, when operating under the terms of organized society, legal officials have the power to determine the legal relations of others, specifying, clarifying, and adjudicating legal duties. Any such power runs the risk of creating pernicious hierarchies. Nevertheless, constitutional justice transforms this power to an agent of political equality, through the rule of law. This kind of institutional framework, which works under the guidance of general rules and principles and meets the basic tests of constitutional justice, I call a system of jurisdiction.

A jurisdiction encompasses the whole set of rule-based decision-making from law-making to law-applying, enforcement, and adjudication. It serves to reassure everyone under its dominion that the public rights and duties announced by the law will be truly given effect through public but also reasonable institutions that determine legal relations in a legitimate and authoritative manner. Without this assurance, the legal order is uncertain and vulnerable to collapse.[84]

Kant used different terminology to make essentially the same point. He called a system of government a system of 'public right'. He argued that we have a 'natural

[81] See Ronald Dworkin, *Law's Empire* (London: Fontana, 1986) 82–90.

[82] See Eleftheriadis, 'Power and Principle in Constitutional Law' (n. 79) 48–52.

[83] John Locke, *Two Treatises of Government*, edited by Peter Laslett (Cambridge: Cambridge University Press, 1988), Second Treatise, ch. VI, §54, p. 303.

[84] For the idea of assurance in public law, see Arthur Ripstein, 'Authority and Coercion' (2004) 32 *Philosophy and Public Affairs* 2.

duty of justice' to leave the state of nature and enter a system of 'public right' because this was the only way in which we can live in society with other human beings while respecting them as equal citizens. Kant argued that in any given society legal rights and duties, unlike merely moral rights and duties, are always correlative and interlinked. A right to do something entails a correlative restriction on the options of someone else. The mutual moral responsibility that arises from social life is fully reflected in the structures of law and the correlativity of rights and duties.[85] The structure of social life makes it necessary that institutions should be available for determining the content of rights, assessing evidence and, if necessary, enforcing remedies. These tasks cannot be done voluntarily. If we were to perform them through self-help, reciprocity would break down.[86] Kant explains the point as follows: 'A unilateral will cannot serve as a coercive law for everyone . . . , since that would infringe upon freedom in accordance with universal laws'.[87] Bernd Ludwig puts the point as follows: 'Kant's concept of state . . . is nothing but the elaboration of the concept of a set of rules and institutions necessary for playing the *Rechtslehre* game in its most extensive version: a game of *persons* who share a world of external objects of choice'. Universality is failed, Kant argued, if we make, determine, and enforce the law to our own case. Kant's alternative answer is to outline a set of public institutions, to which he gives the name 'public right', that will put everyone under the same obligation of compliance and provide everyone the assurance that their lawful freedom is protected.[88] This is not merely a stage of enforcement that supposedly follows an act of violation. Putting the matter this way would misunderstand the role of institutions. Coercive legal structures are not a further stage to substantive rights. Reciprocal constraint is part of the very definition of legal rights and duties.[89] Jurisdiction is thus a rule-bound procedure of decision-making under general (or 'universal') laws.[90]

[85] For a detailed analysis of this Kantian insight especially in relation to Hohfeld's account of legal rights and duties as bilateral relations see Pavlos Eleftheriadis, *Legal Rights* (Oxford: Oxford University Press, 2008) 114–19.

[86] See Bernd Ludwig, 'Whence Public Right? The Role of Theoretical and Practical Reasoning in Kant's Doctrine of Right' in Mark Timmons (ed.), *Kant's Metaphysics of Morals: Interpretive Essays* (Oxford: Oxford University Press, 2002) 159–84, at 181.

[87] Immanuel Kant, *Metaphysics of Morals* in Kant, *Practical Philosophy*, edited by Allen Wood and trans. by Mary Gregor (Cambridge: Cambridge University Press, 1996) 6: 256, p. 409.

[88] ibid.

[89] Kant writes, in his discussion of the emergence of property rights: 'I am therefore not under obligation to leave external objects belonging to others untouched unless everyone else provides me assurance that he will behave in accordance with the same principle with regard to what is mine. This assurance does not require a special act to establish a right, but is already contained in the concept of an obligation corresponding to an external right, since the universality, and with it the reciprocity, of obligation arises from a universal rule'; ibid.

[90] There are various ways of putting this point about equality. I have relied on Kant's way, but I also find support for this view in more recent arguments, for example in Kolodny's idea of 'social equality' in Nico Kolodny, 'Rule Over None II: Social Equality and the Justification of Democracy' 42 *Philosophy and Public Affairs* (2014) 287–336; and in Elizabeth Anderson's analysis of equality in Elizabeth Anderson, 'What is the Point of Equality?' 109 *Ethics* (1999) 287–337.

If, then, a state is a jurisdiction that meets the tests of constitutional justice, international law must be a law in a very different sense. By definition there cannot be an international 'jurisdiction' because if there was, there would be no jurisdiction of states. The international institutions would effectively absorb the domestic ones. It follows that international law can only be law in a different sense to that of a jurisdiction. Although it relies on the same ideas of the rule of law, it recognizes the independence of states towards one another. Dworkin's account of international law offers a simple account of the pluralism of the international community and the need to protect states from one another. He explains that the interpretation of international legal documents must make:

> the best sense of the text, given the underlying aim of international law, which is taken to be the creation of an international order that protects political communities from external aggression, protects citizens of those communities from domestic barbarism, facilitates coordination when this is essential, and provides some measure of participation by people in their own governance across the world.[91]

From this point of view, the idea of dualism between national and international law is a doctrine that entails no paradox. Domestic law is the law of a jurisdiction while international law is the law among states or the law of nations. If domestic law is the law of a jurisdiction and international law the law of nations, then there cannot be a constitutional conflict between the two of the kind described by MacCormick. If an international treaty creates obligations that ought to be domestically enforced, for example, a double taxation treaty or a bilateral investment treaty, or a human rights treaty, then domestic law must create new domestic obligations that incorporate international law into the domestic system. Until such an incorporation happens, the international rules create no domestic remedies, even though they create legal effects in international law and the relations among states.

Constitutional dualism accommodates the effects of international law within the domestic sphere through a process of incorporation. This allows for the coexistence not only of national and international law but also of several national jurisdictions side by side. But if such incorporation does not take place, then international matters are not 'justiciable' before national courts. Such a substantive dualist view is not merely a theoretical construct. This position is in evidence whenever courts are invited to apply international or foreign law.[92] The test whether foreign law will apply domestically is ultimately one of substance, not form.

91 Ronald Dworkin, 'A New Philosophy for International Law' 41 *Philosophy and Public Affairs* (2013) 1, at 22.

92 See in general Philip Sales and Joanne Clement, 'International Law in Domestic Courts: The Developing Framework' 124 *Law Quarterly Review* (2008) 388.

It is a very old rule of the English law of contract that a contract may be unenforceable in England if it is illegal in foreign law, other than the law applicable to the contract. For example, the English courts did not enforce a contract the recognition of which could have constituted a hostile act against a foreign friendly government (this would now be considered a matter of 'public policy'). Thus in the 1824 case of *De Wütz v Hendricks* the plaintiff, in order to raise a loan in support of the Greek revolutionaries against the Ottoman Empire, deposited with the defendant certain papers.[93] After the loan agreement fell through, the plaintiff sought to recover the papers. Yet, because the purpose of the transaction which encompassed the overthrow of a friendly government was unlawful, the plaintiff could not recover the papers under the contract. Similarly, in *Regazzoni v K. C. Sethia (1944) Ltd*, a contract to export a commodity from India to South Africa contrary to the law of the former country was held unenforceable.[94] In short, it is a matter of English law if the courts also refuse to enforce a contract where the common intention of the parties was to violate the law of a foreign friendly state.[95] It is also a longstanding rule that English courts will not enforce a contract where performance of that contract is forbidden by the law of the place where it must be performed, at least whenever English law is the law governing the contract.[96]

Such examples show that the reception of foreign law is a matter of substance, not of form. Some legal rules develop full legal effects even though they originate in what appears to be an external 'legal system'. The positivist theory must say that such rules are not rules at all, since they originate in the wrong 'system'. This is not, however, how judges think about foreign or international law. Their reception does not depend on the primacy of a foreign or international rule of recognition, but on the merits of each case. There is therefore nothing radical or novel in the proposition that under a dualist framework domestic law may recognize and respect foreign or international law on account of its *substance*, the content of which is beyond the control of domestic law.

Dualism here is not just about 'who decides' to have international law received. It is always the domestic court that has to decide and does decide and it does so on the basis of what is required by the substance of the case. The national forum is always the starting point, since it cannot be otherwise. Yet its choices are based on substantive criteria, not on a formal hierarchy of 'rules'.

93 (1824) 2 Bing 314. See J.G. Collier, 'Is International Law Really Part of the Law of England?' 38 *International and Comparative Law Quarterly* (1989) 924–35. The law now is covered by the 1980 Rome Convention on the law applicable to contractual obligations, see OJ C 27 of 26.01.1998.

94 [1958] AC 301.

95 *Foster v Driscoll* [1929] 1 KB 470; *Soleimany v Soleimany* (1998) CLC 779, 792: 'Nor will it [i.e. English law] enforce a contract governed by the law of a foreign and friendly state, or which requires performance in such a country, if performance is illegal by the law of that country.'

96 For example, *Ralli Bros v Compania Naviera Sota y Aznar* [1920] 2 KB 287; *Libyan Arab Foreign Bank v Bankers Trust Co* [1989] QB 728.

This is exactly the way in which English law treats international law. An example is the law of sovereign immunity. The State Immunity Act 1978, in line with international practice, exempts foreign governments and their officials from the jurisdiction of UK courts. The function of the 1978 Act is to give effect to customary international law by granting immunity from certain types of legal proceedings in the government and government officials of a foreign state but also provide certain exceptions. Part of the logic of the statute is that English law has no say over the matter of who is an official of such a government. In other words, the statute relies on dualism: some issues are to be resolved authoritatively by foreign law. In the case of *Jones v Saudi Arabia* the House of Lords ruled that two Saudi government officials could not be sued for damages before English courts on the basis of alleged torture they were responsible for in Saudi Arabia.[97]

This case recognized Saudi law as authoritative as to who is a government official. It also recognized the power of international law to outline the limits of jurisdiction over foreign governments. In the course of his opinion, Lord Bingham explicitly relied on international law to support this conclusion that international law gives states the right to claim immunity for its own officials. It was a matter of international law, following explicit judgments of the international court of justice, which the United Kingdom courts could not ignore. Even a breach of a *jus cogens* norm of international law would not suffice to confer jurisdiction, in Lord Bingham's view.[98] The Court therefore had to defer to international law. This is because the State Immunity Act incorporates the principles of international law on state immunity, as they stand at the relevant time.

Similarly, in *Holland v Lampen-Wolfe*, another case of sovereign immunity, Lord Millet suggested that there is not even a *prima facie* breach of Article 6 of the ECHR, if a state fails to make available a jurisdiction which it does not possess.[99] He added that state immunity is not a 'self-imposed restriction on the jurisdiction of [the] courts' but a 'limitation imposed from without'.[100] The '*without*' is, evidently, public international law. Whether the United Kingdom possesses jurisdiction to hear a claim against a sovereign state is not a matter for the United Kingdom to decide.

These issues have now received extensive discussion by the United Kingdom Supreme Court. The question on the role of state immunity and the rights to a fair trial under Article 6 of the ECHR where raised again in the employment case of *Benkharbouche*, which concerned the possibility of a third country national

[97] *Jones v Saudi Arabia* [2006] UKHL 26; [2007] 1 AC 270; [2006] HRLR 32.

[98] ibid par. 24. Lord Bingham referred to the ICJ case *Democratic Republic of the Congo v Rwanda*, 3 February 2006, par. 64.

[99] *Holland v Lampen-Wolfe* [2000] 1 WLR 1573, at 1588 (endorsed by Lord Hofmann in *Jones v Saudi Arabia*, par. 64).

[100] ibid 1588 (Lord Millet): 'State immunity, as I have explained, is a creature of customary international law and derives from the equality of sovereign states. It is not a self-imposed restriction on the jurisdiction of its courts which the United Kingdom has chosen to adopt. It is a limitation imposed from without upon the sovereignty of the United Kingdom itself.'

bringing an employment claim against his or her former employers, a foreign Embassy in London.[101] The Supreme Court examined the provisions of the State Immunity Act and held that section 16(1)(c) was contrary to Article 6 ECHR because it barred employment law claims against states brought by ordinary employees. The reasoning of the Court, outlined by Lord Sumption (with whom all the other Justices agreed) was that in the absence of a rule of customary international law requiring such claims to be barred, the more generous domestic grant of immunity was a disproportionate interference with Article 6 of the ECHR. Here, the court's reasoning relied entirely on what it considered to be customary international law, implying that the requirements of customary international law would have been proportionate interferences with Article 6. The Court held that customary international law requires immunity only in cases where the functions of the employee involve the exercise of sovereign power, or if the case engages some other sovereign interest of the state. From that conclusion it followed that the more generous provisions of the State Immunity Act were contrary to the Human Rights Act—and subject to a declaration of incompatibility.

Lord Sumption explained the general point of law as follows: 'If it is necessary to decide a point of international law in order to resolve a justiciable issue and there is an ascertainable answer, then the court is bound to supply that answer. In the present cases, the law requires us to measure sections 4(2)(b) and 16(1)(a) [of the State Immunity Act] against the requirements of customary international law, something that we cannot do without deciding what those requirements are.'[102] After examining the relevant authorities in great detail Lord Sumption reached this conclusion: 'The rule of customary international law is that a state is entitled to immunity only in respect of acts done in the exercise of sovereign authority. In the absence of a special rule to some different effect applicable to employees in the position of Ms Janah and Ms Benkharbouche, that is the default position.'[103] By looking at international case law Lord Sumption showed that the contracts of employment of domestic staff were generally treated as private acts, not acts of sovereignty. There was no basis in customary international law for the application of state immunity to acts of a private law character.[104]

Interestingly, the question was not only looked at from an international law perspective. Lord Sumption also looked at the case law of several different jurisdictions. He cited Austrian, Italian, Belgian, Swiss, German, Norwegian, and Dutch cases.[105] He concluded:

[101] *Benkharbouche (Respondent) v Secretary of State for Foreign and Commonwealth Affairs (Appellant) and Secretary of State for Foreign and Commonwealth Affairs and Libya (Appellants) v Janah (Respondent)* [2017] UKSC 62. For similar theoretical issues see *R (Corner House Research) v Serious Fraud Office* [2009] 1 AC 756.

[102] *Benkharbouche* (n. 101) par. 35.

[103] *Benkharbouche* (n. 101) par. 38.

[104] *Benkharbouche* (n. 101) par. 63.

[105] *Benkharbouche* (n. 101) par. 66.

> The considerable body of comparative law material before us suggests that unless constrained by a statutory rule the general practice of states is to apply the classic distinction between *acts jure imperii* and *jure gestionis*, irrespective of the nationality or residence of the claimant. Indeed, the courts of a significant number of jurisdictions have refused to apply the immunity as between states which are not both party to the Convention, unless they performed functions directly related to the exercise of the state's sovereign authority, on the ground that the requirements of general international law differed on this point from those of the Convention.[106]

This wide-ranging judgment continues and renews the attitude of the English courts towards international law, which is a *substantive* and *interpretive* dualism. Under dualism, a court looks at the substance of the relevant rule of international law and interprets it in relation to the instant case. In *Benkharbouche* the Supreme Court examined international custom, the relevant treaties (and draft treaties) as well as comparative practice in order to understand the substance and point of the relevant rule of international law. The Court accepted without hesitation the authority of public international law for matters that concern relations between states, which in this case concerned the immunities of state representatives. The court's dualism did not deny the effects of international law or of foreign law. It interpreted the rule in order to apply it to the domestic case, in case the claimants had a good case for a remedy against the defendants.

In this sense interpretive dualism fully recognizes international and foreign law as an ordinary kind of law. It does so because it looks at the substance of the law of nations and not at a supposedly content-independent structure of a 'legal system'. The distinction between domestic and international law does not entail a formal hierarchical relationship between legal systems, as suggested by Kelsen, Hart, and MacCormick—and Nico Krisch. There is no question of deciding which legal system prevails over or excludes the other. No such choice is necessary. All courts have the task of applying substantive principles of law according to the best interpretation of the law as it stands. According to this division of labour, international law deals with the law of nations and domestic law deals with the law of a particular jurisdiction. Under the dualist framework, it is perfectly possible for domestic constitutional law to apply international law without compromising the state's sovereignty.

[106] *Benkharbouche* (n. 101) par. 66.

4
Incorporation

How exactly does constitutional dualism apply to the reception of European Union law by the law of the member states? It is now time to look at the practice of European Union law in light of the theories I discussed in Chapter 3. In the example of state immunity that I examined the problem was simple. We were dealing with a single question of international law which was by definition a matter of the law of nations, namely the treatment of one sovereign state by the courts of another. European Union law is different, however. It creates its own laws which alongside the treaties develop direct effects over a broad range of policy areas. EU law covers subject matters that are traditionally domestic, such as commercial law, environmental law, consumer protection, the regulation of banking and financial services, public procurement, and competition policy to mention but a few. EU law goes well beyond the interaction among nations. Is dualism applicable here?

It is not unusual to see international law affect private relationships. As we saw in *Benkharbouche*, customary international law may end up affecting the law of the domestic jurisdiction and ultimately the relations between one person and his or her employer. European Union law is similarly based on a treaty that establishes international obligations on the basis of reciprocity between states. Just like the principles of customary international law, the EU treaties impose direct obligations that states and their courts must respect with implications for the rights and obligations of individuals. There is nothing strange in the process of adjusting domestic law in order to accommodate international obligations. Courts always have the substantive interpretive task of working out their powers and their duties, as I showed in Chapter 3. The same problem arises in the European Union.

In this chapter I will show that the question of the role of EU law can be answered with the same dualism that accommodates international law. I will also seek to show that most domestic courts have incorporated EU law on the basis of substantive and interpretive dualism. I will argue that they have rejected the most extreme versions of the theory of a 'new legal order'. The national courts have instead received EU law on the basis of three unique principles that follow from dualism: 'conditional primacy', 'institutional tolerance', and 'integrity'. Although I will focus primarily on English and German Courts, the argument applies equally to all other member states.

A Union of Peoples. Pavlos Eleftheriadis. Oxford University Press (2020). © Oxford University Press.
DOI: 10.1093/oso/9780198854173.001.0001

4.1 The 'New Legal Order' and the Court

I turn first to the question of the primacy of European Union law over domestic law under the doctrine of a 'new legal order'. Primacy is a unique feature of European Union law, because it requires not only that domestic law makes room for the EU rule, but also grants it primacy over any contrary domestic law. According to the Court of Justice of the European Union, the founding treaties of the European Union unlike 'ordinary' international treaties establish a 'new legal order of international law' that possesses its own institutions and for the sake of which the member states have limited their sovereign rights in a series of fields.[1] Indeed this and other fundamental cases of the Court of Justice leave no doubt that the 'new legal order' is supposed to be independent on the domestic legal order. This is why it is 'unlike international law'. This impression is strengthened by Article 19(1) TEU, according to which the CJEU constitutes the legal guardian of a European legal order thus created by the treaties.[2] The standard argument is that primacy follows directly from the nature of the 'new legal order'. In this sense the making of the treaties was, in the words of Judge Mancini, the 'making of a Constitution for Europe'.[3]

The argument appears at first sight to rule out a theory of dualism. As I discussed in Chapter 1, the Court of Justice has frequently stated that EU law is 'autonomous' and the Court of Justice has exclusive jurisdiction to rule on matters pertaining to EU law (see section 1.1). It is arguable that the Court of Justice is giving effect to precisely this view. If EU law is autonomous, it will not depend on incorporation. If it does not depend on national acceptance then EU law is a 'monist' system whereby the national legal order has been merged with the European one. In this chapter I offer an argument for the opposite conclusion. The Court has not endorsed monism. Although some cases leave the question open, a more detailed look at the case law shows that the Court has stopped short of endorsing monism. The most plausible reading of the case law of the Court of Justice is that of dualism. This is the only theory that can accommodate the doctrine of the relations between EU law and domestic law as set out by the Court of Justice.

In *Van Gend* the court said that direct effect operates 'independently of national legislation'. It is easy to draw the inference that because EU law is independent of national law, it is therefore superior to it. If a type of law is to be read independently of others it must be true whatever these other types of law say about the same matter. It is logical, for example, that in a constitutional order such as that of the

[1] Case 26/62 *van Gend en Loos v Nederlandse Administratis der Belastingen* [1963] ECR 1; Case C-6/64 *Flaminio Costa v E N E L* [1964] ECR I-01141.

[2] Opinion of the Court 1/09 [2011] ECR I-01137, paras 65–7; Joined Cases C-402 and 415/05 *Kadi and Al Barakaat International Foundation v Council and Commission* [2008] ECR I-06351, paras 282, 285.

[3] G. Federico Mancini, 'The Making of a Constitution for Europe' (1989) 26 *CML Rev* 595.

United States or Germany we read the written constitution 'independently' of what statutes determine. It should be the same perhaps with European Union law. This was suggested in *Van Gend* and was confirmed a few years later in the case of *Costa v E N E L*.[4] This was one of the most important cases in EU law and it is worth spending some time understanding the Court's reasoning in that case too.

The case first arose in an Italian court where Mr Costa argued that the nationalization of the Italian electricity company, of which he was a shareholder, was contrary to the European rules on the prohibition of state aids and free movement of services. Irrespective of the substantive question, the claim raised a constitutional question. If the offending Italian statute was indeed in conflict with the European treaties, should the treaties prevail? If the treaties and the statute were thought to be of equal standing, then the later one should prevail, namely the Italian statute. The same would occur if the statute was deemed to be higher than the treaty. Hence the only possibility that in this case the treaties would be relevant to the case would have been if *they* prevailed over the Italian statute, because they were hierarchically superior.

The Court in *Costa* did not hesitate to draw what appeared to be a natural conclusion from *Van Gend's* reference to a 'new legal order'. It concluded as is well known that the Treaty was superior to all national statutes whenever passed. The first argument the Court gave in support of this conclusion was very broad and is the most ambitious. The European Economic Community (EEC) Treaty, as it then was, had created its own legal system: 'By contrast with ordinary international treaties, the EEC Treaty has created its own legal system which, on the entry into force of the Treaty, became an integral part of the legal systems of the Member States and which their courts are bound to apply.' The first step to the Court's argument is thus the 'independence' of the legal system of the Community, which is combined as we see with its direct effect: the legal system of the Community is an 'integral part' of the law of the member states. Primacy follows from this premise, as follows:

> By creating a Community of unlimited duration, having its own institutions, its own personality, its own legal capacity and capacity of representation on the international plane and, more particularly, real powers stemming from a limitation of sovereignty or a transfer of powers from the States to the Community, the Member States have limited their sovereign rights, albeit within limited fields, and have thus created a body of law which binds both their nationals and themselves.

The Court explains here that the primacy of EU law comes as a result of what the states did. By creating the EEC on the basis of international treaties, the member states have 'limited their own sovereignty' and transferred powers from the states

[4] Case 6/64 *Flaminio Costa v E N E L* [1964] ECR 585.

to the Community. The primacy of EEC law was thus based on this transfer. The argument is that the independence and primacy of the law of the treaties is the result of a willing act of foundation by the member states. The court thus starts from the premise that the foundation of a new legal order is a delegation by the member states by virtue of public international law. This is not enough for primacy though.

It all depends on a second argument. The effectiveness of the general scheme of the Treaty requires the supremacy of its provisions, the Court said. The judgment went on as follows:

> The integration into the laws of each Member State of provisions which derive from the Community, and more generally the terms and the spirit of the Treaty, make it impossible for the States, as a corollary, to accord precedence to a unilateral and subsequent measure over a legal system accepted by them on a basis of reciprocity. Such a measure cannot therefore be inconsistent with that legal system. The executive force of Community law cannot vary from one state to another in deference to subsequent domestic laws, without jeopardizing the attainment of the objectives of the Treaty set out in Article 5 (2) and giving rise to the discrimination prohibited by Article 7.

Efficiency leads to primacy. Yet the argument from efficiency does not lead to unconditional primacy. It is true that the objective of the treaties in creating an internal market would be compromised by inconsistent national laws. Nevertheless, the treaty leaves a great deal of space to the national authorities. States are supposed to enjoy wide discretion and significant exceptions to, and indeed opt-outs from, the process of integration. These powers are also part of the treaties. They too deserve 'effectiveness'. Indeed, the very idea of direct effect, as I showed above, is based on the premise that the legal orders remain distinct. Hence the efficiency of one part of the treaty, that concerning integration, may be cancelled out by the efficiency of the other part of the treaty which grants states reasonable powers to exercise their own policy choices. Effectiveness must apply to every part of the treaty. States also have a claim to effectiveness for their own policies and priorities. The argument for effectiveness does not, therefore, lead to unconditional primacy.

So we must return to the argument that European Union law is 'independent' for a general theoretical reason, which derives from the nature of the EU. But that argument is weak too. The argument for independence assumes that at some point in time the member states willingly transferred sovereignty. There is little evidence of such a transfer ever having taken place. The treaties do not mark such a transfer.

Indeed the Court of Justice has given little textual evidence to the effect that the scheme of treaties requires or implies supremacy. The Court relied on what is currently Article 288 of the Treaty on the Functioning of the European Union (TFEU) and was then Article 189, as follows:

> The precedence of Community law is confirmed by Article [288 TFEU, formerly 249 EC, ex 189 EC] whereby a regulation 'shall be binding' and 'directly applicable in all Member States'. This provisions, which is subject to no reservation, would be quite meaningless if a state could prevail over Community law.

The argument appears to be that supremacy is necessary if the explicitly provided for direct applicability of regulations is to make sense. This is a strikingly poor argument. Whether regulations have direct effect is entirely unrelated to primacy. Direct effect can exist without primacy at all. It makes perfect sense to consider that regulations may have direct applicability while operating at the same level as domestic statutes. They could be binding only until they were replaced by new domestic statutes. This would not be a 'meaningless' possibility, as the Court suggests, although it would signal a very different and very much weaker Union. So this textual argument is not convincing.

Another formulation of the argument for the primacy of European Union law was offered in another famous case originating in Italy and reaching the Court of Justice by means of a preliminary reference.[5] In *Simmenthal* the Court had to deal with a new procedural question. An Italian statute had already been found to contravene European law by the Court. The ordinary Italian courts, however, did not have the power under constitutional rules to strike down or 'disapply' a national law, even after the Court of Justice had found it unlawful. Whenever such a question arose they had to refer the matter to the Italian Constitutional Court which alone had the power to do so. To do so in this case would have entailed considerable delay, hence an Italian judge on the case sent a preliminary reference to the Court of Justice asking if the supremacy of European law meant that he should ignore the procedural obligation to refer the matter to the Italian Constitutional Court.

The Court of Justice answered affirmatively. It said that the primacy principle means that the national court must immediately set aside any provisions of national law that were contrary to directly applicable European law, irrespective of procedural complications. The reason for this was 'effectiveness' but also something that had to do with the institutional structure of the treaty. This was partly due to Article 267 TFEU (formerly 234 TEC, ex 177 EC). The Court said:

> The same conclusion emerges from the structure of article [267 TFEU, then 177 EC] of the Treaty which provides that any court or tribunal of a member state is entitled to make a reference to the court whenever it considers that a preliminary ruling on a question of interpretation or validity relating to Community law is

[5] Case 106/78 *Amministrazione delle Finanze dello Stato v Simmenthal SpA* [1978] ECR 629.

> necessary to enable it to give judgment. The effectiveness of that provision would be impaired if the national court were prevented from forthwith applying community law in accordance with the decision or the case-law of the court.[6]

Nevertheless, this textual argument is also inconclusive. The preliminary reference procedure does not *entail* primacy. Under European Union law we do have a principle of national procedural autonomy. It is almost always the case that as a matter of EU law the application and enforcement of EU-based obligations are a matter of national procedures. In any case, the system of preliminary reference does not require unconditional supremacy. It may well operate under a system of *conditional* supremacy. After all the national court has the last word after receiving the judgment of the Court in any preliminary reference procedure.

The Court in *Simmenthal* concluded that every national court 'must, in a case within its jurisdiction, apply Community law in its entirety and protect rights which the latter confers on individuals and must accordingly set aside any provision of national law which may conflict with it, whether prior or subsequent to the Community rule'.[7] The importance of this case lies in the fact that it dealt with an actual conflict between a national constitutional rule and the requirements of Community law. It was a real test of what happens in case of conflict, whereas in *Costa* the conflict was only theoretical.

The substantive effect of *Simmenthal* is that all national courts must henceforth directly and immediately enforce a clear and unconditional provision of European Union law of whatever kind and status even if there is a contrary national law of whatever kind and hierarchical status. Whenever a national court finds a national measure contrary to EU law it must disapply it immediately without procedural or other delay. For the Court of Justice supremacy is unconditional.

Nevertheless the argument for the 'independence' and thus the primacy of EU law was not directly addressed by the *Simmenthal* court. Other than the reference to the process of preliminary references to the Court from national courts (under Article 177 as it then was), there was no extended discussion in the case of any textual support for the proposition that the member states had signalled their willingness to transfer 'sovereign' powers to the Community. There was also no discussion of other aspects of the treaty that suggested the opposite outcome, namely the *dependence* of European law on national laws and procedures, as I showed in Chapter 3. We saw there that Neil MacCormick had noticed how dependent EU law and law-making was on the institutions of the member states. McCormick noted that the effective legislature for the Community is the Council of Ministers 'whose members are identifiable only by reference to the place they hold according to state-systems of law', and the fact that 'the process of constitutional

[6] ibid 19–20.
[7] ibid 21–2.

amendment for both Union and Community remains a process of treaty-making among member states'.[8] I have already drawn the same conclusion as MacCormick, namely that the legal orders of the member states are not intended to 'retain validity' only through the mediation of EU law.[9] None of the arguments offered by the court in *Simmenthal* suggest a different conclusion.

There is, in fact, a different way of reading *Costa* and *Simmenthal*. We may read them as decisions that do not presuppose a monist 'new legal order'. We can see them as decisions that bring about a more limited form of *conditional* primacy that follows from dualism. The cases may affirm the significance of uniformity, without, however, taking the view that EU law is 'autonomous' from national law.

Everything said in *Costa* and *Simmenthal* is compatible with the idea that EU law requires national law to take a *constitutional* step of *ex ante* incorporation. If we take this view, we say that primacy is achieved only through the constitutional decision of the member state to incorporate EU law as law that is superior to ordinary domestic claw. Primacy is thus achieved *through* incorporation. But if primacy is a matter of the domestic constitution, then the national courts are right to say that EU law must be in conformity with the national constitution.

This is precisely the way in which states deal with public international law in general. Primacy is not a novel idea in international law, as we have already seen.[10] It is generally accepted that international law binds states irrespective of national laws. Article 27 of the Vienna Convention on the Law of Treaties (VCLT) states: 'A party may not invoke the provisions of its internal law as justification for its failure to perform a treaty.' It is perhaps natural to say that the same applies to the EU treaties. The treaties bind the member states in their mutual relations, very much like any treaty among states. In this sense Article 27 of VCLT gives precedence to Treaties in the mutual relations of states, so that their mutual relations in international law cannot be determined by unilateral laws by one of them. EU law, however, has an added dimension, which we have just examined. Unlike ordinary treaties, EU law has direct effect in domestic law. The EU Treaties develop effects in the domestic legal order and are expected to be applied by the national courts directly and immediately. So the reading of conditional primacy is eminently plausible.

I now wish to argue, however, that conditional primacy is the *only* possible reading of *Costa* and *Simmenthal*. We cannot interpret those cases as requiring unconditional supremacy. This is so because the radical autonomy argument is actually *self-contradictory*. The reason is very simple.

There is immediately something paradoxical in the idea that a provision of a treaty may give that treaty its supreme character. For any provision of the treaty

[8] Neil MacCormick, *Questioning Sovereignty* (Oxford: Oxford University Press, 1999) 117.

[9] ibid.

[10] This was already noticed by Derrick Wyatt, 'New Legal Order, or Old?' 7 *European Law Review* (1982) 147.

depends on the effect of that treaty. A legal text cannot lift itself up from its own bootstraps so to speak. What if there was a provision in the Treaties saying that 'this treaty is primary and has direct effect in the legal systems of all the member states'? If such provision were part of the Treaty it would certainly create a clear international obligation of the states agreeing it towards one another. The states would have to recognize primacy and direct effect through incorporation. But they could only do so through their own laws. A treaty provision like this would only have the effect and force of a treaty of public international law. So such a provision would not answer the question of the 'autonomy' of the Treaty from domestic law, because its own authority was that of a treaty, which by definition is not so 'autonomous'.

When the European Communities were first set up no one doubted that the new entity was some kind of international organization whose status was subject, more or less, to public international law. Under the founding treaties the Communities possessed powers of legislation and had organs with penetrating competences—at least within designated subject-matters. Although this made the Communities the most integrated international entity, it created no claim for them to be a self-sufficient legal order separate from the international agreements that bound the member states. But with the judgments we have just surveyed, which were handed down in the 1960s and 1970s, the Court of Justice spoke of the law of the European Communities as a 'new legal order' that is binding on the member states irrespective of their own constitutions. This transformation, however, was not a result of any political process. It simply developed as a doctrine of the Court of Justice over a period of careful and gradual appraisal of the law.

The Court's apparent monism relies, at least implicitly, on the theory of law outlined by Kelsen and his followers. As I showed in Chapter 3, for Kelsen a legal order exists when a set of rules is based on a single higher norm that determines validity by way of a 'first constitution'.[11] Seeing the Treaties as a first or in any event a formal constitution allows one to say that the EU has become a new legal order or system. The European legal order can be an independent legal order because it created a new hierarchy of European legal norms with its own 'Grundnorm' at the top, is the implicit argument.

Nevertheless, the Kelsenian argument for the 'new legal order' of EU law is in the end self-defeating.[12] The argument requires that the domestic courts recognize the new legal order and, as a consequence, set aside their own previous 'basic norms' in order to put the EU treaties in its place. But in Kelsen's own theory such a change cannot be *lawful*—or unlawful. It is something *outside* the realm of legal validity. The argument for a 'new legal order' entails a legal revolution as correctly noticed

[11] See explicitly *Partie Ecologiste—Les Verts v European Parliament*, Case 294/83, [1987] 2 CMLR 343, at 371. In this case, however, the supremacy of European law was not at issue.

[12] I explained this in greater detail in Pavlos Eleftheriadis, 'Aspects of European Constitutionalism' 21 *European Law Review* (1996) 32; Pavlos Eleftheriadis, 'Begging the Constitutional Question' 36 *Journal of Common Market Studies* (1998) 255.

by William Wade.[13] A legal revolution cannot be a matter of legal duty however. One cannot have a legal duty to bring about a legal revolution.

If the Court of Justice's doctrine of the 'new legal order' changes the basis of validity, then it cannot be subject to the test of validity. In other words it cannot be legally valid. It follows that the doctrine cannot bind the courts of the member states in the way of valid law. Its acceptance or rejection escapes legal doctrine. Thus the 'new legal order' cannot take effect. The doctrine is self-defeating.

It is therefore not surprising that all domestic courts have refused to read the doctrine of a 'new legal order' in this way.[14] The idea of a 'new legal order' that binds domestic courts can only survive if we take it to be a manifestation of real law, or the law of nations. Dualism and conditional primacy are thus the only plausible ways to interpret *Costa* and *Simmenthal*.

4.2 Conditional Primacy

Everything said in *Costa* and *Simmenthal* is compatible with the idea that EU law requires member states to take a *constitutional* step of *ex ante* incorporation. If we take this view, we say that primacy is achieved only through the constitutional decision of the member state to incorporate EU law. The process of incorporation creates primacy. This is a very different theory to that of monism although in practice it may amount to the same thing in practice, if domestic law is serious about avoiding any contradiction to EU law.

Under the monist view, we recall, law exists when it is organized in a system of rules, with a master rule at the top called either the 'basic norm' (for Kelsen) or the 'rule of recognition (for Hart). Monism guarantees success for any part of EU law, since it assumes that the master rule is European. The national courts have to make a choice along the lines proposed by Mattias Kumm: they would have to decide which legal order prevailed as a whole.[15] The choice is therefore wholesale or 'constitutional'.[16] If such a choice was to be made in favour of EU law, then the whole of

[13] H.W.R. Wade, 'Sovereignty—Revolution or Evolution?' 112 *Law Quarterly Review* (1996) 568–75.

[14] This argument for a more or less revolutionary 'new legal order' was put to the court in *Thoburn* by Eleanor Sharpston who was then counsel of the claimants and later became the last Advocate General of the United Kingdom; see *Thoburn v Sunderland City Council* [2002] EWHC 195 (Admin), [2003] QB 151. The argument was explicitly rejected by Sir John Laws—and his rejection was endorsed by the Supreme Court in *HS2 (R v Buckinghamshire)*.

[15] See the discussion in the Chapter 1, section 1.2. Mattias Kumm's proposal is in Mattias Kumm, 'The Jurisprudence of Constitutional Conflict: Constitutional Supremacy in Europe before and after the Constitutional Treaty' 11 *European Law Journal* (2005) 262–307, at 286.

[16] Recall that according to Kumm's view the relevant question is this: 'what is the best understanding of the relationship between national and European constitutions, given the normative commitments underlying legal practice in Europe, seen as a whole? What is the interpretation of the relationship between national constitutions and the EU constitution that *best fits and justifies legal practices in the European Union*? What makes national and European constitutional practices in Europe appear in their best light?' ibid at 287.

EU law would prevail. If it was made in favour of national law, then all national law would prevail.

Although Kumm deploys the logic of a constitutional conflict, which normally leads to monism, he is not himself a monist. As we have seen, he proposes a 'pluralist' reading of European Union law whereby courts apply both national and European constitutional principles at the same time. This is because monism must lead to a very different model—which evidently Kumm rejects. Under monism, the inferior legal system cannot be recognized as a legal system. This is shown much more clearly if we stay within the Kelsen and Hart formal analysis of the legal order. Since a legal order or system requires a basic norm or a rule of recognition in order to exist then the dominant legal system will provide the *only* relevant basic norm or rule of recognition. If so then the inferior system must have stopped being a legal system at all.

Under the terms of the question asked by Kelsen and Hart, the answer must be that there is only one legal system in place since there is only one basic norm or rule of recognition. Understood in these terms the question of the relationship between two legal systems cannot arise in the case of the EU: the larger system has absorbed the local ones.

The pluralist view is different. It believes that whereas the conflict between legal systems is real, the courts need not make a decision between them. We need not say that the broader system 'absorbs' the local ones nor that the domestic system 'prevails' over the European. But even for pluralists there can only be one *relevant* legal system at any particular time. Pluralists cannot describe the legal architecture as one of standing between two legal systems *all the time*.

It must be obvious that the idea of 'incorporation' under monism is far more radical than it first seemed. Remember: monism is a strict view. It proposes the construction of a single legal system, where all law-making elements must be incorporated into a single hierarchical structure. The logic of formal validity does not work in any other way. Monism does not deal with relations *between* legal orders, since there can only be one *relevant* legal order: the one determined by the rule of recognition or 'Grundnorm'. Monism does not incorporate laws into the dominant legal system since it cannot recognize any other law as the product of any other system. It may incorporate rules or words but it cannot incorporate laws for there are no laws outside the system.

Hence, under a monist reading of international law the ruling of the US Supreme Court which accepted the reality of international law as law made outside the United States was false. By recognizing a separate domain of law it challenged the idea of a single legal system with one master rule. This is why from the point of view of a Kelsenian legal system, monism is a logical entailment of legal positivism. For the same reasons the primacy of EU law under a monist perspective must entail that all the domestic jurisdictions should be held as components of one legal system: that of the European Union.

I now return to the doctrine of autonomy of EU law, as proposed by René Barents, which I discussed in Chapter 1.[17] Does Barents, ultimately, propose a doctrine of European Union monism? Surprisingly, perhaps, he does not. Barents, who as we saw is the main exponent of the idea of the 'autonomy' of EU law, does not accept the Kelsenian framework. He explicitly rejects the 'monist' reading of the EU treaties along Kelsenian lines by observing that monism denies the autonomy of national legal orders and organizes EU law on the basis of a revolutionary new basic norm under which 'national constitutions would have been transformed into constitutions of federated states'.[18] He finds this interpretation unrealistic and rejects it. But then what follows? Barents argues that his proposed theoretical account of EU law emerges from its substance and its 'Community character'.[19] He argues that from the 'Community' character follows the 'intrinsic unity' of Community law, its 'self-referential' character, and its 'independence from other systems of law'. But this comes with qualifications. The strengthened position of Community law vis-à-vis national legal orders, he says, 'should not conceal the fact that in spite of its autonomy, this order remains to a large extent factually dependent on national legal orders ... [I]n the autonomous identification of what constitutes 'the law' of the Community legal order, within certain limits due account should be taken of the facts, i.e. national law'.[20] In other words, 'the concept of autonomy itself implies that the full effect of Community law is and remains dependent on national legal orders'.[21] Here we reach a surprising position: EU law is both 'autonomous' and dependent on national law. Barents finally concludes that EU law is autonomous but 'does not represent a common constitutional conception reflecting a particular political identity'.[22] It is constitutional law without a state, helping explain 'the process of globalization of law'.[23]

This conclusion is, with all due respect, self-contradictory. It cannot be the case that a legal order is both autonomous from other legal orders and also dependent on other legal orders. Barents' view appears to be that EU law is autonomous only in that it is *partly* immune from the legal effects of national law. Barents accepts that EU law has no real power to impose itself on national law. He explains this as follows: 'These observations demonstrate again that the concept of autonomy of Community [law] relates to an inherent quality of Community law, not to a particular power of the community to change the 'facts' at will. Furthermore, it appears that there is no contradiction between the autonomy of Community law and its dependence on national law.'[24]

[17] Rene Barents, *The Autonomy of Community Law* (The Hague: Kluwer Law International, 2004).
[18] ibid 185.
[19] ibid 239.
[20] ibid 270.
[21] ibid 271.
[22] ibid 315.
[23] ibid 318.
[24] ibid 267.

This particular argument seems to confuse the issue of effectiveness with the issue of lawfulness. EU law does not seek to exercise force onto the member states. This is why the law needs not only judges, but also security guards, police, bailiffs, and other officers of the law. Law is a criterion, not a force. It sets standards of lawful conduct. If EU law is autonomous, it must be an autonomous standard or test for the actions of state authorities. It is not clear, from what Barents says, that EU law is such an autonomous criterion for national bodies. If it was he would have endorsed monism.

Barents' position avoids contradiction only if law is not even a criterion for decision-making. If law is taken to be a merely technical or hypothetical set of concepts, with little relevance to practice, then its incoherence would not matter. This is a particular understanding of legal positivism, familiar from Kelsen, Hart, and Raz, where validity appears to be in principle a technical matter, irrelevant to practical reasoning. But if one takes a more robust view of the practical relevance of law, Barents' view is untenable. If law is the justification of a claim of right enforceable on demand, then the requirements of EU law—and, of course, of international law—must make sense alongside the requirements of ordinary domestic law.[25] Legal reasons cannot work if they are incoherent.

It turns out that the idea of the 'autonomy' of EU law offered by Barents leads to a highly implausible conception of positive law—as some kind of fictitious reality with little relevance to legal practice. Neither version of Barents' theory can be accepted. And in any event not even the most vocal supporters of the 'autonomy' of EU law adopt a monist perspective.

More importantly perhaps, not even the Court of Justice makes the monist claim to the singularity of a 'European' legal system. The doctrine of primacy as set out by the Court of Justice does not entail that contrary domestic law is non-existent. The Court only says that domestic law that is contrary to EU law is merely *inapplicable* and has to be 'set aside'. In the classic case that established the doctrine of primacy of EU law—*Simmenthal*—the Court of Justice took a very subtle view of primacy.[26] An Italian statute had already been found by the Court to contravene EU law in an earlier case. But Italian judges did not at the time have the right under Italian constitutional rules to strike down or disapply a national statute. They had to refer the matter to the Italian Constitutional Court which alone had the power to do so. This would have entailed considerable delay. So the Italian court that sent a further preliminary reference to the Court of Justice asking if the supremacy of EU law meant that the Italian Court should also ignore the procedural obligation to refer

25 The phrase is from Ronald Dworkin, *Justice for Hedgehogs* (Cambridge, Mass.: Harvard University Press, 2011) 405. The relevant paragraph reads: 'We construct a conception of law—an account of the grounds needed to support a claim of right enforceable on demand in that way—by finding a justification of those practices in a larger integrated network of political value. We construct a theory of law, that is, in the same way we construct a theory of other political values—of equality, liberty, and democracy.'

26 Case 106/78 *Amministrazione delle Finanze dello Stato v Simmenthal SpA* [1978] ECR 629.

the matter to the Italian Constitutional Court. The Court of Justice said yes. It set out the primacy principle and insisted that it meant that the national court must immediately 'set aside', but not invalidate, any provisions of national law that were contrary to directly applicable EU law, irrespective of procedural complications.

The Court said that a national court 'must, in a case within its jurisdiction, apply European Union law in its entirety and protect rights which the latter confers on individuals and must accordingly set aside any provision of national law which may conflict with it, whether prior or subsequent to the Community rule'.[27] The effect of *Simmenthal* is that all national courts must directly and immediately apply a clear and unconditional provision of EU law of whatever kind and status, even if there is a contrary national law of whatever kind. But the obligation of primacy does not entail that the domestic law is void.

The Court had an opportunity to confirm this ruling two decades later when the Court received another procedural reference from Italy, this time concerning limitation periods for civil and tax matters.[28] In that case, the Court asked itself if an Italian tax law contradicting EU law was void. If it was, the longer civil claim limitation would apply. The Court replied in the negative. The fact that the Italian tax law was contrary to EU law did not mean it was void. It was merely to be set aside. But this meant that the relevant limitation period was the shorter one, applicable to tax disputes.[29] The Court said:

> It cannot therefore, contrary to the Commission's contention, be inferred from the judgment in *Simmenthal* that the incompatibility with Community law of a subsequently adopted rule of national law has the effect of rendering that rule of national law non-existent. Faced with such a situation, the national court is, however, obliged to disapply that rule, provided always that this obligation does not restrict the power of the competent national courts to apply, from among the various procedures available under national law, those which are appropriate for protecting the individual rights conferred by Community law.[30]

It is clear, I think, that the Court of Justice does not accept the monist reading. If it had accepted monism it would have said that any contrary law to the law of the EU would be void. But the Court is not saying this.

The Court's ruling is subtle. It recognizes the main element of dualism: EU law applies on the basis of institutions set up by domestic law, in a two-step process. Domestic courts have a constitutional as well as a European duty to set aside law that contradicts EU law.

[27] ibid paras 21–2.
[28] Joined Cases 10-22/97 *Ministero delle Finanze v IN CO GE '90 Srl et al.* [1998] ECR 6307.
[29] ibid paras 20–1.
[30] ibid par. 21. The Court also referred to Case 34/67 *Lück v Hauptzollamt Köln-Rheinau* [1968] ECR 245.

This was not a unique judgment. In the recent *Achmea* case the Court had the opportunity to revisit the issue of the relations between the EU and the domestic legal orders and again spoke of a two-step process in the application of EU law.[31] In this case, a preliminary reference from the Netherlands, the court was invited to explain the place in EU law of bilateral investment treaties binding two member states, concluded before one of them, Slovakia, became a member state. The question of practice was whether the special arbitration process for investors protected under the pre-existing Bilateral Investment Treaty between Slovakia and the Netherlands was compatible with the ordinary law protecting investors from the EU under the Treaties.

The court, in its Grand Chamber composition, took the opportunity to speak broadly of the relations between EU law, international law, and domestic law. The court made clear that even though the EU treaties are an 'independent' source of law, EU law exists alongside the laws of the member states. EU law and domestic law co-exist, by way of a 'structured network of principles, rules and mutually interdependent legal relations binding the EU and its Member States reciprocally and binding its Member States to each other'.[32]

The Court then put this relationship as one of mutual respect and reciprocity:

> EU law is thus based on the fundamental premiss that each Member State shares with all the other Member States, and recognises that they share with it, a set of common values on which the EU is founded, as stated in Article 2 TEU. That premiss implies and justifies the existence of mutual trust between the Member States that those values will be recognised, and therefore that the law of the EU that implements them will be respected. It is precisely in that context that the Member States are obliged, by reason inter alia of the principle of sincere cooperation set out in the first subparagraph of Article 4(3) TEU, to ensure in their respective territories the application of and respect for EU law, and to take for those purposes any appropriate measure, whether general or particular, to ensure fulfilment of the obligations arising out of the Treaties or resulting from the acts of the institutions of the EU.[33]

This way of describing the 'interdependence' of EU law and member state law is incompatible with monism. If monism was true, there would be no complex duty of 'sincere cooperation' among separate states and institutions or distinct legal orders. There would have been a much simpler and direct duty of member state

[31] Case C-284/16 *Slovak Republic v Achmea BV*, 08 March 2018 (Grand Chamber), ECLI:EU:C:2018:158.

[32] ibid 33. The Court referred here to Opinion 2/13 *Accession of the EU to the ECHR*, 18 December 2014, EU:C:2014:2454, paras 165–7.

[33] ibid par. 34. The Court referred here to Opinion 2/13 *Accession of the EU to the ECHR*, 18 December 2014, EU:C:2014:2454, paras 168–73 and the case law cited there.

authorities complying with 'higher' law within a single legal order. But EU law does not work like this. It does presuppose that there are distinct legal orders that do not compete but complement each other. Once again the Court implies that there is a two-step process. It is not enough that EU law is created. It must also be endorsed by domestic law and given full effect. In *Achmea* the Court once again spoke of EU law in dualist not monist terms.

What the member states need to do is to apply EU law that binds them as states. The member states are under an obligation, which can only be understood as an obligation of the law of nations to incorporate the relevant rules or principles and, whenever necessary, to set aside domestic law that conflicts with EU law. What they have to do is take 'appropriate' measures, whether general or particular, in order to fulfil the obligations arising out of the Treaties or resulting from the acts of the institutions. This is the logic of dualism.

The duties are not only relevant to legislatures but also to courts. The Court said that:

> it is for the national courts and tribunals and the Court of Justice to ensure the full application of EU law in all Member States and to ensure judicial protection of the rights of individuals under that law. (. . .) In particular, the judicial system as thus conceived has as its keystone the preliminary ruling procedure provided for in Article 267 TFEU, which, by setting up a dialogue between one court and another, specifically between the Court of Justice and the courts and tribunals of the Member States, has the object of securing uniform interpretation of EU law, thereby serving to ensure its consistency, its full effect and its autonomy as well as, ultimately, the particular nature of the law established by the Treaties.[34]

It is apparent, therefore that the Court of Justice does not endorse the 'monist' reading. The obligations of the judiciary as those of an ongoing 'dialogue' between one court and another 'in accordance with Article 19 TEU'. The European legal order does not compete with the legal orders of the member states. The Court is not saying that a 'constitutional conflict' needs to be resolved.

But the Court is not endorsing pluralism either. Under radical pluralism there cannot be any *legal* duties to do anything when we happen to be between legal systems. According to pluralism's analysis, navigating a course between legal systems is an *extra-legal* question, the result of political privilege or personal choice. Pluralism tells us that it only makes sense to look at each question from within a single legal system, although courts are not forced to choose which one this will be. As a result, pluralism does not tell us which legal system to comply with. Nevertheless, the Court of Justice clearly rejects that point of view because it says

[34] ibid paras 36–7.

that courts have real legal duties to each other. These are the duties of *cooperation* and *dialogue*: the national courts are to set aside national legislation when it conflicts with EU law. This duty does not follow from pluralism.

The only way in which we can make sense of these legal duties of dialogue that arise for domestic courts under EU law is under a dualist framework whereby both national law and EU law are laws in the proper sense of the term. They are both laws but do not compete because they apply to separate subject matters: the national law applies to a domestic jurisdiction whereas EU law applies to the relations between states as part of the law of nations. They have their own substantive principles and processes according to their functions and aims. Dualism illuminates the court's reasoning in *Simmenthal*. EU law is not aiming to replace the domestic constitutional order, nor does it compete with it. It merely creates transnational obligations to the other member states and the EU itself.

In turn, the member state is under an obligation to the other member states and to the EU under the law of nations to give European Union law direct effect and supremacy in order to realize the idea of a uniform single market on the basis of reciprocal limitations to sovereignty. One of those obligations—*Simmenthal* tells us—is to require national courts to set aside laws that are contrary to directly effective EU law. Of course the rule to set aside contrary law requires a prior constitutional accommodation. But this is done by adjusting domestic constitutional law not by supposing that EU law has replaced the domestic constitution. In this sense the member states incorporate EU law in two steps: first by adjusting their constitution, and then by legislating in *ad hoc* cases wherever required to do so, by a Directive for example. The constitutional arrangement does not involve any constitutional conflict however. The incorporation of EU law is a matter for the domestic constitutional order.

This is not only the way in which the Court of Justice sees EU law. It is also the way in which the national courts have interpreted EU law and its primacy. They see it as a true legal obligation that binds them under the treaties. The courts of the member states have indeed accepted that EU law has direct effect and primacy. But they accepted it because it is derived from domestic constitutional provisions that give effect to the EU treaties. In all cases there is some kind of constitutional incorporation of the laws that the European Union designates as directly effective. The clearest example of this dualist reading of EU law is the case law of the German constitutional Court. The Court has to start from the provisions of the German Basic Law which provides in Article 24(1) that: 'The Federation may be a law transfer sovereign to international organisations.' This provision provides for a formal reception of any treaty-based law. With effect form 1992 a new Article 23 (1) specifically provides for the effect of EU law as follows:

> With a view to establishing a united Europe, the Federal Republic of Germany shall participate in the development of the European Union that is committed to

> democratic, social, and federal principles to the rule of law, and to the principle of subsidiarity, and that guarantees a level of protection of basic rights essentially comparable to that afforded by this Basic Law. To this end the Federation may transfer sovereign powers by a law with the consent of the Bundesrat'.

It is evident that the recognition of EU law in Germany is not unconditional. It depends on the European Union being committed to relevant constitutional principles. But if the European Union meets those tests, then its laws prevail over national law, according to both the German Constitution and the EU Treaties.

This was set out in detail in the judgment of the Federal Constitutional Court on the Lisbon treaty.[35] In its wide-ranging judgment the German Constitutional Court explained that the primacy of European Union law was conditional on the German constitution and in any event did not affect the validity of national law:

> As prescribed by the Basic Law, federal law shall take precedence over conflicting *Land* law (see Article 31 of the Basic Law). The supranationally based law does not have such a derogating effect to the extent that it annuls law. The primacy of application of European law does not affect the claim to validity of conflicting law in the Member States; it only inhibits its application to the extent required by the treaties and permitted by them under national legislation adopted to give effect to them within the Member States (...). Law of a Member State that is contrary to Community and Union law is rendered inapplicable merely to the extent required by the conflicting regulatory content of Community and Union law.[36]

The Court went on to recall its earlier case law, according to which the Federal Constitutional Court had suspended its general competence 'to review the application of European Community law in Germany against the standard of the fundamental rights of the German constitution' because it recognized that a similar function was well performed by the Court of Justice of the EU (CJEU). Nevertheless, the German Court insisted that it retained the sovereign power to review EU law—which was still 'international law' for all practical purposes—if this became necessary: 'In view of the position of the Community institutions, which is derived from international treaties however, the Federal Constitutional Court could recognise the final character of the decisions of the Court of Justice only "in principle".'[37]

A very similar process of conditional primacy has been provided by courts in Italy, France, Poland, the Czech Republic, and other jurisdictions.[38] Most

[35] *Re the Lisbon Treaty*, 2 BvE 2/08 et al., Federal Constitutional Court, 2009 *Entscheidungen des Bundesverfassungsgerichts* 123, 267 (June 30, 2009).
[36] ibid par. 335.
[37] ibid par. 337.
[38] French Conseil Constitutionnel, *Décision* No 2006-540 DC, 27 July 2006, French Conseil Constitutionnel, *Décision* No 2006-543 DC, 30 November 2006, Italian Corte Costituzionale, *Sentenza*

impressive of all is the adjustment that the United Kingdom brought about in order to give effect to EU law. The problems there were starker because the United Kingdom has an unwritten constitution which gives primacy to Acts of Parliament. Under the constitution of the United Kingdom Acts of the Westminster Parliament are the supreme law of the land. It was originally thought that this left no room for the primacy of EU law because any subsequent Act of Parliament would 'impliedly repeal' the European Communities Act 1972, by virtue of which EU law took effect in the UK. Nevertheless, in the case of *Factortame*, the House of Lords did what British constitutional authors had thought was impossible.[39] It declared that the European Communities Act 1972 could not be 'impliedly repealed' by a later Act of Parliament.

In that case the Merchant Shipping Act 1988, which had introduced directly discriminatory restrictions on EU businesses contrary to the fundamental freedoms of the EU treaties, was effectively set aside by a court. According to constitutional orthodoxy 'there is under the English Constitution no marked or clear distinction between laws that are not fundamental or constitutional and laws which are fundamental or constitutional'.[40] Nevertheless, the House of Lords introduced a distinction between ordinary Acts of Parliament and Acts that could not be impliedly repealed on account of their constitutional importance. This distinction was further formalized in the case of *Thoburn* where the court had to deal with the claim that the Weights and Measures Act 1985 was incompatible with the requirements of a UK statutory instrument giving effect to an EU Directive (requiring the use of kilograms and grams for the sale of groceries). The claimants argued that, contrary to *Factortame*, the domestic law should prevail and EU law be set aside. The judgment, by the distinguished judge John Laws, drew a distinction between higher and ordinary Acts of Parliament. The judge called the former 'constitutional' statutes. A constitutional statute determines how an ordinary statute is to be read: 'Ordinary statutes may be impliedly repealed. Constitutional statutes may not. For the repeal of a constitutional Act or the abrogation of a fundamental right to be effected by statute, the court would apply this test: is it shown that the legislature's actual—not imputed, constructive or presumed—intention was to effect the repeal or abrogation? … the ordinary rule of implied repeal … has no application to constitutional statutes.'[41]

183/73, *Frontini*, 27 December 1973, *Sentenza* 170/84, Granital 8 June 1984, Spanish Tribunal Constitucional, *Declaracion* 1/2004, 13 December 2004, Czech Constitutional Court, Pl US 50/04, 8 March 2006 and PI Us 66/04, 3 May 2006, Pl US 19/08, 26 November 2008 and Pl Us 29.09, 3 November 2009, Polish Trybunal Konstytucyjny, K 32/09, 24 November 2010.

[39] *R v Secretary of State for Transport, ex p Factortame Ltd (No. 2)* [1991] 1 AC 603.

[40] Albert Venn Dicey, *Introduction to the Study of the Law of the Constitution* (Indianapolis: Liberty Fund, 1982) p. 37.

[41] *Thoburn v Sunderland City Council* [2003] QB 151, par. 63.

According to the court's view Parliament creates constitutional statutes in the ordinary process. What marks out a statute as constitutional is not the way it is made but its subject matter. This view was further endorsed by the Supreme Court in *Buckinghamshire* and more recently in *Miller*.[42] In effect, the United Kingdom courts have ruled that membership in the European Union has created a new method of law-making, whereby European institutions create laws that take effect in the UK directly without any other prior act of specific incorporation.

The fact that Parliament decided to enter into this power-sharing agreement with other European states on the basis of treaties was a constitutional decision of the highest significance. This explains what Lord Bridge had already said in *Factortame*:

> If the supremacy within the European Community of Community law over the national law of member states was not always inherent in the EEC Treaty it was certainly well established in the jurisprudence of the Court of Justice long before the United Kingdom joined the Community. Thus, whatever limitation of its sovereignty Parliament accepted when it enacted the European Communities Act 1972 was entirely voluntary. Under the terms of the 1972 Act it has always been clear that it was the duty of a United Kingdom court, when delivering final judgment, to override any rule of national law found to be in conflict with any directly enforceable rule of Community law.[43]

This gradual adjustment of the law of the United Kingdom was, however, a domestic constitutional process. John Laws, writing extrajudicially, has explained that the primacy of EU law was something created by Parliament on conditions set out by the United Kingdom Constitution, so that 'the reach of European law is ultimately a function of Parliament's will; and it is of course not to be assumed that Parliament has given the European legislature *carte blanche*'.[44] This is the same solution accepted in Germany, France, and all the other member states of the Union: EU law is subject to the domestic constitution but not subject to ordinary statutes. Here is then how our overview ends. Even the unwritten constitution of the United Kingdom has adopted a two-step process for applying EU law. EU law does not apply automatically but must be incorporated into the law of the United

[42] *R (on the application of Buckinghamshire CC) v Secretary of State for Transport* [2014] UKSC 3, par. 207; *R (on the application of Miller and another) v Secretary of State for Exiting the European Union* [2017] UKSC 5; [2017] 2 WLR 583. See Pavlos Eleftheriadis, 'Two Doctrines of the Unwritten Constitution' 13 *European Constitutional Law Review* (2017) 525–50.

[43] *Factortame (No 2)* [1991] 1 AC 603 at p. 658.

[44] John Laws, *The Common Law Constitution* (Cambridge: Cambridge University Press, 2014) p. 70. See also *Pham v Secretary of State for the Home Department* [2015] UKSC 19, [2015] 1 WLR 1591 [2015] 2 CMLR 49, where Lord Mance said (at par. 76) that EU law is part of the law of the UK because Parliament legislated, in the European Communities Act 1972, that it should be.

Kingdom. This is what the European Communities Act 1972 achieved in its capacity as a 'constitutional statute'.[45]

This short discussion of the various decisions by the Court of Justice and the national courts has shown that both sides recognize that the other side produces law. None of them say that theirs is the only valid legal order. So they all reject monism. They accept that domestic law and EU law are both real types of law and presuppose a division of labour whereby national courts deal with the main institutional issues of a legal order and the European courts deal with the obligations arising out of the treaties. Time and again they insist that the relations between the legal orders are a matter of law, not a matter of political privilege or extra-legal discretion. So they reject pluralism too.

I believe that the only way in which we can make sense of this case law is through a doctrine of dualism that leads to conditional primacy for EU law. The EU recognizes that its laws must be incorporated by the laws of the various member states. But, equally, the constitutional law of the member states accepts that it owes respect to the European Union and its laws. If one understands the domestic legal order as a constitutional jurisdiction and the EU legal order as part of the law of nations, one avoids the dilemma of a constitutional conflict. There is no constitutional conflict if two legal orders are created or designed to achieve different institutional purposes. This is the meaning of dualism.

4.3 Institutional Tolerance

I now turn to the second general principle, or set of related principles, of the reception of EU law by the domestic courts. This is a principle of 'institutional tolerance', which answers a further question arising out of the coexistence of European and domestic law-making institutions. Conditional primacy answers the question of the place of EU law in the legal order of the member state, after it has been validly made. It tells us that a national law that contradicts EU law is to be set aside and not applied in relation to EU matters, although it may be valid for other purposes. The opposite question arises, when EU law fails to respect the division of labour set out in the treaties between the EU and the member states. In principle this will be sorted out by the CJEU which has the power to invalidate unlawful EU laws. But what happens if EU law is not validly made and is, in the language of administrative law, 'ultra vires' and the CJEU fails to spot it?

Again, a monist view would perhaps say that such an EU law should be void for the domestic court. But this is not what the national courts have said. In principle,

[45] It also follows that the act that finally organizes the departure of the United Kingdom from the EU, the European Union (Withdrawal Agreement) Act 2020, which was given the Royal Assent on 23 January 2020, must also be a constitutional statute.

the national courts have addressed the question on the basis of their own constitutions but with a clear intention to respect the integrity of the European Union's legal order and the Court of Justice as an institution.

Inevitably, national courts have the first and the last word on such matters whenever they arise in domestic litigation. The CJEU could only be involved if a national court made a preliminary reference. Since the treaties derive from the power of states to make them, their authority depends on the constitutional authority of the member states. Thus one would have expected to subsume the powers of the EU to an interpretation of the Treaties offered by each member state's courts. Nevertheless, such fragmentation would be highly damaging to a union that seeks to build a single market and set up common standards in various fields. This is why fragmentation has been carefully avoided, both in the way the treaties are set up, but also in the practice of the member states.

The member states courts have recognized that the European institutions and the CJEU enjoy a special privilege in enforcing the division of labour between the EU and the states. Their possible mistakes are in a way 'tolerated'. Hence, the principle of 'institutional tolerance': national courts will not rule any EU law invalid unless its failing is both important and manifest. The validity of EU laws is a matter best left to the CJEU as far as practically possible.

The clearest example of this approach is again that of the German Constitutional Court.[46] The Court has explicitly passed judgment on the tests under which EU legislation or judicial decisions must pass if they are not to be rejected as lying outside the competences of the EU.[47] The Court outlined its position in the *Honeywell* case.[48] In that case the German Constitutional Court was faced with a claim that the Federal Employment Court had wrongly given effect to the *Mangold* principle of age discrimination.[49] That judgment of the CJEU had found that the principle of age discrimination was a true principle of EU law and applied to employment relations directly, even though the implementation period of the relevant Directive had not yet expired (and the member state was not yet required to give it effect). The claimant before the German Constitutional Court submitted that the *Mangold* judgment was so wrong: that in effect it was an 'ultra vires' action which German authorities ought to ignore. The mistake engaged the principles first outlined in the *Maastricht* and *Lisbon* judgments of the German Constitutional Court and entailed that the judgment could not be enforced by German courts. The court took the opportunity to offer a general overview of the doctrine of competences of the European Union. It rejected the claimant's submission.

[46] See *Re the Maastricht Treaty* and *Re the Lisbon Treaty*.

[47] The Court has also created a parallel doctrine the idea of the 'identity review', concerning proposed EU treaties, from the point of view of the constitutional identity of the member state. But the approach is similar for both cases.

[48] *Honeywell*, BVerfG, 2 BvR 2661.06 of 06.07.2010, Rn (1-116).

[49] Case C-144/04, *Mangold v Helm* [2005] ECR I-9981, [2006] 1 CMLR 43, ECLI:EU:C:2005:709.

The German court restated the principle of primacy of EU law and noted that it 'does not lead to a situation in which contrary national law is null and void'.[50] Even when it contradicts EU law, the national law continues to apply in areas outside the domain of EU law. The court grounded this primacy both on the inherent need for uniformity of EU law but also on the constitutional 'empowerment' of Article 23.1 of the German Constitution, in accordance with which sovereign powers can be transferred to the European Union. For the court this provision contains 'a promise of effectiveness and implementation corresponding to the primacy of application of Union law'.[51] Whether primacy applies, however, depends on whether EU law exists in the first place. When the Court turned to the 'ultra vires' doctrine, it returned to the treaties as the immediate ground for the EU's competence and the principle of conferral of Article 5 TEU. Any expansion to the EU's powers must happen through treaty reform.[52] Surprisingly, however, the Court did not say that anything outside the explicit terms of the treaties was automatically *ultra vires*.

The German Constitutional Court suggested that national courts could tolerate some departure from the established division of work between national and European in the following way:

> The Federal Constitutional Court is hence empowered and obliged to review acts on the part of the European bodies and institutions with regard to whether they take place on the basis of *manifest transgressions of competence or on the basis of the exercise of competence in the area of constitutional identity which is not assignable* (Article 79.3 in conjunction with Article 1 and Article 20 of the Basic Law) ... and where appropriate to declare the inapplicability of acts for the German legal system which exceed competences.[53]

This conclusion was surprising because it does not follow from the premise. If the European Union's powers are grounded solely in the treaties, then *any* transgression of those treaties would be sufficient to create invalidity. A measure created unlawfully must be invalid under normal administrative law principles. Yet, the German Constitutional Court went on to say that this does not follow in the case of EU law. Some transgressions are to be tolerated if they are not 'manifest', it said. But what does this qualification mean and what is its purpose?

The German Constitutional Court distinguished between two different issues: the fact of manifest violation and the fact of 'structural significance'. The court said: 'the act of the authority of the European Union must be manifestly in violation of competences and that the impugned act is highly significant in the structure

50 *Honeywell* (n. 48) par. 53.
51 ibid par. 53.
52 ibid par. 55.
53 ibid par. 55.

of competences between the Member States and the Union with regard to the principle of conferral and to the binding nature of the statute under the rule of law'.[54] Although these tests are not clear, they do suggest that only the most significant of transgressions will lead to a remedy.

The court explained that the reason for this adjustment was the value of *uniformity* for the European Union, something to which obviously Germany subscribed when it joined. Because the EU is a union of states—where uniformity is both paramount but also difficult—given that the member states have their own jurisdictions and systems of courts, the national courts must accept the unifying interpretations of the CJEU even when they do not fully agree with them. The complexity of the EU's institutional architecture as a union of peoples is laid bare in the Court's reasoning. The Court said that if each member state sought to decide for itself where the powers of the European Union stop, we would have no uniform application of EU law. So it is in the nature of the treaties to promote uniformity under the terms set out by the EU institutions, including the Court of Justice. Since this is something that the member states signed up to in the treaties, it follows that they have delegated the ordinary matters of the division of labour to the EU's institutions. Because uniformity is now an aim shared by the member states, they accept that they have to tolerate decisions that may go against their own judgment. But they do not give up the power to stop the EU when the disagreement is not merely one of opinion but is a matter of a 'manifest' transgression. This of course will be a very rare occasion, but it needs to be taken into account.

The court asked, rhetorically, what would happen if the member states gave up completely any check over *ultra vires* review. This would basically mean the transfer of power of oversight of the treaties from the states to the European Union. Although the court did not use this language, it implied that this solution would be one akin to monism. The Court rejected this reading of EU law. It adopted instead what is clearly a 'dualist' framework of analysis, whereby the European Court retains the power to police the separation of powers, but where national courts keep the ultimate power to step in if a *manifest* error takes place. The court concluded: 'The tensions, which are basically unavoidable according to this construction, are to be harmonised cooperatively in accordance with the European integration idea and relaxed through mutual consideration.'[55] It is a pragmatic solution, fully in accordance with the nature of the European Union as a union of peoples—a project of self-governing independent states.

This is then what 'institutional tolerance' means. The German Constitutional Court considers that the national courts should be slow to find an EU law measure *ultra vires*, even though they clearly have the constitutional power to do so. It suggests that disagreements should be resolved through 'mutual consideration'. One

[54] ibid par. 61.
[55] ibid par. 57.

way of doing so is by the practice of preliminary reference of Article 267 TFEU. The court stated that before it would make any *ultra vires* ruling, it would give the CJEU the opportunity to express its own view as to the law, according to the procedure for preliminary reference. The German court said that it would not find any inapplicability of Union law in Germany, as long as the Court of Justice did not have an opportunity to rule on the question.[56]

This is precisely the method followed in the case of the Outright Monetary Transactions (OMT) programme. In 2014 the Federal Court found that the European Central Bank's OMT programme was likely to meet the Honeywell test of manifest transgression of competences with structural significance and therefore made a reference to the CJEU.[57] The Court of Justice responded adopting the narrow reading of the OMT suggested by the German court.[58] In the end the German Constitutional Court did not make a finding of manifest breach.[59] This was a process of judicial dialogue at work—fully in line with a dualist interpretation of EU law and the methods of judicial oversight provided by the Treaties.[60]

4.4 Integrity

The principle of conditional primacy of EU law ensures that domestic law remains valid even when it is contrary to EU law. The principle of institutional tolerance means that EU law remains valid, even when it is contrary to the domestic interpretation of the treaties. These two principles are mirror images of each other. They coexist under dualism. They are based on the fact that both legal orders are truly legal and must organize their mutual relations on the basis of legal principle. We therefore say that the legal order of each member state is the legal order of a jurisdiction and that the legal order of the European Union is an order of the law of nations. Both orders accept each other order as a *relevant dimension* of law. They take effect by being recognized and therefore 'incorporated' into each order's own process of legal reasoning.[61]

[56] ibid par. 60.

[57] *Re the OMT Programme*, Federal Constitutional Court, Order of 14 January 2014, Case 2 BvR 2728/13.

[58] Case C-62/14 *Gauweiler et al. v Deutscher Bundestag*.

[59] *Re the OMT Programme*, Federal Constitutional Court, Judgment of 21 June 2016, Case 2 BvR 2728/13. For a general discussion see Mehrdad Payandeh, 'The OMT Judgment of the German Federal Constitutional Court: Repositioning the Court within the European Constitutional Architecture' 13 *European Constitutional Law Review* (2017) 400–16.

[60] I discuss some of the case law in detail in Chapter 5 on accountability.

[61] For a very similar argument regarding the principle of 'limited and shared jurisdiction' between EU law and the European Convention on Human Rights see the illuminating arguments of Piet Eeckhout, 'Human Rights and the Autonomy of EU Law: Pluralism or Integration?' 66 *Current Legal Problems* (2013) 169–202.

What is being incorporated, however, is not a particular form of words, or sentence, or paragraph written in some legal text. What is being incorporated is a set of purposive interpretations about the respective aims and functions of the EU and the member states. This is where EU law creates a new obligation of *integrity* of the laws as they apply to the European Union.

Integrity is an obligation of consistent interpretation. This is something we observed in the judgment of the German Constitutional Court in *Honeywell*. Conscious of the difficulty of reconciling the law of the various states and the law of the European Union, the German Court said that the tensions between the various courts, which are 'basically unavoidable', ought to be 'harmonised cooperatively in accordance with the European integration idea and relaxed through mutual consideration'. This cannot mean that the aim is merely for the decisions of the various courts to be compatible so that one could comply with them both without contradiction. This is too little given what the European legal order aims to achieve. It would be possible for a person to comply with conflicting court decisions if one decision prohibited one action and the other permitted it: by voluntarily not doing the contested action one complies with both judgments. This would not be enough. EU law requires more of the legal orders of the member states. Coordination between the legal orders requires agreement in the process and principles of *reasoning*. A harmonious relationship requires coherent common legal principles. This is the aim implied by the words 'mutual consideration'. The consideration at issue refers to each other's reasons.

That courts should take a consistent view of the law is an ancient idea. It is encapsulated in the doctrine of precedent of the common law. It is similarly adopted as a principle of the CJEU. Precedent has its own technical rules, but it is illuminated and guided by a moral and political value. This is a value that applies to the legal order as a whole and which Ronald Dworkin called the value of 'integrity'. Integrity means that the judge in a given legal order ought to aim to achieve consistency with relevant decisions that preceded his or hers, not only in outcome but also in the reasons offered for those outcomes. Integrity in this sense proceeds from a conception of law as a deliberative practice organized and structured by coherent moral ideas.[62]

Precisely because law is a series of practical arguments and judgments made within an institutional context by officials operating under the terms of a jurisdiction, it is important that it makes sense as a single or coherent order of principle. This is what the value of integrity seeks to capture. We may distinguish, following Dworkin, between integrity in legislation and integrity in adjudication. Applied

[62] This is the view defended by Ronald Dworkin, *Law's Empire* (London: Fontana, 1986). I defend a similar practical and constructivist view of law in Pavlos Eleftheriadis, *Legal Rights* (Oxford: Oxford University Press, 2008) and in Pavlos Eleftheriadis, 'Power and Principle in Constitutional Law' 45 *Netherlands Journal of Legal Philosophy* (2016) 37–56.

to adjudication, integrity explains 'why judges must conceive of the body of law they administer as a whole rather than as a set of discrete decisions they are free to make or amend one by one, with nothing but a strategic interest in the rest'.[63] The coherence required by integrity is practical, not historical. It does not require that we always comply with the decisions of the past. Sometimes, when there is sufficient reason to do so, integrity requires that we acknowledge that the decisions of the past were wrong, or have been superseded and must be abandoned. Either way, overruling precedent by giving reasons does recognize the practical weight of the earlier decision. Integrity does not require absolute conformity, merely respect for the institutional decisions of the past.[64] That decision was binding on us, but it was not categorically so. A judge's public acknowledgment of a change of direction would be an application of precisely the value of integrity.

Can this value apply to the relations between European courts and domestic courts? It evidently can and must apply to them. This follows from the two principles of 'conditional primacy' and 'institutional tolerance'. If the law of the European Union is received into the law of the member states as a constitutional requirement, it then becomes part of that law. If the interpretation of EU law is delegated by virtue of the EU treaties to the CJEU, then its judgments are relevant institutional decisions for all member states. The principles of EU law are now constitutional principles of the legal orders of the member states. This is precisely the explicit view of English law, as far as incorporated treaties are concerned:

> Where, for instance, a treaty is directly incorporated into English law by Act of the legislature, its terms become subject to the interpretative jurisdiction of the court in the same way as any other Act of the legislature. ... Again, it is well established that where a statute is enacted in order to give effect to the United Kingdom's obligations under a treaty, the terms of the treaty may have to be considered and, if necessary, construed in order to resolve any ambiguity or obscurity as to the meaning or scope of the statute.[65]

Something like this is said explicitly in the *Honeywell* judgment about EU law but taking into account the principle of 'institutional tolerance'. The court notes that 'the Union understands itself as a legal community' and is 'bound by the principle of conferral and by the fundamental rights, and it respects the constitutional identity of the Member States'.[66] The German legal order endorses the same principles and therefore exercises its powers 'in a manner that is reserved and open

[63] Dworkin, *Law's Empire* (n. 62) 127.

[64] This is well shown by Scott Hershovitz in his 'Integrity and *Stare Decisis*' in Scott Hershovitz (ed.), *Exploring Law's Empire: The Jurisprudence of Ronald Dworkin* (Oxford: Oxford University Press, 2008) 103–18.

[65] *J H Rayner v DTI (International Tin Council)* [1990] 2 AC 418, at 500.

[66] *Honeywell* (n. 48) par. 59.

towards European law'.[67] The court thus outlines its own duty of allowing some margin for error in the CJEU: '... the Court of Justice has a right to tolerance of error. It is hence not a matter for the Federal Constitutional Court in questions of the interpretation of Union law which with a methodical interpretation of the statute can lead to different outcomes in the usual legal science discussion framework, to supplant the interpretation of the Court of Justice with an interpretation of its own.'[68] The Court of Justice must be given its due respect as a court with recognized powers within the German legal order.

It follows that even though the European Union is divided up into as many jurisdictions as there are member states, the content of EU law is common to them all, as is the recognition of the authority of the CJEU in each separate jurisdiction. This reception of EU law is not different, however, to the reception of customary international law and of any treaties of public international law that the member states have ratified, according to standard constitutional principle. Precisely because law is practical and is not a formal order or hierarchy of rules, it is perfectly possible to say that the jurisdictions are separate but the European legal order—as an order of international law—is shared.

The principle of integrity captures, I hope, the proposal made by George Letsas which I examined in Chapter 1, according to which European Union law seeks to be 'harmonious' with domestic law and does not need rules of conflict between legal systems as proposed by legal positivists.[69] For Letsas, the task for the Court of Justice is to provide a unified moral and political theory of the European Union that can be shared by all courts. As I argued above, that theory must proceed from the assumption that both legal orders are legitimate and binding in their own substantive spheres. Harmony must proceed from dualism. But once this qualification is made, Letsas' conclusion is easily accepted. Harmonious law is what the principle of integrity seeks to achieve.

Ronald Dworkin wrote that in the ideal case, integrity is appropriate to a 'community of principle'. Whenever integrity is well followed by the appropriate institutions, the community becomes a 'genuine' political community under a 'model of principle'. He wrote that a genuine community insists that 'people are members of a genuine political community only when they accept that their fates are linked in the following strong way: they accept that they are governed by common principles, not just by rules hammered out in political compromise'.[70] This argument cannot apply without qualification to the European Union.[71] As I explained in

[67] ibid par. 60.

[68] ibid par. 66.

[69] See George Letsas, 'Harmonic Law: The Case Against Pluralism' in Julie Dickson and Pavlos Eleftheriadis (eds), *Philosophical Foundations of European Union Law* (Oxford: Oxford University Press, 2012) 77.

[70] Dworkin, *Law's Empire* (n. 62) 211.

[71] Dworkin goes on to say: 'Politics has a different character for such people. It is a theatre of debate about which principles the community should adopt as a system, which view it should take of justice, fairness, and due process, not the different story, appropriate to the other models, in which each person

Chapter 2, the member states are independent political communities with their own claims to self-government. So integrity cannot apply in exactly the same way to the European Union. It can only apply to European Union law on the basis that the EU is a community of communities of principle. The same ideals of a community of principle apply to the European Union as a whole, when seen as a union of peoples that come together on the basis of the law of nations. In order for this principled interpretation of EU law to succeed, we need to have principles that are appropriate for a union of peoples—not just those that apply to a single jurisdiction.[72]

When integrity applies to the relations between different jurisdictions, it needs principles that explain how the self-governing states relate to one another. This structure of principled reciprocity requires that we distinguish between principles that concern states in their mutual relations in the manner of the *law of nations*, principles that determine relations between states and their citizens in the manner of *public law*, and principles that in an entirely novel way determine relations between states and the citizens of other states, which we may call, following Kant, principles of '*cosmopolitan law*'.[73] The first group are horizontal principles that are grounded in the equal standing of states, which was itself a reason for deploying dualism. The second are vertical principles that track both the member states' commitments to human rights and democracy but also the fundamental freedoms recognized by the Treaty. The third set of principles addresses the questions arising out of the idea of European citizenship and the rights of free movement. Bringing these ideas together under a single theory of European Union law—that makes sense both of the self-government of the member state but also of their explicit commitment to share political power in novel ways—is the task set out by the principle of integrity. Integrity tells us to look at the European Union both as a union of peoples and as a community of principle.

tries to plan the flag of his convictions over as large a domain of power or rules as possible. Members of a society of principle accept that their political rights and duties are not exhausted by the particular decisions their political institutions have reached, but depend, more generally, on the scheme of principles those decisions presuppose and endorse'. ibid 211.

[72] I discuss some of the complexities of these analogies in Pavlos Eleftheriadis, 'The Idea of a European Constitution' 27 *Oxford Journal of Legal Studies* (2007) 1.

[73] See for further elaboration of this point Pavlos Eleftheriadis, 'Cosmopolitan Law' 9 *European Law Journal* (2003) 241–63; Pavlos Eleftheriadis, 'The European Constitution and Cosmopolitan Ideals' 7 *The Columbia Journal of European Law* (2001) 21–39.

5
A Community of Principle

In the last two chapters I looked at the way in which member states adopt the law of the European Union and suggested a new theory of transnational legal institutions. I rejected monism and pluralism as theories of EU law for two reasons. First, because they proceed from an inadequate model of law offered by the legal positivism of Kelsen and Hart. Second, because they turn EU law into a paradox which does not fit with the way the Court of Justice and the national courts routinely interpret and apply EU law.

I defended a different theory, a theory of interpretive dualism, according to which the law of the European Union is part of the law of nations. I argued that a practical or deliberative understanding of law provides an account of the relationship between domestic and EU law without paradox. Dualism and the deliberative framework go hand-in-hand in this argument: they stand or fall together. I argued that the example of the European Union shows that legal positivism is self-defeating as a theory of law. It makes no sense in theory and is ignored in practice.

This argument relied on a fundamental distinction that should be of use to any theory of law: the distinction between state law as the law of a jurisdiction and international law as the law of nations. The distinction is based on political fundamentals that we had a chance to examine in Chapter 2. It arises from the deeper distinction between the substantive functions or purposes that are appropriate to states and the parallel functions of international organizations that are agreed among states. It is now time to turn our attention more closely to these political fundamentals. In order to understand the law of the European Union, we need to discuss in some detail the political interpretations that have underpinned the legal doctrines. We need now to turn our attention to the political and ethical reasons and arguments that turned the law of the European Union into the most progressive part of the law of nations.

5.1 In Search of a Theory

What kind of political and ethical project is the European Union? It is an international project whose aims, purposes, and powers respect the self-government of its member states. It ensures that all member states are sovereign and self-governing. This institutional arrangement is endorsed by all member state courts, with only minor local variations. For the domestic courts the Union's treaties do

A Union of Peoples. Pavlos Eleftheriadis. Oxford University Press (2020). © Oxford University Press.
DOI: 10.1093/oso/9780198854173.001.0001

not operate as a new 'Constitution', but only as treaties of public international law that are to be given effect through domestic law. They are received by the domestic legal order through the doctrine of dualism and in accordance with appropriate constitutional requirements.

Nevertheless, the European Union is a special kind of international institution. The member states have committed themselves to handing over very significant powers of decision-making to its supranational bodies: the Commission, the Council, the European Parliament, the European Central Bank, and the Court of Justice, whose powers are circumscribed by the treaties under the principle of conferral. Decisions are not always taken with unanimous consent there. Under this arrangement, EU laws that a member state may have objected to, may have direct effect in its domestic law and apply immediately to its legal order, enjoying a status of primacy. As we have seen, the member states have various constitutional mechanisms for accommodating EU law all of which manifest a theory of constitutional dualism, distinguishing state law from EU law as a law of nations.

I argued that national law receives EU law through the development of three parallel constitutional principles that seek to preserve an equilibrium between national and EU law: the principle of 'conditional primacy', which concerns the effectiveness of EU law, the principle of 'institutional tolerance', which requires member states to heed the need for uniformity, and perhaps the most fundamental of all, the principle of 'integrity', which requires EU law to become a coherent and principled area of law in accordance with the domestic constitutional architecture.

These legal strategies create many theoretical puzzles, however. They do not fit the standard constitutional narrative as I explained in Chapters 3 and 4. They do not deploy the standard tools of constitutional theory, for example the separation of powers or the principle of democracy. So they often seem to offer too little, too late: they do not address what many call Europe's 'democratic deficit'.

The reason why the European Union does not meet the tests of constitutional legitimacy is that it does not need to. Since it is not a state, it is not set up to answer the ethical concerns of a constitution. The European Union is a different project altogether. This is why we need a fresh political interpretation of the European Union which will help us make sense of the international elements of its legal architecture.

I will argue, in this and the next three chapters, that the best public philosophy of the European Union must be one of progressive internationalism. While dualism is the legal theory in which we find a uniform and coherent way of dealing with the various legal systems of the member states, progressive internationalism is the political theory that animates the most compelling interpretation of the European Union.

Many distinguished experts in EU law see it differently. Some version of federalism dominates the current political interpretations of the EU, so we need to understand that argument better. Any internationalist point of view is rejected by these theories as a seemingly 'backward' step in the process of integration. Indeed the Court is praised for having gone beyond the treaties in the direction of 'ever closer union' which is taken to be the 'progressive' view. The Court of Justice has often appeared to have adopted a maximalist attitude to the nature of EU law, especially when it issued its judgments on direct effect and supremacy. For many the idea of the 'autonomy' of EU law points to 'monism' as its official theory of law. While I have rejected this reading of the Court's case law, the general impression remains: the Court is looking to federalism for political and ethical inspiration.

There is some truth in the federalist reading. Progress has been achieved by the bold steps of the Court of Justice which were often put in the guise of a federal 'ever closer union'. But it does not follow that federalism is the appropriate *general* framework for our understanding of the European Union. It must be rejected if it does not fit the architecture of the treaties and the case law of the courts. Moreover, internationalism can be equally progressive. The European Union may be a pioneer of a new internationalism which it can hold up as an example to the world. The EU may well be a model for redrawing the map of sovereignty around the world, especially as new global challenges require coordinated global response. The crisis of climate change or the experience of coordinated attacks on democracies by well-organized autocracies are only two recent examples of much-needed progressive international cooperation.

Indeed, federalism seems to have a dark side. It has provoked some backlash against Europe.[1] I explained in Chapter 4 that some member states courts do understand the Court of Justice to have demanded monism and they have explicitly rejected it. This is why for some legal commentators we are facing a 'constitutional conflict',[2] or a constitutional paradox.[3] The reasoning is that if European institutions are federalist, while the member state institutions are statist we are set for a political confrontation that we do not know how to resolve.

In this chapter I argue that the European Union needs neither federalism nor statism. I also argue that neither the Court of Justice nor any other European institution has consistently relied on a federalist reading of the European Union. In any event the federalist reading is not at all necessary. Although a small number of the Court's judgments reflected a monist theory in the 1960s and 1970s, a different pattern has emerged in subsequent years. As the European Union developed through the Single European Act—the Maastricht, Nice, and Amsterdam treaties—its constitutional theory has become more sophisticated and more clearly

[1] For a sophisticated discussion of some of these challenges to the European Union see Ivan Krastev, *After Europe* (Philadelphia: University of Pennsylvania Press, 2017).

[2] Mattias Kumm, 'The Jurisprudence of Constitutional Conflict: Constitutional Supremacy in Europe before and after the Constitutional Treaty' 11 *European Law Journal* (2005) 262–307.

[3] Miguel Poiares Maduro, 'Europe and the Constitution: What if this Is as Good as it Gets?' in J.H.H. Weiler and Marlene Wind (eds), *European Constitutionalism Beyond the State* (Cambridge: Cambridge University Press, 2003) 74, at 95–100.

'internationalist'. The recent case law accommodates much better the twin requirements for the uniformity of EU law and the self-government of the member states.

I believe that during this later period practically all the significant judgments of the Court of Justice have been both dualist in legal theory and internationalist in political interpretation. In this chapter I explore in detail this broad political interpretation. The task is not simply to report on what the Court of Justice has said but also to offer a constructive interpretation of the political principles that have animated the EU treaties and the Court's case law.

I shall discuss three general theories: three interpretations of the legal and political framework of the European Union. These theories offer rival accounts under which the European Union could be a community of principle in a way consistent with the dualist practice we observed in the previous chapters. These theories are 'federalism', 'statism', and 'internationalism'. I will argue that the third model, that of internationalism, is the most attractive and the one that fits our legal materials in the best way. I will argue that the European Union relies on a sophisticated political theory of progressive internationalism, which sees the European Union as a union of peoples organized on the basis of a progressive reinvention of the law of nations in order to manage the economic and social interdependence of the member states.

5.2 Constitutional Federalism

There are several variations of federalism. I divide them up, somewhat arbitrarily, into four different categories: 'constitutional federalism', 'demoicracy', 'pluralist federalism', and 'aspirational federalism'. I discuss them in turn below. By way of introduction, I should say that federalism as a political doctrine is ambiguous. Viewed from the point of view of a unitary state, federalism is de-centralizing. Viewed from the vantage point of a loose association of states, however, it is centralizing. In the context of the EU, where we start from treaties of international law, federalism generally means a step towards close integration, i.e. towards a 'supranational' or 'constitutional' framework.

Robert Schütze, one of the most articulate defenders of federalism in the EU, speaks of it as a 'uniform normative frame that allows for national diversities'.[4] This is an excellent definition because it highlights both the ambition for uniformity as well as its and open-endedness. This is also the sense in which 'federalism' was used in one of the earliest discussions of federalism in the EU by Koen Lenaerts, who went on to become President of the Court of Justice of the EU:

[4] Robert Schütze, *From Dual to Cooperative Federalism: The Changing Structure of European Law* (Oxford: Oxford University Press, 2009) 352. See also Robert Schütze, *European Constitutional Law*, 2nd edn (Cambridge: Cambridge University Press, 2016).

> The other dimension, the *vertical* division of powers between the Community and the Member States, was equally constitutionalized when the Court had to explain in the landmark *Van Gend & Loos* ruling of 1962 that although the EEC Treaty presents itself as a compact among sovereign States, it is in reality—due to its substance—a 'constitution' of a central legal order, federally related to the legal orders of the Member States.[5]

Lenaerts was using here the terms 'constitution' and 'federally' as elements of an architecture of the European Union that explicitly turned away from the international model. He introduced the term 'federal' to describe a 'vertical' and therefore a hierarchical relationship between member states and the Union under the idea of a 'new legal order'. For Lenaerts the direct effect of the Treaties followed the logic of a central legal order imposing uniformity onto the member states. This is what the 'constitutional' logic was meant to achieve. In this argument federalism calls for more integration not less.[6]

A similar argument for federalism was made a few years later by the distinguished EU law scholar and former Advocate General at the Court of Justice of the European Union Walter van Gerven. For van Gerven federalism was a viable interpretation of the legal materials as they stood at the time. Van Gerven argued that the EU responded to political principles according to which the EU ought to be organized are those of an 'accountable executive government', on the basis that the EU already exercised executive government under a single constitutional framework.[7] Although van Gerven conceded that the EU is not on the way to becoming a federal state,[8] he argued that the appropriate constitutional framework for the EU was one where the values of domestic democracy ought to be strictly adhered to. In his concluding chapter van Gerven compared parliamentary and presidential systems of government and considered which one of them may be the most appropriate form of government for the EU. This comparison assumes, at least implicitly, that the problems addressed by domestic and EU institutions are the same.[9] He concluded that a European democratic government should encompass an elected parliament, a 'multiparty consensus government' relying upon the Commission, a Commission that is fully accountable to Parliament, a Council of Ministers, and a European Council.[10]

[5] Koen Lenaerts, 'Constitutionalism and the Many Faces of Federalism' (1990) 38 *American Journal of Comparative Law* 205, 208.

[6] See also Koen Lenaerts, 'Federalism and the Rule of Law: Perspectives from the European Court of Justice' 33 *Fordham International Law Review* (2011) 1338–87, where Lenaerts describes the 'pervasive' effect of EU law, even in areas that do not, strictly speaking, fall under the competence of the EU.

[7] Walter van Gerven, *The European Union: A Polity of States and Peoples* (Oxford: Hart, 2005).

[8] ibid 60.

[9] ibid 309–74.

[10] ibid 373–4.

But van Gerven's arguments for a federalist reading of the EU suffers from an important omission. His account fails to discuss the treaty-making process which involves an 'intergovernmental conference' as well as the process of ratification by all member states.[11] This complex process has always been the highest law-making authority in the European Union. This is the diplomatic conference that agrees the European Union Treaties. It has full powers to redraft them entirely, on the condition that it secures the ratification of all the member states of the texts it agrees, according to standard practices of public international law. If there is an EU constitution, then the intergovernmental conference and the member states are its authors. It is surprising that van Gerven does not discuss this process of treaty-making, since it is a superior source of law to any law made by the European Parliament. Had he discussed it, he would have to find some other way of accounting for such an 'undemocratic' process. As is well known in public international law all states are equal irrespective of size.

There is no way of accommodating such a process of creating treaties into any democratic framework as it is conventionally understood. Treaty-making cannot be captured by any model of democracy, since it provides for the disproportionate representation of states, all of which enjoy powers of veto irrespective of the size of their populations. Van Gerven's analysis has left no room for the absolute equal standing of all member states qua subjects of public international law nor does he mention the other ways in which states have equal standing in the EU institutions.[12] When we include this fundamental institutional feature of the Union under the Treaties, the federal and democratic model seems out of place. Either the EU fails the tests of political legitimacy or we have applied the wrong tests.

The most extensive and thorough defence of a constitutionally federalist theory has been offered, however, by Professor Robert Schütze in a series of highly original publications. Schütze argues that the institutional structure of the European Union started as an international project but has evolved. It was originally compatible with a model of 'dual federalism', according to which the EU had 'dual sovereignty' so that the 'federal' and state governments were 'sovereign co-equals' and each was operating independently in a separate sphere. But Professor Schütze believes that the EU has now moved to a different model, which he calls 'cooperative federalism'. In this model the Union and the member states are 'complementary parts in a shared legal sphere'.[13] This has happened gradually, he argues, as the European Union has seen more and more competences transferred to its institutions and as the Court of Justice has been offering ever more centralising interpretations of EU

[11] The amendment of treaties is set out in article 48 TEU. For brevity, I do not discuss here the simplified amendment process, since it makes little difference in practice.

[12] See Pavlos Eleftheriadis, 'The Standing of States in the European Union' in Nicholas Tsagourias (ed.), *Transnational Constitutionalism: International and European Perspectives* (Cambridge: Cambridge University Press, 2007).

[13] Schütze, *From Dual to Cooperative Federalism* (n. 4) 346.

law. Schütze borrows from the federal theory of the United States to argue that the Union and the states are in effect 'mutually complementary parts of a *single* governmental mechanism all of whose powers are intended to realize the current purposes of government according to their applicability to the problem at hand'.[14]

This federalist institutional analysis follows Schütze's monist analysis of the legal architecture of the European Union according to which the Treaties are now the 'Grundnorm' of the European legal order.[15]

Schütze addresses directly the question of the constitution-making of the EU by way of international treaties.[16] He argues that according to the Court of Justice the limits of the European Union's powers are determined by its own constitutional identity. This means that 'within these constitutional boundaries, it is for the [Union] itself to determine the scope of its powers'.[17] His argument relies on Article 352 TFEU (ex Article 308 TEC) which provides that: 'If action by the Union should prove necessary, within the framework of the policies defined in the Treaties, to attain one of the objectives set out in the Treaties, and the Treaties have not provided the necessary powers, the Council, acting unanimously on a proposal from the Commission and after obtaining the consent of the European Parliament, shall adopt the appropriate measures.' This article has often been used to expand the powers of the EU. Schütze, however, interprets it as providing plenary and unlimited power to expand the powers of the EU. He says that even though this article 'a*ppears* like an ordinary competence', in fact has 'an almost unlimited scope'.[18] He believes that in fact it establishes '*legislative* competence-competence' for the EU.

This argument, however, does not effectively respond to the problem of the international nature of the EU: it is open to the states to repeal Article 352 in their next treaty amendment. The problem we identified above, in relation to van Gerven's argument, applies equally to the argument offered by Schütze. How can a Union have power of 'unlimited scope', when its founding documents, the treaties, are in the hands of the inter-governmental conference and the member states ratification process? Schütze accepts that it still 'depends on the Member States to determine the fundamental structure of [the EU's] institutions: its constitutional identity'.[19] He thus qualifies his argument by admitting that the EU's constitutional competence is '*bounded* competence-competence' or 'partial competence-competence' and that 'this characterization aligns itself with the idea of divided or partial sovereignty and thus captures the federal nature of the Community legal order best'.[20]

14 ibid 243.
15 See Schütze, *European Constitutional Law* (n. 4) 43–76.
16 See Schütze, *From Dual to Cooperative Federalism* (n. 4) 151 ff.
17 ibid 152.
18 Schütze, *From Dual to Cooperative Federalism* (n. 4) 155.
19 ibid 156.
20 ibid 156.

These arguments, however are not convincing. There is a choice to be made between a *constitutional* framework and an *international* framework. We cannot say that states are sovereign and they are not sovereign. A constitutional structure is a comprehensive and coercive order of law, or in the terminology I have adopted, a 'jurisdiction' of a sovereign state.[21] International legal structures do not create such a structure for the world. Nor do the European treaties. As Schütze accepts, the powers of the EU derive from the treaties under public international law. The treaties derive their legal authority from the joint action and power of the member states that create them. Everything depends on international law. The analogy of the European Union legal order with a federal framework does not work.

5.3 'Demoicracy'

'Demoicracy' is one of the most interesting arguments to have emerged in recent European Union scholarship, mostly in the writings of the Oxford political theorist Kalypso Nicolaïdis. In my reading, which I hope is not uncharitable, the theory of 'demoicracy' is a variation on federalism. Nicolaïdis argues that the European Union must not be understood as a federal 'state' but instead as a federal 'union'.[22] What is the difference? The key to Nicolaïdis' distinction is that Europe is not supposed to be a single 'demos' but a community of different 'demoi'. She is proposing the novel term 'demoicracy' to refer to the multiple 'demoi' that jointly compose a coherent institutional union.[23] A demoicracy, she says, is a union of peoples who govern together but not *as one*.

As the Constitutional Treaty was being negotiated about fifteen years ago, Nicolaïdis commented as follows: '... today's constitution does not call for a homogeneous community or for laws grounded on the will of a single European demos. Rather, it makes mutual respect for national identities and institutions one of its foremost principles'.[24] The key here is that the institutional architecture does not centralize power among the various peoples but allows the various parts to retain their independence.

[21] See section 2.7.

[22] Kalypso Nicolaïdis, 'We, the Peoples of Europe' 83 *Foreign Affairs* (2004) 97–110, at 102. See also Kalypso Nicolaïdis, 'The Idea of European Demoicracy' in Julie Dickson and Pavlos Eleftheriadis (eds), *Philosophical Foundations of European Union Law* (Oxford: Oxford University Press, 2012) 247–74 and Kalypso Nicolaïdis, 'European Demoicracy and its Crisis' 51 *Journal of Common Market Studies* (2013) 351–69.

[23] Similar arguments about 'demoicracy' were made by Francis Cheneval and Frank Schimmelfenning, 'The Case for Demoicracy in the European Union' 51 *Journal of Common Market Studies* (2013) 334–50. The term 'demoicracy' was coined, I believe, by Philippe van Parijs, 'Should the EU Become More Democratic?' in Andreas Follesdal and Peter Koslowski (eds), *Democracy and the European Union* (Berlin: Springer, 1997).

[24] Nicolaïdis, 'We the Peoples of Europe' (n. 22) 102.

Is this federalism? Nicolaïdis relies heavily on the fact that under the then proposed constitutional treaty member states have the explicit right to withdraw. She draws the conclusion that the treaty 'firmly establishes the EU as a federal union, rather than a federal state, which … is defined by the very denial of that right'.[25] It is clear, I think, that Nicolaïdis' conclusions are correct in relation to a federal 'state'. Given that the option for all member states to leave the Union is always open (under what has now become Article 50 TEU), then one cannot call the structure one of statehood, as has been recently confirmed by the *Wightman* judgment of the Court of Justice.[26] This will necessarily be the case for as long as the union is based on treaties of public international law. So the EU is certainly a union of states not a state itself. Nevertheless, the states are a 'federal union'. What does this mean?

In more recent work Nicolaïdis, writing with the Swiss philosopher Francis Cheneval, has sought to give a more complete account of 'demoicracy'.[27] Their argument is not one concerning the institutions of the EU, but the underlying social conditions that make possible a 'social reality of demoicracy' that could be 'acted out in the democratic experience and self-awareness of its peoples'.[28] They argue that it is possible to see popular sovereignty being exercised by several rather than just one demos without contradiction. The argument offers a carefully structured account of what they call 'collective intentions of togetherness and co-sovereignty' among various peoples. They hope that such intentions can achieve consensus while remaining aloof from substantive moral commitments, if they exhibit ethical open-endedness. This makes possible, they argue, a feeling of loyalty towards an ambiguous political union.

Interestingly Koen Lenaerts recently endorsed the analysis of Nicolaïdis and Cheneval and offered his own account of 'demoicracy' in the European Union.[29] He argues that the term 'demoicracy' captures the fact that European Union rests on 'a dual structure of democratic legitimacy' which is composed 'not only of the body of EU citizens collectively, but also of the various individual peoples of Europe organized in and by their national constitutions'.[30] Such a 'dual structure' does not seek to replace the democratic structure of the states but only to 'supplement' them. If, however, one sees the European Union legal order as one creating a single order of law, so that European institutions act together as a 'federal union', then the overarching democratic structure should replace the state one. Lenaerts,

[25] ibid 105.

[26] Case C-621/18, *Wightman et al. v Secretary of State for Exiting the European Union*, Court of Justice of the European Union (Full Court), 10 December 2018, ECLI:EU:C:2018:999.

[27] Francis Cheneval and Kalypso Nicolaïdis, 'The Social Construction of Demoicracy in the European Union' 16 *European Journal of Political Theory* (2017) 235–60.

[28] ibid 238.

[29] Koen Lenaerts, 'Demoicracy, Constitutional Pluralism, and the Court of Justice of the European Union' in Luuk van Middelaar and Philippe van Parijs (eds), *After the Storm: How to Save Democracy in Europe* (Tielt: Lannoo, 2015) 123–38.

[30] ibid 128.

following Nicolaïdis, feels that he does not need to resolve this tension. How the two levels are related can remain open-ended—or one governed by 'pluralism' (something which I will discuss in the next section).

But can we call a structure of 'demoicracy' a 'federal union'? What is the word 'federal' doing here exactly? Perhaps it means a 'federation', in the sense that some people distinguish between a federal state and a federation. A federation has been defined by a leading political scientist as:

> a compound polity combining constituent units and a general government, each possessing power delegated to it by the people through a constitution, each empowered to deal directly with the citizens in the exercise of a significant portion of its legislative, administrative, and taxing powers, and each directly elected by its citizens.[31]

This account of federation is close to what Lenaerts was speaking of, i.e. of a constitution imposing order in a vertical ordering as the Court of Justice has consistently said since the 1960s. It seems not to cover, however, Nicolaïdis' idea of a federal 'union', which sounds much closer to a 'confederation'.

In a confederation the institutions are not organized according to a single constitution, nor do they seek their legitimacy in the representation of a people. Instead, power there is exercised by the delegates of the constituent units and is justified on the basis of their reciprocal agreements, not on the basis of an independent electoral base. So: 'by contrast with federation, in which each government operates directly on the citizens, in confederations the direct relationship lies between the shared institutions and the governments of the member states'.[32]

Philippe Van Parijs distinguishes between a confederation, where 'all significant powers are entrenched at the level of the components', a federation, where 'some of them are entrenched at the centre', and a federal state 'when those entrenched at the centre include the ultimate authority over physical coercion, compulsory education and compulsory redistribution'.[33] It is obvious from the points made by Lenaerts, Nicolaïdis, and Van Parijs that the EU is somewhere in between a federation and a confederation. But what is the point of these distinctions? If we were political scientists, we could perhaps refrain from choosing one among them. We might be able to say that the EU is a *sui generis* case. In due course its success and

[31] Ronald L. Watts, 'Federalism, Federal Political Systems, and Federation' 1 *Annual Review of Political Science* (1998) 117–37, 121. For important essays on federalism and the EU see Kalypso Nicolaïdis and Robert Howse (eds), *The Federal Vision: Legitimacy and Levels of Governance in the United States and the European Union* (Oxford: Oxford University Press, 2001) and Sergio Fabbrini (ed.), *Democracy and Federalism in the European Union and the United States: Exploring Post-National Governance* (London: Routledge, 2005)

[32] Watts, 'Federalism' (n. 31) 121.

[33] Philippe van Parijs, 'Justifying Europe' in Luuk van Middelaar and Philippe van Parijs (eds), *After the Storm: How to Save Democracy in Europe* (Tielt: Lannoo, 2015) 247–62, at 252.

imitation elsewhere (or its possibly unceremonious demise) would tell political scientists all they needed to know.

But our question is not one of classification. We are not looking to provide merely descriptive accuracy or explain a social phenomenon from the point of view of political sociology. We are seeking to *interpret* a set of political principles with a view to organizing our normative arguments about the EU in law. Legal interpretation, we have seen, is constructive and interpretive on the basis of a theory of political legitimacy.[34] By choosing an appropriate intellectual framework for the EU, we are opting for a particular way of reading the existing law or outlining legal duties, so that our deliberations about the free movement of goods and persons, competition law, the law of state aid, or the protection of the environment will be affected. The questions before us are practical not descriptive.

Hence the federalist reading of EU law will produce a different reading of the law to one that is internationalist. It is possible that these differences provide a different account of direct effect, or of supremacy, or of citizenship. From a practical or legal doctrinal standpoint, we need to make up our minds whether the principles of the constitutional *state*, federal or otherwise, apply to the European Union or not. This is not a question of degree, but a question of yes or no.

Lenearts' argument does not actually engage with this doctrinal dilemma. He does not offer any arguments why the EU ought to be seen as a federation in the making or as something else. Nicolaïdis is also happy to leave the issue undecided, giving the EU the ambiguous term of 'demoicracy'. But the practical dilemma between the constitutional and the international framework is real and pressing.

The argument from 'demoicracy' is sophisticated and attractive, but does not address the central question of the political legitimacy of the European Union. When we address issues of legal interpretation we need to make a choice between a framework of constitutionalism and a framework of internationalism.[35] I believe that 'demoicracy' effectively, although not always explicitly, chooses the latter when it says that the EU's institutional structure is not governing 'as one'. Yet, the position is not always clear. Although such an ambivalent attitude may be descriptively accurate, it does not lead to a sustainable legal interpretation of the general framework of EU law.

There is an alternative position: that no such choice is necessary. Theorists of 'demoicracy' may insist that there is no practical urgency to our dilemma. This is

[34] I discussed this process in detail in Pavlos Eleftheriadis, 'The Idea of a European Constitution' 27 *Oxford Journal of Legal Studies* (2007) 1.

[35] Indeed the institutional framework of what I see as transnational accountability among peoples that Cheneval and Nicolaïdis outline in their essay is very close to the internationalist framework that I will set out in the next few chapters. My disagreement with them about 'demoicracy' is not practical, but strictly *interpretive*. I do not consider 'demoicracy' a genuinely middle position, but an interpretation of EU law from within internationalism.

a view often defended as 'pluralism' and is a very popular position in EU law. We need to discuss this view now in some detail.

5.4 Pluralist Federalism

I now turn to the version of federalism that is the most popular among legal scholars, 'pluralist federalism'. This is the idea that some form of federalism is an appropriate constitutional interpretation of EU law while at the same time allowing for the equal standing of states. Such a view combines federalism and self-government by way of 'pluralism'.[36] How is this possible? Koen Lenaerts first spoke of it in his 1990 article on federalism, which spoke of 'diversity in unity':

> *Devolutionary federalism* ... refers to a constitutional order that redistributes the powers of a previously unitary State among its component entities; these entities obtain an autonomous status within their fields of responsibility. The principal concern is to organize diversity in unity. The system will only be in balance when the shift from a single-sovereign towards a multi-sovereign structure is no longer resented as a merely centrifugal movement threatening national cohesion.[37]

Lenaerts used this idea to describe features of the then European Communities that signalled disintegration rather than integration. He used federalism as a formal idea which can be deployed both for integration and occasionally for disintegration. He concluded that European federalism is 'dual federalism' according to which the Court of Justice 'pursues a constitutional model in which the legal orders of the Community and the Member States are as strictly separated as possible'.[38] Rather than signalling the failure of federalism, for Lenaerts the existence of two or more 'legal orders' in the Union signalled just another manifestation of federalism.[39] The key structural features of the EU, which set it apart from all states and all international organizations was its 'divided sovereignty'.

[36] On pluralism and the EU see Neil Walker, 'The Idea of Constitutional Pluralism' 65 Modern Law Review (2002) 317–59; Neil MacCormick, *Questioning Sovereignty: Law, State and Nation in the European Commonwealth* (Oxford: Oxford University Press, 1999); Nico Krisch, *Beyond Constitutionalism: The Pluralist Structure of Postnational Law* (Oxford: Oxford University Press, 2010); Pavlos Eleftheriadis, 'Pluralism and Integrity' 23 *Ratio Juris* (2010) 365. As I will argue in the next section, some of the 'pluralists' can best be seen as internationalists.

[37] Lenaerts, 'Constitutionalism and the Many Faces of Federalism' (n. 5) 206.

[38] ibid 260.

[39] Something similar has been accepted by Mattias Kumm when he says that the EU has a 'constitution' even though there is no way of establishing what is the supreme law: 'The authority of EU law is possibly a question of degree. It may depend on the degree to which republican principles are realized by EU institutions. It admits to the possibility that neither EU Law nor national constitutional law effectively establishes the supreme law of the land'; in Mattias Kumm, 'Beyond Golf Clubs and the Judicialization of Politics: Why Europe Has a Constitution Properly so Called' 54 *American Journal of Comparative Law* (2006) 505–30 at 523.

> Federalism is present whenever a divided sovereignty is guaranteed by the national or supranational constitution and umpired by the supreme court of the common legal order. Both sovereigns enact laws with direct operation upon those to whom they are addressed. There is—in principle at least—no political oversight of one sovereign over the other. The normal enforcement mechanism of the constitutional balance is of a judicial nature and in case of conflict between validly enacted federal and component-entity laws, the former prevail over the latter.[40]

Lenaerts' solution was to say that a federation does not need *political* oversight but only *judicial* oversight over the allocation of competences. In other words, the member states do not owe accountability to a single political institution, but are subject to the oversight of the Court of Justice of the EU. There may be many 'legal orders', but only one responsible court for a federation to exist, he argued. The Court of Justice, the federal court whose judgments prevail over all national courts, may well be what holds the union together.

Can this argument work? I do not think so. We saw above that Van Gerven's constitutional federalism cannot accommodate the *international* nature of the treaties. The same problem occurs here. Lenaerts's argument fails to show any real oversight over the actions of the states. It cannot show that there are any accountability mechanisms or any other democratic tests for the intergovernmental process of treaty change, for example. Because the diplomatic representatives are delegates of equal states under public international law, no common European institutions can test them. The states are only accountable separately to their own constitutional bodies, following their own separate arrangements.

This model of separate accountability is an institutional model occurring in many aspects of the EU such as, for example, the election of members of the European Parliament or the appointment of commissioners and judges. It is a model of an international order, not of a federation (or federal 'union'). The member states' actions are not accountable to any European body but only to each other.

Lenaerts' pluralist federalism faces exactly the same problem as van Gerven's constitutional federalism. There is no way of accommodating the public international law elements of the Union through the supposed dominant jurisdiction of the Court of Justice. The Court has no power to interpret national law, nor can it hold it invalid (it can only require it to be 'set aside'). The amendment of treaties is something wholly beyond the control of the Court of Justice, although not outside the remit of the member state courts as shown in the examples of the ratification of the Maastricht and Lisbon Treaties, where several courts were invited to express a view. This means that the most important law-making power within EU law lies

[40] Lenaerts, 'Constitutionalism and the Many Faces of Federalism' (n. 5) 263.

wholly outside what Lenaerts calls a 'federal court' and wholly outside the union's supposedly 'federal' constitutional law.

Other institutional elements too are also outside the Union's scope. For example, the composition of the European Parliament is also determined exclusively by state law and adjudicated by state courts.[41] The domestic compliance of the member states' institution with EU law is also in principle outside the jurisdiction of the Court of Justice. The Court receives references for a preliminary ruling but cannot hear claims from persons against their states. When the Commission brings an action against a member state it launches a judicial procedure that is, in principle, international. The Court of Justice has very strong and important powers. But its scheme of jurisdiction has not replaced those of the member states. If there is no central constitutional law and no central jurisdiction, then there is no federation.

Could perhaps this argument for constitutional federalism be saved by presupposing that the 'constitution' of the EU includes both the EU treaties and the member state constitutions under a common set of general principles? Something like that is being proposed by Mattias Kumm. He argues that the Treaties are 'a constitution in a strong normative sense' even if they are not the 'supreme law of the land' and that 'common principles of European republicanism, and not an ultimate rule either of national or European constitutional supremacy, provide the ultimate norms for guiding European constitutional practices'.[42] Kumm's argument, however, is ambivalent between monism and dualism. What he describes can be both monist and dualist.

Nicole Roughan has offered a similar reading of supranational law. She proposes the idea of 'relative authority' or relative claims to legitimacy, according to which

> when there are multiple *prima facie* legitimate authorities in interacting or overlapping domains, and there is no outweighing reason to have just one singular authority, then those *prima facie* legitimate authorities can have only relative authority and must coordinate or cooperate or tolerate one another in order to be legitimate for their subjects.[43]

Her argument seeks the unity of law and the legal order not in a 'rule of recognition' or the creation of a positive 'authority' by some kind of fact—a legal theory she rejects—[44] but in considerations of substantive practical reasoning including the questions of legitimacy and authority.

[41] See for example Case C-208/03P *Le Pen v European Parliament* [2005] ECR I-6051.

[42] Kumm, 'Beyond Golf Clubs' (n. 39) 527–8. See also, for an earlier defence of the same argument, Mattias Kumm, 'The Jurisprudence of Constitutional Conflict: Constitutional Supremacy in Europe before and after the Constitutional Treaty' 11 *European Law Journal* (2005) 262–307.

[43] Nicole Roughan, *Authorities: Conflict, Cooperation and Transnational Legal Theory* (Oxford: Oxford University Press, 2013) 158.

[44] She states that her books sets out to: 'to treat plurality and relationships between legal orders/institutions/officials/norms as matters concerning legitimate authority, and thus as being part of any question about the existence and/or legitimacy of authority over subjects'; ibid 3.

On the basis of this practical view of law Roughan explains how relative authority 'is simply a claim to have legitimate authority through appropriate relationships with other authorities'.[45] Her argument is not about legal systems, but about the substantive content of law as an attempt to meet the tests of justice and legitimacy while regulating social life.

Nevertheless, neither Kumm nor Roughan address the substantive moral argument supporting a single public scheme of authority. This is what Malcolm calls 'sovereignty', and Kant calls 'public right', and Locke a 'commonwealth'. This is the scheme of comprehensive and coercive public laws that seek to achieve the moral purposes of political authority, as we saw in Chapter 2. At the heart of the distinction between the law of a jurisdiction and the law of nations lies this moral argument. A constitution is an *indispensable* institutional requirement for equal citizenship. How can we give this up, for 'relative' authority? This is why sovereignty is 'indivisible'. A constitution fails in its very purpose if it does not claim and possess comprehensive authority. The idea of shared or ambiguous 'sovereignty' fails our basic tests of political legitimacy.

5.5 Aspirational Federalism

Theories that insist that the appropriate political framework for the EU *should* one day become that of constitutionalism, even though it is not applicable yet, should properly be called 'aspirationally federalist'. The argument in favour of a federal transformation of the EU has been offered by Jürgen Habermas in various ways. In his 2001 essay 'Why Europe Needs a Constitution', Habermas outlined an argument for a European Constitution that was partly historical and partly political.[46] The main objective of the European Union, for Habermas, was to maintain the specific form of social solidarity achieved in Europe, against the pressures of globalization and 'neoliberalism'.[47] He wrote as follows:

> The question therefore is: can any of our small or medium, entangled and accommodating nation-states preserve a separate capacity to escape enforced assimilation to the social model now imposed by the predominant global economic regime? This model is informed by an anthropological image of 'man' as rational chooser and entrepreneur, exploiting his or her labour-power; by a moral view of

[45] ibid 158.

[46] Jürgen Habermas, 'Why Europe Needs a Constitution' 11 *New Left Review* (2001) 5–26. For further arguments in the same direction see Pablo de Greiff and Ciaran Cronin (eds) *Habermas, The Inclusion of the Other: Studies in Political Theory* (Cambridge, Mass.: MIT Press, 1998).

[47] I do not believe the term 'neoliberalism' has any meaningful application in political or legal theory. It refers loosely to very many different theories and processes. Nevertheless, Habermas uses it extensively in this and other essays.

> society that accepts growing cleavages and exclusions; and by a political doctrine that trades a shrinking scope of democracy for freedoms of the market. These are the building blocks of a neo-liberal vision that does not sit well with the kind of normative self-understanding so far prevalent across Europe as a whole.[48]

In order to protect their achievements against these dark forces of globalization, Habermas argues that we need a 're-regulation' of global economy. It follows, for Habermas, that European nations 'have a reason for building a stronger Union with greater international influence'.[49] This means not only stronger internal institutions but also the capacity to act in the international scene: 'With a view to the future of a highly stratified world society, we Europeans have a legitimate interest in getting our voice heard in an international context that is at present dominated by a vision quite different from ours.'[50] Both for social cohesion and for articulating an international voice we need to promote closer European integration through a new Constitution.

But what are the preconditions for closer integration through a new Constitution? It is clear that we cannot create society afresh by fiat. Habermas concedes that any closer institutional integration in Europe needs to build on a common consciousness or a minimum of cultural and political cohesion. Without a pan-European 'civic solidarity' the project will fail, since it will not be endorsed by the public it is intended to serve.

What is needed is that European citizens share, therefore, something like a public sphere of a vibrant democracy: 'There will be no remedy for the legitimation deficit, however, without a European-wide public sphere—a network that gives citizens of all member states an equal opportunity to take part in an encompassing process of focused political communication.'[51] This public sphere and the civic solidarity it brings about support state institutions but are also created by them in a 'circular process'. This is the key to Habermas' argument for a new constitution. History tells us that constitutions can act as catalysts in the creation of nations. Habermas notes that 'national consciousness emerged as much from the mass communication of formally educated readers as from the mobilization of enfranchised voters and drafted soldiers. It has been shaped as much by the intellectual construction of national histories as by the discourse of competing parties, struggling for political power.'

Habermas' argument for the constitution is therefore that it can work as a catalyst for further developments that would make Europe stronger. A European Constitution is thus a means for defending Europe against globalization and

[48] Habermas, 'Why Europe Needs a Constitution' (n. 46) 12.
[49] ibid 12.
[50] ibid 12.
[51] ibid 17.

asserting its voice in the international scene. Habermas said that 'the European project can be seen as a common attempt by the national governments to recover in Brussels something of the capacity for intervention that they have lost at home.[52] Europe ought to positively promote and, if necessary, actively engineer a continental public culture and a European public sphere both through institutional and cultural measures.

What are we to make of this argument? There are some obvious difficulties with it. First, why is social democracy the privileged identity of Europe, in preference to various liberal, conservative, leftist or populist political outlooks? What are we to make of these other political views, especially those that are in favour of globalization and openness? Second, how can a constitution be a historical catalyst? And third, what is to be lost by the creation of a pan-European public sphere? This is clearly a reversal of the argument made by Larry Siedentop in *Democracy in Europe*.[53] Siedentop had noted that the preconditions for a genuine democracy—the kinds of things that Tocqueville noticed in his study of America—were lacking in Europe. There was no common political tradition, no common language, no particular identification with other communities, no mutual trust. Siedentop's conclusion was that we should hold up the federalist project, at least until the conditions were closer to being met. Habermas' argument is the reverse: we must proceed with federalism precisely because we need to accelerate the process of 'creating a public sphere' at the European level. If necessary, we are to engineer a common public sphere through the process of constitution-building.

Habermas has recently renewed this argument in response to the Eurozone crisis. In a recent essay he advocates a 'supranational democracy' in Europe which would be set up by turning the European Monetary Union (EMU) into a full political union. Habermas accepts that this signals the loss of sovereignty for the member states, but welcomes it as a principled *choice*:

> The decision for such a core Europe would amount to more than merely a further evolutionary step in the transfer of particular sovereign rights. With the establishment of a common economic government the red line of the classical understanding of sovereignty would be crossed. The idea that the nation-states are the 'sovereign subject of the Treaties' would have to be abandoned.[54]

This is a clear call for a federal transformation. Nevertheless, Habermas qualifies it by adding that the state would continue to play a significant role. He says that in his view 'confederation' versus 'federal state' is a false alternative.

52 ibid 14.

53 Larry Siedentop, *Democracy in Europe* (London: Penguin, 2000).

54 Jürgen Habermas, 'Democracy, Solidarity, and the European Crisis' in Luuk van Middelaar and Philippe van Parijs (eds), *After the Storm: How to Save Democracy in Europe* (Tielt: Lannoo, 2015) 95–107, at 102–3.

I find this qualification difficult to understand. If the reforms Habermas proposes came to pass, what would be left of member-state sovereignty? Habermas argues that 'the nation-states can well preserve their integrity as states within a supranational democracy by retaining both their roles of the implementing administration and the final custodian of civil liberties'.[55] This description suggests to me that we have already moved away from 'confederation' to a model of full 'federal' union. The qualification does not really change the point that the nation-states must lose their ultimate or constitutional decision-making power.

That sovereignty should be abandoned is also the view of the leading economist Dani Rodrik, who has argued that the project of monetary union had made it necessary to proceed to 'EU-wide democracy'. Rodrik adds, moreover, that the present arrangement is unsustainable. Having transferred monetary policy to the European Central Bank (ECB) we have rendered our overall arrangements undemocratic. For Rodrik we cannot escape the 'trilemma' of democracy, sovereignty, and globalization. It is impossible to have all three of them at the same time. For the European transnational institutions to succeed, its member states must compromise sovereignty further by creating a federal democracy. Rodrik's conclusion is uncompromising:

> Europe's leaders have been misleading their voters, delaying the Europeanization of democratic politics, and raising the political and economic costs of the ultimate reckoning. Simply put, the European integration project has hinged on restrictions on national sovereignty. If its future is now in doubt, it is because sovereignty stand in the way once again.... [56]

Rodrik argues that the transfer of monetary policy to the ECB was not just an act of 'democratic delegation', which is something that democracies regularly do without harm to their institutions. He believes that the EU faces a 'stark choice' between democracy and sovereignty. He argues that 'a single currency and unified financial markets also require harmonization of labour market rules, banking and financial regulations, bankruptcy procedures, and a good deal of fiscal policy as well'.[57] Rodrik argues that 'as the American example illustrates', it is possible to give up on sovereignty. He suggests that the members of the EU should do just that in order to protect democracy. This is the only way, he believes, in which the project of integration can carry on, without compromising its democratic principles.[58]

These arguments for federalism are, in effect, instrumental. Habermas and Rodrik propose a constitutional model for the union, in order to accelerate the

[55] ibid 103.

[56] Dani Rodrik, 'The Future of European Democracy' in van Middelaar and Van Parijs (eds), After the Storm: How to Save Democracy in Europe (n. 54) 55–65, at 61.

[57] ibid 62.

[58] ibid 63.

formation of an adequate European political system, which is the only way to overcome the current crisis. I do not wish to discuss the substance of these arguments. But such arguments cannot work as a *legal* interpretation. Any legal and constitutional interpretation must stay loyal to the materials as they stand. And as long as the treaties remain as they are, aspirational federalism remains just that, an aspiration. Habermas' argument, whatever its merits, does not offer an interpretation of the treaties as they are. It suggests what they *ought to become* sometime in the future, if the states agree to have a treaty amendment.

I should say here, however, that Habermas' call for political union fails to give credit to the value of self-government for the member states. Many of the smaller states in particular achieved their political integration after wars of liberation from Empires, or civil wars or other important events (think of Belgium, Greece, Ireland, and the Eastern European members). Their public life is informed by these common memories. It would be a great loss to them —and to the experience of their citizens—if a common political structure were to replace these domestic constitutions.

Such a view is defended by those theories that emphasize self-government and the EU, or 'statist theories'. It is now time to turn to the way these theories view the European Union.

5.6 The Self-Government Model

All arguments for federalism are open to the objection that they undermine established and valuable institutions of self-government.

John Rawls raised these questions in a private debate with Philippe van Parijs on the moral purposes of the European Union:

> One question the Europeans should ask themselves, if I may hazard a suggestion, is how far-reaching they want their union to be. It seems to me that much would be lost if the European Union became a federal union like the United States. Here there is a common language of political discourse and a ready willingness to move from one state to another. Isn't there a conflict between a large free and open market comprising all of Europe and the individual nation-states, each with its separate political and social institutions, historical memories, and forms and traditions of social policy. Surely these are of great value to the citizens of these countries and give meaning to their life. The large open market including all of Europe is the aim of the large banks and the capitalist business class whose main goal is simply larger profit. The idea of economic growth, onwards and upwards, with no specific end in sight, fits this class perfectly. If they speak about distribution, it is [al]most always in terms of trickle down. The long-term result of this—which we

> already have in the United States—is a civil society awash in a meaningless consumerism of some kind. I can't believe that that is what you want.[59]

John Rawls was only offering here a preliminary view in the course of private correspondence that was not intended to be published. But what he says there is perfectly focused on the most important issue: what is the point of 'ever closer union' or a smooth single market, if our political and moral values are to be compromised? Is our aim to arrive the largest possible society of meaningless consumerism?

I call this the argument from 'self-government'. It argues that the European Union opens up a possibility for giving up sovereignty for the sake of integration, and that when this choice is presented, we ought to choose sovereignty. This is the view, which we looked at in the preface, of the British historian (and polemical Eurosceptic) Noel Malcolm. What is at issue, he argues, is not just the sharing of political 'power' with the EU but the sharing of the states' sovereignty'.[60]

Malcolm shows that 'sovereignty' is not 'power', and that whereas power can be shared, sovereignty cannot. Whereas a nation may have to share power with its neighbours, it alone will remain sovereign over its decision to do so. He said: 'Sovereignty means constitutional independence, the exercise of plenary and exclusive political authority in a legal order. The idea that constitutional independence can be "pooled" is therefore an evident absurdity. Why do people believe in this idea, or say that they believe in it?'[61]

What Malcolm discusses here is not the 'fact' of sovereignty but sovereignty as constitutional authority appropriate to a state. Behind it lies a legal or moral argument about constitutional self-government and independence. This is the only way we can understand the idea of 'plenary and exclusive' political authority, as something allocated or defined by higher law or the law of the constitution. This is then the challenge of self-government to the EU. If the sharing of sovereignty undermines the constitutional ideal, then the EU is bad for the self-governing constitution.[62]

[59] John Rawls and Philippe van Parijs, 'Three Letters on the Law of Peoples and the European Union' (2003) 7 *Revue de philosophie économique* 7–20.

[60] Noel Malcolm, *Sense on Sovereignty* (London: Centre for Policy Studies, 1991), reprinted in Martin Holmes (ed.), *The Eurosceptical Reader* (London: Palgrave, 1996) 342–67. See also Noel Malcolm, 'The Case Against "Europe"' *Foreign Affairs* (1995).

[61] Malcolm, *Sense on Sovereignty* (n. 60) 25.

[62] Noel Malcolm restated the same point in his contribution to the referendum debate: 'For me, the most important issue is the one that flows directly from these problems: the loss of democracy. This huge artificial structure would indeed be paralysed if all decisions required unanimity. But once our laws and policies are made by EU majority voting, we begin to sacrifice the most precious thing of all: the principle that those who make our laws and rule us are chosen by us, and can be removed by us. European elections, and tinkering with the so-called democratic deficit in Brussels, are entirely beside the point here, as the EU is not, for any of its member populations, the primary political community, the 'demos' on which genuine democracy is based'; Noel Malcolm, 'The Great EU Power Trap' *The Spectator*, 28 May 2016.

One of the most eloquent defences of this view was articulated by the historian of ideas Richard Tuck.[63] In his article, which was meant to respond to the European Union referendum debate in the United Kingdom, Tuck contrasted the 'democratic state'—which enables Left-wing policies to be carried out—to Europe's 'neo-liberal' institutional framework—which as currently configured would 'prevent' a socialist agenda from being carried out. Tuck explained this contrast as follows: 'As the jurisprudence of the EU has developed, it has consistently undermined standard left policies such as state aid to industries and nationalization. Constitutional structures that are largely outside the reach of citizens have, in the modern world, tended almost invariably to block the kind of radical policies that the left has traditionally believed in.'[64] The argument is, legally speaking, false. The state aid rules do not prevent nationalizations, such as those advocated by some people on the Left. Nothing in EU law blocks 'left-wing' policies.[65] But Tuck's point has a general constitutional purchase: there is something wrong in our constitution, if a whole section of the electorate may be prevented from effectively pursuing some of its preferred policies because of treaty commitments. If this is true of the EU, then the treaties undermine democracy in the member states. The argument is theoretically sound in principle. However, in Tuck's version it is manifestly false. The idea that EU law prevents nationalizations and other Left-wing policies is not correct.

A similar point, although more closely focused on more general constitutional principle rather than any particular political agenda, has been offered by the Oxford political philosopher David Miller. Miller has argued that the arguments for a common European public sphere or a European political union fail to overcome the division of a multicultural and multi-state demos.[66] Miller noted that the international character of the EU meant that the 'factions' that condemn any political community to failure are evident in the EU. There is no common culture or history, no common language, and no common purpose. Miller said that the mere fact of being subject to the same political system is not sufficient. Miller concludes that a 'large conglomerate', such as the EU, is unsuitable for democratic politics.[67] This is a more interesting version of the self-government argument because it identifies the

[63] Richard Tuck, 'The Left Case for Brexit' *Dissent*, 6 June 2016.

[64] ibid. This argument is common in the United Kingdom, but is false. The policies of state aid do not preclude nationalizations or state support in certain industries—mostly through 'Block Exemptions' but in other ways as well.

[65] In any event, the policies that Tuck has in mind are not policies that any recent government wishes to pursue. In effect, these policies are not blocked by the EU but by the electorates that consistently reject them at the polls.

[66] David Miller, 'Republicanism, National Identity and Europe' in Cecile Laborde and John Maynor (eds), *Republicanism and Political Theory* (Oxford: Blackwell, 2008). Miller renewed his argument in his 'A Plea for Pluralism' in van Middelaar and van Parijs (eds), *After the Storm*, 179–88, where he concludes: 'For a democratic Europe, therefore, the main signal should give national—and subnational—democracy the air to breathe' (p. 188).

[67] ibid 154.

problem not in the endorsement of any particular policy by the European Union but in the process by which decisions are taken.

The upshot of such scepticism has been well described by the lawyer and academic Dieter Grimm. In his wide ranging book *The Constitution of European Democracy*, Grimm gives detailed reasons against a Europe-wide federation.[68] He notes that the European Parliament, although elected, has not been sufficient to respond to the problems with legitimacy. Because Europe's politics is fragmented among the several member states, its institutions are not sufficient to provide legitimacy. They can only do that when combined with the institutions of the member states. Hence, the most important political institution of the EU is not the European Parliament, but the Council of Ministers. Unfortunately, the Commission and the Court of Justice are not always aware of these problems with legitimacy. Their maximalist theory of EU law has failed to give national law its due:

> If the EU's legitimacy problem stems from the fact that its executive and judicial institutions have separated themselves from the will of the legitimating Member States, and that they make decisions of great political importance through non-political means, then measures must be taken to limit this separation and ensure that political decisions are made in a political manner. And if it is true that the EU will long remain dependent on the Member States for its democratic legitimacy, then one must ensure that this flow of legitimacy is not hindered by reconfiguring the EU according to a nation-state model.[69]

But how is the EU to be 'reconfigured', if not according to the nation-state model? Grimm proposes that the EU Treaties should be radically simplified. He would have removed almost the whole of the TFEU from the treaties, to allow for the policies on the internal market and the four freedoms to be shaped by EU secondary legislation.

The underlying constitutional theory in Grimm's argument distinguishes—in exactly the same way as Noel Malcolm—between 'power' (which can be shared) and 'sovereignty' which cannot be shared. Grimm thus asks the crucial question: What is the difference between sovereignty and public powers?[70] His answer is: self-government, or the sovereign power to determine your own government:

> Sovereignty in the EU lies with the Member States since they are the 'Masters of the Treaties' and hold the Kompetenz-Kompetenz. This is indeed the difference between a federal state and other types of federations. The EU does not have

[68] Dieter Grimm, *The Constitution of European Democracy* (Oxford: Oxford University Press, 2017).
[69] ibid 17.
[70] ibid 46.

> the right to self-determination about its existence, its legal basis, and its competencies. The decision about these matters is in the hands of the Member States. They decide by way of concluding a treaty under international law, and that means: unanimously.[71]

Grimm rejects Habermas' suggestion that the EU may have a 'double source' of sovereignty: in the states and the EU. After examining how the Treaties are to be amended post-Lisbon, he concludes that the states retain the ultimate power to shape the treaties as they see fit, with unanimity.

In the end, Grimm proposes that national constitutional courts must put a stop to the slow transformation of the EU in line with a 'state centred' model through treaty amendments or through the case law of the Court of Justice. Grimm concludes that the principle of conferral must also be preserved:

> The Kompetenz-Kompetenz—the power to determine the division of powers between the EU and the Member States—must not be relinquished to the EU. Likewise, the EU institution in which the Member States are represented—the Council—must remain the central institution of the (non-state) EU and must not be subordinated to the other institutions. Moreover, as an EU Member State, the Federal Republic and its Parliament must retain political powers sufficient to make Germany's elections more than mere formalities, and to ensure that the election results have consequences for decisions that affect German citizens.[72]

I shall call Grimm's view of self-government, perhaps somewhat unfairly, the 'statist' view, because it does not tell us how the EU may become legitimate. He only tells us where the legitimacy of the EU stops, namely at the point where states are self-determining political communities, possessing what Grimm calls '*Kompetenz-Kompetenz*'. The Union's legitimacy remains entirely derivative in this view, or in any case obscure.

This view is in my view too one-sided. It only addresses the value of self-government, without considering how self-government requires relations of reciprocity with other self-governing peoples and can be reconciled with international co-operation or 'integratin'. Any self-governing state has ethical obligations to other states. The European Union is, after all, a *voluntary* union of states. No state entered contrary to its will. If membership in the European Union is a democratic decision, then the power the EU enjoys by virtue of the Treaties is democratically legitimate for that reason.

Moreover, this delegation creates a new institutional environment that is relevant to domestic constitutional law. Indeed, as Robert O. Keohane, Stephen

[71] ibid 46–7.
[72] ibid 237–8.

Macedo, and Andrew Moravcsik have argued, multi-lateral commitments may be enhancing domestic democracy by helping control special interests, making democracy more inclusive by protecting individual and minority rights, and facilitating collective deliberation.[73] In this sense self-government is enhanced by membership in the EU. Indeed, it is possible that through this route the self-government argument may vindicate the European Union law as a necessary stage of democratic politics. Failing to see this connection weakens the statist arguments. This one-sided view of self-government cannot be the appropriate way in which to interpret European Union law.

5.7 A Union of Peoples

I now turn to a positive presentation of the internationalist argument for the EU as a 'Union of Peoples'. Neither federalism nor statist self-government provide an appropriate political model for the European Union. I wish to argue for a rival view. I endorse the distinction between sovereignty and power as drawn by Dieter Grimm and I also accept the argument for self-government as put forward by David Miller: sovereignty is not to be given up for the sake of integration. But I reject the possible conclusion that self-government appears to rule out democratically legitimate supranational law-making such as we see in the European Union.

On the contrary, I will argue that self-government is an argument for progressive European integration. To put the point in a sound bite, my argument is that self-government requires more Europe, not less. I will argue that international institutions *enhance* domestic constitutional democracy and help it satisfy the substantive tests of political legitimacy that applies to democracies. Democracy has, by definition, a cosmopolitan dimension.

I start with the argument from self-government made by Noel Malcolm. There are two reasons to reject it. The first reason is that as a matter of fact the European Union does *not* threaten sovereignty—as I showed in my discussion of 'dualism' in Chapter 3. As an international legal order, the European Union does not compete with domestic jurisdiction. The second reason, however, is equally important. Noel Malcolm's argument against further European integration was based on an equivocation between power and sovereignty. He appears to consider that sovereignty is a matter of the amount of power a state has. This is shown where he expresses a concern that the United Kingdom may be giving up *too much* power as it participates in the process of European integration. He says that little by little the United Kingdom may find itself without sovereignty.

[73] Robert O. Keohane, Stephen Macedo, and Andrew Moravcsik, 'Democracy-Enhancing Multilateralism' 63 *International Organisation* (2009) 1–31.

Malcolm says that in the case of the EU, sovereignty can be lost if the 'pretensions' of the European Parliament were gradually accepted by more and more people. He says that the more this acceptance happens 'the more likely it is that the [EU] will become a fully federal state; for this Assembly is the sole body that can convey political legitimacy directly from the citizens of the member states to the supranational structures of the EEC'.[74] There is an idea here of a slippery slope to federalism. It is an ancient idea: sovereignty is plenary power, power that is irresistible, so if power slips away from the sovereign state which stops being irresistible, it will gradually stop being sovereign. This arresting image, however, is mistaken. It confuses legal authority with political power.

Malcolm's reading of the EU forgets that sovereignty is a legal manifestation of one kind of power, namely constitutional authority. Constitutional authority is not a matter of the quantity of power a state or an institution has, but of its kind. Malcolm confuses political power and constitutional authority when he warns us against the dangers of the European Union gradually taking over more power. No accumulation of more power is sufficient to change the nature of a sovereign state, since all such transfers are a result of the state's power to delegate to other institutions. All such transfers are conditional on the constitutional process that enabled membership in the European Union.

This point is better made by Dieter Grimm, whose discussion of sovereignty in relation to the European Union is instructive. Grimm shows that self-government is a particular set of rules about the exercise of political power. Grimm follows the analysis of the European Union one finds in the German Constitutional Court's judgments on the Maastricht and Lisbon Treaties, namely the view that sovereignty is a kind of 'Kompetenz-Kompetenz', or in other words the 'power to determine power'.

I find the term 'Kompetenz-Komptenz' highly perplexing and will not use it. It makes no sense as a point about political power or a point about legal power. If an institution or body has the political, physical, or psychological power to determine what another person does, then it has first order political power. But this is all there is. There cannot be second order power in this sense, i.e. political power over political power. There is only one type of political power, power to influence another person's actions.

Similarly, if a body or institution has a *legal* power over another person's *legal* powers in the sense, for example, described by Hohfeld's powers and immunities, then this body or institution enjoys that legal power by virtue of another more fundamental legal rule. If so, it enjoys law-making powers because it is subject to an enabling legal rule. If so, that person or body or institution is subject to law like everybody else. It does not have power over it. I conclude that in a legal order no

[74] Malcolm, 'Sense on Sovereignty' (n. 60) 29.

person or body or institution has 'Kompetenz-Komptenz', since everyone operates *under* the law. Amendments can only be legal if subject to a lawful framework of legal change. I cannot, therefore, understand the idea of '*Kompetenz-Kompetenz*' and will avoid using it.[75]

The German Constitutional Court has used a different expression to refer to a similar idea, namely the 'identity' of the member states as an inherent limit to the powers of the European Union.[76] In a recent case the German Constitutional Court refused to give effect to a European Arrest Warrant on such grounds.[77] The Court restated the doctrine that the German courts ought to review the acts of an institution or agency of the European Union with the question whether these acts may have an effect on Germany's 'constitutional identity' and especially the protection of human dignity and fundamental rights.

If an EU institution violates those principles, it effectively acts *ultra vires*, because the German accession to the treaties never had the meaning of authorizing such a violation. For the Court, the German Constitution 'cannot transfer sovereign powers to the European Union which, if exercised, would affect the constitutional identity protected by Art. 79 sec. 3 GG'.[78] The court concluded that: 'Within the framework of the identity review, one has to review whether the principles laid down as inalienable by Art. 79 sec. 3 GG are affected by an act of the European Union.'[79]

The German Constitutional Court is correct to connect the required review with a matter of the fundamental constitutional structure of a member state. This follows from the fact that the sovereignty of each member derives from its constitutional power, or power under a constitution. It is the legal authority to make and amend any law, including the law of the constitution, according to the ordinary deliberative practices of a legal order.[80] This comprehensive and self-reflective power is not absolute. It is by definition limited, because it is legally constituted. However, that power belongs to the states, not to the European Union. The powers that the EU exercises are derived from the constitutional power or sovereignty of the states, the power to make and amend a constitution as higher law.

[75] I explain this point in greater detail in Pavlos Eleftheriadis, 'Law and Sovereignty' 29 *Law and Philosophy* (2010) 535 and in Pavlos Eleftheriadis, 'Power and Principle in Constitutional Law' 45 *Netherlands Journal of Legal Philosophy* (2016) 37–56.

[76] The German Constitutional Court has derived this principle from Article 79(3) of the Basic Law, which states: 'Amendments to this Basic Law affecting the division of the Federation into Länder, their participation on principle in the legislative process, or the principles laid down in Articles 1 and 20 shall be inadmissible.'

[77] Federal Constitutional Court, Order of the Second Senate of 15 December 2015, 2BvR 2735/14.

[78] ibid par. 42.

[79] ibid par. 43.

[80] See Pavlos Eleftheriadis, 'Constitutional Change Through Deliberation' in Ron Levy, Hoi Kong, Graeme Orr, and Jeff King (eds), *The Cambridge Handbook of Deliberative Constitutionalism* (Cambridge University Press, 2018).

Who, therefore, has sovereignty in a constitutional state? The answer can only be that no single person has it. Sovereignty belongs to the citizens of that state, but only when they are acting as a single political community under the terms of their common laws through representative institutions. The sovereignty of equal citizens does not mean that the electorate, or a majority of it, can do as it pleases. This would contradict the very idea of equal citizenship in a community of law. The citizens have sovereignty only when they are acting jointly according to the standing law. Sovereignty, very much like Rousseau's '*volonté generale*', exists when our actions respect the constitutional rules in place.

In this sense sovereignty is only an abstract idea, not a property or power that belongs to a person or group. In a constitutional state, no other answer is compatible with the principle of equal citizenship. Sovereignty is held by the people, when the various institutions—their courts, the government, parliament, and the civil service—are operating under laws in their proper way. Under a constitutional government, therefore, the idea of 'sovereignty' becomes irrelevant since no particular person or institution is strictly speaking 'sovereign' and the contours of sovereignty are identical to constitutional government. Sovereignty, however, remains highly relevant to international law, since it marks the equality of all states in the eyes of the law of nations.[81]

We are thus ready to see how the European Union may be a union of sovereign peoples, under international law, without undermining self-government. The member states retain the power to decide how the power is divided among them, for they can amend the EU treaties. But the European institutions are granted significant powers in a great number of policies, on the basis of these treaties. The general architecture is familiar from public international law, although the actual powers given to the European Union are substantial and similar to what happens in some federations. But the federal model creates a very different institutional environment. In the United States, for example, the federal constitution enjoys supremacy over state law and federal courts have priority over state courts. It is the federal constitution and the federal courts that determine the division of labour between federation and the state.

Nothing like it exists in the European Union.[82] As both van Gerven and Lenaerts admit, the European legal systems and the domestic legal systems work

[81] For this point see Benedict Kingsbury, 'Sovereignty and Inequality' 9 *European Journal of International Law* (1998) 599.

[82] For a detailed comparison between the arrangements of competence between the centre and the participating states in the US and the EU see Daniel Halberstam, 'Of Power and Responsibility: The Political Morality of Federal Systems' 90 *Virginia Law Review* (2004) 732–834. Halberstam speaks of both systems as 'federal', but his own study shows that the terminology cannot properly apply to the EU. Halberstam notes that in contrast to Germany the EU 'does not have the general power to tax and has only limited resources of its own' and, in addition, 'its member states control what is still the most important legislative chamber (the Council), and each is the home to a largely self-contained "public sphere" of civil engagement'; ibid p. 764. In addition, Halberstam fails to note that the ultimate legislator in the European Union is not the Council or the Commission but the making of Treaties, which is a process of public international law controlled by the member states. He also does not point out that

in parallel, without a single scheme of constitutional rules applying to both and without common judicial oversight. The CJEU does not hear appeals from the national courts, nor does it review them at a final stage. Its role is to give preliminary references in the course of domestic proceedings. The last word remains with the domestic courts, which, however, do not have jurisdiction to pass judgment on EU law.

Kumm and Roughan argue that this lack of finality is not a reason to say that there is no robust constitution. Such an ambivalence, they believe, is compatible with a federal constitutional interpretation. This is perhaps what is meant by the terms 'federation' and 'confederation', both of which avoid the decisive dominance of either the federal centre (the case of a 'federal state') or the component entities (the case of a 'unitary state').

The arrangement they propose is constitutionally inappropriate, however. Our constitutional institutions cannot accommodate a fundamental ambivalence about their nature and scope. The independence of the member states under the treaties can only by accommodated by an account of the European Union as an international organization, which respects the integrity of the member states and relies on the distinction between national and international powers and a dualist theory of the legal orders involved. Internationalism, which derives from the duty of justice to support a legitimate constitution, is the public philosophy of the European Union.

The Treaties support this view. The first Articles of the Treaty of the European Union, some of which were added by the Lisbon Treaty in 2009, set this out without any doubt. Article 1 TEU states:

> By this Treaty, the HIGH CONTRACTING PARTIES establish among themselves a EUROPEAN UNION, hereinafter called 'the Union', on which the Member States confer competences to attain objectives they have in common.

The Treaty is clear here that all the powers of the Union have been transferred by the states, through a process of public international law, in order to attain common objectives. And after outlining the Union's objectives, the Treaty further states at Article 4(2) TEU that the competence of the Union are enumerated and that the Union is to respect the independence of the member states:

the European Court of Justice has very limited jurisdiction, unlike the German Federal Constitutional Court. Halberstam draws correctly the distinction with the US, when he notes that whereas the US constitution 'was ratified in the name of a single people', the EU treaties 'were expressly concluded as sovereign actions of the individual member states' (ibid p. 801). Nevertheless, he does not draw what appears to me to be the correct conclusion from this observation, namely that the EU is not a federal union, but a union of peoples under the law of nations.

> The Union shall respect the equality of Member States before the Treaties as well as their national identities, inherent in their fundamental structures, political and constitutional, inclusive of regional and local self-government. It shall respect their essential State functions, including ensuring the territorial integrity of the State, maintaining law and order and safeguarding national security. In particular, national security remains the sole responsibility of each Member State'.

This article, which was introduced by the Lisbon Treaty, leaves no doubt that the Union is not supposed to challenge the self-government of the states.[83] And Article 5 (2) TEU restates the familiar principle of conferral of powers, so that 'under the principle of conferral, the Union shall act only within the limits of the competences conferred upon it by the Member States in the Treaties to attain the objectives set out therein'. It follows that competences not conferred upon the Union in the Treaties remain with the member states.

Does this vindicate Dieter Grimm's vision of 'self-government'? I think it does not. The treaties give effect to self-government, but also add the international dimension of the pursuit of common objectives through shared institutions. The member states have exercised their sovereignty and willingly created a method for pursuing public policies together. As the preamble says: the treaties are created by the states in order 'to attain objectives they have in common'. The two projects complement each other: the international project sits alongside the domestic one. This commitment follows, implicitly if not explicitly, a Kantian fundamental assumption: self-government fails when it is not backed up by a cosmopolitan dimension.

This argument has gone unnoticed, while legal theorists were tied to the idea of EU law as a 'Kelsenian' legal system. If we fail to see the difference between domestic and international law, then it is easy to interpret the EU legal system as inherently in conflict with the domestic legal system. This is so because in Kelsen's theory (and Hart's similar one) there can only be one 'Grundnorm' (or 'rule of recognition'). The antagonism of the two 'systems' is the necessary result. This was in effect Neil MacCormick's analysis of the European Union legal order, which was written from the point of view of Hart's theory of law. However, when we abandon the Kelsen-Hart straitjacket, we see law as a moral idea that has *two distinct manifestations* in the law of a jurisdiction and the law of nations. These are not in conflict. They support one another in their quest for political legitimacy.

In this sense the EU is above all its own cosmopolitan 'order of law'. It is international in origin, but is given effect through the national constitutions. There is no doubt that EU law is a 'legal order' in this sense, and to that extent its specialists are right to treat it as an independent system of ideas and arguments. EU law has its own organizing principles and techniques of reasoning, which are continuously

[83] For a sophisticated interpretation see Elke Cloots, *National Identity in EU Law* (Oxford: Oxford University Press, 2015).

refined and reworked by the Court of Justice and European legal scholarship. But just like international law EU law is not a jurisdiction. The Commission, the Council, and the Court of Justice do not constitute a comprehensive institutional order. The EU has no police force or other enforcement mechanisms securing respect for its laws. It has no complete system of courts. This is evident both in its founding treaties and its ordinary practice.

EU law is thus a law among states, not a new constitution for a new political society. It does not seek to regulate comprehensively the legal relations of those living under its jurisdiction, nor does it have a complete public law organizing the relations between citizens and political power. This finding does not entail that EU law is in any way less significant or less authoritative. The creation and maintenance of EU law as a law among states is something with great moral and legal authority of its own. The members of the European Union have not created a new constitutional order but have, nevertheless, created something which is legally authoritative and which has changed their constitutional laws for good: a voluntary 'union of peoples' according to law.

Kant describes such a 'congress' or federation of states as follows:

> By a *congress* is here understood only a voluntary coalition of different states which can be dissolved at any time, not a federation (like that of the American states) which is based on a constitution and can therefore not be dissolved.—Only by such a congress can the idea of a public right of nations be realized, one to be established for deciding their disputes in a civil way, as if by a lawsuit, rather than in a barbaric way the way of savages, namely by war.[84]

Many critics of Kant find this formulation unacceptable. The fact that the federation of peace is the result of voluntary action appears to them to make it optional. But for Kant it is *legally* optional, but *morally* a matter of duty. The idea of a public right of nations is part of the framework of justice. Such a public right is voluntary only in the sense that any moral action is voluntary.

The duty to set up a federation of peace arises from the same grounds as the duty to create institutions of public law:

> Since the earth's surface is not unlimited but closed, the concepts of the right of a state and of a right of nations lead inevitably to the idea of a *right for a state of nations* (*ius gentium*) or *cosmopolitan right* (*ius cosmopoliticum*). So if the principle of outer freedom limited by law is lacking in any of these three possible forms of

[84] Immanuel Kant, *Metaphysics of Morals* in *Practical Philosophy*, edited by Allen Wood (Cambridge: Cambridge University Press, 1996) 488 (henceforth, 'Kant, MM').

rightful condition, the framework for all the others is unavoidably undermined and must finally collapse.[85]

In other words, states are internally unjust, if they fail to respect and maintain the public law of nations. So in Kant's framework the structure of an international congress of nations is continuous with, and does not replace, the structure of domestic constitutional law. It follows directly from the idea of a domestic order of a civil condition.

We can say exactly the same thing about the EU as a voluntary 'congress' of states under public laws. The EU does not replace the relation between citizens and political power. It does not establish a new constitutional law that replaces the national ones. It is, primarily, a new way of organizing the relations between the various member states, whose equality as jurisdictions it fully respects. But the member states will fail to respect their own constitutional principles if they fail to grant sufficient recognition to the rights and duties created by the EU Treaties they have entered into. They have willingly signed and ratified those treaties on the basis of reciprocity and they are bound by them in public international law. EU law is therefore a composite legal order, consisting of principles of EU law, applied through principles and institutions of domestic and international law.

5.8 Integrity Revisited

If the EU is an international project in the way just described, its legal principles must be principles consonant with the law of nations. They must recognize the equal sovereignty of the member states as the source of the primacy of EU law through the treaties under a political architecture of internationalism. Does this make any difference as to the way in which integrity applies to EU law? We have seen that international law does not organize its own structures of power but depends on national law for its complete recognition and effect. On a number of key issues, public international law relies unconditionally on national law and vice versa.[86] The same applies to EU law. The European Union does not have its own system of courts and civil procedure. It does not have its own civil service, police,

[85] ibid 455. The Kantian argument is very well restated by Mattias Kumm, 'The Cosmopolitan Turn in Constitutionalism: An Integrative Conception of Public Law' 20 *Indiana Journal of Global Legal Studies* (2013) 605–28. Kumm concludes as follows: 'The constitutional legitimacy of national law depends, in part, on being adequately integrated into an appropriately structured international legal system. And the legitimacy of the international legal system depends, in part, on states having an adequate constitutional structure. The standards of constitutional legitimacy are to be derived from an integrative conception of public law that spans the national-international divide' (ibid p. 625). I agree with the first two sentences, but not with the third.

[86] For some of these issues of international law see Yuval Shany, *Regulating Jurisdictional Relations Between National and International Courts* (Oxford: Oxford University Press, 2007).

or army. For all of these functions it relies on the laws and institutions of the state. Its relations to the national jurisdictions remain a matter that is shared between the two legal orders: EU law and national law. Both EU and national have something to say about it, and the result changes from jurisdiction to jurisdiction. So the relationship is not determined and is not supposed to be determined by a single set of general principles of public law and no 'constitution' organizing and regulating the Union as a whole. This must be one of our guiding interpretive principles.

How then can the European Union legal order be a coherent legal order? By virtue of what do the various systems of jurisdiction of the twenty-eight member states come together in a single scheme? What principles and purposes guide the division of labour between them? For any arrangement of this kind to work, the law of the EU must provide organizing principles that provide principles of the allocation of power. If the legal order of the EU is to respect the demands of integrity, it cannot simply throw courts, treaties, and constitutions together and hope for the best. There must be an organizing framework of principle that make the division both intelligible and workable.

In the next three chapters I will argue that the European Union does this successfully under a framework of progressive internationalism. I will show that it has already adopted principles appropriate for a Union of Peoples, that respect both self-government and progressive integration under common values. Before I do that I will briefly discuss here the 'federalist' arguments that must be set aside, if we are to respect the integrity of EU law as an internationalist project.

In his impressive argument on the constitutional structure of the European Union Robert Schütze argues that the EU has proceeded from a system of 'dual federalism' to one of 'cooperative' federalism. He says that 'dual federalism' is based on the idea of 'dual sovereignty', such that the 'federal government and the State governments are "sovereign" co-equals and each is operating independently in a separate sphere.'[87] 'Cooperative federalism' on the other hand, stands for the idea that both governments work together: they are complementary parts in a shared legal sphere. Schütze believes that the European Union—and in particular the structure of its law—has evolved from dual to cooperative federalism. Schütze insists that under cooperative federalism the EU legal order envelops the orders of the members states. He argues in great detail that in the last thirty years, the European Union has 'constitutionalized the philosophy of cooperative federalism by means of two constitutional devices: the principle of subsidiarity and complementary competences.'[88] His position however has moved even further than that. He now argues for a monist understanding of the European Union legal order, under which EU Law is the 'grundnorm' of the European legal order.[89] This idea, however, fails

[87] Schütze, *From Dual to Cooperative Federalism* (n. 4) 346.
[88] ibid 242–86.
[89] See Robert Schütze, *European Constitutional Law* (Cambridge: Cambridge University Press, 2016) 43–76, where Schütze speaks of the EU as a 'Federation of States'.

to capture the dimension of the European Union as an international project. It cannot accommodate the international nature of EU law and cannot account for constitutional dualism.

In the same way, Koen Lenaerts and Tim Corthaut are wrong to argue that the 'primacy' rules of EU law is simple because it is based on uniformity.[90] Lenaerts and Corthaut have argued that: 'whenever a national rule conflicts with a rule of Community law the rule of Community law is to trump national law, irrespective of the status of that rule of national law in the national legal order and irrespective of whether the Community rule is one of primary or secondary law'.[91] They argue that primacy works even when the EU rule in question does not have direct effect. They assume, therefore, that a principle of uniformity is at work and argue that the EU legal order is very much like a domestic legal order where uniformity is a requirement of the legal order's coherence and integrity. For them the idea of direct effect applies only to individual rights and does not apply to EU law in general which should in *all circumstances*—not just those of direct effect—be consistent with domestic law. They argue that in all cases the aims of EU law prevail over the aims of domestic law even if EU law creates no rights for individuals:

> It appears from *Costa* that the real concern is consistency: to the extent that a national measure is inconsistent with EC law, it cannot be allowed to apply over EC law. But if we take consistency seriously, there is no need for identifying whether a provision confers rights on individuals. The only thing that matters is that EC law, and by extension EU law, puts forward an identifiable result which cannot be thwarted by incompatible national measures
>
> ....
>
> All this changes, however, when EU law itself grants rights to individuals, which would otherwise not exist in the national legal order. At that stage, we are not merely concerned with removing inconsistencies from the legal order, but with actively imposing a particular burden on an identifiable debtor for the benefit of an identifiable creditor that would otherwise not exist. It is only then that direct effect comes into play.[92]

Such a principle of uniformity is really another way of expressing monism.[93] Lenaerts and Corthaut rely on what the Court of Justice said in *Pfeiffer*, a case

[90] Koen Lenaerts and Tim Corthaut, 'Of Birds and Hedges: The Role of Primacy in Invoking Norms of EU Law' 31 *European Law Review* (2006) 287–315.

[91] ibid 289.

[92] Lenaerts and Corthaut, 'Of Birds and Hedges', 289.

[93] Indeed, Lenaerts and Corthaut draw an explicit link with monism by comparing the adoption of EU law by the member states with the adoption of international law by EU law, which in their view is achieved through a 'monist' doctrine: 'Virtually all of what has been said above in respect of how EU law affects the legal order of the various Member States can be mirrored in respect of the Union itself in its relation towards norms of international law. This is hardly surprising since Art. 300 TEC and Art.24 TEU suggest the existence of a European Union which accepts a monist view of international law. If this

where a directive was taken to apply directly to relations among private persons, and where the Court said that:

> if the application of interpretative methods recognised by national law enables, in certain circumstances, a provision of domestic law to be construed in such a way as to avoid conflict with another rule of domestic law or the scope of that provision to be restricted to that end by applying it only in so far as it is compatible with the rule concerned, the national court is bound to use those methods in order to achieve the result sought by the Directive.[94]

I will argue below that the rule of primacy of EU law is not as simple as Schütze, Lenaerts, and Corthaut take it to be. In my view primacy is a more complex rule because it starts from the assumption that the fundamental rules of the division of labour between the EU and the member states are also domestic in origin, not just European. There is no overarching federal rule of division of labour. EU law merely summarizes the conditions imposed by the domestic constitutions. The coherence of EU law is therefore not provided by *uniformity* imposed by a single master or constitutional rule, but it is given by the *coordination* of the laws of the member states achieved under the treaties. Coherence is achieved because the member states have adopted similar, although not identical, constitutional principles of the delimitation of competences according to the treaties they have signed. The architecture of EU law is therefore international not constitutional. For this reason the interpretive readings of Schütze, Lenaerts, and Corthaut cannot be accepted without modification. If this is the case, then the organizing principle of EU law will not be one of 'uniformity' but one of 'consistency', where differentiation follows mutually agreed rules on the basis of the Treaties. I will call this the principle of 'constitutional differentiation' and contrast it to the principle of uniformity.[95] This is not a principle of constitutionalism, but a principle of international law. Its moral basis is not a doctrine of equal citizenship for constitutions, which applies only to a single political society, but a principle of reciprocity under *pacta sunt servanda* according to standard rules of international law.

equivalence is true, however, then it should also be possible to make analogies between the approach of the ECJ in respect of the position of international law in the EU legal order and the position of EU law in the national legal orders. Seen from this perspective, it would appear odd if an ever closer Union, which as we know since *Van Gend & Loos* is an autonomous legal order going beyond the demands of ordinary international law, in practice gave less effect to its legal norms internally than it accords to norms of international law.'

[94] Joined Cases C 397/01-403/01, *Pfeiffer* [2004] ECR I-8835, ECLI:EU:C:2004:584, at par. 116.

[95] I borrow the term from Frank Schimmelfennig and Thomas Winzen, 'Instrumental and Constitutional Differentiation in the European Union' 52 *Journal of Common Market Studies* (2014) 354. See also Anthony Arnull, 'Me and My Shadow: The European Court of Justice and the Disintegration of European Union Law' 31 *Fordham International Law Journal* (2007) 1134–211.

We saw at the start of this discussion John Rawls' letter to Philippe van Parijs. His point there was that states have some unique value. But Rawls also explains how self-governing states can come together to build a rich, rule-based co-operation when they adopt rules for their interdependence. Rawls has explained that when they do this, states adopt the correct attitude about their nature as peoples, and not as self-seeking and power-hungry alliances. Rawls traced the description of that attitude in Raymond Aron's *War and Peace*, where Aron spoke of the peace of 'satisfied peoples', as opposed to 'peace by power' or 'peace by impotence'. Rawls has described the relevant moral attitude as follows:

> I agree with Aron that these conditions are necessary to a lasting peace, and I argue that they would be fulfilled by peoples living under liberal constitutional democracies. These peoples honour a shared principle of legitimate government and are not swayed by the passion for power and glory, or the intoxicating pride of ruling. These passions may move a nobility and lesser aristocracy to earn their social standing and place in the sun; yet this class, or case rather, does not have power in a constitutional regime. Such regimes are not bent on the religious conversion of other societies, since liberal peoples by their constitution have no state religion—they are not confessional states—even if their citizens are highly religious, individually or together in associations. Domination and striving for glory, the excitement of conquest and the pleasure of exercising power over others, do not move them against other peoples.[96]

This position of self-restraint and self-control is the attitude shown by the member states of the European Union. Through this self-restraint it is possible for them to adopt common international institutions of interdependence. Hence, according to the principle of constitutional differentiation as agreed in the Treaties, EU law provides for institutions of *interdependence* among independent and self-governing states, under principles of accountability, liberty, and fairness.

These principles have been agreed by the members states through the treaties of EU law. A careful look at the treaties shows that they do not endorse a monist or federalist model. Their primary task is to outline the division of labour between EU law and institutions and state law and institutions.[97] By endorsing these treaties the member states accept that they owe legal and moral duties to each other on the basis of reciprocity. The authority of these treaties is strengthened by the constitutional endorsement of the supranational mechanisms of accountability they have created, through appropriate domestic institutions. In this sense, the EU is a Union of Peoples with important effects in the constitutional orders of all member states.

[96] John Rawls, *The Law of Peoples* (Cambridge, Mass.: Harvard University Press, 1999) 47.

[97] I have argued for that in some detail in Pavlos Eleftheriadis, 'The Structure of European Union Law' 12 *Cambridge Yearbook of European Legal Studies* (2010) 121–50.

This is then our new view on the integrity of EU law. The most appropriate interpretation of the political legitimacy of the institutions of the European Union must be able to explain *both* the common principles that unite the member states but also those that divide them into self-governing states. As I argued in previous chapters, borders mediate our moral duties to others. Our duties to fellow citizens are different from those to distant strangers. Such duties depend, at least partly, on which side of the border we happen to be. The same applies in the case of the European Union. The rights and duties of European citizens towards other citizens or towards other states will be mediated by the position taken by their government towards the project of the European Union. Member states and their citizens have different rights, obligations, and privileges than non-member states and their citizens. Indeed, some of our duties to others are possible only because our governments have engaged with other governments and states through public international law and have created treaties, such as the World Trade Organization, or bilateral trade, or investment treaties. We need to distinguish between these various cases.

There are some EU principles that apply within borders, which we should call 'constitutional', and other principles that apply across borders, which we should call 'international' when they apply between states and 'cosmopolitan', when they apply between states and the citizens of other states.[98] If a principle is both international and cosmopolitan and no distinction concerning its field of application is necessary, then we should just call it 'transnational'. By drawing these distinctions, we may be able to arrive at principles for legitimacy for the European Union as a Union of Peoples that inform EU law in all its forms. Our challenge is now to develop fully this view of the EU as a Union of Peoples.

This argument takes seriously Rawls' warning about the future of the European Union and the need to pursue progressive integration while at the same time recognizing the virtues of existing political institutions and the practices and attitudes that sustain them. In the chapters that follow I take up this task. Building on this new view of integrity, I focus on three distinct principles that should, and in my view do, inform the EU under a framework of constitutional differentiation and accommodation. The first is *accountability*, the second is *liberty*, and the third is *fairness*. These are the three legal principles that are in my view uniquely appropriate to Europe as a Union of Peoples. I examine them in turn.

[98] I follow here the terminology of Mary J. Gregor (trans. and ed.) Imannuel Kant, 'Toward Perpetual Peace', in Kant (ed.), *Practical Philosophy* (Cambridge: Cambridge University Press, 1996) 8:343, 317–51. Nevertheless, 'cosmopolitan' principles are really international in nature—they are not a third category of law. This was Kant's considered view in *The Metaphysics of Morals*. For this point see B. Sharon Byrd and Joachim Hruschka, *Kant's Doctrine of Right: A Commentary* (Cambridge: Cambridge University Press, 2010) 205–11.

6
Accountability

Accountability, I believe, is the most fundamental principle of the European Union. The basic institutional relations within the Union are designed to hold the member states as well as the European institutions to account. In the normal case, an international institution has few mechanisms for the enforcement of treaty obligations. Compliance depends on the internal mechanisms of states. This, however, gives states too much discretion and creates mutual distrust. The European Union has adopted a different strategy. Its members have agreed to give up their discretion over the way they keep their agreements. They have created joint institutions of enforcement deploying novel processes of law. They thus hope to achieve close integration, for the benefit of all of their citizens, by sharing reciprocal forms of accountability. It has become possible because the member states offer each other practical assurances that they will respect and enforce the treaties. This is a novel arrangement of intensive multilateralism based on a new principle of accountability.

The term 'accountability' needs clarification, however.[1] It is not used much in constitutional or international law. Accountability is normally subsumed under the doctrine of the separation of powers. Within the constitutional order of a state, power is checked by other power through mechanisms of transparency and control, which are sometimes described as a system of 'checks and balances'. The European Union does not follow this pattern. The distinction between the legislature, the executive, and the judiciary is imperfect or in any event entirely different in practice. The member states and their institutions play an equally important role and cannot fit in the traditional model of a separation of powers. The architecture of the European Union is thus unfamiliar and more fragmented. This creates uncertainty because this fragmentation is taken to be absence of principle. I hope to show, however, that the fragmentation we see in the European Union is a principled position that follows from the idea of constitutional differentiation under the treaties.

I attempt to show in this chapter that within the European Union's legal architecture, accountability is a legal principle at work. It requires all decision makers to respect the law, to make decisions transparently, and to honour the rights of others. The key to this argument is to see that accountability is not only targeted towards European institutions, but also to the member states, their parliaments, and their

[1] For an excellent discussion of the concept of accountability see Carol Harlow, *Accountability in the European Union* (Oxford: Oxford University Press, 2002) ch. 1.

A Union of Peoples. Pavlos Eleftheriadis. Oxford University Press (2020). © Oxford University Press.
DOI: 10.1093/oso/9780198854173.001.0001

courts. At the epicentre of these processes are the Commission and the Court of Justice, but the national institutions must play their own part. The general network of European accountability is, therefore, very broad.. Every decision is subject to scrutiny and review on the basis of common rules. Accountability is the first principle of the Union's law.

6.1 Accountability, Equality, Reciprocity

Accountability is a mechanism for the control of a decision based on institutions and public rules. In order to understand accountability, we need to draw a distinction between accountability and representation. An elected representative is entitled to make decisions for you, because of a reason of procedural fairness, namely that you have elected them in advance. You are bound by your implied or explicit consent to the representative's decisions on your behalf.

Accountability works in an entirely different way. It is not based on procedural fairness or consent. It means a process by which political decision makers, whether representative or not, are subject to *ex post facto* review on the basis of substantive public standards of conduct. Here what matters is the content of each decision. A process of accountability enables the reviewer to assess and perhaps impose some sanction on the person or body being reviewed.[2] Not all constraints on power are reviews of content in this sense and are not all necessarily manifestations of accountability. We would not, for example, say that the competition for the leadership of a party by two rivals is in effect a system of accountability. This would be a contest of power or of persuasion among the relevant electorate of party members.

What makes the difference between a power contest and a process of accountability is the presence of public standards of conduct applied by an independent institution or body. Accountability is invariably rule based and institutional.

Representation, by contrast, is an alternative to accountability—and this is true even though some representatives can also be held accountable after they are elected to represent us. Representative bodies, such as parliaments, are often held to be supreme and therefore unaccountable to anyone else other than their voters. This is the official constitutional doctrine in the United Kingdom (although not the USA or Germany, where the rule of law imposes constraints to parliament). Governments on the other hand are accountable to the elected parliament. Hence, parliamentary government combines representation (in the parliament chamber) with accountability (by parliament over the Executive). Throughout its term of office, a government remains accountable to parliament, which appoints and dismisses it. Parliamentary democracy combines representation with accountability

[2] I borrow this definition from Ruth W. Grant and Robert O. Keohane, 'Accountability and Abuses of Power in World Politics' 99 *American Political Science Review* (2005) 29–43.

only with the help of political parties which give meaning to periodic elections. The voters, aware of where political parties stand on various issues, are invited to reward or punish the political party in government through the election of members of parliament. Parliamentary systems combine, therefore, representation with accountability in indirect and subtle ways.

EU institutions are different, however. They do not follow a clear pattern borrowed from constitutional law. There is no single moment of democratic election, or a single executive making decisions. Decisions are not neatly divided between executive functions and legislative functions. Indeed, the states play a party in both of them. What the EU institutions achieve, I believe, is a novel process of 'impartial' and not strictly political or partisan accountability. This is not entirely unknown in constitutional systems. The French political theorist Pierre Rosanvallon has described a transformation of constitutional democracy from a simple method of representation to a more complex pattern of political legitimacy, through the ideas of 'impartiality', 'reflexivity', and 'proximity'.[3] This perceptive observation applies not only to domestic accountability but also to the method adopted by the EU. Accountability in an international context requires the help of novel processes that connect institutions of a transnational nature with domestic institutions. In this case accountability occurs between states or between a state and the citizen of other states. The distinctness of the processes of the European Union is due to its four permanent institutions: the European Commission, the Council of Ministers, the Court of Justice, and the European Parliament. All four of them are self-standing in that they are not just diplomatic conferences bringing together representatives of states (although the Council brings together government ministers under an EU institutional framework). These institutions are organized according to rules of collective decision-making procedures provided in detail by the EU treaties as well as their own 'rules of procedure'. As we will see in some detail below, these institutions occupy a 'transnational' space, because they stand between the member states' governments and their citizens. Their decisions apply both between states, i.e. in an 'international' way, and between member states and the citizens of other member states, i.e. in a 'cosmopolitan' way.

The Commission, the Court, and the European Parliament play an 'international' role, because they interact with the member states directly. The Commission, for example, can issue proceedings against a member state before the Court of Justice. The Council is in a position to conclude international agreements between the EU and third parties, thereby binding the member states, if the agreement lies within the EU's exclusive competence. In all these ways the EU institutions are both international and cosmopolitan in that they affect the relations among states as well as the lives of every EU citizen irrespective of nationality.

[3] See Pierre Rosanvallon, *Democratic Legitimacy: Impartiality, Reflexivity, Proximity*, Arthur Goldhammer trans. (Princeton: Princeton University Press, 2011).

Although much anti-EU rhetoric—very prominent in the media of the United Kingdom—suggests that the EU is run by an obscure 'bureaucracy', the reality is that the European Union's institutions work in tandem with states. The member states hold each other to account through the assistance of the four institutions, mostly the Council and the Parliament, but also in more legally defined ways by the Commission and the Court. The member states are largely accountable to each other.[4]

The key to understanding how the member states hold each other to account, is to distinguish between the strict equality of states which applies generally in public international law and what I shall call the 'reciprocity principle' that applies within the European Union. Strict equality means that each state follows rules agreed in advance that aim to deliver returns of more or less equivalent value. Reciprocity means, by contrast, undertaking obligations that may be beneficial overall, but not necessarily in a precisely symmetrical way. Whereas equality is the logic of bilateral agreements, reciprocity is the logic of multilateral and long-term agreements.[5] The European Union Treaties adopt both ideas: some areas are decided according to equality and others according to reciprocity. I will spend some time here describing how this works under the treaties.

In principle, the member states stand as equals. They are the equal authors of the treaties. Under the treaties, the states have in principle equal standing, not dependent on the size of their populations or the size of their territory. Their most important rights of equality are in the making and amending of the EU Treaties, where they all enjoy a veto under a principle of unanimity. But the member states also appoint one member at the Commission, one member at the Court, and one minister representing them in the Council, although qualified majority voting now takes into account the size of population.[6] In all these ways, the EU Treaties respect the strict equality of states. This should not be surprising. The equality of states is a standard feature of international law. Their equality is unequivocally recognized in Article 2(1) of the Charter of the United Nations, according to which the UN is based on 'the principle of the sovereign equality of its Members'.

Indeed, sovereignty was the cornerstone of international law even before the United Nations were founded and it remains so. Treaties of international law are based on sovereignty because they assume that their creators are equal partners, capable of binding themselves on their word when they want to. Just as in private

[4] The working theory of the European Union is therefore entirely different from that which applies to federal systems. For a detailed account of such systems see Daniel Halberstam, 'Of Power and Responsibility: The Political Morality of Federal Systems', 90 *Virginia Law Review* (2004) 731, 739–62.

[5] For this distinction, which is put in a different way as the distinction between 'specific reciprocity' and 'diffuse reciprocity' see Robert O. Keohane, 'Reciprocity in International Relations' 40 *International Organization* (1986) 1–27, at 4–5 and the analysis offered there.

[6] The European Parliament, however, follows a different pattern of regressively proportionate representation: all states are represented according to their population, with the smaller states given increased representation.

law, treaties go under the rule of 'privity of contract': those parties that choose not to join are not bound by the decisions of others. Treaties are thus parallel to contracts, although they lack the mechanism of enforcement through civil procedure that normally accompanies private agreements within a jurisdiction. Unlike contracts, the enforcement of Treaties is not entrusted in any higher executive or judicial body, but is left to the states' own devices.

Under this arrangement, every state respects the status of every other as an equal member of the international community. This rule means that each state has one vote in a collective decision process irrespective of its size. The rule departs from a general 'democratic principle' that would apply to institutions under standard principles of constitutionalism and which would have required that there should be as many votes as there are people affected by a decision. If this was the applicable principle within the EU, then sovereignty and self-government would disappear from the states. The making of the EU's constitutional documents would, perhaps, have to become a matter of a vote in the European Parliament, which means of course that they would cease being treaties of public international law. Such a transformation, however, would mean that within the European Union the larger states would completely dominate the smaller ones. The largest electorates would decide everything. The same would follow if the United Nations adopted a simple democratic principle for its decision-making. If it relied on the vote of populations, then everything would be decided by India and China (assuming for a moment that China permitted such an election). The equal status of states, or in other words their 'external sovereignty', protects their own self-government and their own democracy.

The equality of states has various manifestations in international law. In some international bodies equality requires that either all have a power of veto (unanimity rule) or that none do (majority rule). The first variation, the unanimity rule, is endorsed, for example by the procedures of the Council of the North Atlantic Treaty Organization (NATO), which makes decisions only with the consent of each of the representatives of the member countries. The second variation of formal equality, the majority rule, is adopted by the Committee of Ministers of the Council of Europe, where some issues require unanimity of votes cast, others a two thirds majority, and others a simple majority.[7] The voting power of states in these cases is still equal, however, because no distinction is drawn between the various states on account of their size, their economic or military power, or any other criteria. Everyone has one vote, the significance of which is determined by the particular decision mechanism: unanimity, or two-thirds, or simple majority.

States occasionally agree to be bound by a different sense of equality. They choose to adopt collective decision-making by way of an *unequal* number of votes.

[7] See, for example, Article 20 of the Statute of the Council of Europe.

They may follow size of population, or monetary contributions, or some other relevant criterion for voting power. Such a system would not really be one of inequality but, perhaps, one of proportionality: each state will have rights in proportion to the relevant test, e.g. population. An example of such proportional equality is the allocation of votes in the Board of Governors of the International Monetary Fund. This is the organization's highest decision-making body, which allocates votes according to the participating countries' financial contributions to the Fund, in terms of IMF quotas of Special Drawing Rights.[8] Members of the IMF have a vote equal to their quotas. The EU itself now has a voting rule that provides that a qualified majority requires also a majority of populations, not merely majority of member states. Neither the General Assembly of the UN nor any other collective body in the United Nations adopts a criterion of population.

The equal standing of states is not an absolute rule in multilateral treaties, however. Inequality occasionally occurs. In order to make common decisions possible, states occasionally come together and accept that some of them will enjoy higher status over the decisions of this or that international body. This occurs, for example, in the composition of the Security Council, where the five strongest states in the world have a permanent seat in the fifteen member body. This also works in the voting procedures of the Security Council, because the permanent members do have a veto power over its decisions. The 'concurring' vote of the permanent members must be included among the nine necessary votes for a decision.[9] The role of the members of the UN is therefore unequal. The permanent members of the Security Council have more powers because the UN Charter says so. This is true irrespective of their current power, influence, population, or of any other criteria. In one sense, the rule is one that still respects the member states' equality as original law-makers. It exists solely on the basis of the text of the UN Charter that was agreed in 1945. This explains how India, South Africa, and Brazil are not on the Security Council even though their economic power has increased significantly since the UN Charter was agreed.

It must be apparent from this short discussion that the equality of states in international law is compatible with much inequality. States are happy to give up their equality in return for long term benefits or clear ways of decision-making. It is possible, as we saw above that states agree to have fewer votes or offices than other states. The logic of these multilateral agreements, I believe, is not equality, but *reciprocity*. The parties agree to be bound by a set of rules in uneven ways because they expect to share, more or less, in the benefits of cooperation over a long period. They

[8] The quota determines a member's voting power in IMF decisions. Each IMF member has 250 basic votes plus one additional vote for each SDR 100,000 of quota. Accordingly, the United States has 371,743 votes (17.1% of the total), and Palau has 281 votes (0.013% of the total).

[9] See Articles 23 and 27 of the Charter of the United Nations. An abstention by a permanent member does not defeat a resolution.

do so under a principle of reciprocity, because the rules leave them all equally open to the uncertainties of the institutional architecture.

International relations are full of such examples, where states willingly enter into such arrangements. One striking example is the procedure according to which a member state of the European Union may lose its voting rights if it is found guilty of risking a breach of democratic principles, the rule of law and human rights, as provided for in Article 7 of the Treaty on European Union. Such states lose the right to vote at the meeting where such sanctions against them may be decided. This procedure has not yet been applied by the EU, but it shows that states are willing to submit each other to strict rules, for the sake of a common goal, such as commitment to the principles of the rule of law. Given the alternatives, this type of long-term reciprocity expresses a realistic commitment of all states to peace and to the rule of law in their mutual relations.[10]

How reciprocity replaces equality is in my view most clearly evident in the case of the Security Council, to which I now return. As we saw above, this was an *ad hoc* guarantee of stability in the circumstances of post-war peace. The strongest states in the world needed some safeguards in order to abide by a multilateral system of peace. This is because they had the most to lose by submitting to international law. The most powerful nations have most to lose by abandoning the recourse to power and war. They were, thus, given additional power in the Security Council because the institutions of peace needed to reassure them that their self-interest would be safeguarded. They needed a guarantee that the Security Council would not turn against them. Their veto power is that guarantee. This was not a matter of unilateral imposition, but an agreement for maintaining peace and trust among the strongest nations of the world. Given the alternatives, this type of reciprocity expresses a realistic commitment to peace.[11]

What do these types of reciprocity teach us about collective decisions in international law? In principle, the law of the European Union does not take a different view of sovereignty compared to that of international law. All states are equal. Their sovereignty is protected, as I explained in Chapter 3. Article 4 of the Treaty of the European Union (TEU) makes this explicit by providing as follows: 'The Union shall respect the equality of Member States before the Treaties as well as their national identities, inherent in their fundamental structures, political and constitutional, inclusive of regional and local self-government' The provision states that European institutions are not meant to replace national institutions but work

[10] Benedict Kingsbury has persuasively argued that the formal system of equal sovereignty is a far more realistic system for managing inequality than any of the proposed alternatives. See Benedict Kingsbury, 'Sovereignty and Inequality' 8 *European Journal of International Law* (1998) 599–625.

[11] Reciprocity over many interactions offers another model for why states obey international law. See for example the conclusions drawn by Harold Koh, 'Why Do Nations Obey International Law?' 106 *Yale Law Journal* (1997) 2599–659; Robert O. Keohane, *After Hegemony: Cooperation and Discord in the World Political Economy* (Princeton: Princeton University Press, 1984) 214.

alongside them. This arrangement is possible precisely because the EU is a creation of public international law. The EU is an international organization based on treaties and for that reason it remains under the full control of the states. In principle, a unanimous desire by the states to change everything in the EU could bring that about. To that extent the architecture of the European Union is more fluid than any national constitution. Everything can be changed.

At the same time, the European Union Treaties provide for deeper integration of decision-making beyond what we see anywhere else in international practice, which I shall call 'deep multilateralism'. The four main institutions—the Council, the Commission, the European Parliament, and the Court of Justice—all have significant decision-making powers in ways that supplement the primary law of the treaties. They all work independently of the wishes of a single state, since there is, in principle, no right to veto on most decisions. And within the scope of EU law, the enactment of a directive or a regulation is binding even on those Member States that voted against it, where majority voting applies, or absented, in cases where unanimity is required.

This is why when we look at the institutions of the EU we must speak not simply of the equality but also of the 'reciprocity' of the member states. The states are connected by deep interdependence in their institutions, their economy, and their social life. They have agreed to share their decision-making and to open themselves to the powers of the Court of Justice. They recognize the power of shared institutions to impose transnational standards, to form policies, and issue binding decisions.[12] What makes this process different from formal equality is the fact that all states are subject to the decisions of common EU institutions without secured parity in outcomes. How each decision is going to affect them is unknowable. As many observers have noted, this means that voting in the Council tends to be consensual, even though consensus is not normally required. Paraphrasing the words of Robert Keohane we may say that the member states rely on 'diffuse reciprocity' because they 'typically view diffuse reciprocity as an ongoing series of sequential actions which may continue indefinitely, never balancing but continuing to entail mutual concessions within the context of shared commitments and values'.[13]

6.2 Transnational Institutions

How does this flexible reciprocity work in practice? European institutions commit the states to respecting common rules of decision-making on the basis

[12] Keohane calls this 'diffuse reciprocity'; see Keohane, 'Reciprocity in International Relations' (n. 5) p. 4.

[13] ibid.

of reciprocity. Yet law-making is always moderated by the impartial services of the European Commission, which is the most original institution of the European Union.

a) The Commission

The Commission has a wide remit: to promote the general interest of the Union and take appropriate initiatives to that end; to ensure the application of the Treaties, and of measures adopted by the institutions pursuant to them; to oversee the application of Union law under the control of the Court of Justice of the European Union; to execute the budget and manage programmes, and finally to exercise coordinating, executive, and management functions, as laid down in the Treaties, among other things (see Article 17 TEU). It has no counterpart in a domestic constitution or in any other international body.

It would thus be a mistake to consider the Commission to be the Executive power of the European Union. It does not have the requisite powers or the required political legitimacy. In some ways the Commission is entrusted with important executive decisions, especially in resolving competition disputes and complaints, concluding an international trade agreement or publishing reports on the economic health of the member states (as well as running programmes of economic assistance for them). But the Commission also has legislative and law enforcement roles. It has the unique 'right of initiative' or the right to propose new secondary laws under the treaties. It also has the task of operating as the enforcer of the law. In pursuing both tasks it is supposed to serve the general interest, conceived quite independently from that of the particular interests of any of the members states. It takes a truly transnational point of view.

The Commission's uniqueness is not just due to its powers, however. It is also due to its composition. In the past the largest states had two Commissioners and smaller states one. Since 1 May 2004 the rule has been that each state has a single Commissioner. The members of the Commission are appointed by the European Council in a complex procedure outlined in Article 17(7) TEU, which is aimed at reflecting somewhat the results of the immediately preceding election for the European Parliament. The Council proposes to the European Parliament its choice for the position of President of the Commission, 'taking into account the elections to the European Parliament and after having held the appropriate consultations'. This candidate may be elected by the European Parliament by a majority of its component members. This laborious process ensures that the President of the Commissions enjoys political prestige and legitimacy sufficient for him to take important initiatives in his five-year term.

In 2014 the parties of the European Parliament volunteered to only accept as President of the Commission a person nominated by each one of them, according to the majority of seats achieved in the European election. Effectively this meant that either the representative of the European People's Party or the representative of the European Socialists and Progressives had a chance. This was the so-called system of the '*Spitzenkandidaten*' which was aimed to give democratic legitimacy to the Commission. Although the European Council chose Jean-Claude Juncker, the representative of the EPP after it had won the most seats in the European Parliament, the member states have refused to accept the practice for the future. The process was not followed in 2019. The eventual Commission President, Ursula von der Leyen, was imposed by the member states even though she had not run as a candidate of any political party. The *Spitzenkandidaten* experiment is in my view of questionable legitimacy. First, the Treaties empower the member states to make a free choice. Since the foundation of the European Union lies in the Treaties, it is really surprising to suggest that legitimacy might be improved, if the Treaties are misapplied. Second, the *Spitzenkandidaten* system contradicts the nature of the Commission, which is not a government, but a central transnational executive set up by the governments. Since the Commission aims at achieving impartial and non-political accountability, its role is closer to a common civil service than to a common government. It would be wrong, therefore, to turn this impartial executive into a partisan quasi-government.

Finally, the appointment of the Commission is consensual, not party-political. Once a President of the Commission is elected, the Council, by common accord with the President-elect, adopts the list of the other persons whom it proposes for appointment as members of the Commission. They are selected on the basis of the suggestions made by member states, not on the basis of their political persuasion. Each government appoints a Commissioner close to its own political affiliation, not to the affiliation of the Commission President. Still the Commissioners do not sit as representatives of the states and supposed to be independent. Their term of office is independent of that of the government that appointed them. Finally, the members of the Commission cannot be dismissed by the European Council or the member state that suggested them.[14] So it would be wrong to consider the Commission to be the 'government' of the EU.

The Commission's role, however, is not exactly that of a domestic civil service. The Commission, more than any other institution, embodies the common *transnational* interest of the Union. The Commissioners are supposed to be independent of the government that appointed them and are not expected to seek or take instructions from them. They are chosen on the ground of 'their general competence and European commitment from persons whose independence is beyond doubt'.[15] Member states have a duty to respect their independence and must not seek to

[14] Only the Commission as a whole can be dismissed by a vote of the European Parliament, see Article 17(8) TEU.

[15] Article 17(2) TEU.

influence them in the performance of their duties.[16] Commissioners are bound by the Commission's Rules of Procedure.[17] Given that they are not accountable to the governments that appoint them, in the event of any breach of their obligations it is the Court of Justice that has the final word, on application by the Council. In the one case that has become before the Court of Justice, the Court ruled that 'it is... the duty of Members of the Commission to ensure that the general interest of the Community takes precedence at all times, not only over national interests, but also over personal interests'.[18] Under the Treaties the Commission as a body, shall be 'responsible' to the European Parliament, which can dismiss it—and once came close to doing so.[19] Commissioners frequently appear and are questioned before Committees of the European Parliament.

Equally as important as its composition is its mode of operation. The Commission is not organized according to party lines, divided on a Left to Right axis. It is instead a collegiate body where the members seek consensus among all, irrespective of national or political origin. In that sense, it follows a mode of operation that is entirely unknown in parliamentary governments. This is also provided for explicitly by the Treaties. The Commission is supposed to act as a collegiate body, debating every decision and deciding by majority.[20] The Commission's meetings are not public and its contents are confidential.[21] This mode of operation has also been affirmed by the Court of Justice, which stated that the Treaties have established a principle of 'collegial responsibility' of the Commissioners, which is based on the 'equal participation of the Members of the Commission in the adoption of decisions' and which entails that 'decisions should be the subject of collective deliberation and that all the members of the College of Commissioners bear collective responsibility on the political level for all decisions adopted'.[22] The main function of the Commission is not political.

The way in which the independence of the Commission strengthens transnational accountability is nowhere more evident than in the process of law *enforcement*. The Commission has the power to commence infringement proceedings before the Court of Justice.[23] The Commission has always been the guardian of the Treaties. Article 17 TEU now states that it 'shall ensure the application of the Treaties, and of measures adopted by the institutions'.[24] In order to perform these

[16] Article 245 TFEU (ex 213 TEC).

[17] Rules of Procedure of the Commission (C(2000) 3614), OJ L 308 of 8.12.2000 and Consolidated Version as amended by Commission Decision 2007/65/EC of 15 December 2006, OJ L 32/144, 6.2.2007.

[18] Case C-432/04 *Commission of the European Communities v Édith Cresson* [2006] ECR I-06387 par. 71.

[19] Article 17(8) TEU.

[20] Article 250 (ex 219 TEC).

[21] Commission Rules of Procedure, Article 9.

[22] Case 5/85 *AKZO Chemi v Commission* [1986] ECR 2585, par. 30; see also Joined Cases 97-99/87 *Dow Chemica Ibérica v Commission* [1989] ECR 3165, par. 58.

[23] Case C-191/95 *Commission v Germany* [1998] ECR I-5449, paras 33–7.

[24] Article 17 TEU (ex 211 TEC).

broad tasks, the Commission has certain specific powers, namely the power to collect any information,[25] the power to bring a member state before the Court of Justice,[26] and the power to bring an action for annulment for failure to act in the Court of Justice under Article 265 TFEU (ex 232 TEC). The court has stated that decisions to issue the reasoned opinion and to commence proceedings are also subject to that principle of collegiate responsibility.[27] Recourse to this process provides one of the means by which the Commission ensures that the member states give effect to the provisions of the Treaty and those adopted under the Treaty by the institutions. [28] The decisions to issue a reasoned opinion and to commence proceedings before the Court thus come within the general scope of the supervisory task entrusted to the Commission under the Treaty.

If a member state does not comply with the Court's judgment, the Commission may bring a further action before the Court of Justice, specifying the amount of the lump sum or penalty payment to be paid by the member state concerned which it considers appropriate in the circumstances.[29] The Commission may apply for the fines immediately in case where the Commission brings a case before the Court on the grounds that the member state concerned has failed to fulfil its obligation to notify measures transposing a directive adopted under a legislative procedure.[30] The Commission, in short, is an institution that is intended to ensure that the member states are constantly under review. In order for it to do that without any suggestion of bias or partisanship, it is organized in order to remain entirely independent and is generally thought to be so.

b) The European Parliament

The European Parliament is an entirely different institution. Its composition is clearly not a matter of equality, since the states do not have the same number of MEPs, but a number that is proportionate to their populations with a minimum number guaranteed for the smallest states—a system occasionally called one of 'degressive proportionality'. From the Lisbon Treaty and until the United Kingdom's departure, for example, the European Parliament had 754 members, of which Germany had 99, France 74, the United Kingdom and Italy 73, Greece and Belgium

[25] Article 337 TFEU (ex 284 TEC).
[26] Article 258 TFEU (ex 226 TEC).
[27] Case C-191/95, par. 34.
[28] ibid par. 35; Case C-422/92 *Commission v Germany* [1995] ECR I-1097, par. 16.
[29] Article 260(2) TFEU (ex 228 TEC). See *Information from the Commission—Memorandum on applying Article 171 of the EC Treaty* (96/C 242/07), OJ C/242/6, 21/08/1996. Some cases where this power was exercised are Case C-387/97 *Commission v Greece* [2000] ECR I-5047, Case C-278/01 *Commission v Spain* [2003] ECR I-14141, Case C-119/04 *Commission v Italy* [2006] ECR I-6885, and Case C-121/07 *Commission v France* [2008] ECR 2008 I-09159.
[30] Article 260(3) TFEU (ex 228 TEC).

22, Cyprus, Luxembourg, and Malta 6. The European Parliament follows therefore neither formal equality based on sovereignty nor a simple criterion of the size of populations. Its composition is a mixture of criteria of population and statehood.[31]

c) Voting Procedures

The situation is more complex when we turn our attention to voting procedures for secondary legislation, i.e. directives and regulations. The question is complicated by the fact that there are many processes of law-making. Co-decision is now the main law-making mechanism for secondary legislation by the Council and the Parliament in the ordinary legislative procedure. As is well known, the process involves the Commission, the Council, and the Parliament. In most cases (except when it wishes to approve an amendment to which the Commission objects) the Council decides in this procedure by qualified majority, i.e. on the basis of an allocation of weighted votes.

Whereas the composition of the Council of Ministers reflects formal equality, since every member state has one representative, the standing of each state as reflected on voting power varies (on account of their different voting rights). The main voting method currently follows the size of each country's population. A qualified majority is reached when two conditions are met: 55% of member states vote in favour (this means 16 out of 28) and the proposal is supported by member states representing at least 65% of the total EU population. This procedure is also known as the 'double majority' rule. A blocking minority must include at least four members states representing more than 35% of the EU population. We now have, therefore, a mixture of a formal principle, as the first majority is based on the formal equality of all member states, and a criterial principle, since the second majority is dependent on population.

This solution for law-making shows that the EU avoids—in most cases—the principle of formal equality and endorses some variation of the principle of voting according to population. Nevertheless the most fundamental process of law-making in the EU is not this one. It is the making of the Treaties. This is a process which also involves deciding who is to be a member. Here, in the area of the most fundamental decisions of the EU, we find a strict adherence to formal equality. Unanimity is the only decision-making rule. The procedure is that of public international law, allowing states to freely enter into or reject international treaties.

[31] The principle is reaffirmed in the Treaty Establishing the Constitution for Europe, *OJ* C 310, 16 December 2004: Articles 1–20, par. 2. 'The European Parliament shall be composed of representatives of the Union's citizens. They shall not exceed seven hundred and fifty in number. Representation of citizens shall be degressively proportional, with a minimum threshold of six members per Member State. . . . '.

There is no difference to standing or to representation among states and all decisions are taken by unanimity.

d) The Court of Justice

The Court of Justice is the most distinctive legal institutions of the European Union. It is perhaps the most important institution in securing compliance with the Treaties. Much of the Commission's effect and prestige depends on the background role of the Court of Justice, which complements that of the Commission. The Commission's powers would be pointless if the Court of Justice had not been steadfast in its willingness to apply the law even against the will of the most powerful state. Just like the Commission, the Court is entirely independent of the member states. Unlike a federal court, the composition of the Court of Justice is formally representative, since there is one judge from each member state. The judges and the Advocates General of the Court are appointed by the governments. The Court has jurisdiction to hear applications by the Commission against the member states but also, and uniquely, to hear preliminary references from national courts on issues of EU law.

Because of the doctrines of direct effect and supremacy, to which I return below, the national courts are called upon to apply EU law as part of their ordinary tasks. However, when we look at the procedural law and judicial architecture of the EU in Chapter 3, we reach an interesting and perhaps surprising conclusion. Despite the theoretical construct of the 'new legal order', the judicial powers of the EU are limited by dualism. The CJEU is not the highest appellate court for the member states. It is the highest court of the Union, but its institutional relationship with the courts of the member states is not hierarchical, but one of partnership. It is a well-known feature of the EU that the legal systems of the member states remain in principle independent of that of the Union.

In the *Huber* judgment, for example, the Court stated quite clearly that national law is something distinct from Community law:

> None the less, Commission approval of a national aid programme does not in any way have the effect of conferring on that programme the nature of an act of Community law. In those circumstances, where an aid contract is incompatible with the programme approved by the Commission, it is for the national courts to draw the appropriate inferences from this in regard to national law, by taking account of the relevant Community law in applying national law.[32]

[32] Case C-336/00, *Republik Österreich v Martin Huber* [2002] ECR I-7736, par. 40. See also Case 33/67, *Dietrich Kurrer v Council* [1968] ECR 179, at 193, where the Court had declared that the Community is 'composed of States, each of which retains its own national legal order'.

Although the doctrines of direct effect and supremacy have brought national law and European law very close to one another, the general rule is that they remain distinct.

The point is well illustrated by looking at the complex rules regarding the jurisdiction of the Court of Justice. There are five routes by which a case comes before the Court of Justice and none of these routes implies a hierarchical relation with a national court. The Court has jurisdiction to hear a case when a state takes action against another state, when the Commission takes action against a state, when a national court makes a preliminary reference a propos of a domestic case, and finally when it hears—via the General Court—a direct action by an individual or an EU institution against an act of an institution. It is obvious that the Court of Justice is not a 'supreme court' of Europe. The missing link is that it cannot hear appeals from national courts. This means that it does not deliver judgments on domestic law, only on the interpretation of EU law. Since, in addition, individuals have very limited direct access to the court as a forum of first instance, the judicial function of the Court for the member states remains limited. This does not mean that the Court is weak. It only suggests that the Court, for all its power, influence, and prestige, is not a higher appellate court. It is not a court with the power to issue decisions binding on the interpretation of state law. It only speaks on EU law.

The two institutions—the Commission and the Court of Justice—give teeth to the arrangement of reciprocity among the member states. Their roles complement each other. What the Commission and the Court come to decide, either as a legislative proposal or as a judicial decision, comes to unite the member states on the basis of a reciprocal arrangement of mutual respect. The member states have not dissolved their institutional or judicial systems inside the European Union, yet they offer the Commission and the Court almost unconditional recognition. They remain distinct constitutions and distinct legal systems that nevertheless recognize the power of the Commission and the Court to determine the terms of their own co-operation in in the EU independently of the states' particular wishes.

6.3 Legal Accountability

The institutional arrangements we have just outlined offer only a partial view of EU law and institutions. There is fine detail in the way these institutions function. We must now proceed to examine the powers that these institutions are called upon to exercise and the way in which they are designed to check the powers of the member states on a basis of reciprocity. It is common ground that the ultimate rules for the exercise of any powers by the EU institutions lie with the Treaties. There is no 'inherent jurisdiction' or customary sources of power, such that we find in English law of civil procedure, for example.[33] The treaties are the ultimate source of power in the EU.

In some sense this reflects well-established constitutional practice in states that have a written constitution, especially when interpreted by a dedicated constitutional court, e.g. Germany, Italy, or South Africa. The European Court of Justice (ECJ), similarly, follows a strict line on the sources of EU law and the relations between the Union and the states. Nevertheless, in the case of the European Union, these self-imposed limitations also reflect the fact that the foundation of the Union is an international Treaty. This Treaty is created by self-governing states with their own legal systems. It is not a legal system that replaces in any meaningful sense these pre-existing systems.

There are many examples of the narrow interpretation of the European Union's powers under the Treaties. In the leading *Marshall* case, for example, in spite of elaborate arguments to the contrary offered by counsel in the case and powerful academic literature,[34] the Court of Justice refused to extend the direct effect of directives to horizontal relations. The Court said that this would be incompatible with the explicit distinction between directive and regulation established by the Treaty:

> With regard to the argument that a Directive may not be relied upon against an individual, it must be emphasized that according to Article 189 (now 249) of the EEC Treaty the binding nature of a Directive, which constitutes the basis for the possibility of relying on the Directive before a national court, exists only in relation to 'each member state to which it is addressed'. It follows that a Directive may not of itself impose obligations on an individual and that a provision of a Directive may not be relied upon, as such, against individual.[35]

A similar argument was made by the Court in a case regarding the admissibility of direct challenges to a EU measure, where the Advocate General Jacobs and counsel for the claimant offered powerful arguments in favour of opening up the court to individual challengers and showing that the current law for challenging EU acts, which required 'individual concern', was too restrictive and prevented claimants from bringing good cases.[36] The Court said that the Treaty 'established

[33] See Adrian Zuckerman, *Zuckerman on Civil Procedure: Principles of Practice*, 3rd edn (London: Sweet & Maxwell, 2013) 2.10 and by way of illustration *Langley v North West Water Authority* [1991] 1 WLR 697, [1991] 3 All ER 610, where the Court of Appeal confirmed that the county court had an 'inherent jurisdiction' to make directions regulating its own procedure provided that no such direction was inconsistent with rules of court or statutory provisions.

[34] For these arguments see Paul Craig, 'The Legal Effect of Directives: Policy, Rules and Exceptions' 34 *European Law Review* (2009) 349.

[35] Case 152/84, *Marshall v Southampton and South-West Hampshire Area Health Authority (Teaching)* [1986] ECR 723, par. 48; see also Case C-91/92, *Paola Faccini Dori v Recreb Srl* [1994] ECR I-3325, Case C-192/94 *El Corte Inglés SA v Cristina Blázquez Rivero* [1996] ECR I-1281; [1996] 2 CMLR 507 at [15]; Case C-80/06 *Carp Snc di L Moleri e v Corsi v Ecorad Srl* [2007] ECR I-4473 at [20].

[36] Case C-50/00P, *Unión de Pequeños Agricultores v Council of the European Union*, [2002] ECR I-6719, ECLI:EU:C:2002:462.

a complete system of legal remedies and procedures designed to ensure judicial review of the legality of acts of the institutions, and has entrusted such review to the Community Courts'.[37] This system was for the member states to establish and perhaps amend, not the court:

> […]. While it is, admittedly, possible to envisage a system of judicial review of the legality of Community measures of general application different from that established by the founding Treaty and never amended as to its principles, it is for the Member States, if necessary, in accordance with Article 48 EU, to reform the system currently in force.[38]

In these and other cases, the court has persisted with a narrow reading of the treaties. There is nothing wrong or surprising about these interpretations. The task of the court is to apply the law as it is set out in the Treaties. This is an expression, once again, of the equality of states and their power to shape the nature of the European Union. It implies a duty on each state to respect its agreements with the other members and with the EU itself. Hence, a reason for the strict compliance with the letter of the treaties need not be a theory of constitutional formalism for the EU, but more plausibly a matter of respect owed to the equality of states and to their self-government. So one of the most secure principles of EU law is the principle of conferral, that all its powers must be explicitly based on the treaties and that all secondary law issuing from the EU (and all national law in the relevant areas) must conform to the treaties. There are many examples of this restriction having real effects.

The most sensitive such area of the Treaties is, naturally, the list of competence of the European Union. The EU Treaties introduce very clear legislative guidance as to the division of labour between the European Union and the member states. The Treaties outline a principle of enumerated powers for the Union as a whole. Article 5 TEU (ex Article 5 TEC), provides that: 'The limits of Union competences are governed by the principle of conferral. The use of Union competences is governed by the principles of subsidiarity and proportionality' and that 'the Union shall act only within the limits of the competences conferred upon it by the Member States in the Treaties to attain the objectives set out therein'. Competences not conferred to the Union therefore remain with the member states. In general the Treaty will provide for the necessary powers in certain policy spheres and will specify the procedures according to which the measure is to be agreed.

The principle of enumerated powers can often create disagreements, especially when there are two possible bases for EU action, providing for different decision procedures. There are two types of problems. The first is the question of whether

[37] Case 50/00 P, *Unión de Pequeños Agricultores*, par. 40.

[38] ibid paras 44–5.

the legal basis is the right one, which matters for procedural reasons. The second is whether the competence exists at all.

The first type of question was illustrated by the case of the *Working Time Directive*,[39] where the United Kingdom sought the annulment of a directive concerned with the organization of working time in various fields of the economy.[40] The Directive had been adopted on the basis of what was at the time Article 118A EC, which provided for a qualified majority in the Council in areas of health and safety at work. The United Kingdom claimed that the measure should have been proposed under what was at the time Article 94 (ex 100) EC,[41] which provided for unanimity in areas that affect the establishment of the Common Market. The Court ruled that the Directive was properly adopted except for one minor provision that had to be annulled.

The second type of problem arose in the *Tobacco Advertising Case*.[42] Here the question raised by Germany was not as to the precise basis of a measure from amongst many possible bases in the Treaty and the relevant procedures, but on whether the power existed anywhere in the Treaty at all. The measure was claimed by the Commission and the Council to fall under what was at the time Article 95 EC, the provision that provides for measures promoting the 'establishment and functioning of the internal market'. The Court held that 'a measure adopted on the basis of Article 95 EC must genuinely have as its object the improvement of the conditions for the establishment and functioning of the internal market'.[43] The task of the Court was accordingly to examine if the measure in question pursued the objectives stated. The problem with the Directive under review was that it did not make it easier to buy and sell tobacco products on the internal market, but that it sought to make it more difficult. By banning advertising of tobacco in Europe it made the rules the same for all, but these rules were not rules designed to achieve an internal market in tobacco products, but were making it harder to advertise smoking in order to protect consumers from its harmful effects. The Court found that what was at the time Article 95 EC was wrongly invoked and that the Directive had to be annulled in its entirety. The Union cannot act in areas where it does not have competence on the basis of the Treaties.

The rules of competence that we outlined above are a particular expression of the Union's commitment to the rule of law. The role of the Court of Justice is to give effect to the Treaties, as they have been agreed by the states. Both types of problems, namely the precise legal basis and the question of the very existence of a competence, can be traced to the obligation of the Union institutions (and the Court) to

[39] Council Directive 93/104/EC of 23 November 1993 Concerning Certain Aspects of the organization of Working Time, OJ 1993 L 307.

[40] Case C-84/94, *United Kingdom v Council of the European Union* [1996] ECR I-5755.

[41] Previously Article 100 of the EC Treaty prior to amendment.

[42] Case C-376/98, *Germany v Parliament and Council* [2000] ECR I-8419.

[43] See (n. 23), par. 84.

respect the rights of states. In the first case, the correct legal basis safeguards the role of states in the appropriate decision-making procedure. In the second case, the rights of states guarantee them exclusive powers to regulate a particular field.

The principle of subsidiarity was introduced in the Maastricht Treaty and rephrased in the Amsterdam Treaty.[44] Article 5 TEU provides that under the principle of subsidiarity, in areas which do not fall within its exclusive competence, the Union shall act only if and in so far as the objectives of the proposed action cannot be sufficiently achieved by the member states, either at central level or at regional and local level, but can rather, by reason of the scale or effects of the proposed action, be better achieved at Union level. The principle of subsidiarity was meant to check the creeping expansion of the Community's powers, and it applies only in areas of 'shared competence'. Yet, it has been hard to apply by the courts. The Court of Justice has rarely used it. Even the *Tobacco Advertising* judgment did not employ the principle of subsidiarity, despite the fact that the German Government raised it. One of the problems is that the principle requires us to make a judgment as to who can achieve 'better' the objectives of the Community, the States, or the Community itself. This is a very indeterminate criterion and the Court has rightly refrained from invoking it.

Proportionality, on the other hand, means that a measure must be appropriate and necessary to achieve its objectives. The standard expression used by the Court of Justice is whether the measure employs means that correspond to the importance of the aim and whether it is necessary for the achievement of that aim.[45] There are, therefore, two dimensions to proportionality. First, the criterion of 'suitability': is the measure in question suitable to achieve a legitimate aim? The second is the criterion of 'necessity': is the measure necessary to achieve that aim or are there less restrictive alternatives? At the heart of the second criterion lies a consideration for the individual freedom or other interests that may be compromised by the aim in question. It is obvious that the balance to be achieved here is between the effectiveness and uniformity of Union policies on the one hand and something like the rights of states to self-government on the other. This is why proportionality is required: the EU should not compromise self-government without good reason.

The Court of Justice recognized that proportionality was important for the Union competences even before the Maastricht Treaty came about (which brought into force what is now Article 5 TEU). In a case decided in 1987 the Court stated the principle as follows:

> It is settled case-law that in order to establish whether a provision of Community law complies with the principle of proportionality, it must be ascertained whether

[44] See Takis Tridimas, *The General Principles of EC Law*, 2nd edn (Oxford: Oxford University Press, 2006) 175–92.

[45] For further discussion see ibid, p. 177 ff.

> the means which it employs are suitable for the purpose of achieving the desired objective and whether they do not go beyond what is necessary to achieve it. Furthermore ... if a measure is patently unsuited to the objective, which the competent institution seeks to pursue this may affect its legality.[46]

According to the Court's case law, in order to establish whether a provision of EU law complies with the principle of proportionality, it must be ascertained whether the means which it employs are suitable for the purpose of achieving the desired objective and whether they do not go beyond what is necessary to achieve it. Nevertheless, the court considers that for a measure to fail the second criterion it must be 'manifestly disproportionate'.[47] In this area, therefore, the review by the Court will be only at the margins.

Similar constraints bind the Commission. Its powers are extensive in some areas, for example in competition and external trade, but they do not extend to the full range of modern executive action by national governments.[48] There is no power over the main political issues of the day, such as criminal law, family law, pensions, taxation, defence, or foreign affairs. The restrictions to the Commission's executive powers are the same as in legislation. The competences of the EU are arranged for the union as a whole, not for particular institutions. Hence, the disabilities that apply to legislative action apply, *mutatis mutandis*, to executive actions: powers must be expressly granted by law and they must be exercised according to the principles of subsidiarity and proportionality.

6.4 Direct Effect

Perhaps the most distinctive mechanism for legal accountability of the member states to one another and to the European institutions is the principle of direct effect. It is not always clear that this is a mechanism of reciprocal accountability among states, because it is seen as a consequence of a vertical effect of the 'new legal order'. A closer look at it, however, shows that direct effect is structurally different from the vertical effect of legislation in a constitutional order. The principle of direct effect empowers the domestic courts to hold their own governments accountable for any breaches of EU law. It grants rights and duties to individuals

[46] Joined Cases 279/84, 280/84, 285/84, and 286/84 *Walter Rau Lebensmittelwerke and Others v Commission* [1987] ECR 1069, par. 34.

[47] Case C-426/93, *Germany v Council of the European Union* [1995] ECR I-3723, par. 49.

[48] See Andrew Moravcsik, 'In Defence of the "Democratic Deficit": Reassessing Legitimacy in the European Union' 40 *Journal of Common Market Studies* (2002) 603–24; Andrew Moravcsik, 'The European Constitutional Compromise and the Neofunctionalist Legacy' 12 *Journal of European Public Policy* (2005) 349–86. Dashwood also observes that the Commission lacks the ordinary powers of coercive action normally enjoyed by national executives: see Alan Dashwood, 'States in the European Union' 23 *European Law Review* (1998) 201, at 211.

against their own but also against foreign governments. This why it is easy to see this as a 'constitutional' principle. A fuller account, however, will show that its institutional logic is *international*, not constitutional. Through direct effect the enforcement of EU law becomes a matter for any national law-enforcing mechanism, so that the member states become accountable *to each other*. The principle of direct effect creates a decentralized or diffuse system of transnational legal control of the member states on the basis of EU law.[49]

The direct effect of the Treaties marks a fundamental difference between EU law and all other laws or treaties made under public international law. The treaties do not explicitly make any reference to it, other than as a feature of regulations. The direct effect of the treaties emerged through a gradual development by the case law of the ECJ. In developing the principle the Court outlined its fundamental constitutional position that the EU is a 'new legal order'. This doctrine can be linked to monism, so that the EU legal order and the domestic legal orders can be taken to be effectively one. I rejected that reading in Chapters 3 and 4.

Here we can look at direct effect as a mechanism of accountability among states in some detail. We have been saying that the European Union is a Union of Peoples and its legal principles are to be interpreted in light of a framework determined by the law of nations. What role is there for direct effect? Properly conceived, the doctrine of direct effect is neutral among the various interpretations of EU law. It is compatible with all of the rival theories that we outlined above, i.e. federalism, statism, and union of peoples. It is also compatible with both monism and dualism. The monist reading is obvious whereas the dualist reading less so.

Direct effect can be seen as the manifestation of mature dualism in international law. As we have seen, international treaties normally have effects only among states. If a state violates a Treaty obligation, the other party to the Treaty may impose sanctions on the first one. This is set out in the principles of state responsibility in public international law. This kind of accountability to each other, however, is highly imperfect. The power of a state to impose a sanction depends on its size or its economic power. A small state can never force a large one to comply with a Treaty obligation in this way. At the same time, an individual cannot normally rely on a Treaty against a government. A claim by a private individual against one's own government on the basis of the UN Charter will not normally be allowed. For the claim to succeed, the UN Charter would have to have been 'incorporated' into national law before it developed any effects in domestic law. In that sense the UN Charter is not a source of domestic law in the United Kingdom, since Britain has not incorporated the Charter in its law.

[49] This mechanism is well described by Bruno de Witte, 'Direct Effect, Primacy and the Nature of the Legal Order' in P. Craig and G. de Burca (eds), *The Evolution of EU Law*, 2nd edn (Oxford: Oxford University Press, 2011) 323.

It is now well established that the effect of the EU Treaties is quite different. Under certain conditions, the EU Treaties develop effects in domestic law for the benefit of individuals without incorporation. The question was first posed in 1962 when the Netherlands violated one of their obligations under the Treaty. The then Article 12 (later 25 TEC) created an obligation on the member states not to impose new customs duties. The Netherlands had imposed such a new duty and were, therefore, in breach of their obligations under EU law. A case was brought by a private citizen before a Dutch Court. Could a private citizen derive rights from the EU Treaty? Did the Treaty develop effects before domestic courts? The Court rejected the argument made by the Netherlands, that the Treaty was just another international treaty without immediate domestic effects and that what was then the law of the EEC was to be enforced by the Commission, by way of an action before the Court of Justice if necessary, not by individuals before national courts.

The Court made the following, now famous, general statement on the legal order of the Community as a 'new legal order':

> The conclusion to be drawn from this is that the Community constitutes a new legal order of international law for the benefit of which the states have limited their sovereign rights, albeit within limited fields, and the subjects of which comprise not only Member States but also their nationals. Independently of the legislation of Member States, Community law therefore not only imposes obligations on individuals but is also intended to confer upon them rights which become part of their legal heritage. These rights arise not only where they are expressly granted by the Treaty, but also by reason of obligations which the Treaty imposes in a clearly defined way upon individuals as well as upon the Member States and upon the institutions of the Community.[50]

As a result of this judgment EU law does not need to be transposed to the member state's legal system to have domestic effects. The court has confirmed the direct effect of the EU Treaties in numerous cases since. The decisive test is now, slightly amending the *Van Gend* ruling, whether the content of the Treaty provision is 'clear and unconditional and not contingent on any discretionary implementing measure'.[51] On the basis of this doctrine we now say that if the content of a Treaty provision is sufficiently clear and unconditional, it is to be followed immediately by the national courts.

In their leading treatise on the law of the EU, Lenaerts and van Nuffel summarized the position as follows: 'The application of the Community Treaties in the Member States does not depend on whether they have been transposed into

[50] Case 26/62 *N V Algemene Transporten Expeditie Onderneming van Gend en Loos v Nederlandse Administratie der Belastingen* [1963] ECR 1.

[51] Case 44/84 *Hurd v Jones* [1986] ECR 29, par. 47 at 83.

the national legal system'.[52] Nevertheless, it is questionable whether this monist reading of the doctrine of direct effect was established by the *Van Gend* judgment, or if it is part of EU law at all.

It was quickly noticed by the most sophisticated legal commentators that the judgment in *Van Gend* was really about two different things. The first issue was the character of the EU Treaty as a 'self-executing' treaty, i.e. as a treaty which as a matter of its contents 'private individuals can always ask the national administrative organs and … the courts to apply'.[53] The second issue was the substantive content of the provision at issue and the question whether Article 12 EC created enforceable rights on individuals or simply changes one's legal position in other ways.[54] The judgment answered most clearly the second question, by ruling that the provisions of the Treaty were not simply addressed to the member states but also to their citizens. Such a question, however, was not about the wording of any particular provision that could or could not have 'direct effect', but a matter for the interpretation of the scheme of the Treaty as a whole.[55] Hence, as a matter of the constitutional architecture of the EU, whenever an obligation is created in EU law such obligations are not just owed to the other member states or to the Commission, but also to the citizens of the member states.[56]

The court answered the first question in the affirmative, but it did so on a different basis. It said that the Treaty was meant to create justiciable rights and obligations before national courts, because of the nature of the substantive rights involved. The Treaty was directly applicable, because this was the only method of making the obligations of member states to their own citizens properly enforceable. The Commission would not be possible to monitor and intervene in each individual case within a domestic jurisdictions. Hence, the character of the Treaty, which at the time was the Treaty on the European Community, as directly applicable was determined by its contents. The Court concluded:

> The objective of the EC Treaty, which is to establish a common market, the functioning of which is of direct concern to interested parties in the community, implies that this treaty is more than an agreement which merely creates mutual obligations between the contracting states.

[52] Koen Lenaerts and Piet Van Nuffel, *Constitutional Law of the European Union*, 2nd edn (London: Sweet & Maxwell, 2005) 702.

[53] J. A. Winter, 'Direct Applicability and Direct Effect: Two Distinct and Different Concepts in Community Law' 9 *CMLRev* (1972) 425 at 427. I discussed Winter's distinctions in Pavlos Eleftheriadis, 'The Direct Effect of Community Law: Conceptual Issues' 16 *Yearbook of European Law* (1996) 205.

[54] ibid 437.

[55] This point is misunderstood by those who, like Winter, wish to draw a distinction between 'direct applicability' and 'direct effect' as properties of particular Treaty provisions. For this argument see ibid 209–12.

[56] Case 26/62 *Van Gend en Loos*.

Hence, the principle of direct effect amounts to these two statements. First, that the Treaty creates rights that are enforceable by individuals against member states and, second, that such rights are meant to be effective before domestic courts as a matter of EU law.

These two propositions do not need the doctrine of a 'new legal order'. The idea of a new legal order adds something more. The two positions identified above are quite distinct from the position taken by Lenaerts and Van Nuffel, for whom: 'the application of the EU Treaties in the Member States does not depend on whether they have been transposed into the national legal system'.[57] This is a third thesis, inspired perhaps by the Courts' turn of phrase to the effect that the direct effect obtains 'independently of the legislation of Member States'.

Nevertheless, this cannot be taken to mean that EU law is independent of national law, as Lenaerts and Van Nuffel assume. The difference between this third statement and the narrower view on direct effect that I gave above is in the fact that this third position concerns the national legal systems. Whereas the first two points tell us that the EU Treaty is about individuals (i.e. it creates individual rights) and that it is self-executing (i.e. it is supposed to find effect internally), this third premise tells us that the national treatment and incorporation of the EU treaties is irrelevant to its domestic effect. This was not part of the *Van Gend* judgment.

There are two reasons for this, the first procedural and the second substantive. The procedural reason is that the court cannot give any ruling on such a doctrine. Any preliminary reference concerns EU alone. It does not concern the constitutional law of a member state. So the Court has no power to pronounce on how Dutch law is to receive EU law. The Court, by definition, interprets EU law alone. So it follows that the *Van Gend* judgment cannot be a ruling on a 'new legal order' as interpreted by Lenaerts and Van Nuffel.

The substantive reason is that on the facts of the case, the relevance of national constitutional law was never at stake. The Netherlands is a legal system that gives direct effect to *all* treaties on their ratification. Hence, the precise means of incorporation of the EU treaties in the Netherlands was never an issue in the case and did not affect its outcome. The national constitutional law makes perfectly adequate provision for the domestic effect of EU on the basis of a very generous provision for all public international law treaties.

Van Gend, therefore, concerned the meaning of the Treaty, not its transposition in the Netherlands. Whatever the content of the Treaty, the Dutch law was perfectly willing to accept it. This is not a unique feature of Dutch law, of course. All national jurisdictions have ratified and endorsed internally the EU Treaties one way or another. Even the strictly dualist United Kingdom introduced explicit statutory provision to that effect in the European Communities Act 1972. So the

[57] Lenaerts and Van Nuffel, *Constitutional Law of the European Union* (n. 52) 702.

conclusion that the *Van Gend* ruling means that EU law is a new legal order that is 'independent' of national law is a misreading. A closer reading of the case shows that the *Van Gend* ruling is perfectly compatible with the view that the effect of the EU Treaties in domestic law depends on the constitutional arrangements set up by the member states. The 'new legal order', if this is what EU law is, can be as dependent on domestic law as public international law. There is no need to distinguish between them.

The view followed by Lenaerts and Van Nuffel proposes therefore a third concept of direct effect. This is an idea of independence of EU law from national laws, which amounts to the *radical autonomy* of EU law. Such autonomy means that unlike other international laws, EU law does not rely on incorporation into national law but operates there on the basis of its own status.[58] This doctrine creates a more or less constitutional relationship between the treaties and the member states and entails some form of monism. If it was correct, then the Treaty would not only develop direct effects and grant rights to individuals before national courts, but it would do so irrespective of what any national constitutions said. Such theory has been put forward in a well-argued work by René Barents, whose views I examined in detail in Chapter 4.[59] Barents' case for radical autonomy was bold and simple: 'the autonomous nature of Community law is entirely the result of its contents, i.e. its 'Community' character. Autonomy, for Barents, followed from the contents of Community law. It must be obvious that the doctrine of the autonomy of EU law as proposed by Barents and Lenaerts and van Nuffel, is not the same thing as the doctrine of direct effect set out in *Van Gend.*

In short, direct effect is a matter of the EU treaties, not a matter of national law. Hence, the explication of this doctrine does not need to affect national law. What national law is expected to do is to incorporate the treaties in the constitutionally appropriate way. Once incorporation is complete, then direct effect applies to it. It is obvious that the question of the supposed autonomy of EU law from national law does not affect direct effect. A doctrine of dependence of EU law on domestic law is equally open to direct effect. The result is no different to that achieved if we dispensed with the need for domestic incorporation—as Lenaerts and van Nuffel suggest. If, under a theory of the radically autonomous nature of EU law we said that incorporation was not necessary, then direct effect would work immediately and irrespective of constitutional law. But the doctrine of direct effect does not rely on such a radical idea. It is perfectly serviceable by national incorporating mechanisms, when they succeed in incorporating EU law (which they do, normally through their national constitutions).

[58] That the idea of 'incorporation' was separate from the other aspects of direct effect was also noticed by Winter, 'Direct Applicability and Direct Effect (n. 53) 427–8.

[59] René Barents, *The Autonomy of Community Law* (The Hague: Kluwer Law International, 2004).

When we approach the question in this way, we can see that the very logic of direct effect, which makes various distinctions between the effect of the Treaty, directives, and regulations, presupposes two distinct legal orders: that of the EU and that of the member state. Acts of the Westminster Parliament, for example, do not have 'direct effect' in the United Kingdom. They just are the laws of the realm, and this is the case even though we recognize three separate legal systems within it: England and Wales, Scotland, and Northern Ireland.

The very question of direct effect arises from the presupposition that the European legal order and the domestic jurisdictions do not form a single area of law. The European Union may well be a legal order on its own, but it does not encompass those of the member states. It remains part of the law of nations. Whatever the merits of the idea of the 'new legal order', it must be obvious that the doctrine of direct effect does not need it. Direct effect as set out by the CJEU in its most famous judgments is perfectly consistent with a dualist framework according to which EU law is deployed in the domestic courts as a test of accountability for all member states.

6.5 Interdependence

I now return, very briefly, to the doctrine of primacy of EU law as a tool for accountability. I discussed the doctrine of primacy in some detail in Chapters 2 and 3. I return to it now only in order to examine it as an institutional mechanism of accountability. As we have seen national legal orders have incorporated the Treaties and given appropriate effect to the secondary laws created under them. But what is the precise place of EU law in these domestic legal orders? From the point of view of legal theory a great deal depends on whether this incorporation is *conditional* or *unconditional*, as explained in Chapter 4. Dualism suggests that EU law has conditional primacy because it enjoys the same status as that of the constitutional or statutory provision that incorporate it. Nevertheless, this debate is unimportant from the point of view of accountability.

Primacy makes the national courts guardians of EU law vis-à-vis the national executive and legislatures. EU law thus prevails in practice against any contrary law or executive action. How exactly this takes place in legal or constitutional theory is not important. One way or another, the national institutions *monitor* compliance with EU law. Primacy thus protects the uniformity of EU law at least as well—and probably better—than a doctrine of unconditional primacy.

In effect, primacy creates institutions that are interdependent. EU law and domestic law coexist, sharing principles as well as mechanisms of enforcement. When we look at the practical applications of EU law, it becomes evident that EU law prevails not because it is 'radical autonomous', but because it is deeply *interdependent* with national law.[60] In practice EU law explicitly relies on domestic law in order to bring about mechanisms of accountability. This is evident in many areas of EU law, but I will only concentrate on three in order to illustrate the point. The first is the doctrine of the 'indirect effect of EU law', the second is the doctrine of effective remedies, and the third is the area of electoral law as it applies to the European Parliament. In all these areas the accountability of member state institutions depends explicitly on *domestic* processes that apply EU law.

a) Indirect Effect

As we have seen, some articles of the treaties, regulations, and in some respects directives, have direct effect in the law of the member states. In some cases, however, EU law does not have that effect even though its purposes are clear. In *Van Colson* the Court of Justice said that the courts of the member states are under an obligation to 'achieve the result envisaged by the Directive' by taking 'all appropriate measures, general or particular, to ensure the fulfilment of that obligation'.[61] This has been called the doctrine of indirect effect or the doctrine of 'consistent interpretation'.

In *Factortame*, the Court of Justice required that national courts have 'the power to do everything necessary' at the moment of application of [EU] law 'to set aside national legislative provisions which might prevent, even temporarily Community rules from having full force and effect'.[62] This doctrine was meant to supplement that of direct effect. And in a later case, *Marleasing*, the court held that that national courts should interpret domestic law in the light of the wording and purpose of the directive in order to achieve the result pursued by the latter 'so far as possible'.[63] Developing this doctrine the Court said that the Directive could not develop effects between private parties, even though it was 'clear, precise and unconditional'.[64] Yet, the Court added that national courts still were under an obligation when applying domestic law 'and in particular legislative provisions specifically adopted for the purpose of implementing the requirements of a directive' to interpret national law: 'so far as possible, in the light of the wording and the purpose of the directive concerned in order to achieve the result sought by the directive'.[65]

[60] Or, in the words of the Court of Justice, their 'mutual interdependence'; see Case C-284/16 *Slovak Republic v Achmea BV*, ECLI:EU:C:2018:158, (Grand Chamber) 06 March 2018, par. 33.

[61] Case 14/83 *Sabine von Colson and Elisabeth Kamann v Land Nordrhein-Westfalen* [1984] ECR 1891, par. 26.

[62] Case C-213/89 *R v Secretary of State for Transport ex p Factortame Ltd* [1990] ECR I-2433, par. 20. This led, in that case, to an entirely novel grant of relief: the suspension of the operation of a Westminster statute. See also Case 14/83, *Van Colson and Kamann v Land Nordrhein-Westfalen* ECLI:EU:C:1984:153.

[63] Case C-106/89 *Marleasing v Comercial Internacional de Alimentación* [1991] 1 ECR 4135 par. 8. See also Case C-91/02 *Dori v Recreb Srl* [1994] ECR I-3325 par. 26.

[64] Joined Cases C-397-403/01 *Pfeiffer* [2004] ECRI-8835, para 109. For similar statements see Case C-212/04 *Adeneler* [2006] ECR I-6057.

[65] *Pfeiffer* (n. 64) par. 113.

This requirement, the court said was 'inherent in the system of the Treaty, since it permits the national court, for the matters within its jurisdiction, to ensure the full effectiveness of Community law when it determines the dispute before it'.[66] It is generally acknowledged that the doctrine has had far reaching effects in the application of EU law by the member states.[67]

The doctrine, however, has limits. The Court recognizes that courts cannot do things that are contrary to the domestic legal order, or contrary to legal certainty, or the rule of law in general.[68] Hence, in Case C-268/06 *Impact*, the court explained that the doctrine of consistent interpretation requires national courts to do whatever lies within their jurisdiction through the interpretative methods recognized by domestic law, with a view to achieving an outcome consistent with the objective pursued by a directive, but was equally clear that the doctrine was limited by the law of the member states.[69] It cannot operate *contra legem*. The same view has been taken by the English courts. In *Clarke v Kato, Smith and General Accident, Fire & Life Assurance Corporation plc*, Lord Clyde said that 'the exercise must still be one of construction and it should not exceed the limits of what is reasonable'.[70] In *R v Durham City Council ex p Huddleston* it was held that the primary legislation was simply incompatible with the Directive and a 'convergent construction' was not possible.[71]

b) Procedural Autonomy

EU law relies on the procedural law of the member states for its enforcement. It is generally accepted that the states enjoy 'procedural autonomy', even though no such explicit principle exists in the treaties. In *Rewe-Zentralfinanz* the referring Dutch Court wanted advice on the effect of national time-limits to the legal challenge to an unlawful customs duty. The domestic law of procedure was thought to be a barrier to the true direct effect of the duties arising from the Treaty, since the

66 ibid 114.

67 Michal Bobak, now an Advocate General at the Court, has written: 'Originally perhaps construed as an alternative to direct effect, it soon became arguably more important than direct effect itself, and can reach into situations and relationships where direct effect cannot. In quantitative terms, consistent interpretation became the most important avenue for EU law penetration of the national legal orders in the process of adjudication.' Michal Bobak, 'The Effects of EU Law in the National Legal Systems' in Catherine Barnard and Steve Peers (eds), *European Union Law* (Oxford: Oxford University Press, 2014) 140–73, at 158.

68 See Case 80/86 *Kolpinghuis Nijmegen* [1987] ECR 3969, par. 13, and *Adeneler and Others*, par. 110, and Case C-105/03 *Pupino* [2005] ECR I-5285, paras 44 and 47.

69 Case C-268/06,*Impact v Minister for Agriculture and Food* [2008] ECR I-24, ECLI:EU:C:2008:223.

70 *Clarke v Kato, Smith and General Accident, Fire & Life Assurance Corporation plc,* [1998] 1 WLR 1647, at 1656.

71 *R v Durham City Council ex p Huddleston* [2000] 1 WLR 1484. For further analysis see S. Drake, 'Twenty Years after *Von Colson*: The Impact of "Indirect Effect" on the Protection of the Individual's Community Rights' (2005) 30 *European Law Review* 329.

short time limit left allowed the effects of an unlawful custom duty. The Court recognized the conditional autonomy of national jurisdictions with these words:

> [I]n the absence of Community rules on this subject, it is for the domestic legal system of each Member State to designate the courts having jurisdiction and to determine the procedural conditions governing actions at law intended to ensure the protection of the rights which citizens have from the direct effect of Community law, it being understood that such conditions cannot be less favourable than those relating to similar actions of a domestic nature.[72]

The national institutions are autonomous on the condition that they respect the both effectiveness and equivalence.[73] Although it is for the domestic legal systems of each member state to designate the courts having jurisdiction and to lay down the rules governing actions intended to ensure the protection of rights conferred by EU law, states must not render the exercise of EU law rights 'virtually impossible' or 'excessively difficult'. In a leading case the Court said that 'in the interests of legal certainty, which protects both the taxpayer and the administration, it is compatible with Community law to lay down reasonable time-limits for bringing proceedings'.[74]

A good example of procedural independence is the *IN.CO.GE.* judgment.[75] In this case an Italian Court asked the Court of Justice assistance with classifying a claim that a number of Italian companies had against the Italian state. The claim concerned payment of a 'registration charge' that all Italian companies had to pay the Italian state, contrary to a Directive. EU law affected jurisdiction in this way: if the illegal charge was void and non-existent, the claim was a claim properly heard by a civil court. If the charge was of a fiscal nature, it fell under the jurisdiction of special tax courts. If the charge was a tax, it was subject to a three-year limitation. If not, to a ten-year limitation. So the question of classification affected both jurisdiction and the level of potential reimbursement. During the hearing the Commission argued that an unlawful charge would be non-existent because it was contrary to EU law, according to the doctrine of supremacy under *Simmenthal*. The court, however, thought otherwise. It explained that in *Simmenthal*, the Court held that 'every national court must, in a case within its jurisdiction, apply Community law in its entirety and protect rights which the latter confers on individuals, setting aside any provision of national law which may conflict with it, whether prior or

[72] Case 33/76 *Rewe-Zentralfinanz eG and Rewe-Zentral AG v Landwirtschaftskammer fur das Saarland* [1976] ECR 1989. For a very clear discussion of the cases see Robert Schütze, *European Constitutional Law* (Cambridge: Cambridge University Press, 2012) 381–408.

[73] See e.g. Case C-432/05 *Unibet Ltd v Justitiekanslern* [2007] ECR I-2271, par. 41.

[74] Case C-62/00 *Marks and Spencer v Commissioners of Customs and Excise* [2002] ECR I-6348, [2003] QB 866, par. 35.

[75] Joined Cases 10-22/97 *Ministero delle Finanze v IN.CO.GE.'90 Srl et al.* [1998] ECR 6307.

subsequent to the Community rule'. But the instant case was different. The question here was not whether the law was to be 'set aside' but whether it was 'non-existent'. The court therefore ruled against the claimant:

> It cannot therefore, contrary to the Commission's contention, be inferred from the judgment in *Simmenthal* that the incompatibility with Community law of a subsequently adopted rule of national law has the effect of rendering that rule of national law non-existent. Faced with such a situation, the national court is, however, obliged to disapply that rule, provided always that this obligation does not restrict the power of the competent national courts to apply, from among the various procedures available under national law, those which are appropriate for protecting the individual rights conferred by Community law (. . .).[76]

In other words, the procedural independence of the member states entails that law that may be contrary to EU law will have at least some procedural effects. The national courts may well disapply national laws in appropriate cases, but cannot question their existence or validity.

The Court, in other words, accepts that national law is not entirely and in every respect subject to the law of the EU treaties. This is partly a recognition of political realities but also of the fact that the consequences of the effectiveness or priority of EU law are to be sorted out by the national courts themselves. The ECJ here stopped short of affirming the most ambitious reading of the doctrine of supremacy and allowed for the role of domestic law.

c) Electoral Law

The third example of independence is the simplest. It concerns the election of members to the European Parliament. Even though the European Parliament appears to be the most important democratic institution of the European Union, its composition is entirely a matter of domestic law. Indeed, there is no common European method of electing members of the European Parliament. In the absence of such a law, the election and powers of MEPs is a matter entirely for domestic law. That this is so was confirmed in the case of *Jean-Marie Le Pen*.[77] Jean Marie Le Pen, a French politician, was convicted for assault by a French Court after having been elected a Member of the European Parliament in 1999. As a result of his sentence, Mr Le Pen lost under French law his seat at the Parliament. Once the French Ministry of Foreign Affairs notified Mr Le Pen and the President of the European Parliament,

[76] Joined Cases 10-22/97 *Ministero delle Finanze v IN.CO.GE.'90 Srl et al.* par. 21.

[77] Case C-208/03 P, *Jean-Marie Le Pen v European Parliament* [2005] ECR I-06051, ECLI:EU:C:2005:429.

the disqualification was put into effect. Mr Le Pen brought an action against the European Parliament. Yet, both the Court of First Instance and on appeal the CJEU rejected his application saying that the process of election and disqualification of members of the European Parliament were matters for domestic law alone, which operated entirely independently of EU law. In effect, Mr Le Pen had not been disqualified by the European Parliament, but by France.

This legal arrangement was first set out in Decision 76/787 'relating to the Act concerning the election of the representatives of the Assembly by direct universal suffrage'. It is generally known as the 1976 Act.[78] In effect, the Act (in Article 12) allocates the election of members of the European Parliament and their legal standing entirely to the law of the member states: '(1) Pending the entry into force of the uniform electoral procedure referred to in Article 7(1) and subject to the other provisions of this Act, each Member State shall lay down appropriate procedures for filling any seat which falls vacant during the five-year term of office referred to in Article 3 for the remainder of that period.' The Act also provided that: 'Where a seat falls vacant pursuant to national provisions in force in a Member State, the latter shall inform the [Parliament], which shall take note of that fact'. It follows that the election and continuous standing of the members of the European Parliament is not a matter of EU law, but a matter of domestic law. As in so many other areas, the continuing effect and operation of the European Union relies, unconditionally, on the operation of the domestic legal system. Their interdependence is constant and deep.

6.6 Conclusion

In this chapter I examined in detail the ways in which members states as well as institutions of the EU are held to account through the operation of EU law. The EU's legal architecture organizes the division of labour between member states and the Union in mixed legislative, executive, and judicial functions. This is a very different arrangement from the standard separation of powers that we find in domestic constitutions. The allocation of powers between member states and the Union in the EU is a system of transnational accountability, whereby the EU and the members states are accountable to each other for their decisions and actions under a system of the rule of law set up by Treaties of public international law. This is not a doctrine of the 'autonomy' of EU law or of the creation of a *sui generis* 'new legal order', but a doctrine of interdependence according to standard assumptions of constitutional law and the law of nations under a doctrine of dualism.

[78] OJ 1976 L 278, p. 1. The Act was amended in 2002 by Decision 2002/772/EC, Euratom of the Council of 25 June 2002 and of 23 September 2002.

In a widely discussed article Tony Arnull argued a few years ago that the strategy of 'constitutionalization' of the Treaties that had been pursued by the CJEU since the 1960s had created a different kind of adjustment which he summarized as 'fragmentation'.[79] The process had in fact led to the 'disintegration' of EU law. Arnull observed that the member states had deployed strategies that aimed at containing the power of the Court either through Treaty amendment or through their own constitutional doctrines. Arnull concluded that the Court was responsible for a largely unstable and 'unhealthy' relationship with the member states. Arnull's conclusion was: 'It is hard to deny that this ad hoc legal disintegration is partly attributable to the record of the Court.'[80] My argument thus far is that the 'disintegration' of EU law has a limit set by public international law. Whatever steps the member states take to limit the Court's alleged or emerging 'monism' are cast in terms of public international law, which is the effective constitutional backstop for EU law.

EU law appears a lot of the time to be uniform. In fact it is not. It permits a great deal of flexibility as the above examples of deployment of international law show (or indeed the example of the ESM Treaty shows, in another context). The member states are accountable to each other through various mechanisms of law, yet none of these mechanisms is truly constitutional. This is how EU law has survived its many crises. By giving states the required flexibility on the basis of international law, not on the basis of an emerging constitution. In my view, therefore, the position of EU law is the opposite of that envisaged by the Court of Justice. EU law does not owe its success to its supposed 'autonomy', but on the contrary, to its full *dependence* on international law. Both in theory and in practice, as we saw above, EU law is not an 'independent' source of law but is always dependent, as we have seen, on domestic constitutional law as well as on public international law. EU law is a form of international law. This is how the states manage to hold each other to account.

[79] A. Arnull, 'Me and My Shadow: The European Court of Justice and the Disintegration of European Union Law' 31 *Fordham International Law Journal* (2007) 1174–211.
[80] ibid p. 1208.

7
Liberty

I argued in Chapter 6 that transnational accountability is the central institutional principle that connects member states to one another and to the European Union as an international institution. A second principle operates in a different domain: it connects member states directly with ordinary people. I call it a principle of 'European liberty', or simply the principle of liberty. Since it connects states directly with the citizens of other states, this is the most important 'cosmopolitan' principle of EU law.

The principle of liberty lifts borders for the benefit of member state nationals and others. Before the European Union was created, European states assumed that persons were either national citizens or complete strangers. A state was free to discriminate against non-citizens. Indeed, admission to a state was a discretionary prerogative of each government. Those who settled permanently in foreign lands could be economic immigrants or perhaps political 'exiles' like Rousseau and Marx were a few generations ago (which is a special category of person with its own moral requirements and challenges).[1] By definition, however, all non-citizens suffered various legal disabilities in the host country. European liberty eliminates those disabilities by creating a common European liberty, which removes all barriers as well as any discrimination for those who move from one member state to another. This has a uniquely liberating effect, since it enables persons to move, reside, study, and work throughout the territory of the European Union without administrative obstacles or fear of a change in circumstances. The principle of liberty for all citizens of the member states is one of the most significant novelties of the progressive internationalism of the European Union.

Under traditional public international law, the rights of strangers are the minimum humanitarian ones provided, say, by human rights treaties or the conventions concerning refugees or the laws of war. There is no right to move to a foreign country, against the wishes of the authorities of that country. The creation of the European Economic Community in 1958 marked a great departure from that model, however. It created a new set of rights for persons to move to another member state and to seek employment there without discrimination. Over the years, however, these rules were developed beyond economically active persons and covered other categories, such as students, pensioners, and those of

[1] See Judith N. Shklar, 'The Bonds of Exile' in Stanley Hoffmann (ed.), *Political Thought and Political Thinkers* (Chicago: The University of Chicago Press, 1998) 56–72.

A Union of Peoples. Pavlos Eleftheriadis. Oxford University Press (2020). © Oxford University Press.
DOI: 10.1093/oso/9780198854173.001.0001

independent means who did not need social assistance by the host state. The rights of persons of those categories have now acquired an independent rationale that extends beyond the single market. The rights of non-discrimination have now been expanded to cover all nationals of the member states under the name of 'European Citizenship'.

This idea of European citizenship was introduced by the Treaty of Maastricht. It was an addition to the earlier trade-related rights of the free movement of persons. The Treaty on the Functioning of the European Union provides now, at Article 20, that 'every person holding the nationality of a Member State shall be a citizen of the Union', yet this status 'shall be additional to and not replace national citizenship'. Over the years citizenship has expanded in meaning and assumed a new significance, assisting many people in securing various rights in the host states even when they were not economically active. The principle, however, covers still something different from the citizenship of a constitutional state.

Like accountability, liberty is a *transnational* principle. It is fundamental to the European Union, not because it marks the creation of a new 'demos', as some of its original supporters hoped, but because it assists the persons who live under a union of peoples to achieve their aims on the basis of reciprocity and fairness. This kind of transnational liberty is not a new status of 'citizenship' but a new set of individual rights that allows them to take control over their lives. By extending such rights to outsiders on the basis of equality and reciprocity, the members of the European Union have created a novel principle of 'cosmopolitan liberty'.

7.1 The Idea of Citizenship

Becoming a citizen means you enjoy equal standing within a political community under its public laws.[2] This is true whatever particular features you may have on account of your work, your origin, or your achievements. This idea of equal, moral standing or formal equality enables everyone to be able to bring a claim before a court, to be party to a contract, to own property, and to vote and stand in elections. It is now a universally accepted principle of civil and political equality. This is not all, however. In modern Europe, legal and political equality is accompanied by a particular kind of economic equality. T. H. Marshall is famous for bringing these together: 'Citizenship is a status bestowed on those who are full members of a community. All who possess the status are equal with respect to the rights and duties with which the status is endowed ... Social class, on the other hand is a system of

[2] The next few paragraphs are partly based on Pavlos Eleftheriadis, 'The Content of European Citizenship' 15 *German Law Journal* (2014) 777.

inequality. And it, too, like citizenship can be based on a set of ideals, beliefs and values.'[3]

Marshall explained how the drive towards equality has enriched the idea of citizenship. It led to a different understanding of common membership with the 'incorporation of social rights in the status of citizenship and thus creating a universal right to real income which is not proportionate to the market value of the claimant'.[4] Marshall is referring to the social welfare state that European states have created after the Second World War. Philosophers now speak of the welfare state as a matter of justice, not simply a matter for satisfying the urgent needs of the poor or even that of building much needed fellow feeling. The social welfare state is a standard element of the European political landscape.[5]

Within the European social model citizens enjoy free tangible services, such as education and health, whereas they are also due payments to support their housing or other needs if they are out of work and do not have sufficient assets.[6] These benefits may take the form of unconditional benefits, or of benefits linked to some insurance scheme related to work. Citizenship under Marshall's distinctions involves therefore three elements: legal status, political status, and social status. All of them entail some kind of equal treatment. In the first case, that of legal status, they involve the formal equality of access to property rights and to standing before courts of law. In the second case, of political status, they involve the equal right to vote and stand for election. In the third they involve, in Marshall's own words, 'the whole range from the right to a modicum of economic welfare and security to the right to share to the full in the social heritage and to live the life of a civilized being according to the standards prevailing in the society'.[7] The various rights are of course interconnected. Marshall wrote, for example, that education is a precondition of 'civil freedom'.[8] Citizenship is then the result of all those rights and duties. It is the result of an egalitarian philosophy of the state and of corresponding legal doctrine.

When it was first created, European citizenship created an expectation that it might work in the way of state citizenship as a direct and special political relationship of member-state nationals with the Union itself. It was the strongest signal that the Treaties adopted much of the institutional logic of a constitution. Advocate

[3] T. H. Marshall, *Citizenship and Social Class and Other* Essays (Cambridge: Cambridge University Press, 1950) 28–9.

[4] ibid 29.

[5] For a very positive general discussion see Steven Hill, *Europe's Promise: Why the European Way Is the Best Hope in an Insecure Age* (Berkeley: University of California Press, 2010).

[6] For a discussion of Marshall's arguments and their contemporary relevance see John D. Stephens, 'The Social Rights of Citizenship' in Francis G. Castles, Stephan Leibfried, Jane Lewis, Herbert Obinger, and Christopher Pierson (eds), *The Oxford Handbook of the Welfare State* (Oxford: Oxford University Press, 2010) 511.

[7] T. H. Marshall, *Citizenship and Social Class* (n. 3).

[8] ibid 26.

General Francis Jacobs described it in one of the earlier cases on European citizenship as: 'a commonality of rights and obligations uniting Union citizens by a common bond transcending Member State nationality'.[9] In the same Opinion he went on to add:

> The introduction of that notion was largely inspired by the concern to bring the Union closer to its citizens and to give expression to its character as more than a purely economic union. That concern was reflected in the removal of the word "economic" from the Community's name (also effected by the Treaty on European Union) and by the progressive introduction into the EC Treaty of a wide range of activities and policies transcending the field of the economy.[10]

Citizenship was part of the long-term effort to complete the process of 'ever closer Union' and to expand European integration into new areas of public policy. In reality, however, citizenship never worked in exactly that way.

What kind of 'common bond' or 'special relationship' did European Citizenship create? A special relationship is assumed by almost any citizenship code for a nation or a state. It is also assumed by most of theoretical approaches, whatever the nuances and transformations resulting under the twin pressures of globalization and mass migrations.[11] It is true that some sociological accounts present a model of citizenship with many of its components 'disaggregated' and broken down as overlapping identifications.[12] Even such theories, however, presuppose that the primary case of citizenship is some kind of special belonging or attachment to a political community. Multiple ethnic or other cultural identities do not challenge the idea of a single bundle of rights of citizenship and do not compete with it. Constitutional citizenship is based on the idea of a single bond to a political community. As Judith Shklar put it: 'Citizenship as nationality is the legal recognition, both domestic and international, that a person is a member, native-born or naturalized, of a state.'[13] Shklar was also very clear about its moral significance. She considered being 'stateless' as one 'of the most dreadful political fates that can befall anyone in the modern world'.[14]

It is clear that European citizenship does not serve the same moral or legal function as constitutional citizenship. The bond it creates between the person and a political community is not direct. European citizenship connects a person with the

[9] Case C-274/96 *Bickel and Franz* [1998] ECR *I-0763*, Opinion of the Advocate General, par. 23.

[10] ibid.

[11] See, for example, J.G.A. Pocock, 'The Idea of Citizenship since Classical Times' in Ronald Beiner (ed.), *Theorizing Citizenship* (New York: State University of New York Press, 1995) 29–52.

[12] See e.g. Jean Cohen, 'Changing Paradigms of Citizenship and the Exclusiveness of the Demos' 14 *International Sociology* (1999) 245–68.

[13] See Judith Shklar, *American Citizenship: The Search for Inclusion* (Cambridge, Mass.: Harvard University Press, 1991) 4.

[14] ibid.

government of the host state not directly but only through the mechanisms of EU law. It remains a *transnational* bond. It connects a person to several states at the same time, since under EU citizenship a person can enjoy rights in more than one state (for example a German national living in Nice and working in Genoa). This kind of citizenship does not create a link with a central authority, i.e. the European Union itself.[15]

European citizenship clearly overlaps—or perhaps competes—with the pre-existing bond that the European citizen has with his or her own state. This bond continues to exist and to define his or her relations with the other member states and the Union. As a result EU citizenship does not give one an unconditional right to reside everywhere in the territory of the European Union. The right exists in other states of the EU only under certain conditions. This is made explicit in the most central legislation on citizenship and residence: the EU Residence Directive 2004/38 on the right of citizens of the Union and their family members to move and reside freely within the territory of the member state. Under this Directive third country nationals who are family members of a Union citizen derive rights to enter and reside in a member state, only if the Union citizen has already exercised his or her right of free movement in another member state. According to Article 3, the Directive does not apply if the Union citizen remains in the state of his or her citizenship.[16]

It appears therefore that, paradoxically, in EU law the right of citizenship is weakest wherever the bond of community is strongest: in one's own state. Or, in other words, European citizenship only works for a citizen who is already disconnected from his or her place of national citizenship. So a UK citizen cannot bring her family into the UK under the Directive or under European Citizenship, but can bring them to live with her if she has moved to France. Her rights under EU law are stronger where her citizenship is only European, and weaker where European and national citizenship overlap.

This solution is perfectly understandable under the law of the free movement of persons, but sits uneasily with a logic of constitutional citizenship. So whatever rights European citizenship creates, they are not similar to those of national citizenship. It is therefore not true of European citizenship what Judge Cardozo said of United States citizenship, namely that 'the people of the several states must sink or swim together'.[17] European member states are very much independent of each other.

[15] The right to citizenship does not create, for example, an independent 'right to vote' in European Union law. See Case C-145/04 *Spain v United Kingdom* [2006] ECR I-7917, and Case 300/04 *Eman and Sevinger v College van Burgemeester en Wethouders van den Haag* [2006] ECR I-8055.

[16] Similar restrictions apply to other secondary law providing for free movement, such as Regulation (EU) No 492/2011 and Directive 2014/54/EU, as well as the coordination of social security systems, covered by Regulation (EC) No 883/2004.

[17] *Baldwin v GAF Seelig Inc* 294 US 522 [1935] at § 523.

7.2 Theories and Conjectures

What kind of citizenship grants you more rights abroad than at home? European citizenship appears not only to be something less than constitutional citizenship, but something entirely different from it. We can summarize here some of the deficiencies of European citizenship: under its coverage, citizens do not enjoy full rights of residence everywhere in the European Union, do not have a right to vote in national elections, and do not have unconditional social welfare entitlements. Both the political but also the social components of citizenship are incomplete. Indeed, Catherine Barnard summarized the EU's own arrangements of social policy as a 'patchwork', rather than 'a fully-fledged social policy with welfare institutions and cradle-to-grave protection', since it 'makes no provision for what is generally agreed to be the central core of social policy: social insurance, public assistance, health and welfare services, education and housing policy'.[18] In all these ways, the most important political and social rights of EU citizens are exercised through their member states, not through the Union. European citizenship does not signify a special relationship to the European Union in a way that begins to compare with the relationship signified by the domestic case. What kind of principle is it?

These theoretical difficulties have not stopped the Court of Justice from adopting very ambitious language in relation to European citizenship. It has said that citizenship is 'intended to be the fundamental status of nationals of the Member States', implying that it does not yet enjoy this status.[19] But statements of this kind replace the first puzzle with a second: they derive rights from a fundamental status that does not yet exist. This tension resurfaced in a remarkable series of cases before the Court of Justice of the EU starting in 2011. In the first case, *Ruiz Zambrano*,[20] the Court had to deal with the case of the two Belgian children of a Colombian couple who lived in Belgium.. The couple claimed an EU right to residence in Belgium as family members of their children on the basis of European citizenship. Since the children had never been outside Belgium, the Directive did not apply, however. One would have expected this to be a 'purely internal situation', where Belgian law would dispose of the case. The Court, however, thought otherwise. It repeated the well-known doctrine that 'citizenship is intended to be the fundamental status of nationals of the Member States'[21] and concluded that Article 20 TFEU precludes national measures which have the effect of depriving citizens of the 'genuine enjoyment of the substance of the rights conferred by virtue of that status'.[22]

[18] Catherine Barnard, *EC Employment Law*, 3rd edn (Oxford: Oxford University Press, 2006) 49.

[19] Case C-184/99 *Grzelczyk* [2001] ECR I-6193, par. 31; Case C-413/99 *Baumbast and R* [2002] ECR I-7091, par. 82.

[20] Case C-34/09, *Ruiz Zambrano v Office national de l'emploi (ONEm)* (Grand Chamber), [2011] ECR I-01177, ECLI:EU:C:2011:124.

[21] ibid par. 41.

[22] ibid par. 42.

A refusal to grant a right of residence to the parents of those dependent minors would have this effect, namely that the children would be 'unable to exercise the substance of the rights conferred on them by virtue of their status as citizens of the Union'.[23] So citizenship protects the 'exercise' of the 'substance' of those rights. This odd expression was tested within a few weeks in the case of *McCarthy*.[24] In this case it was clear that Mrs McCarthy could not reasonably claim to be 'deprived' of the genuine enjoyment of the substance of the rights associated with her status as a Union citizen since she had never exercised any rights of free movement. The *Zambrano* precedent was of no assistance to her. These issues returned in *Dereci*, which concerned five separate cases of third country nationals seeking residence rights in Austria, where the precise effect of various family relationships were put before the Court.[25] None of them related to dependent school-age children with their parents. None of them succeeded.

Advocate General Mengozzi noted that the *Zambrano* and *McCarthy* cases raise certain questions 'which could be seen as stumbling blocks, or at least as paradoxes', namely that a citizen can enjoy EU rights of citizenship only if they abandon the state of their citizenship.[26] In *Dereci*, the court embraced the paradoxes. It ruled that 'the criterion relating to the denial of the genuine enjoyment of the substance of the rights conferred by virtue of European Union citizen status refers to situations in which the Union citizen has, in fact, to leave not only the territory of the Member State of which he is a national but also the territory of the Union as a whole'.[27] It then noted that this criterion is 'specific' in that 'a right of residence may not, exceptionally, be refused to a third country national, who is a family member of a Member State national, as the effectiveness of Union citizenship enjoyed by that national would otherwise be undermined'. In *Zambrano* Advocate General Sharpston said that 'lottery rather than logic would seem to be governing the exercise of EU citizenship rights'.[28] In spite of the efforts of the Court of Justice to clarify the confusion in *Dereci*, the lottery seems to go on and on.

What are we to make of these puzzles? Some theorists seek to overcome the paradoxes of EU citizenship by referring to the supposed 'progressive' evolution of its contents or its inherent 'dynamic'. They see these problems as temporary troubles, which will not stop European citizenship one day becoming itself—in the sense of a full constitutional citizenship. Armin von Bogdandy, for example, concludes that even though the various principles of EU law are paradoxical, in that they never settle on a consistent scheme of principle between unity and diversity,

23 ibid par. 44.
24 Case C-434/09 *McCarthy v Secretary of State for the Home* Department [2011] ECR I-03375, ECLI:EU:C:2011:277.
25 Case C-256/11 *Dereci and Others v Bundesministerium für Inneres*, [2011] ECR I-11315, ECLI:EU:C:2011:734.
26 ibid. Opinion of AG Mengozzi, par. 43.
27 ibid par. 66.
28 ibid par. 88.

this is just a 'tension' that is normal in any 'real' federation.[29] Von Bogdandy concludes by embracing and almost praising the indeterminacy of European citizenship as follows: 'Carl Schmitt was likely right on one point: substantial stability is largely impossible in a real—that is, heterogeneous—federation. However, it is more likely that, in a rapidly changing interdependent world, substantial stability is an outdated, illusory, pipedream.'[30] This argument suggests that citizenship is not an ordinary legal principle like, for example, the principle of freedom from arbitrary arrest, whose content is specified in legislation and applied by the police and the courts every day, but a very different kind of legal principle, intentionally unstable and open-ended. In an equally ambivalent discussion, Jo Shaw suggests that European citizenship 'has not found a secure and comfortable position in debates about a "new" constitutionalism of the Union'.[31] Nevertheless, she insists, like von Bogdandy, that this is a dynamic process of 'polity' building. These assertions of an emerging new principle of citizenship have no grounding in law whatsoever.

These theorists, I believe, put the cart before the horse. They assume that the aim of European citizenship is indeed to prepare the ground for real citizenship. Yet EU citizenship has none of the features of constitutional citizenship and performs an entirely different function. The comparison to national citizenship strengthens the sense of paradox and ultimately creates great legal uncertainty in very sensitive cases of immigration, residence, and personal status, as is evident from the facts in the cases of *Zambrano, McCarthy*, and *Dereci*.

The recent judgment by the Grand Chamber in *Chavez*, issued in May 2017, confirmed the principle of *Zambrano*, ruling that a mother enjoys a right of residence in the country of her child's citizenship. The logic, again, is that the child should not be forced to accompany his or her mother abroad, in case she is forced to leave the country.[32] The Grand Chamber's restatement will perhaps settle matters, and is certainly welcome, but it does not touch on the fundamental questions. The court repeated the *Zambrano* doctrine without explanation or any further refinement. We still lack a coherent and comprehensive theory of European citizenship. The future and livelihood of persons involved in all kinds of immigration proceedings depend on a clear application of the principles of citizenship of EU law. It is therefore essential that we provide clear and coherent guidance on EU citizenship. The theories of imminent nation-building seem wide of the mark.

[29] See Armin von Bogdandy, 'Founding Principles' in Armin von Bogdandy and Jurgen Bast (eds), *Principles of European Constitutional Law* (Oxford: Hart, 2009) 11–54. For a similar attitude of resignation see also Stefan Kadelbach, 'Union Citizenship' in ibid 443–78.

[30] ibid p. 54. Of course, stability can be the result of incoherence. Bad law or corrupt law often fails to surprise those living under it.

[31] Jo Shaw, 'Citizenship: Contrasting Dynamics' in Paul Craig and Grainne de Burca (eds), *The Evolution of EU Law*, 2nd edn (Oxford: Oxford University Press, 2011) 575, at 597.

[32] Case C-133/15 *Chavez-Vilchez and Others v Raad van bestuur van de Sociale verzekeringsbank* (Grand Chamber), ECLI:EU:C:2017:354, [2018] QB 103.

7.3 Transnational Liberty

In my view, the comparison of European citizenship to some kind of constitutional citizenship fails in at least three ways. First, European citizenship does not even attempt to provide equal or uniform standing to citizens as persons. This is a matter entirely left to domestic constitutional law. It is done separately for each jurisdiction, hence it entails that there will not be a *single* bundle of rights of European citizenship. There will be as many bundles as there are member states. Second, the EU does not itself attempt to award equal political rights to citizens, only the states can do so. Third, the EU does not have the power to raise revenue via taxation in order to distribute the benefits and burdens of social life by way of a social citizenship. Again, this is something that the states do. So, in effect, EU citizenship is not a principle of equality at all.[33]

For all these reasons, European citizenship is a different principle to that of constitutional citizenship. It is a principle appropriate to transnational organizations. It consists of a reciprocal arrangement between the member states of the EU to avoid some of the worst inequalities that result from being a foreigner. EU law awards some rights of equality to persons who happen to be under the jurisdiction of another state, as in *Grzelczyk*,[34] *Zambrano, Baumbast*,[35] and *Zhu and Chen*.[36] These cases show that the purpose of European citizenship is not to create a floor or basic set of rights (and duties) of citizenship common to all European citizens. These are things left to the member states.[37] The member states are only under a different obligation to give the same social rights that they give to their own nationals to the citizens of the EU if the latter have a 'real link' with the host member states. Under this principle, if a member state offers a very low and perhaps inadequate unemployment benefit, and no other support to being unemployed, then EU citizenship offers no other remedy. There is no minimum duty of assistance or social justice or solidarity under EU law. There is only a right of equal treatment for those that qualify. Such an arrangement is something entirely different to that

[33] A similar conclusion is drawn by Floris de Witte, *Justice in the EU: The Emergence of Transnational Solidarity* (Oxford: Oxford University Press, 2015) 124, where he concludes: 'In elaborating the commitments of communitarian solidarity it seems that the Court is led by the desire to force Member States to undertake this exercise of opening up their national citizenships, rather than to elaborate a range of normative commitments that supranational communitarian solidarity would require all Member States to converge around.'

[34] Case C-184/99 *Grzelczyk* [2001] ECR I-6193.

[35] Case C–413/99 *Baumbast* [2001] ECR I-7091.

[36] Case C-200/02 *Zhu and Chen* [2004] ECR I-9925

[37] See e. g. Case C-224/98 *D'Hoop* [2002] ECR I-6191, par. 38, Case C-138/02 *Collins* [2004] ECR I-2703, par. 69; Case C-258/04 *Ioannidis* [2005] ECR I-8275, par. 30; Case C-209/03 *Bidar* [2005] ECR I-2119, paras 55 and 56. By contrast, in the US such entitlements are automatic with residence. See for example *Edwards v California*, 314 US 160 (1941); *Shapiro v Thompson*, 394 US 618 (1969); *Saenz v Roe*, 526 US 489 (1999). See A. P. van der Mei, 'Freedom of Movement for Indigents: A Comparative Analysis of American Constitutional Law and European Community Law' 19 *Arizona Journal of International & Comparative Law* (2002) 803.

which applies to constitutional citizenship. This feature of European citizenship shows that it is a very different political principle to ordinary 'citizenship'.

Something similar in fact has taken place with the protection of fundamental rights in the EU. The Charter of Fundamental Rights does not create a uniform law of human rights in the EU. Article 6(1) TEU provides that the Charter has the same legal value as the Treaties. Yet the Charter is not designed to have exactly the same effect. Whereas it fully binds EU law-making bodies—and has given rise to some remarkable judgments striking down EU legislation—[38] it applies in a much less rigorous way vis-à-vis the member states. Article 53 of the Charter states that 'Nothing in this Charter shall be interpreted as restricting or adversely affecting human rights and fundamental freedoms as recognised, in their respective fields of application, by Union law and international law and by international agreements ... and by the Member States' constitutions.' The provision is not entirely clear and interpretations vary.[39] Aida Torres Pérez in fact argues that the 'commitment to the European integration process does not in itself justify homogenizing fundamental rights'.[40] Whatever the best interpretation, it is clear that, just as with citizenship, the protection of fundamental rights by the European Union is something that is shared with the legal orders of the member states. It is not something that the European Union can do on its own without at the same time taking into account domestic law. European citizenship, just like the protection of fundamental rights under EU law, is not about creating a single and uniform law of rights and duties of citizenship that are common in all the member states. It aims instead at creating reciprocal commitments of *equal* treatment—not *uniform* treatment.

Here we need to return to our discussion of reciprocity, which I started in Chapter 6. I showed there how international legal structures in the EU have created transnational accountability on the basis of reciprocity.[41] Here we are dealing with another manifestation of the same idea. When the member states introduced European citizenship as a principle in the Maastricht Treaty, they effectively created a multilateral and reciprocal arrangement to treat other's citizens with fairness. They established that those citizens who, for one reason or another, acquired a permanent link with a host state would be protected by the same rights that applied to that state's citizens. Once a European citizen participated in the economy

[38] See Joined Cases C-293/12 and C-594/12 *Digital Rights Ireland et al*, 08 April 2014, ECLI:EU:C:2014:238, where the court found that Directive 2006/24 on date retention was invalid as an unacceptable interference with fundamental rights.

[39] For interpretations see Koen Lenaerts, 'Exploring the Limits of the EU Charter of Fundamental Rights' 8 *European Constitutional Law Review* (2012) 375–403; Aida Torres Pérez, *Conflicts of Rights in the European Union: A Theory of Supranational Adjudication* (Oxford: Oxford University Press, 2009) 76–84.

[40] ibid 92.

[41] See for example Robert O. Keohane, 'Reciprocity in International Relations' 40 *International Relations* (1986) 1–27.

of a host state as a contributor and stakeholder in its success, he or she gained equal standing which lasted even after they stopped being economically active.

This reciprocal protection of persons who have become - or used to be - economic agents in a host state is of course something very different from recognizing a common constitutional citizenship for all. It is not a formal recognition of membership or a legal act with permanent and formal, legal and political, results. It does not create a new bond with a political community. It just creates new legal consequences for the existing one. European citizenship arises only after the real participation of the economic agent in a cooperative activity in the host state and after his or her active engagement in a productive role there. An economically active resident becomes a kind of joint investor in the collective well-being of an economic community. A citizen may come and go as he or she pleases without losing the rights of citizenship. Citizenship is formal. Active residence, however, is substantive. The nationals of the European Union do not derive citizenship rights from being nationals of member states alone, but by having become active agents within another member state.

The way in which reciprocity explains European citizenship is evident in *Baumbast*, the first case on European citizenship and one of the most important. In this case for the first time and against the contrary submissions of the Commission, the United Kingdom, and Germany, the Court of Justice established the independent status of a right to citizenship in EU law. Mr Baumbast was a German national who had spent several years as a migrant worker in the United Kingdom but who was no longer employed there. His wife, a third country national, was refused renewal of her residence permit in United Kingdom while he was being employed abroad, on the ground that she could not derive any rights from Mr Baumbast's rights as a migrant worker or under the then valid residence Directives.

The Court of Justice decided that the citizenship provisions of the Treaty were a sufficient legal basis to ground a right of residence for Mr Baumbast and his family. The Court said that Mr Baumbast, as a citizen of the European Union who no longer enjoyed a right of residence as a migrant worker, could enjoy there a right of residence by direct application of the [then Article 18(1) EC], but with some important conditions, including whether he had sufficient means to support his family. The court ruled that the exercise of that right was subject to the limitations and conditions referred to in that provision subject to the principle of proportionality. Such conditions are now recast by the 2004 Directive, but the essence of the judgment remains valid.

What kinds of rights did Mr Baumbast enjoy under the status of citizenship and why? The Court relied on the provisions of the then valid residence directive and in particular the test of being a burden on the social services of the host member state to establish conditions for citizenship rights. What gave Mr Baumbast his rights as a European citizenship was not just his German nationality, but the fact that he was of independent means and had medical insurance in Germany. Without them he would not have enjoyed rights of residence in the United Kingdom:

> As regards the limitations and conditions resulting from the provisions of secondary legislation, Article 1(1) of Directive 90/364 provides that Member States can require of the nationals of a Member State who wish to enjoy the right to reside within their territory that they themselves and the members of their families be covered by sickness insurance in respect of all risks in the host Member State and have sufficient resources to avoid becoming a burden on the social assistance system of the host Member State during their period of residence... In any event, the limitations and conditions which are referred to in Article 18 EC and laid down by Directive 90/364 are based on the idea that the exercise of the right of residence of citizens of the Union can be subordinated to the legitimate interests of the Member States. In that regard, according to the fourth recital in the preamble to Directive 90/364 beneficiaries of the right of residence must not become an unreasonable burden on the public finances of the host Member State.'[42]

The Court was not taking European citizenship to depend only on the formal rights of legal citizenship related perhaps to political membership. There was no suggestion that Mr Baumbast has participated in the 'polity-building' process that Jo Shaw took citizenship to be. There is no test of having voted or participated in any political activity whatsoever. Moreover, there was no formality in the rights identified by the Court. The rights of residence would have been lost if the circumstances changed. So neither nationality, nor formal citizenship were at issue.

What decided the case was Mr Baumbast's economic agency, or the fact that he had been part of the workforce in the United Kingdom and had created some corresponding duties of fairness. The Court declared that as a matter of reciprocal arrangement between the member states any of their citizens who have been economically active in the EU and are not a burden on social services should enjoy rights of residence. This has now been formalized in the new Directive on residence. The mechanism for granting those rights, however, is the fact of having become a *stakeholder* in the relevant society, by being economically active—as Mr Baumbast had been active in the past and his family were continuing to be active—in the host state and not imposing any burden on it.

A similar principle was stated in the equally well known case of *Collins*.[43] The Court was asked to assess the eligibility of a jobseeker from Ireland in the United Kingdom a few days after his arrival. Under what conditions do European citizens derive rights of social assistance? The court ruled once again that the Court repeated the well-known principle that nationals of a member state seeking

[42] Case C-413/99 *Baumbast* [2001] ECR I-7091, paras 87–90.
[43] Case C-138/02 *Collins* [2004] ECR I-2703.

employment in another member state may have rights to access the labour market but not rights to 'social and tax advantages'. The Court of Justice held that, while the residence requirement applied by the United Kingdom was indirectly discriminatory, it could be justified if a residency requirement was a necessary and proportionate means to establish a 'real' or 'genuine' link between the jobseeker and the labour market. No such test can be justified on the basis of a doctrine of nationality or formal citizenship. What the principle of 'real link' requires is active economic membership, such that creates the ordinary rights and duties of *reciprocity*.

At the start of my argument I set out Francis Jacobs's elegant formulation of European citizenship as 'a commonality of rights and obligations uniting Union citizens by a common bond transcending Member State nationality'.[44] I have been searching for this common bond in the last few pages. We cannot find it in the constitutional analogy. The European Union is neither a community of national membership nor an egalitarian political community providing its members equal rights by virtue of its laws. As we have seen, the rights associated by European Union citizenship are rights recognized by the individual member states and extended to certain persons under EU law, on the basis of reciprocity. As we have seen, the fact that the analogy with constitutional citizenship does not work does not mean that European citizenship is empty or without meaning. The rights and duties of European citizenship are real and constitute a form of transnational citizenship under a principle of reciprocity.[45] But they are not comparable to constitutional citizenship'.

We have found that European citizenship becomes engaged when a national of a member state moves to another member state in order to work, or to study, or as a person of independent means. In all three cases he or she actively participates in the economic life of the host state. By entering the work force, studying, or settling in that state, this person becomes a stakeholder or a participant in a scheme of co-operation. This act creates reciprocal rights and duties under a principle of fairness. The source of these rights is in some sense the European Union itself, but more accurately the member states, which grant particular rights to each other's citizens according to their own laws and on the basis of reciprocity. These rights are rights of equal treatment. They are not self-standing entitlements to membership. They do not signify the creation of a new community or a new social bond—only the extension of the existing ones.

[44] Case C-274/96, *Bickel and Franz* [1998] ECR I-07637, Opinion of the Advocate General, par. 23. AG Jacobs went on to add: 'The introduction of that notion was largely inspired by the concern to bring the Union closer to its citizens and to give expression to its character as more than a purely economic union. That concern is reflected in the removal of the word 'economic' from the Community's name (also effected by the Treaty on European Union) and by the progressive introduction into the EC Treaty of a wide range of activities and policies transcending the field of the economy.'

[45] I am therefore in agreement with Justine Lacroix, 'Is Transnational Citizenship (Still) Enough?' in Dimitry Kochenov, Gráinne de Búrca, and Andrew Williams (eds), *Europe's Justice Deficit?* (London: Hart Publishing, 2015) 177–90.

7.4 Citizenship and Obligation

I have argued that the key to European citizenship is not nation-building but reciprocity. But if citizenship is not about a new political community but about the extension of rights of residence and social support in existing member states on the basis of reciprocity, then, conversely, European citizenship does not create the corresponding duties of constitutional citizenship. Philosophers call this type of obligation 'political obligation', and they think it to citizenship and to membership in a political community.[46] Such an obligation exists independently of other moral obligations. But if the EU is not a political community on its own, then no such kind of obligation to it arises.[47]

This must be true even though the European Union has created not just rules and legal instruments but also legislative and judicial institutions that aim to apply to persons and states directly, without the intervention of any state. It is obvious that these do not create a new state and do not set up a new constitutional citizenship. But do they create new and independent moral obligations to obey them? They seem apt for it, since they are expected to be applicable directly to persons. Yet the problem is that the EU, as a creature of international law, escapes the normal architecture of the state-citizen relationship. So how can the EU generate any political obligation? The EU is perhaps like the WTO or the International Criminal Court, whose decisions take place outside the normal procedures of constitutional process. They are not controlled by political mechanisms accountable to the citizens of any single state, but by state representatives and complex diplomatic conferences.

This is a problem for international law that has been stressed by a number of political philosophers. Jeff McMahan, for example, has raised the issue that the international laws of war have a highly questionable justification. He notes that 'it has not been satisfactorily explained how, by establishing political relations among themselves, people could confer on themselves permission to treat others in ways that would be impermissible in the absence of those relations'.[48] He calls this the challenge of 'collectivism' and he deploys it in an argument that seeks to challenge the coherence of a morality and law of the conduct of war, also known as '*ius in bello*'. He notes that killing is wrong even if under the supposed justification of a declaration of war. How can a state declaring war according to the rules of public international law change the wrongness of killing?[49]

[46] See for example George Klosko, *Political Obligations* (Oxford: Oxford University Press, 2005) and the works discussed below in section 7.2.

[47] I develop this point more fully in Pavlos Eleftheriadis, 'Citizenship and Obligation' in Julie Dickson and Pavlos Eleftheriadis (eds), *Philosophical Foundations of European Union Law* (Oxford: Oxford University Press, 2012) 159–88.

[48] Jeff McMahan, 'Laws of War' in Samantha Besson and John Tasioulas (eds), *The Philosophy of International Law* (Oxford: Oxford University Press, 2010) 493, at 503.

[49] Echoing the same idea, A. John Simmons observes that: 'States are not entitled to demand from unwilling inhabitants anything that one person may not demand from another independent of states.'

Liam Murphy has pursued an analogous argument about the moral responsibility of individuals for the actions of their own states, which international lawyers sometimes call the question of 'international responsibility'. He argues against the 'political view of the state'—namely the view that considers that states have moral standing on the basis of some 'deontological test', according to which 'the state "engages the will" of its subjects when it acts in their name' and therefore creates obligations for them both domestically and internationally.[50] Murphy argues that this view in the end 'personifies' the state.[51] It fails to account for the legitimacy of the state system as we have it today, however, because 'deontological accounts ... are either implausible on their own terms or if plausible do not in fact show the rule of any states over all their subjects to be legitimate (because few people actually consent, for example)'.[52] For these reasons Murphy suggests an instrumental and therefore contingent and specific justification of the state system. For this view there is no room for a theory of the overall legitimacy of the international system. Each particular measure is to be assessed separately on its substantive merits.

The challenge posed by the arguments of Murphy and McMahan are unsettling because they are plausible and far-reaching. If they are right, then international institutions can create no political obligation. The EU will be one of them.. If that is correct, there cannot be *any* political obligation arising from the actions of institutions of an international body such as the United Nations or a regional body such as the European Union.

This argument, however, does not succeed. We need to return to the arguments I made in Chapter 2. I argued there that states have moral standing on account of their institutional structure. If there is a moral duty to obey the laws of a state on account of its constitutional legitimacy, then there will also be a moral duty to obey the international treaties made by legitimate states. Political obligation is fully cosmopolitan when connected to the law of nations.

The law of nations must have the same standing as the laws of the states that jointly create it. If there is a natural duty of justice to respect a legitimate state, then there must be the same duty to respect the law made by legitimate states.

John Rawls, whose arguments we discussed briefly at Chapter 2, explains the 'natural duty' of justice in this way:

> A further feature of natural duties is that they hold between persons irrespective of their institutional relationships; they obtain between all as equal moral

Simmons, 'Justification and Legitimacy' in *Justification and Legitimacy: Essays on Rights and Obligations* (Cambridge: Cambridge University Press, 2001) 122, at 139.

[50] Liam Murphy, 'International Responsibility' in Besson and Tasioulas (eds), *The Philosophy of International Law* (n. 48) 299 at 308.
[51] ibid 313.
[52] ibid 308.

> persons. In this sense the natural duties are owed not only to definite individuals, say to those cooperating together in a particular social arrangement, but to persons generally. This feature in particular suggests the propriety of the adjective 'natural'.[53]

These duties, Rawls tells us, are owed to every person. But if they are owed to persons, and not states, then they may also be owed to other person vis a vis the law of nations.

Kant makes a similar same point about the natural duty of justice. He writes that the civil condition is not simply a union for some common end, but a union which is 'in itself an end' and which is the 'unconditional and first duty in any external relation of people in general, who cannot help mutually affecting one another'.[54] Setting up a commonwealth that complies with the principles of equal liberty is thus the 'supreme formal condition' (*conditio sine qua non*) of all other external duties, without which no external duty is possible. The principle is *necessary* and *formal* because no empirical end can be the focus of a similar agreement: 'for, since people differ in their thinking about happiness and how each would have it constituted, their wills with respect to it cannot be brought under any common principle and so under any external law harmonizing with everyone's freedom'.[55] But if this duty exists for states, it must also exist for the law that states make in their mutual relations.

The European Union is a creation of legitimate states with their own moral standing. When they create the concept of European citizenship, they do not seek to cancel their own statehood or citizenship, but to extend some of the rights of citizenship on the basis of fairness and according to reciprocal arrangements, subject to institutions of transnational accountability. In effect, through European citizenship the member states recognize their own moral standing. Direct effect is not therefore the result of the European Union as an entity replacing the member states, but the result of them *coming together* in order to set up common institutions under the law of nations.

7.5 Liberty and Cosmopolitan Rights

Our argument for a European principle of liberty is based on the moral force of the law of nations, as one dimension of human attempt to live side by side with other

[53] John Rawls, *A Theory of Justice*, revised edition (Oxford: Oxford University Press, 1999) 99.

[54] Immanuel Kant, 'On the Common Saying: That May be Correct in Theory, but is of no Use in Practice' ' in Kant, *Practical Philosophy* trans. and edited by Mary J. Gregor (Cambridge: Cambridge University Press, 1996), 8:289, p. 290.

[55] Kant, 'On the Common Saying', 8:290, p. 291.

persons, while complying with the requirements of justice.[56] This is perhaps why Rawls says that the first familiar and traditional principle of justice among free and democratic peoples is that 'peoples are free and independent, and their freedom and independence are to be respected by other peoples'.[57] Kant, like Rawls, concludes that perpetual peace does not need a world state, but the 'federalism of free states' that come together voluntarily in creating a league of nations.[58] Just like the duty of jurisdiction and the right to hospitality, the duty to set up appropriate institutions of international law is a *moral* requirement. When this duty of setting up international principles of conduct is appropriately exercised, then persons will have a natural duty of civility towards them. The argument proceeds in exactly the same way as in the case for domestic laws.

EU law, just like international law, does not have its own jurisdiction or its own citizenship. It does not compete with states for law application, adjudication, and enforcement. Because EU law does not compete with any constitutional law, it can coexist with all of them without contradiction. We saw above that Jeff McMahan has questioned the idea that the establishment of political relations among one group of people could create duties on outsiders.[59] But the state is not just a set of agreed relations for those involved in them. It is not just a series of transactions. The state is a set of impersonal political institutions consisting of both offices of decision-making and specific conditions of action. The content of political institutions is never merely domestic. Both constitutional law and international law are essential for satisfying the natural duties of justice.

The same argument provides the answer to Murphy. His objection was that the 'political view of the state' personified the state and gave a false account of international responsibility for actions of governments.[60] Yet the cosmopolitan argument offers a different picture. Murphy is right that a despotic government is illegitimate and therefore fails to morally bind its citizens. But this entails the converse result for legitimate government. By electing or otherwise appointing a government we choose officeholders who will run our political and legal affairs. The role of such offices includes the maintenance of foreign relations and the responsibility for those foreigners that happen to arrive—for whatever reason—at our jurisdiction. Hence, when a government engages in internationally unlawful action it is not merely violating international rules. It is also violating *domestic* rules, duties that citizenship requires everyone to respect. In a way there is no difference

[56] For an excellent account of the Kantian moral argument for international law, to which my account owes a great debt and to some extent reproduces, see Amanda Perreau-Saussine, 'Immanuel Kant on International Law' in Besson and Tasioulas (eds), *The Philosophy of International Law* (n. 48) 53.

[57] John Rawls, *The Law of Peoples* (Cambridge, Mass.: Harvard University Press, 1999) 37.

[58] Kant, 'Towards Perpetual Peace', 8:354, in Kant, PP, p. 326.

[59] Jeff McMahan, 'Laws of War' in Samantha Besson and John Tasioulas (eds), *The Philosophy of International Law* (n. 48) 493, at 503.

[60] Murphy, 'International Responsibility' (n. 50) 313.

in moral standing or in source between national and international law and in that sense even monism has a point.

There is, therefore, nothing special about international duties of political obligation. International law is part of the duties of citizenship. But monism is false if it is insists in the simple analogy between the domestic legal order and the international legal order. There cannot be such an analogy. The domestic legal order is one where public rules and principles are given effect through a complete set of institutions of enforcement and adjudication (or institutions of jurisdiction). International law is not a legal system in that sense. It lacks means and principles of enforcement and adjudication, for which it always relies on state institutions. It therefore makes no assurance of public enforcement of any public rules concerning enforcement and adjudication.

There cannot be a truly international legal order that competes with a domestic legal order. By definition, the law of nations and constitutional law address different sets of circumstances. International law has no parallel process to the domestic setting up of an order of public rules and institutions. It promises no institutional enforcement and provides for no such procedure. European institutions complement and do not seek to replace those of the member states. The same applies to European citizenship, which does not seek to *replace* the citizenship of member states but create a new set of cosmopolitan rights for persons. It is for this reason that cosmopolitanism as a principle of transnational reciprocity is the second public principle of the European Union.

European citizenship is thus a principle of liberty. It creates new entitlements for persons to move, reside, and work in other European states, which would have been impossible without the European Union. It removes obstacles created by state institutions for the benefit of all European citizens as well as others. These rights became real precisely because states can trust each other, in a context of reciprocity provided by the single market and the EU institutional framework. The rights of freedom created by the European treaties are not limited to those who wish to work, but are extended also to those who are not working, such as those who have stopped working in order to start a family, students, and pensioners. In some cases, these rights benefit children with European Union citizenship,[61] or persons who may become stateless.[62] The Charter of Fundamental Rights is giving further substance to these rights of liberty. The common thread of these principles and rulings is the reciprocal liberty of the citizens of the member states. In this sense, the European Union is not merely an international, but also a cosmopolitan project. It organizes the law of nations in order to create new rights for persons, not merely governments.

[61] Case C-34/09 *Ruiz Zambrano* [2011].

[62] Case C-135/08 *Rottmann v Freistaat Bayern*.

8
Fairness

I now turn to a new set of questions in order to introduce a new principle of EU law. [1] I call it the principle of fairness. It answers the questions of justice that arise in the relations among the member states. These questions became pressing in Europe when the financial crisis of 2008 affected states in radically differently ways. The Eurozone members took steps to assist the worst affected among them: Greece, Ireland, Portugal, Spain, and Cyprus. The European Union made available funds for emergency loans even though the original assumption was that there would be no state bailouts.[2] In due course, the members of the Eurozone sought to amend and supplement the Treaties. They created a new international institution, the European Stability Mechanism by way of a treaty of international law that is not part of the EU Treaties, with a mandate to assist member states in financial troubles.[3] At the same time, and in a significant shift of policy, the European Central Bank started purchasing sovereign bonds. In the end, the financial assistance programmes helped the burdened states weather the storm so that they all remained in the Eurozone without defaulting on their loans. All of them, however, suffered great economic damage, loss of output, and high rates of unemployment.

The Court of Justice has found that these assistance operations were lawful.[4] But what was their moral character? Were they manifestations of justice, discharging an obligation of solidarity towards the weaker states? Or were they simply instances of prudence, not strictly required by law or morality, only expedient responses to an emergency? Or were these new loans far too generous, unjustly transferring resources from the responsible to the irresponsible? These are still deeply controversial questions. Some believe that the Eurozone did too little to assist its weakest

[1] An earlier version of this chapter was published as 'Corrective Justice Among States' 1 *Jus Cogens* (2020).

[2] Some scholars argued against this initial assumption with regard to Art. 122(2) TFEU. See for example Kaarlo Tuori and Klaus Tuori, *The Eurozone Crisis: A Constitutional Analysis* (Cambridge: Cambridge University Press, 2014) 138 ff.

[3] Extensive and very helpful accounts of the constitutional legal aspects of the crisis are offered in ibid. Alicia Hinarejos, *The Euro Area Crisis in Constitutional Perspective* (Oxford: Oxford University Press, 2015); Federico Fabbrini, *Economic Governance in Europe: Comparative Paradoxes and Constitutional Challenges* (Oxford: Oxford University Press, 2016).

[4] See Case C-370/12, *Pringle*, ECLI:EU:C:2012:756, and Case C-62/14, *Gauweiler et al. v Deutscher Bundestag*, ECLI:EU:C:2015:400, which was a preliminary reference from the German Constitutional Court in BVerfG, Beschluss des Zweiten Senats vom 14. January 2014—2 BvR 2728/13—Rn. (1–24).

A Union of Peoples. Pavlos Eleftheriadis. Oxford University Press (2020). © Oxford University Press.
DOI: 10.1093/oso/9780198854173.001.0001

members.[5] Others think it did too much.[6] All of these positions rely on some conception of what is fair or unfair. These matters depend on our interpretation of the purpose and nature of the Eurozone agreements but they also turn on deeper assumptions about the moral obligations arising out of long-term cooperation.

In this chapter and Chapter 9, I argue that obligations of solidarity from one state to another are real under the treaties. They derive directly both from the treaties and the ongoing practices of the member states. But the rationale of these obligations is not one of fair distribution. Their origin is not in distributive justice. Their rationale is that of fair *redress* for unfairness, which originates in corrective justice. Solidarity in the European Union, I will argue, is a matter of bilateral corrective justice, which informs the established treaties and gives them meaning.[7] This is not just a moral interpretation, but also a legal interpretation, manifested, I will argue, not only in the practice of the member states but also in the judgments of the Court of Justice. Fairness, understood as justice in cooperation, is the third fundamental principle of the European Union as a Union of Peoples.

8.1 From Fairness to Solidarity

The vocabulary of justification is not optional in legal analysis. Fairness is always a matter closely connected to any interpretation of legal agreements between two or more parties. This is so both as a matter of the moral character of law in general, as many legal philosophers have shown,[8] but also as a matter of the specific requirements of agreements, including international agreements.

[5] See Ashoka Mody, *Eurotragedy: A Drama in Nine Acts* (Oxford: Oxford University Press, 2018); Joseph E. Stiglitz, *The Euro: How a Common Currency Threatens the Future of Europe* (New York: Norton, 2016) 85–144.

[6] See Udo di Fabio, 'Karlsruhe Makes a Referral' 15 *German Law Journal* (2014) 107–10; Hans Werner Sinn, *The Euro Trap: On Bursting Bubbles, Budgets, and Beliefs* (Oxford: Oxford University Press, 2014) 343. Sinn thought that rather than new loans, Greece should have been given significant debt relief: 'The right mixture of debt relief, privatization, and wealth levies could be jointly negotiated in a Paris Club debt conference convened to reset the Eurozone. The European debt crisis has many causes, and creditors and debtors alike share the responsibility. A way to distribute the burden fairly should thus be sought—and it is important that it be found soon' (ibid).

[7] The question is relevant to EU law, but any answer would be relevant to any multilateral international framework. If states are agents of justice, as we argued they are in Chapter 2, then we may be able to transpose the principles of private law to other international relations, for example the World Trade Organization or the World Health Organization and others. Such parallels are, of course, a novel issue in the theory of international relations. Political and legal philosophy have not spent much time addressing them. They arose in the course of the twentieth century as the intense interactions between states, companies, and persons created a new modern age of globalization. Given how complex these questions are, lawyers and philosophers have been slow to address them.

[8] I develop this point in Section 3.3. For further arguments on this geneal view of law see Ronald Dworkin, *Law's Empire* (Cambridge, Mass.: Harvard University Press, 1986); N. E. Simmonds, *Law as a Moral Idea* (Oxford: Oxford University Press, 2007); Robert Alexy, *The Argument from Injustice: A Reply to Legal Positivism* (Oxford: Oxford University Press, 2009).

This moral dimension of promises and agreements is well understood by the law of contract. In many jurisdictions the law requires 'good faith' in the interpretation and enforcement of contracts, especially in cases where cooperation is for an indefinite period. The idea of 'good faith' cannot be understood outside a moral framework, however elementary this may be. The distinguished English judge Tom Bingham described the role that fairness plays in the interpretation of long-term agreements in English and foreign law as follows:

> In many civil law systems, and perhaps in most legal systems outside the common law world, the law of obligations recognises and enforces an overriding principle that in making and carrying out contracts parties should act in good faith. This does not simply mean that they should not deceive each other, a principle which any legal system must recognise; its effect is perhaps most aptly conveyed by such metaphorical colloquialisms as 'playing fair', 'coming clean' or 'putting one's cards face upwards on the table.' It is in essence a principle of fair open dealing ... English law has, characteristically, committed itself to no such overriding principle but has developed piecemeal solutions in response to demonstrated problems of unfairness.[9]

In the United States the Second Restatement of Contracts requires that '[e]very contract imposes upon each party a duty of good faith and fair dealing in its performance and enforcement'.[10] English law takes a narrower view, but it too refuses to enforce contracts that parties willingly entered into, if their terms are 'unconscionable' or are the result of undue influence exercised due to unequal bargaining power.[11] Even in English law unfairness can occasionally be a reason for holding a deal unenforceable.

Irrespective of the position in contract law, the principle of 'good faith' is also an established principle of the interpretation of treaties of international law. Article 26 of the Vienna Convention of the Law of Treaties, which bears the title '*pacta sunt servanda*' simply states: 'Every treaty in force is binding upon the parties to it and

[9] *Interfoto Picture Library Ltd v Stilletto Visual Programmes Ltd* [1989] 1 QB 433, at 439. See also *Director General of Fair Trading v First National Bank* [2001] UKHL 52, [2002] 1 AC 507 at [17] (Lord Bingham of Cornhill).

[10] *Restatement (Second) of Contracts* par. 205. cf Uniform Commercial Code ss 1–203. See Robert S. Summers, 'The Conceptualisation of Good Faith in American Contract Law: A General Account' in Zimmermann and Whittaker (eds), *Good Faith in European Contract Law* (Cambridge: Cambridge University Press, 2000) 118–44.

[11] A relevant case is *Lloyds Bank Ltd v Bundy* [1974] EWCA 8, [1975] QB 326, where Lord Denning summarized the doctrine of 'inequality of bargaining power' as follows: 'By virtue of it, the English law gives relief to one who, without independent advice, enters into a contract or transfers property for a consideration which is grossly inadequate, when his bargaining power is grievously impaired by reason of his own needs or desires, or by his own ignorance or infirmity, coupled with undue influences or pressures brought to bear on him by or for the benefit of the other.' The House of Lords has refused to endorse such a wide principle, however.

must be performed by them in good faith.'[12] The reference to 'good faith' means that any interpretation is subject to context and may evolve with the expectations of the parties.[13] The general rules are that a treaty is to be interpreted in good faith in accordance with the ordinary meaning to be given to the terms of the treaty 'in their context' and in 'the light of its object and purpose' because 'each of these elements guide the interpreter in establishing what the Parties actually intended, or their common will'.[14] It follows, therefore, that the justification of the assistance programmes as a matter of the law of treaties of the Eurozone can turn on issues of 'good faith' or fairness. It cannot simply be a matter of the narrow reading of explicit technical rules. Whether the law permits such assistance will depend on the context, intention, and nature of the parties that entered into the Eurozone agreements as these evolved over time.

These general accounts of fairness do not decide the issue of the fairness of the Eurozone. They do, however, put the question of solidarity in context as a specific manifestation of a well-known question. Long-term agreements, be they private or agreements among states, must be interpreted in light of a theory of fairness, but they do not always create obligations of solidarity. Whether fairness requires solidarity will depend on the specific terms and practices of each specific agreement. If the Eurozone agreements do create such obligations, it must be for a reason. Most theorists say that no such reason exists, given how the Eurozone agreements are currently structured.

The philosopher Jürgen Habermas writes that the present economic rationales of the Eurozone are incompatible with social justice and democratic legitimacy: 'A technocracy without democratic roots would not have the motivation to accord sufficient weight to the demands of the electorate for a just distribution of income and property, for status security, public services and collective goods when these conflict with the systemic demands for competitiveness and economic growth.'[15] Habermas contrasts 'technocratic' blueprints for dealing with the crisis and a

[12] For an interpretation see Oliver Dörr, 'Article 26: *Pacta Sunt Servanda*' in Oliver Dörr and Kirsten Schmalenbach (eds), *Vienna Convention on the Law of Treaties* (Berlin: Springer, 2011) 427–51.

[13] For this point see Eirik Bjorge, 'The Vienna Rules, Evolutionary Interpretation, and the Intentions of the Parties' in Andrea Bianchi, Daniel Peat, and Matthew Windsor (eds), *Interpretation in International Law* (Oxford: Oxford University Press, 2015) 189, especially at 203–4.

[14] The quotes are from the 'Decision Regarding Delimitation of the Border between Eritrea and Ethiopia', XXV *Reports of International Arbitral Awards* (2002) 83–195, at pp. 109–10 'The meaning of these Treaties is thus a central feature of this dispute. In interpreting them, the Commission will apply the general rule that a treaty is to be interpreted in good faith in accordance with the ordinary meaning to be given to the terms of the treaty in their context and in the light of its object and purpose. Each of these elements guides the interpreter in establishing what the Parties actually intended, or their "common will," as Lord McNair put it in the *Palena* award.'

[15] Jürgen Habermas, 'Democracy, Solidarity, and the European Crisis' in Luuk van Middelaar and Philippe van Parijs (eds), *After the Storm: How to Save Democracy in Europe* (Tielt: Lannoo, 2015) 95, at 101; Jürgen Habermas, *The Lure of Technocracy* (Cambridge: Polity Press, 2015). For a parallel argument see Rainer Forst, 'Justice, Democracy and the Right to Justification: Reflections on Jürgen Neyer's Normative Theory of the European Union' in Dimitry Kochenov, Gráinne de Búrca, and Andrew Williams (eds) *Europe's Justice Deficit?* (London: Hart Publishing, 2015) 227–34.

project for a 'supranational democracy in the core of Europe'.[16] By the term 'democratic roots' Habermas seems to imply that solidarity needs to be supported by the identification of each person with a single political community as its citizen. He says that the EU's 'technocratic' response runs the risk of lacking 'the motivation to accord sufficient weight to the demands of the electorate for a just distribution of income and property, for status security, public services and collective goods when these conflict with the systemic demands for competitiveness and economic growth'.[17]

Habermas' argument has a compelling logic which is shared by standard defences of the welfare state. He assumes that citizens of the same state will have the psychological motivation to recognize a duty of solidarity to one another, normally expressed by ideas and principles of social justice. This is a very reasonable assumption. Indeed, the EU treaties recognize the division of the Union into states and an associated division of them into welfare states.[18] As a matter of fact European citizens do not feel the same 'identification' with those they consider 'outsiders', inside or outside the European Union. Europe's task, therefore, is to expand outward the bonds of community that exist within each state. This is why Habermas argues that the Union needs to create its own 'democratic roots'.

If this argument is right, then the introduction of meaningful solidarity in the European Union presupposes a profound emotional transformation. The citizens of the member states are to acquire an entirely new attitude towards the citizens of other member states. Habermas is clearly aware of the seriousness of this challenge. He proposes a 'real political union', which will change the social circumstances of European citizens and lead to the required emotional adjustment.[19] Social justice can then become a component of a sharing in power under the institutions of a political community. In order to achieve solidarity, we will need to abandon borders within Europe to produce a single, integrated political community.

Is this a valid argument? I do not think it is. Of course, a political community creates bonds of solidarity. But it does not follow that a duty of solidarity applies only when there are such emotional bonds. In my view obligations of solidarity can arise from less involved relations among persons or, indeed, from relations among states and other collective bodies. Solidarity certainly does not require a relationship of citizenship. Other relations can have the same outcome. The key

[16] ibid 98.

[17] ibid 101.

[18] This point is also well set out in Jürgen Neyer, *The Justification of Europe: A Political Theory of Supranational Integration* (Oxford: Oxford University Press, 2012) 35–55. For an interesting debate on this between Neyer (who sees the European Union as a project that does not seek to be federal) and Forst (who follows Habermas in accepting the federalist interpretation) see Jürgen Neyer, 'Justice and the Right to Justification: Conceptual Reflections' in Dimitry Kochenov, Gráinne de Búrca, and Andrew Williams (eds), *Europe's Justice Deficit?* (Oxford: Hart, 2015) 211–26; Rainer Forst, 'Justice, Democracy and the Right to Justification: Reflections on Jürgen Neyer's Normative Theory of the European Union' in *Europe's Justice Deficit?* 227–34.

[19] Habermas, 'Democracy, Solidarity, and the European Crisis' (n. 15) 100.

to my argument is that obligations of solidarity may arise as acts of mutual aid or redress, as matters of corrective justice. This point has been obscured by most discussions of solidarity in the European Union where the dominant language is that of distributive justice.

8.2 Distributive Claims

The European Union Treaties are not silent on solidarity. Article 3(3) TEU provides that the Union shall 'promote social justice' and promote 'economic, social and territorial cohesion, and solidarity among Member States'. Solidarity is also mentioned in Article 122 TFEU in the context of assistance in emergencies, whereby the Council may decide 'in a spirit of solidarity between member states' on measures assisting a state if 'severe difficulties arise in the supply of certain products, notably in the area of energy'. This article, however, was not invoked in the case of the financial assistance programmes.

It is not entirely clear, however, what these general statements mean. Perhaps, like other general statements in this part of the Treaties, they do not intend to create clear legal obligations, on the institutions of the European Union or the member states.[20] They are supplemented, however, by the mention of solidarity in particular policies. Solidarity is mentioned in the context of asylum policies,[21] the general 'solidarity clause' in case of natural or man-made disasters,[22] and in the detailed mechanism for distributions of funds to the member states. These funds are very important for the distribution of resources from the wealthier states to the poorer ones. They were created at various points in the history of the Union and have complex histories. The European Social Fund is covered by Articles 162 to 164 TFEU. Structural Funds are provided for in Article 175 TFEU. A Regional Development Fund is provided by Article 176 TFEU. The treaty empowers the EU to distribute funds with the aim of improving employment opportunities, strengthening social inclusion, fighting poverty, promoting education, skills, and life-long learning and developing active, comprehensive, and sustainable inclusion policies.[23]

[20] See Esin Küçük, 'Solidarity in EU Law: An Elusive Political Statement or a Legal Principle with Substance?' 23 *Maastricht Journal of European and Comparative Law* (2016) 965–83; Malcolm Ross, 'Solidarity—A New Constitutional Paradigm for the EU?' in M. Ross and Y. Borgmann-Prebil (eds), *Promoting Solidarity in the European Union* (Oxford University Press, 2010) 23–45. For a discussion of the (relatively limited) role of the Charter of Fundamental Rights in the protection of social welfare rights see Síofra O'Leary, 'Solidarity and Citizenship Rights in the Charter of Fundamental Rights of the European Union' in Grainne De Burca (ed), *EU Law, and the Welfare State: In Search of Solidarity* (Oxford: Oxford University Press, 2005) 39–87.

[21] See Article 67 TFEU and Article 80 TFEU. The principle has not, however, made any difference in practice. See Joined Cases C-411/10 and C-493/10 *N S and M E*, EU:C:2011:865, par. 93.

[22] Article 222 TFEU.

[23] The rules of distribution of these sums are set out in Regulation (EU) No 1304/2013 of the European Parliament and of the Council of 17 December 2013 on the European Social Fund and repealing Council Regulation (EC) No 1081/2006, OJ L 347, 20.12.2013, 470–86. The Regulation provides

Nevertheless, the total amount of spending on such projects is very small in relation to the overall EU economy. It is also very small in proportion to funds available within each state for social purposes. In the member states the equivalent spending ranges between 35% and 58% of Gross Domestic Product. In the total EU budget the equivalent amount is about 1% of the Gross National Income of the twenty-eight member states.[24] According to an estimate made by the Institute of Fiscal Studies, the EU's total spending on structural, cohesion, agriculture, and rural development funds accounted for about 38% of the total EU spending in 2014. The scale of redistribution involved is very modest indeed. The direct European Union social spending is about twenty or thirty times less than what occurs within a member state. The small size of these transfers strengthens the argument that solidarity in the European Union is not really a functioning principle. Solidarity may be an exclusive preserve of the member states.

Many sophisticated commentators observe that the social dimension of the EU is minimal. Commenting on the 'patchwork' of social justice provisions in EU law, Gráinne de Búrca writes that solidarity had a 'constructive potential' which could gradually 'promote a degree of solidarity and mutual responsibility—however tentative and limited at first—between states, citizens, and other residents within the enlarging European space'.[25] Such cautious endorsements of solidarity, however, cannot hide the fact that social justice is a very small part of the EU. Many authors thus take the view that, since the EU is not a state, the normal rules of distributive justice do not apply to it. Since solidarity or social justice is a principle that only applies within states (or equivalent political communities), no solidarity principle applies in the European Union, at least not yet.[26]

In this vein, Professor Christian Joerges, a leading scholar on EU law, argues that the European Union is incapable of having a proper policy towards social justice. Joerges refers to an argument made by Friedrich Carl von Savigny, the leading German legal scholar of the nineteenth century, that justice applies to private

for common principles for the implementation of five European Structural and Investment Funds: the European Regional Development Fund (ERDF), the European Social Fund (ESF), the Cohesion Fund, the European Agricultural Fund for Rural Development (EAFRD), and the European Maritime and Fisheries Fund (EMFF). The treaty articles are also supplemented by Protocol No 28 on economic, social, and territorial cohesion.

24 See James Browne, Paul Johnson, and David Phillips, *The Budget of the European Union: A Guide: IFS Briefing Note BN181* (London: Institute of Fiscal Studies, 2016).

25 Gráinne de Búrca, 'Towards European Welfare?' in Gráinne de Búrca (ed.), *EU Law, and the Welfare State: In Search of Solidarity* (Oxford: Oxford University Press, 2005) 9.

26 This is a view reflected in the writings of influential legal scholars. It is the view, for example, defended by Andrew Williams, *The Ethos of Europe: Values, Law and Justice in the EU* (Cambridge: Cambridge University Press, 2010); Alexander Somek, 'The Preoccupation with Rights and the Embrace of Inclusion: A Critique' in Dimitry Kochenov, Gráinne de Búrca, Andrew Williams (eds), *Europe's Justice Deficit?* (Oxford: Hart, 2015) 295–310; Neil Walker, 'Justice in and of the European Union', in Dimitry Kochenov, Gráinne de Búrca, Andrew Williams (eds), *Europe's Justice Deficit?*) 247–58.

relations but not to the relations between states. In Joerges' reading, Savigny has shown that 'interstate relations . . . remain in an unruly state of nature governed by power and politics rather than law'.[27] From Savigny's premise, Joerges draws the conclusion that the European Monetary Union is incapable of imposing a uniform architecture of social policy. It does not have the means. Europe has instead created a competitive 'single market' where each state seeks to have a social policy on its own, allowing for great 'socioeconomic diversity', which the institutions of the EU cannot address.

Joerges adds that the various economies have diverged rather than converged since the creation of the Union. Europe's idea of 'a highly competitive social market economy' results in the undermining of social justice and solidarity everywhere in the EU. He says that 'the socioeconomic diversity of the Union was treated with benign neglect and an institutional framework with the potential to manage the implication of this move was not established'.[28] He finds this 'fateful' for the 'prospects of Social Europe'.[29] The only policy that, for Joerges, is working at EU level is that emanating from the European Central Bank, which in his view is insensitive to the concerns of social justice. Hence, he says, the 'Maastricht arrangement was an ill-defined political compromise, rather than a sustainable accomplishment of constitutional validity and strength', which has led to 'authoritarian managerialism'.[30] The only way of overcoming this stalemate, for Joerges, is through the creation of a 'transnational democracy' through federal institutions. He insists that such a transformation is urgent, because the present arrangements do not provide a solid basis for solidarity and social justice.[31]

A similar view has been taken by Floris de Witte, who has offered an extensive and original discussion of the question of social justice in the EU. De Witte argues that justice is an 'associative commitment'. He says 'it is born and sustained by the interaction between particular groups of citizens'.[32] Nevertheless, de Witte's discussion locates justice firmly within the framework and architecture of the institutions of a *single* state. De Witte argues that the existence of the European Union 'ensures that the associative connections between citizens across borders are incorporated

[27] Christian Joerges, 'Social Justice in an Ever More Diverse Union' in Frank Vandenbroucke, Catherine Barnard, and Geert de Baere (eds), *A European Social Union after the Crisis* (Cambridge: Cambridge University Press, 2017) 92–119, at 94 (citing from Savigny's *System des Heutigen Römischen Rects*, vol. III, 1849).

[28] ibid 107.

[29] ibid 107.

[30] ibid 111. Joerges follows here similar arguments made by Fritz W. Scharpf, 'The European Social Model: Coping with the Challenges of Diversity' 40 *Journal of Common Market Studies* (2002) 645–70.

[31] A similar view is taken by Frank Vandenbroucke, who proposes a new 'Social Union' as the appropriate response to the current absence of proper institutions of solidarity. See Frank Vandenbroucke, 'The Idea of a European Social Union: A Normative Introduction' in Frank Vandenbroucke, Catherine Barnard, and Geert de Baere (eds), *A European Social Union after the Crisis* (Cambridge: Cambridge University Press, 2017) 3–46.

[32] F. de Witte, *Justice in the EU: The Emergence of Transnational Solidarity* (Oxford: Oxford University Press, 2008) 208.

within the pursuit of justice on the national level'.[33] In effect, the EU brings citizens closer to one another, by putting them 'in a social relationship' in the sense that 'all EU citizens are part of the incipient and ill-defined European polity' but also on 'the national level, where citizens of different nationalities engage with each other through a whole range of social interactions'.[34] But de Witte concludes that since the EU is in effect an international project, it does not have the potential for justice: 'The EU does not dispose of the institutional sophistication required in order legitimately to articulate an autonomous conception of supranational justice .... In consequence, the EU cannot engage in the definition of supranational ideas of equality, fairness, or distributive justice in a legitimate way'.[35]

Surprisingly perhaps, Joerges and De Witte are in agreement with the former Finance Minister of Germany, Wolfgang Schäuble. In a widely leaked 'non-paper' to the ministers of the Eurogroup on the occasion of his departure from his post in November 2017, Dr Schäuble gave a detailed account of his overall assessment of the Eurozone, where he also expressed scepticism about the potential of the European Union to achieve social justice. He said that it lacks both the mechanism for redistribution and the required institutions of democratic accountability. The paper stated that in the Ministry's view fiscal responsibilities and fiscal control belong together. It observed that there were only two ways in which the EU could maintain the symmetry of responsibilities and control:

> Either we transfer parts of national sovereignty and control of fiscal rules to the EU level ('Euro Finance Minister'), together with a greater democratic legitimacy. This would certainly require EU treaty changes to be credible. Or we agree on an intergovernmental solution.[36]

The real choice here appears to be between full union and loose intergovernmentalism. The 'non-paper' by the Finance Ministry, just like Joerges, De Witte, and Habermas, relies on the assumption that an intergovernmental institutional setting is an inappropriate institutional arrangement for the operation of solidarity. The paper therefore proposes further political union through treaty change as a priority for the future. But, as long as 'there is little willingness for treaty changes, we should follow a pragmatic two-step approach: Intergovernmental solution now, to be transposed into EU law later on'.[37]

[33] ibid 208.
[34] ibid 123.
[35] ibid 210.
[36] Available at: https://www.scribd.com/document/361120275/German-finance-ministry-non-paper-on-Eurozone-reforms.
[37] These views seem to correspond to standard views among German economists. It is commonplace in German economics departments that within the Eurozone 'ever member country has to do its homework and that relying on bailouts from others distorts incentives'; Markus K. Brunnermeier, Harold James, Jean-Pierre Landau, *The Euro and the Battle of Ideas* (Princeton: Princeton University Press, 2016) 97.

Habermas, Joerges, and De Witte share a negative claim. They suggest that solidarity is strictly limited to the national domain and cannot develop in an international context. I will now argue that this assumption is mistaken. I reject the premise that solidarity applies only within states and that solidarity does not apply to international or intergovernmental structures.

Solidarity is not identical to distribution. Solidarity, I will argue, has in fact two distinct grounds: one in distributive justice and one in corrective justice. Only distributive justice is restricted to the domestic case.

8.3 Distributive and Corrective Justice

Although the distinction between distributive and corrective justice is old and well understood, it has not, for the most part, been deployed in the debates concerning international justice.[38] When scholars refer to justice in the international context they tend to have in mind distributive claims. If distributive claims cannot be justified, then justice is irrelevant.[39] These views seem to work on a mental picture of justice relying on a central distribution of a good to beneficiaries according to criteria of need or merit. This is the typical model of the distribution of fair shares outlined by Aristotle and repeated many times in modern philosophy. It is the standard model of justice in distribution.

John Rawls too identifies social justice with distributive justice when he says on the 'subject of justice' that: 'the primary subject of [social] justice is the basic structure of society, or more exactly, the way in which the major social institutions *distribute* fundamental rights and duties and determine the division of advantages from social cooperation' (emphasis added).[40] In the case of the state, the distribution takes place through central taxation and social welfare schemes. The distribution is not from state resources, but effectively from the mostly better off taxpayers to the least well off, as they receive public assistance through public funds or through freely available services such as education and health care.

It is clear that such a model of justice cannot apply to the European Union. First, there is no central taxing authority collecting public funds. Second, there is no central spending power of such funds. Third, there are not in place any institutions with the appropriate democratic powers for deciding on the appropriate test of distribution, since the European Parliament cannot have such powers. Fourth, we do

[38] See for a valuable exception, Thana Campos, *The Global Health Crisis: Ethical Responsibilities* (Cambridge: Cambridge University Press, 2017), where the right to health is recast as an obligation of corrective or 'commutative' justice and not 'distributive' justice.

[39] This assumption is implicit, I think, in Thomas Nagel, 'The Problem of Global Justice' (2005) 33 *Philosophy and Public Affairs* 113, where 'social justice' is identified with justice in distribution. My discussion in Chapter 2 assumes that social justice is the same thing as distributive justice.

[40] John Rawls, *A Theory of Justice*, rev edn (Oxford: Oxford University Press, 1999) 6. Rawls refers to Aristotle's *Nicomachean Ethics* 1129b–1130b in support of his view of social justice; ibid 9.

not have clear institutions for the accountability of such decisions. Fifth, we do not have the underlying 'community' or 'demos' which would see the public support the transfer of funds from one part of the community to another and give meaning to mechanisms of participation as we—more or less—have in the conventional welfare systems of the states. For these reasons the advocates of political union as a pre-condition of institutions of solidarity, such as Habermas, di Fabio, and Joerges, must be right to rule out a general distributive principle for the European Union under the present institutional arrangements. If social justice makes sense only within a territorial state, then it cannot apply to the European Union as it is today.

This argument, however, is not the end of the matter. It fails to take into account the way in which solidarity works in other ways, without involving distribution. The relations between states just like the relations of persons are subject to a second dimension of justice, which since Aristotle we call 'corrective justice'. Corrective justice does not provide for the distribution of something from a central source or state but accounts for the just relations among two or more parties in the event of cooperation, exchange, or reparation.[41] Corrective justice addresses injustice by restoring the original positions between a person that suffered a loss and the person who gained a profit from the other's expense. The just redress is the arithmetic mean between the part of the earner and the part of the loser.[42]

In Ernest Weinrib's apt description, the organizing idea is that of correlativity. The 'elements of liability under corrective justice can be explicated only in terms of concepts whose normative force applies simultaneously to both parties'.[43] Unlike distributive justice, corrective justice takes the parties to be equal. For corrective justice 'liability involves a conception of fairness that recognizes the equal normative status of the two parties and treats their normative positions as mirror images of each other'.[44] These ideas have generated some very sophisticated arguments about the substance of the law of tort, contract, and unjust enrichment. There is no need to rely on these theories in any detail here. What we need for the purposes of our argument is only the idea that states are independent agents—similar to corporations or other collective agents—and subject to private law when they are co-operating towards a common project, sharing in the process rights, obligations, and risks. Such relations create mutual moral obligations from each state to all others that are analogous to legal obligations arising in contract law. I say that are merely analogous and not identical, because there is no contract law in the international sphere. Strictly speaking, there cannot be anything like contract law. There

41 For a general historical account of Aristotle's distinction between distributive and corrective justice see Izhak Englard, *Corrective and Distributive Justice: From Aristotle to Modern Times* (Oxford: Oxford University Press, 2009).

42 See ibid 8.

43 Ernest J. Weinrib, *Corrective Justice* (Oxford: Oxford University Press, 2012) 10.

44 ibid.

is no central power of enforcement in international law, so that all legal obligations are to some extent provisional.

Under international law, states can have obligations of law to one another, but they cannot rely on the jurisdiction of a common court to enforce them. So the analogy with contract is incomplete. States nevertheless owe each other duties on the basis of public international law and their agreements.

That states have mutual obligations to one another is not an original thought. In the *Law of Peoples*, Rawls argues that the international community must be based on principles of fairness that apply to states. He argues that such principles would have been adopted by well-ordered peoples in a hypothetical original position for the 'law of peoples'. In Rawls' account, the relevant agents are peoples and not citizens. He argues that inequalities between states are unjust 'because of their unjust effects on the basic structure of the Society of Peoples, and on relations among peoples and among their members'.[45] He further argues that in a scenario of an 'original position' among peoples, the parties will 'formulate guidelines for setting up cooperative organizations, and will agree to standards of fairness for trade as well as to certain provisions for mutual assistance'.[46] Nevertheless, the relevant principle of justice does not presuppose a central distributing power. It applies in a decentralized way among the various states, as a self-imposed constraint on their foreign policies by way of 'cooperative organizations' and other agreements.

In this account, the principles of international justice bind states in their mutual relations: they create obligations to exercise a particular kind of policy or to discharge their natural duties to each other. A principle of mutual aid is part of these obligations. One of the eight principles of the law of peoples is that 'peoples have a duty to assist other peoples living under unfavourable conditions that prevent their having a just or decent political and social regime'.[47] The obligation to assist binds peoples, but exists only up the point at which societies overcome 'unfavourable conditions'. This is not strictly speaking a matter of the distribution of resources between the parties, but the one off lifting of our fellow human beings from a state of destitution. Rawls' principle of aid is solidarity in assistance, not solidarity in achieving fair shares.[48]

[45] John Rawls, *The Law of Peoples* (Cambridge, Mass.: Harvard University Press, 1999) 113.

[46] ibid 115.

[47] ibid 37.

[48] There is an analogy with the idea of a duty of mutual aid among strangers. Such a duty is ethically fundamental outside any legal or institutional framework. I follow here Barbara Herman, 'Mutual Aid and Respect for Persons' 94 *Ethics* (1984) 577–602, who applies the idea of the 'dependence' of human beings to the process of the categorical imperative and concludes: 'The duty of mutual aid has its ground in the facts that we are dependent beings with ends it is not rational for us to forgo: ends set by "true needs" whose satisfaction is a necessary condition for the exercise of rationality. As we are rational agents, we set ends ... As a person's true needs are those which must be met if he is to function (or continue to function) as a rational, end-setting agent, respecting the humanity of others involves acknowledging the duty of mutual aid: one must be prepared to support the conditions of the rationality of others (their capacity to set and act for ends) when they are unable to do so without help' (ibid 597).

Although Rawls does not use the term 'corrective justice' for this type of bilateral obligation, it is clear that what he has in mind for the *Law of Peoples* is very different from the kind of justice that applies to the basic structure of a single political community. It is not a principle of distribution of fair shares, but a bilateral relationship created by encounter of one state or one people with another. The claim arises because of a desperate need of the burdened state or people, not because of a pattern of distribution. This is a different moral relationship to that of citizenship. When we encounter each other as citizens we look at the whole picture in relation to a vertically organized system of authority to which we both contribute and to which we owe allegiance. The question of inequality among citizens is a question that takes its special character precisely because all citizens are equally subject to the directions of common authority. The relevant relationship is very different in the international domain. Here, by contrast, our encounters are structured in a purely horizontal way by way of cooperative agreements, without a vertically organized system of power binding us.

Rawls thus presents the obligations of solidarity in the international case as arising only out of the reasonable terms under which peoples would join a system of international law as equals. Rawls' argument introduces in this way the idea that fairness should be a precondition of general international law, whatever else agreements may establish as binding obligations.

In this way a horizontal principle of fairness serves as the background condition for the continuing legitimacy of the international community. The best way in which we can understand such a non-distributive principle of fairness is as a principle of corrective justice, similar to that giving rise to a duty of mutual aid. It arises—just as it does with persons—from the very fact of the vulnerability of states towards natural disasters or other misfortunes.[49] If a prosperous state is in a position to provide aid to a burdened state without risk to itself, it has a duty to do so. A similar principle of corrective justice covers the cooperative practices of international law in the following way. If states engage with one another—as they should—in setting up complex cooperative arrangements in the course of international relations, then they are bound by terms of fairness towards one another, just like motorists sharing a road are bound by the rules of negligence for accidents. We often call this aspect of justice 'cooperative justice'.

The distinction between distributive and corrective justice has one important consequence for the European Union. It suggests that the simple disjunction drawn by Habermas and Joerges between independence and solidarity was not correct. Remember that they assumed that there were only two ways forward as

See also Barbara Herman, 'Being Helped and Being Grateful: Imperfect Duties, the Ethics of Possession, and the Unity of Morality' 109 *Journal of Philosophy* (2012) 391–411.

49 By analogy with dependent human beings, as in ibid.

far as the future of the Eurozone was concerned: either a decentralized and international fiscal order in which each country was exclusively liable for its own debt, or a fully integrated fiscal union in which spending powers are transferred to a European authority. The distinction necessarily assumed that there could not be a sharing of burdens or a practice of solidarity, without some form of integrated political union. This is correct, only as far as distributive justice is concerned. If there is no single political power to tax the parties and distribute the shares justly, then it makes no sense to speak of 'just shares'. The question is very different if we are asking about something else. Solidarity in the form of *mutual* aid does make sense without a central authority doing the sharing. Corrective justice that arises from international cooperation does not require political union.

The question that corrective justice asks is not one of fair shares, but of fair redress for a wrong. If parties provide redress to one another for the wrongs they committed, they exhibit solidarity outside a distributive framework. If I drive carelessly and I cause a cyclist to lose their balance, I owe them a duty of reparation, even if it is only an apology. If I have injured them, I must provide appropriate redress. If I ignore my moral obligation to another person in need of aid, I show—among other things—a lack of solidarity. It is the same with states. A state may owe to another state some form of redress, for example the return of a cultural artefact stolen by some of the first state's citizens or compensation for an oil spill caused by a military vessel. This sense of solidarity is entirely familiar from private law. There is no reason for not following the same principle in international relations.

The best example of this kind of obligation in international relations is the granting of debt forgiveness as an obligation under the doctrine of 'odious debt' in international law.[50] Under certain—very demanding—conditions, the debts assumed by a corrupt government may not be held to bind a subsequent democratic government. The doctrine of 'odious debt' holds that the debt is unlawful and therefore invalid. A lender should not seek to exploit a dictator's greed for one's personal profit. Under that doctrine, Cuba and the United States refused to recognize Cuba's debts that had been taken by the Spanish colonial government just before Cuba's independence.[51] The same applied to loans taken by the Costa Rican government in the dying days of the dictator Federico Tinoco's corrupt regime.[52] In all these cases, fairness in substance was deemed more important than the formalities of a contract. The agreement was invalid.

Of course, the theory of 'odious debt' cannot conceivably apply to the members of the European Union. The issues here are entirely different. All the members

[50] Robert Howse, *The Concept of Odious Debt in Public International Law: UNCTAD Discussion Papers, No. 185* (New York: United Nations, 2007); Jeff King, *The Doctrine of Odious Debt in International Law: A Restatement* (Cambridge: Cambridge University Press, 2016).

[51] See Howse, *The Concept of Odious Debt in Public International Law* (n. 50) 10–11.

[52] *Aguilar-Amory and Royal Bank of Canada Claims* (*Great Britain v Costa Rica)* (1923) 1 RIAA 371. See Howse, *The Concept of Odious Debt in Public International Law* (n. 50) 11–12.

of the Eurozone are democracies and have democratically approved the original accession to the European Monetary Union as well as any amendments to the Treaties. They have borrowed in the international markets exercising their constitutional powers in fiscal policy. Nevertheless, the rule of odious debt may help us understand the basic principle, namely that fairness applies more generally as a background principle for all international institutional arrangements.[53]

The general point is this: if cooperative fairness creates international obligations under a principle of corrective justice in some cases of international interaction, then it can also create obligations in a process of market integration such as that provided for by the European Union Treaties. In the most direct case, if a state suffers a loss because of the wrongful action of another state, it is then entitled to redress and failure to provide it is a failure to exhibit appropriate *solidarity*. Indeed, the European Union has created exactly such mechanisms. It provides redress for violations of the law through the Commission and the Court of Justice. But we are entitled to ask if corrective justice creates further moral obligations of fairness or solidarity among states on the basis of their cooperation. We need to refine the argument by asking in particular who can be responsible for the joint decisions of a cooperative agreement such as the European Union.

8.4 Structural Responsibility

The principle of mutual aid applies between two parties that encounter each other in a certain way. The case of international cooperation in trade agreements is more complex. The parties organize their relationship based on common rules and monitored by multi-lateral institutions. Here the argument for a principle of cooperative fairness must take a modified form. By entering the founding treaties, the member states jointly created institutions of cooperation, such as the Commission, the Council, the European Parliament and—more recently—the European Central Bank. Such institutions make decisions in the name of the organization as a whole. Some of these decisions are highly consequential.

These common institutions are not entirely independent nor do they enjoy comprehensive powers. The member states retain economic decision-making and exercise some element of control through the Council of Ministers (and through their delegates at the European Parliament). The member states remain, therefore, key decision-makers and are to that extent *responsible* for what the EU does.[54] At the

[53] An attempt to interpret Greece's debt as 'odious debt' is made in Ilias Bantekas and Renaud Vivien, 'On the Odiousness of Greek Debt' 22 *European Law Journal* (2016) 539–65. In my view the argument cannot possibly succeed. Greece's democratically elected governments created the debt mountain in the period between 1980 to 2010.

[54] This follows from my argument above that the European Union is an international and not a federal project. For this argument see also Stephen Weatherill, *Law and Values in the European Union* (Oxford: Oxford University Press, 2016).

same time, we cannot hold the states responsible for everything that the EU does. But since the member states created the basic structure, such as the single market and the free movement of persons, goods, services, and capital, then they can be held responsible for what it does. If we can detect some economic outcomes—positive or negative—of those structures, then the member states can be held to be jointly responsible for them.

This is not an entirely original thought. Something similar may already exist in the structures of the global economy. It is common ground that the current structures of economic globalization are the conscious result of policy decisions made by the leading economic powers, for example the global financial architecture, the World Trade Organization, and numerous other multilateral agreements that make trade possible.[55] The philosopher Thomas Pogge argues, for example, that world poverty is partly the result of the joint actions of developed states, which make it possible for dictators and corrupt politicians to siphon their ill-gotten gains to tax heavens around the world.[56]

The most extensive argument in this respect is offered by the American philosopher Aaron James. In his book *Fairness in Practice* he describes the process of creating institutions of international trade as an international 'social practice', a practice of 'mutual reliance on common markets' which, in his view, creates 'a distinctive class of fairness responsibilities'.[57] These responsibilities go beyond the explicit commitments of the parties. They are structural in that they require that the structures of international trade meet certain requirements of 'structural equity'. James argues that the states that create these structures of international trade are jointly responsible for any harm and unfairness that such structures bring about. In James' argument, a states' negotiation has the same effect as direct legislation.[58] The states are structurally responsible for their processes of negotiation, just as much as if they were directly legislating the resulting consensus. What are the structural principles of fairness that bind the states, when they act in this way? For James, these principles require 'due care' for those who unfairly lose out from the system overall, principles of 'fair distribution among states' and 'fair distribution within states'.[59] The states that participate in the international social practice of trade are *jointly responsible* for

[55] See for example Joseph E. Stiglitz, *Globalization and its Discontents* (London: Penguin, 2002), where he describes the developments brought about by 'global institutions'. See also Dani Rodrik, *The Globalization Paradox* (Oxford: Oxford University Press, 2011).

[56] Thomas Pogge, *World Poverty and Human Rights: Cosmopolitan Responsibilities and Reforms*, 2nd edn (Cambridge: Polity, 2008) 97–123. For a powerful account of these processes by an investigative journalist see Oliver Bullough, *Moneyland: Why Thieves and Crooks Now Rule the World and How to Take it Back* (London: Profile Book, 2018).

[57] See Aaron James, *Fairness in Practice: A Social Contract for a Global Economy* (Oxford: Oxford University Press, 2012) 131.

[58] ibid 91–3.

[59] ibid 203–45.

setting up mechanisms for compensation to the losers of free trade, as well as mechanisms for maintaining equality in the distribution of benefits among states and among populations within states.

An argument along these lines concerning structural responsibility is clearly applicable to the European Union, where the member states have legislated the terms of their own cooperation. They have created legally binding treaties and enforcement mechanisms. Their actions have gone much beyond a mere 'practice' of international trade, as described by James. In the case of the European Union the structural responsibility of the states is even more direct than that of the creators of diffuse systems of cooperation, such as the World Trade Organization or systems of international arbitration.

Cooperative structural fairness applies thus to the member states in two stages. At the first stage, which we may call 'basic fairness', the principle of fairness asks if an agreement to cooperate, given its formation and substantive content, is fair overall at the point the parties first enter it. This test requires, for example, that when the parties enter into some agreement to cooperate, they do so willingly and having been in a relatively even bargaining position to one another. The principle also assumes that, absent special circumstances, the cooperating parties would strike an agreement by which they would receive a fair return on their investment over time. Otherwise, the agreement might have been the result of exploitation or undue pressure.

At a second stage, which we may call 'fairness in practice', the principle asks if the parties acted fairly as their agreement unfolded in the course of time. This aspect of fairness asks of the content of the obligations of the parties after the agreement is put into effect. John Rawls explains the relevance of fairness in practice in a remarkably clear way. He says that fairness creates obligations on the participants in a mutually advantageous cooperative venture to continue to acquiesce by its terms.[60] As Rawls puts it: 'we are not to gain from the cooperative labors of others without doing our fair share'.[61] This goes beyond the basic fairness that was in place at the original starting point. Whether we are fairly treated by others depends on how they treated us in the process of *cooperation over time*. Although some of the ongoing cooperation will be based on the original rules and commitments, the relevant obligations will also arise from the conduct, practices, and expectations created and relied upon by others after the cooperative project started. So a cooperative project may be fair to begin with, but can fail to remain fair because of the subsequently unreasonable conduct of one of the parties.

[60] Rawls, *A Theory of Justice* (n. 40) 96. Rawls was also referring to H.L.A. Hart, 'Are There any Natural Rights?' 64 *Philosophical Review* (1955) 185.
[61] Rawls, *A Theory of Justice* (n. 40) 96.

8.5 The Symmetry Principle

I now turn to a fuller discussion of the idea of basic fairness. My focus remains the framework of multi-party cooperation and principles of corrective justice among states. We are not asking about the ideal distribution of shares or about a certain ratio of return to investment. No such ratio of 'fair return' exists in the absence of a central distributing mechanism. The outcomes of any trade agreements are determined by economic practice, or in effect by a mixture of political judgment, prudent decision-making and, of course, chance. Because cooperative justice is a matter of bilateral relationship structured around the parties' actions, what we are looking for is a standard of wrongness in bilateral relationships. What is fair and what is unfair in cooperation among states?

Basic fairness rules out terms of cooperation that impose unjustified inequalities, or terms that are the result of unfair imposition, monopolies, cartels, and other competitive restrictions.[62] Any such terms must be void and unenforceable. Can we organize these intuitive wrongs in a more coherent whole, so as to cover less obvious but still real unfairness?

There are many ways in which we can interpret fairness in trade agreements. One such way was provided, as we saw above, by Aaron James with reference to the world trade order. James argues that the relation among states must be subject to a principle of 'international relative gains' according to which: 'gains to each trading society, adjusted according to their respective national endowments (e.g. population size, resource base, level of development), are to be distributed equally, unless unequal gains flow (e.g., via special trade privileges) to poor countries'.[63]

Why should the gains be in principle equal? James argues that 'the gains of trade are socially created, by the joint practice of market reliance'.[64] This of course is the starting point for the responsibility of states, although not a sufficient reason for equal shares. He goes on to say: 'Because each trading country has a morally relevant interest in greater rather than lesser national income gains, equal treatment requires equal distribution of gains, unless we can specify a relevant difference among participating countries'.[65] James identifies two such 'relevant' differences as possible grounds for inequality of gain. First, relevant endowments of each country, such as population size, natural resources, degree of economic development. Second, 'inequality of gain is fair if greater benefits flow to people who are worse off in absolute terms'.[66]

I find James' arguments for equal shares unconvincing. What James recognizes as the 'endowments' exception cannot be limited only to the features he sets out.

[62] See John Rawls, *The Law of Peoples* (n. 45) 42–3.
[63] James, *Fairness in Practice* (n. 57) 203.
[64] ibid 221.
[65] ibid 221.
[66] ibid 222.

Other considerations are relevant too. The performance of a state in trading with other states does not depend only on the state structures, but also on the success of private parties: producers, entrepreneurs, and workers who produce relevant tradeable products that appeal to consumers abroad. Economic success or failure cannot therefore be imputed only to each state and its institutions. As long as the background terms of fair competition are respected, the outcome of economic competition will be the result of the 'endowments' that James describes as well as of the capacity—flexibility, agility, and resourcefulness—of firms in producing competitive products and services. This is why James' principle of equality in outcomes seems to me at odds with his general framework. He seems to leave out the element of uncertainty inherent in economic competition. If we allow for the effects of economic competition, equality of outcomes cannot be the default position.

A second argument for fairness is provided by Andrea Sangiovanni, who has offered a sophisticated argument about fairness specifically in the context of the European Union.[67] Sangiovanni takes an 'internationalist' view on the EU. He believes that the best argument for justice in the EU proceeds from the reciprocal commitments the states have made to each other. Sangiovanni argues that: 'According to reciprocity-based internationalism, demands for social solidarity at all levels of governance can be understood as demands for a fair return in the mutual production of important collective goods.[68] Fair return is required because in effect the states have jointly produced the collective goods brought about by the European Union.

Sangiovanni's proposal is to ask what would be a rational insurance policy in case the member states considered the terms of their cooperation in advance of entering into this cooperative project. He asks ' ... what do member states and their citizens owe one another as a fair return for the mutual provision of these goods and the mutual exposure to these risks—goods and risks made possible by opening up their markets, societies and polities to the joint control and supervision of both supranational actors and intergovernmental decision-making?'[69] The answer for Sangiovanni is that the fair return 'which members states owe one another, under member state solidarity, is given by the level at which each state would insure against the potential losses identified above, had they known the distribution of risks but not their place in the distribution'.[70]

Sangiovanni argues that by asking how states would have insured against the 'risks intrinsic to the project of European integration, had they not known what state they would have turned out to be', we eliminate the advantage at the bargaining table of the European social contract obtained by the fact that member

[67] Andrea Sangiovanni, 'Solidarity in the EU' 33 *Oxford Journal of Legal Studies* (2013) 1–29.
[68] ibid 5.
[69] ibid 17.
[70] ibid 17–18.

states know their relative position—including their level of development, population size, welfare regime, type, etc.[71] This argument is ambiguous, however. It is not clear if it proposes 'fair shares' as distributive shares, or a system of minimum insurance against failure. A question of what fair shares are appropriate is, as we have seen, a *distributive* question. It argues for an appropriate allocation among the various parties. Insurance is by contrast a *corrective* question. It is not an allocation of shares but a provision of redress.

I believe that the distinction between distribution and insurance is not clear in Sangiovanni's argument. The aim of insurance is to provide reparation for some loss, under the terms of the insurance agreement. It is not the allocation of fair or equal, or less unequal, distributive shares, all things considered. On the one hand Sangiovanni speaks of an argument based on insurance, but on the other he is seeking fair shares. I believe that his argument needs amendment to make clear that what he is interested in is a basic form of insurance and not a form of distribution. If we are seeking to model our fair background conditions of basic fairness on the basis of a hypothetical insurance scheme, we must envisage returns triggered by a type of wrongful action, not merely inequality in outcomes. The redress must correspond to the wrongful loss actually incurred, or loss in comparison to the position one would have been in without the wrong.

Here is how I believe the argument for basic fairness among states must be restated. Remember that the relevant principle is corrective justice in relation to cooperative projects. We proceed by identifying the threshold of wrongful conduct, which generates a one-off claim for redress from one party to another. We are not looking for a general pattern of fair distribution that should be imposed when it fails to materialize in real life.

I propose the following formulation as the appropriate standard of background cooperative fairness in trading among states, which I call the 'symmetry principle':

> *The Symmetry Principle:* An agreement to cooperate for the purposes of international trade in goods and services is unfair and unenforceable, if it is shown to create asymmetrical opportunities for gain and risks of loss for the parties involved, taking into account the parties' original position, endowments and prospects as the agreement was reached.

Following the principle of symmetry, a structure of cooperation will be unfair, if it creates asymmetrical opportunities for gain and risks of loss. The symmetry here refers both to the level of risk but also the nature of the loss it may cause. Irreparable harms must be given much higher value than temporary harms. Similarly,

[71] ibid 18.

permanent gains (e.g. those associated with education or long-term health) are to be assessed differently from transient gains, economic or social.

The principle of symmetrical risks tries to capture the protective effect of Sangiovanni's approach without resorting to fair shares. This is the thought that an agreement may be fair, if the parties would have been able to agree it as sufficiently beneficial to them, had they entered it without full knowledge of their circumstances.[72] The idea of symmetry of risks seeks to reflect the idea of reciprocity for states that are greatly unequal in size and economic size. Reciprocity entails a form of insurance for all parties: we ask what costs the member states would be willing to pay to offset the risks generated by the project of cooperation.[73]

There are also similarities here with a principle that Aaron James discusses by the name of principle of 'reciprocity of risk', which he eventually rejects.[74] James' idea involves only risk of loss, not opportunity for gain. Yet, his account of reciprocity is the same idea as that behind the 'symmetry principle'. One of the reasons he gives for rejecting the 'reciprocity of risk' principle is that 'current trade practice is clearly a situation of non-reciprocal risk'. This, however, is not a reason to reject the principle. He also notes that symmetry of risks is compatible with terrible losses for both sides, if they are symmetrical.[75] This argument fails, however, for another reason. If a cooperative agreement is open to massive losses of the kind that James has in mind, it will not be struck at all, at least not if we rule out imposition, deception, and the like.

The underlying idea behind the symmetry principle is a requirement of reciprocity. In the philosophical literature, reciprocity commonly refers to the requirement that one returns a benefit they have received from another.[76] In his defence of reciprocity as an ideal of private law Arthur Ripstein introduces it as follows: 'The root idea, fundamental to both fair terms of interaction and the idea of responsibility, is one of reciprocity, the idea that one person may not unilaterally set the terms of his interactions with others.'[77] This is a distinct matter from that of keeping a promise. A promise or an exchange of promises create obligations by virtue of itself alone. Reciprocity creates obligations by virtue of rendering a benefit to another, irrespective of a promise. The economist Serge-Cristoph Kolm, for example, begins his wide-ranging study of reciprocity with a definition that stresses

[72] An analogy may be made between this argument and Rawls' argument for the making of a constitution in a constitutional convention, in the *Theory of Justice*. This stage of law-making, for Rawls, was the second of a 'four stage sequence' where the parties were aware of their individual circumstances (whereas they were not in the 'original position' concerning the basic structure).

[73] The logic of an insurance calculation is the same as set out by Sangiovanni, 'Solidarity' (n. 57) at p. 18.

[74] James, *Fairness in Practice* (n. 57) 233–7.

[75] James, *Fairness in Practice* (n. 57) 235.

[76] See John Rawls, 'Justice as Reciprocity' in Rawls, *Collected Papers*, edited by Samuel Freeman (Cambridge, Mass.: Harvard University Press, 1999) 190.

[77] Arthur Ripstein, *Equality, Responsibility, and the Law* (Cambridge: Cambridge University Press, 1999) 2.

that reciprocity goes beyond a 'binding exchange agreement'.[78] Reciprocity applies beyond agreements, when for example no agreement exists or the one that exists has failed to meet a fair measure of equal return among the parties. In those cases the reason to offer something—or the motivation—is independent of any promise or other undertaking. Some key examples Kolm discusses, for example, are the reciprocity of giving and receiving gifts or reciprocity in family relations.

Philosophers today deploy reciprocity as a political ideal when they discuss the design of a social contract or give other egalitarian arguments for social life. John Rawls, for example, discussed reciprocity alongside legitimacy. He links the idea of a reasonable person with a recognition of the value of reciprocity as follows: 'Reasonable persons [are moved by a desire for] a social world in which they, as free and equal, can cooperate with others on terms all can accept. They insist that reciprocity should hold within that world so that each benefits along with others.'[79] In light of the disagreements we expect to have with others about the terms of co-operation, legitimate political power of one person over another requires that: 'our exercise of political power is fully proper only when it is exercised in accordance with a constitution the essentials of which all citizens as free and equal may reasonably be expected to endorse in the light of principles and ideals acceptable to their common human reason'.[80] For this view political power must fulfil a criterion of reciprocity, in that citizens must reasonably believe that all can reasonably accept a particular set of institutions. Reciprocity is therefore at the heart of corrective justice. As Aristotle put it, voluntary exchanges or instances of cooperation raise issues of corrective justice regarding voluntary transactions.[81] For Aristotle, justice in voluntary transactions involves not simply keeping their parties to their word by way of formal equality—as in a simple commercial contract—but at the same time by being willing to preserve proportionate equality in the fruits of joint activity or cooperation.[82]

8.6 Conclusion

Many prominent legal theorists argue that solidarity will only become relevant at some point in the European Union's future, when new European institutions bring citizens together under a single Europe-wide political community. This chapter argued that these arguments are misleading. They miss the key role played

[78] 'Reciprocity is treating other people as other people treat you voluntarily and not as a result of a binding exchange agreement.' Serge-Cristoph Kolm, *Reciprocity: An Economics of Social Relations* (Cambridge: Cambridge University Press, 2008) 1.

[79] John Rawls, *Political Liberalism* (New York: Columbia University Press, 1993) 50.

[80] ibid 137.

[81] Aristotle, *The Nicomachean Ethics*, trans. H. Rackham (Cambridge, Mass.: Harvard University Press, 1989) V, iv, 1., 273) ('διορθωτικόν δίκαιον, εν τοις συναλλάγμασι τοις εκουσίοις').

[82] ibid V, v. 8.

in international affairs of corrective justice. Unlike distributive justice, which applies *within* states but not *among* states, corrective justice applies to cooperative arrangements creating interdependence among the parties. Corrective justice creates a principle of redress, which requires that those who are unfairly burdened by an agreement should be compensated by those who caused the unfairness. Any state that was unfairly burdened by the Eurozone's flawed architecture, may thus have a claim of redress, if it incurred losses as a result of the unfairness. It is now time to look at this issue in some detail. In Chapter 9 I ask whether the programmes of financial assistance in the Eurozone succeeded in giving effect to European principle of solidarity based on corrective justice.

9
An Unfair Union?

What does the symmetry principle entail for fairness in the European Union? Has it been respected by the member states? Has the EU been structurally fair? If not, what are the reforms that would render it a fair cooperative project among nations? These are some of the most important questions that we can ask of the European Union today. We will move from the heights of theory to the lowlands of practice. Does the symmetry principle help this debate?

It is clear that the European Union Treaties do not introduce anything like a principle of distributive justice for the Union. Habermas and Joerges are right to point this out. The treaties recognize the division of the Union into states and an associated division of them into welfare states.[1] The question of solidarity in the Union will not be, therefore, a distributive matter. As we saw in Chapter 8, solidarity in the EU does not promise social justice among all the various people who live within the geographical territory of the European Union. It promises only redress for wrongs. It follows that the mere fact of great inequalities of wealth between the various nations of the European Union do not by themselves constitute a violation of European solidarity. Such a conclusion would only proceed from distributive justice. It also follows that the fact that the budget of the European Union only corresponds to about 1% of the gross domestic product of its members is not, by itself, unfair. It is not evidence of any neglect to take justice seriously. It is merely a reflection of the fact that the European Union is not a state and does not have its own social welfare functions. The member states have decided to leave such matters to their own domestic political systems. According to OECD data, the member states of the European Union spend the highest percentage of their Gross Domestic Product in social welfare payments in the world.[2]

The question of solidarity from the point of view of corrective justice asks something else. It looks at the relations of the states with one another as they interact in

[1] This point is also well set out in Jürgen Neyer, *The Justification of Europe: A Political Theory of Supranational Integration* (Oxford: Oxford University Press, 2012) 35–55. For an interesting debate on this between Neyer (who sees the European Union as a project that does not seek to be federal) and Forst (who follows Habermas in accepting the federalist interpretation) see Jürgen Neyer, 'Justice and the Right to Justification: Conceptual Reflections' in Dimitry Kochenov, Gráinne de Búrca, and Andrew Williams (eds), *Europe's Justice Deficit?* (Oxford: Hart, 2015) 211–26; Rainer Forst, 'Justice, Democracy and the Right to Justification: Reflections on Jürgen Neyer's Normative Theory of the European Union' in *Europe's Justice Deficit?* 227–34.

[2] OECD, *Society at a Glance 2016: OECD Social Indicators* (Paris: OECD Publishing, 2016).

A Union of Peoples. Pavlos Eleftheriadis. Oxford University Press (2020). © Oxford University Press.
DOI: 10.1093/oso/9780198854173.001.0001

the single market and—for those that participate in it—the European Monetary Union (EMU). We may look at the relevant costs and benefits for each relationship separately or for the relationship of each state with the rest of the European Union considered as a single agent. The relevant tables of actual contributions and receipts from the EU's budget show that some countries are systematic contributors into the budget and others are recipients. Yet that does not, by itself, show any unfairness. The question of the symmetry of risks and losses from membership is not a matter of budget contributions. Member states may be happy to contribute more into the budget because they gain much more through the single market and the opportunities for trade. Perhaps they calculate that they will benefit greatly through an open economy, even if they compensate some of the losers through budget contributions.

The single market has very complex costs and benefits for each economy of the member states through private transfers of goods, services, capital, and of course workers. It is extremely hard to calculate precisely those benefits or costs for each economy. It is even harder to estimate what the risks were at the inception of the single market for each state, although various surveys show that the single market has been largely beneficial for all of them. But such a precise calculation may be in the end unnecessary. What the principle of symmetry requires is a view on whether the *expected* distribution of risks and opportunities is symmetrical or fair, irrespective of whether any of the risks or opportunities were actually realized.

The question we ask is whether it would have been reasonable for each party to take those risks, had they understood them fully at the time. If the answer to this question is no, then the agreement is unfair and its unfairness is not cured by the fact that consent was freely given. We can ask the question with reference to the European Union as a whole. This is a very complex question, given the various layers of cooperation and interdependence and especially the distinction between those who are inside or outside the Eurozone. The question will perhaps be more interesting if we ask the question with reference to the EMU alone. Here is where we have the largest inequalities and the most heated arguments. The question here is not just about the single market but also about monetary union and financial regulation and coordination.

So in what follows I will only ask the question of the fairness of the Eurozone. I will concentrate on the fate of each member separately. As we will see many economists have made the case that the costs and benefits for the member states were unequal both at the start and when the financial crisis struck. I will examine these issues by focusing on three separate points in time: a) the creation of the Eurozone; b) the end of the Eurozone's first decade; and c) the emergency response to the financial crisis starting from 2010.

9.1 On the Basic Fairness of the Eurozone

I start with the question of the basic fairness of the Eurozone at the point of its inception. When the EMU was first proposed, it was hoped that the common currency would create conditions of economic and political convergence among the member states.[3] Looking at the history of the Eurozone, however, it is clear that this aim was not achieved. When we look at the economic performance of the various members we see that the Eurozone remains fragmented between states of the 'core'—that have low unemployment, high rates of investment, and healthy growth—and states of the 'periphery'—which have high unemployment, especially among the young, low levels of savings and investment, and very low rates of growth. Some of the most distinguished commentators have linked this failure to the design of the Eurozone.[4]

The American economist Kenneth Rogoff, who has co-authored one of the leading studies of financial crises,[5] has given a categorical rejection of the Eurozone's design. He has said that 'the problem at the heart of the euro crisis' is that 'the eurozone is a half-built house' and that 'it was a catastrophic mistake to put monetary union ahead of fiscal and political union'.[6] The absence of central fiscal policy, for Rogoff, meant that European policy makers did not have the tools to address the crisis. He concluded: 'Monetary policy is simply one side of fiscal policy. Monetary union without fiscal union is an accident waiting to happen.'[7] Similarly, the distinguished American economist C. Fred Bergsten wrote that 'the European crisis is rooted in a failure of institutional design' and that 'the absence of crucial policy tools constrained Europe's ability to reach a solution quickly, triggering severe market reactions that continue to this day'.[8] In Bergsten's view the response to the crisis required that the members of the Eurozone 'rewrite the eurozone's rule book and complete the half-built euro house'.

It is important to add that this view is not a recent one. Many economists had expressed concern about the structural flaws in the design of the Euro well before it was created. As early as 1971 the British economist Nicolas Kaldor wrote that a common currency in Europe would only succeed if the stronger nations agreed to finance the weaker nations on a permanent basis. In the absence of such transfers

[3] The main case for the Euro had been made in the European Commission's paper, *One Market: One Money; An evaluation of the potential benefits and costs of forming an economic and monetary union* (Brussels, October 1990). For the history of the creation of the EMU see Harold James, *Making the European Monetary Union* (Cambridge, Mass.: Harvard University Press, 2014).

[4] See Jeffrey Franks, Bergljot Barkbu, Rodolphe Blavy, William Oman, and Hanni Schoelerman, 'Economic Convergence in the Euro Area: Coming Together or Drifting Apart?' *IMF Working Paper, 18/10* (January 2018) (Washington, DC: International Monetary Fund, 2018).

[5] Carmen M. Reinhart and Kenneth S. Rogoff, *This Time is Different: Eight Centuries of Financial Folly* (Princeton: Princeton University Press, 2009).

[6] Kenneth S. Rogoff, 'Crash Time' *Project Syndicate*, 8 September 2018.

[7] ibid.

[8] C. Fred Bergsten, 'Why the Euro Will Survive' *Foreign Affairs*, September/October 2012, 216.

a common currency was bound to divide European states rather than unite them.[9] Kaldor wrote that the single market as conceived at the time would presuppose 'full currency convertibility and fixed exchange rates among the members, whilst leaving monetary and fiscal policy to the discretion of the individual member countries'.[10] Such a system, for Kaldor, would entail that some countries would tend to acquire excessive surpluses in their trade with other members, whist others would face corresponding deficits. This could have destabilizing effects. Kaldor concluded that a full monetary and economic union would fail without a full political union bringing about fiscal integration not just fiscal harmonization.

The American economist Martin Feldstein gave a parallel assessment of the common currency a generation later.[11] At a time when the Euro was being introduced, Feldstein wrote that the Euro would not achieve its aims because of its structural flaws. In his view 'the standard of living of the typical European would be lower in the medium term and long term, if EMU goes ahead than if Europe continues with its current economic policies of a single market for trade in goods and services, the free flow of capital and labor, adjustable exchange rates within broad bands, and domestic monetary policies aimed at low inflation'.[12]

The European Commission did not entirely dismiss the risks identified by Kaldor and Feldstein. It noted that the creation of the EMU would create costs in adjusting to economic shocks. But the Commission believed that they would be small:

> The main potential cost of EMU is that represented by the loss of monetary and exchange rate policy as an instrument of economic adjustment at the national level. This loss should not be exaggerated since exchange rate changes by the Community in relation to the rest of the world will remain possible, whereas within the EMS the nominal exchange rate instrument is already largely abandoned, and EMU will reduce the incidence of country-specific shocks. Relative real labour costs will still be able to change; budgetary policies at national and Community levels will also absorb shocks and aid adjustment, and the external current account constraint will disappear.[13]

[9] Nicholas Kaldor, 'The Dynamic Effects of the Common Market' in Nicholas Kaldor, *Further Essays On Applied Economics* (New York: Holmes and Meier, 1978) 187–220.

[10] ibid 202.

[11] Martin Feldstein, 'The Political Economy of the European Economic and Monetary Union: Political Sources of an Economic Liability' 11 *Journal of Economic Perspectives* (1997) 23–42. The standard analysis of 'optimal currency areas' in light of the risk of asymmetric shocks in different parts of a currency area supports Feldstein's scepticism. See Robert Mundell, 'A Theory of Optimum Currency Areas' 51 *American Economic Review* (1961) 509–17. For further discussion see Jean Pisani-Ferry, *The Euro-Crisis and Its Aftermath* (Oxford: Oxford University Press, 2014) 20–5.

[12] Feldstein, 'The Political Economy of the European Economic and Monetary Union: Political Sources of an Economic Liability' (n. 11) 24.

[13] European Commission, *One Market: One Money; An evaluation of the potential benefits and costs of forming an economic and monetary union* (Brussels, October 1990) 11.

Feldstein was not convinced by such arguments. In his view the EMU would deliver some trade benefits to its members, but would still create more significant macroeconomic risks, loss of policy options and, in some cases, higher unemployment. He observed that the members of the EMU would lose the automatic adjustments of their currency in case of a decrease in aggregate demand, namely the decline in the real interest (in response to the decline in the demand for money and credit) and the real value of the currency which would come as a natural result. For Feldstein the member states would also lose the power to adjust interest rates in order to bring down unemployment, since they would be tied to a single interest rate and to a fixed exchange rate.

Feldstein observed that these problems were made worse by the fact that the member states of the EMU differed so much in the structure of their economies. He also noted that in the United States, where the currency union also brings together states with very different economies, such problems were addressed through *fiscal transfers*. In the United States, a fall in demand in one state triggers a set of fiscal transfers from the federal government through various federal social programmes (to which that state will contribute less as its tax income falls). Feldstein calculated that in the US: 'The combination of reduced federal income and profits taxes and increased transfer payments (unemployment benefits and welfare) implies that a $1 fall in a state's GDP is counterbalanced by about a 40 cent change in the net flow between the residents of that state and the federal government in Washington.'[14] There was nothing like that provided for in the EMU blueprint (and even today nothing like that exists in spite of the financial crisis and its aftermath). Feldstein noted that there was 'no similar cyclical net transfer in Europe, since taxes and benefits are almost exclusively the responsibility of the national governments'.[15] His conclusion was therefore unequivocal: 'It is clear that the countries of the European Union do not constitute a natural monetary union and that forcing a single currency on the area would raise cyclical unemployment in response to adverse demand shocks.'[16]

These and other problems of the EMU project were ignored, for Feldstein, because political leaders saw EMU as a means for an eventual federalist union. He found this hope misguided: the economic failure of the monetary union would drive the member states apart, rather than bring them closer together. In a separate article published at about the same time Feldstein warned that the economic failure of the Euro would have serious political consequences: 'Instead of increasing intra-European harmony and global peace, the shift to EMU and the political integration

[14] Feldstein, 'The Political Economy of the European Economic and Monetary Union: Political Sources of an Economic Liability' (n. 11) 36.

[15] ibid.

[16] ibid.

that would follow it would be more likely to lead to increased conflicts within Europe and between Europe and the United States.'[17]

Feldstein returned to his predictions fifteen years later, after the financial crisis had hit the Eurozone. He considered that the subsequent history vindicated his predictions:

> The euro should now be recognized as an experiment that failed. This failure, which has come after just over a dozen years since the euro was introduced, in 1999, was not an accident or the result of bureaucratic mismanagement but rather the inevitable consequence of imposing a single currency on a very heterogeneous group of countries.[18]

The trigger for the Eurozone's failure was the financial crisis, which unleashed forces that were already inherent in the experiment. Feldstein believes that the structural flaws of the Euro created the sovereign debt crisis, weakened European banks, and ultimately created the high levels of unemployment we see in many European countries. Feldstein writes that the tough anti-inflationary policy of the European Central Bank (ECB), which is required by the treaties, caused interest rates to fall sharply but unjustifiably in the countries of the periphery, signalling to households and governments that they could increase their borrowing in response to the lowering of the cost of credit. This created bubbles in real estate in some countries and excessive public deficits in others. The risks were increased by the failure of the market to appreciate the underlying risks:

> The result was rapidly rising ratios of public and private debt to GDP in several countries, including Greece, Ireland, Italy, and Spain. Despite the increased risk to lenders that this implied, global capital markets did not respond by raising interest rates on those countries with increasing debt levels. Bond buyers assumed that a bond issued by one government in the European Monetary Union was equally safe as a bond issued by any other government in the union, ignoring the 'no bailout' provision of the Maastricht Treaty.[19]

The fact that interest rates on Greek and Italian bonds were similar to those of German bonds sent entirely the wrong signal. Rather than reduce a country's borrowing, the market suggested that the risk was negligible. The monetary union eliminated the pre-existing market signals and precluded the rise in interest rates that would otherwise have limited household or state borrowing. The result was

[17] Martin Feldstein, 'EMU and International Conflict' *Foreign Affairs*, November/December 1997.

[18] Martin Feldstein, 'The Failure of the Euro: The Little Currency that Couldn't' *Foreign Affairs*, January/February 2012.

[19] ibid.

that both countries and households borrowed too much. In Feldstein's account the failure was both structural and market driven.

A very similar view of the failure of the Eurozone has been given by Andrew Moravcsik.[20] The causes of the Eurozone crisis, in Moravcsik's account, are mostly structural and they are similar to those identified by Feldstein, namely that the crisis of the Eurozone was 'the result of a fundamental disequilibrium within the single currency zone, which applies a single monetary policy and a single exchange rate to a diverse group of countries'.[21] Nevertheless Moravcsik adds the further dimension that Germany refused to accommodate its own policies to the needs of the other member states during the period before the crisis. He observes that the EMU 'imposed high risks on some European governments', those who had been operating deficits such as Greece and Italy, because they could only survive in the Eurozone if, on entering the Eurozone, they adopted 'German standards of wage discipline, government spending and international competitiveness'. This, however, was practically very difficult. Still, these states were 'betting their future prosperity' on their own abilities of doing so. This was their only way of survival, since they had given up their normal policy tools for offsetting the gap with Germany, namely 'unilateral control over interest rates and the money supply, restrictions on capital flows, and the manipulation of exchange rates'.

Having lost those policy tools, the peripheral states of the Euro were left without a safety net in case of an economic shock—which eventually happened through the 2008 financial crisis. Without their macroeconomic policy tools, when the crisis hit, these states would have to 'act directly to push down economic activity through wages, private consumption, business investment, and government spending. This is a risky course for any government because it imposes immediate and visible costs across the entire society'.[22] Moravcsik also adds that Germany persistently ignored the risks to the economies of the periphery of its own lowering of labour costs, something to which I will return in the next section.

Finally, a similar structural account of the causes of the crisis has also been offered by the former Director of the Bruegel think tank and former advisor to the French President, Jean Pisani-Ferry. In his authoritative account, *The Euro Crisis*

[20] Andrew Moravcsik, 'Europe After the Crisis: How to Sustain a Common Currency' *Foreign Affairs*, May/June 2012, 54–68.

[21] ibid 54–5.

[22] For a similar critique of the design of the Eurozone—peppered with passionate and perhaps unhelpful polemic against the supposed ideology of 'neo-liberalism' that in the author's view lies behind European Monetary Union—see Joseph E. Stiglitz, *The Euro: How a Common Currency Threatens the Future of Europe* (New York: Norton, 2016) 85–144. The book' analysis of the Euro's flaws is compelling—and I rely on it below. But the book treats the Euro as an economic project of a federal union, without recognizing the inherent tensions in achieving consensus among states with conflicting interests that occasionally make decisive (Keynesian) action in practice impossible. The book does not sufficiently deal with the problem that the EU is only a project of the law of nations and it never had the political or economic firepower to attack the financial crisis on its own, in the way the United States as a single federal state did in 2008.

and its Aftermath, Pisani-Ferry effectively agrees with Feldstein and Moravcsik.[23] Pisani-Ferry argues that the economic misgivings that had been expressed by the American economists were acknowledged in Europe as the EMU was being designed, but they were outweighed by three other considerations. First, European economists were strongly averse to exchange rate fluctuations on account of the particular European experience (not shared by the US) with inflation and hyperinflation.[24] Second, the autonomy of monetary policy in Europe was in any case severely limited because of the liberalization of capital movements in the early 1990s. The EU countries could not have stable exchange rates, free capital movement, and independent monetary policy at the same time.[25] By creating the EMU, the member states chose to give up autonomy in order to secure stability. Finally, the third reason was political. French President Mitterrand saw the EMU as a way of binding Germany firmly into European integration.[26] For all these reasons, the members of the EU went ahead with the experiment in full knowledge that it created important risks.

Pisani-Ferry agrees with Feldstein and Moravcsik that the overall architecture was flawed. The criteria for membership were excessively formalistic and did not provide for real convergence between the various economies.[27] The United Kingdom set out its own tests for membership that included substantive convergence, but other countries did not follow in setting out their own preconditions of success.[28] There was no provision for crisis management. The assumption was that there would be no shocks if everybody played by the rules. Pisani-Ferry concludes that the Euro was an 'orphan currency' with serious structural problems:

> The common currency was thus created without significant political foundations. It was logically bereft of any mechanisms for solidarity between countries, since these could not be created without a significant degree of trust, and Europe has made little progress in this field ... In the end, the euro's architects made a choice. In the absence of a proper 'community' to speak of, and in the absence of a European state, each of the participating countries was left to face alone the challenges and risks involved in their participation in the common currency.[29]

[23] Jean Pisani-Ferry, *The Euro Crisis and its Aftermath* (Oxford: Oxford University Press, 2014).
[24] ibid 22–3.
[25] ibid 23–4.
[26] ibid 25, 33–7.
[27] ibid 38–43.
[28] Recently, in its invitation to Bulgaria to start the process of joining the Euro, the Eurogroup set out more substantive tests, including stress tests for the banking system and asset quality reviews. See Mehreen Khan, 'The Euro's Guardians Are Learning their Lessons with Bulgaria' *Financial Times*, 13 July 2018.
[29] Pisani-Ferry, *The Euro Crisis and its Aftermath* (n. 23) 36–7. A similar conclusion is also reached by Ashoka Mody, *Eurotragedy: A Drama in Nine Acts* (Oxford: Oxford University Press, 2018). For the argument that the Eurozone is not an optimum currency area see Paul Krugman, Maurice Obstfeld, and Marc Melitz, *International Economics: Theory and Policy*, 9th edn (London: Pearson, 2011) 587–615.

What are the consequences of this analysis for basic fairness? The test we are applying is the test of the symmetry of risks, which asks whether the expected benefits, costs, and risks of entering into the common currency were symmetrical for the various member states at the point of the Eurozone's creation in 1999. We may draw the following tentative conclusions.

First, the potential opportunities for trade were symmetrically open to all member states of the Eurozone, on the basis of the single market for goods, services, and capital under the effective supervision of the Court of Justice. Those gains, however, required appropriate competitiveness and a rise in productivity to be realized.

Second, the required changes in productivity depend partly on improving an economy's institutional framework.[30] Such structural reforms, however, take a long time to develop. Even if democratic states are in principle free to improve their institutions, by electing reformers, any such process takes a long time to bear results.

Third, the chosen monetary policy target of 2% inflation suited the 'core' countries, such as Germany, Netherlands, and Finland with a strong history of fiscal prudence. It did not suit those countries with a history of more flexible macroeconomic policy who lost traditional policy tools which they could have used otherwise: namely, monetary policy, flexible exchange rate with other members of Euro area.

Fourth, the availability of cheap credit inside the Euro area worked as a disincentive for institutional reform. Research has shown that during the first phase of the currency union, Greece, Italy, and Spain saw a worsening of the institutional delivery indicator, following substantial windfall gains and capital inflows as soon as these states entered the monetary union.[31]

Fifth, the loss of these policy tools affected the most highly indebted states, whose debt from that point on became effectively a debt in a foreign currency. These states assumed a higher risk in case of a crisis, since they had lost their macroeconomic tools for dealing with a sudden loss of demand as well as their lender of last resort. In addition, the loss of the exchange rate mechanism also removed one element of accountability for their economic policy: taxpayers and voters could not take into account the fluctuations of the exchange rate as a market indication of the soundness of their government's economic policies. The Euro Area countries with debt

[30] This is shown both by broad economic reviews, such as Daron Acemoglu and James A. Robinson, *Why Nations Fail: The Origins of Power, Prosperity and* Poverty (London: Profile Books, 2012); Mancur Olson, *The Rise and Decline of Nations: Economic Growth, Stagflation and Social Rigidities* (New Haven: Yale University Press, 1982); but also in more detailed reviews of European economics see Klaus Masuch, Edmund Moshammer, and Beatrice Pierluigi, 'Institutions, Public Debt and Growth in Europe' *ECB Working Papers Series*, No 1963, September 2016. This paper argues, among other things, that the presence of very sound institutions appears able to offset the detrimental effect of high debt on long-term growth.

[31] See Masuch, Moshammer, and Pierluigi, 'Institutions, Public Debt and Growth in Europe' (n. 30) 7; Jesús Fernández-Villaverde, Luis. Garicano, and Tano Santos, 'Political Credit Cycles: The Case of the Eurozone', 27 *Journal of Economic Perspectives* (2013) 145–66.

higher than 60% ratio of debt to GDP in 1999 were: Belgium (113.7%), Germany (60.9%), Greece (100.3%), Spain (62.3%), Italy (113.7%), Netherlands (61.1%), and Austria (67.3%).[32]

Sixth, a further source of instability was the banking system. Although the free movement of financial services and capital turned banking into a continental business, the regulation of banking remained in the member states' hands. There was no common deposit insurance scheme, nor a common mechanism for bank resolution.

What do these tentative observations mean for the symmetry test at the time of the Euro's foundation? It shows that the risks of entering the Eurozone were unreasonable for those states that met three criteria at the start: a) did not have a record of tight fiscal policy; b) had low productivity and weak institutions, which would take several years to repair; and c) were already highly indebted.

Entering the Eurozone under such terms meant that these states assumed *extremely high risks* because they did not have the time at their disposal in which to make structural reforms. The states that met those three tests were heavily *disadvantaged* by the Eurozone agreement, which created for them the risk of sovereign insolvency in the event of a sudden economic downturn or an asymmetric shock, since they had given up the tools that would have allowed them to address it. Their entering into the monetary union was an extremely *unwise* decision. It was unfair even though voluntary. Even though they willingly entered the union they did so on terms that, had they fully understood at the time, they would have considered unreasonable. I shall call them the 'originally disadvantaged' states. Greece and Italy, I believe, fall into this category.

It is therefore arguable that the original Eurozone agreement was unfair towards the originally disadvantaged states. What follows? For the purposes of corrective justice we need to ask if any party was harmed by the unfair agreement. If so, then the harmed party would have a claim for redress. Nevertheless, entering the Eurozone did not harm any party. There was no immediate loss. All the states experienced steady growth for the first ten years, or at least until the financial crisis struck. No claim for redress therefore arose at this point.

9.2 Fairness in Practice: The Euro's First Decade

We can now turn to issues of fairness *in practice* covering the period from the start of monetary union up to the end of its first decade. The narrative is very complex, so we will need to paint with a very broad brush. We need to divide our discussion between what happened before the crisis struck and what happened in response to

[32] See Dagmar Hartwig Lojsch, Marta Rodríguez-Vives, and Michal Slavík, 'The Size and Composition of Government Debt in the Euro Area' *ECB Occasional Paper Series*, No 132, October 2011.

it. This is because the circumstances were very different at each stage. Nevertheless, the assessment must be cumulative for the whole period, since everything that happened has its origin in the agreement as first made. We also need to distinguish between what each state has done towards each partner, for which it is individually responsible, as well as what all states were doing together, through the EU institutions or in other ways, for which all the member states are collectively responsible. We ask: was there unfairness in the way the states treated each other?

All the economic data show that the emergence of the Eurozone did not lead to convergence of the real economies of the member states. It led, for a while, to the convergence of bank lending rates. Yet this convergence was a serious mistake. Cheap credit created bubbles in private lending in Ireland and Spain and in public sector lending in Greece and Portugal. This was partly a failure of market discipline, but it was also a result of state action, since the regulators failed to notice the risks building up in the banking system of the periphery. Neither the Commission, nor the ECB, took action to control this risk.

It seems, however, that the states did not pursue coordinated policies. In some cases the policy of one state was certain to harm the others. Andrew Moravcsik has described how Germany pursued a policy that went beyond what was agreed and helped cause the crisis as it undermined the economies of the periphery. As is well known the Eurozone set a target of 2% for inflation, based on trends in Germany's labour market. Yet, as Moravcsik observes: 'Germany subsequently moved the goalposts by dampening its price and wage growth below that level.'[33] Moravcsik calculates that between 1999 and 2008 the average unit labour cost in the countries that have lived with excessive deficits, i.e. Greece, Italy, Portugal, and Spain, rose by one 1% per year over the target of 2%. So they slowly lost competitiveness towards the other members of the Eurozone. Germany, however, during the same period saw its unit labour cost rise by an average of less than 1% per year, well below the European target. This happened by a combination of slow wage growth, weak domestic consumption, labour market reforms, and cuts in government spending, linked perhaps to the costs with the unification of Germany.

Yet, over time, this disparity of economic policy, with 'excessive rises in unit labor costs in some places and wage suppression elsewhere generated a 25 percent overall gap in competitiveness between Germany and its European partners'.[34] These policies benefited Germany greatly because they allowed Germany's exports to grow everywhere in the Eurozone bringing healthy profits to the exporters, but 'at the expense not just of foreigners but also of German workers and taxpayers, whose wages were not keeping pace with inflation'.[35]

[33] Moravcsik, 'Europe After the Crisis: How to Sustain a Common Currency' (n. 20) 58.
[34] ibid 59.
[35] ibid 59.

Moravcsik is not alone in making the observation that Germany's policies after the establishment of the Euro undermined the prospects of the other member states, who had lost the policy option of replying through the exchange rate. Joseph Stiglitz describes Germany's actions as 'competitive devaluation', which is, he says, a 'form of beggar-thy-neighbor policy: one country gains at the expense of its trading partners'.[36]

Jean Pisany-Ferry, a more dispassionate commentator than Stiglitz, also reports that the policies of Germany departed from those of its partners, so that 'at a time when most European countries—including the United Kingdom and central Europe—were spending, Germany saved'.[37] Pisany-Ferry also reports that the divergence of relative demand, with demand rising in Southern Europe and shrinking or stagnating in Germany, led to external deficits in the South and surpluses in Germany.[38] He concludes that 'the stagnation of demand in Germany can be said to have fuelled the housing boom in Spain'.[39] He concludes that '[f]renzy in the South and lethargy in the North; this was a powerful and self-perpetuating dynamic, which was allowed to go on for far too long.'[40] As a result, Ireland, Spain, Portugal, Cyprus, and Greece were newly 'disadvantaged' states.

I spent a long time discussing the details of this mechanism of financial destruction, so as to establish as clearly as I could that it its operation is now common ground among economists of different persuasions and schools of thought. What is still under discussion is whether the German policy was intentional, which appears to be the view pursued by Joseph Stiglitz, or unintentional, which is the view of Pisani-Ferry. For the purposes of corrective justice the distinction is obviously an important one. Intentional harm is more serious than unintentional harm. This is where the distinction between the period before the crisis and the period after the crisis is significant: after the crisis, it was clear to everyone that the imbalances in the Eurozone had harmed the disadvantaged states. In any event, the European Commission had warned of these imbalances on the occasion of the Euro's tenth anniversary, when it said it reported 'substantial and lasting differences across countries'.[41] After that point the Germany policies must be held to be intentional.

Indeed, after the crisis broke out the European Union legislated changes to the way it monitors the European economies so as to prevent and correct any macroeconomic imbalances under the 'European Semester'.[42] Article 2 of the relevant

[36] Stiglitz, *The Euro* (n. 22) 105.

[37] Pisani-Ferry, *The Euro Crisis and its Aftermath* (n. 23) 49.

[38] ibid 50.

[39] ibid 50

[40] ibid 51. He adds: The German government was reluctant to end the country's penance, and the Spanish government did not want to crash the party. Both pushed on for as long as they could—until the crisis broke out.'

[41] European Commission, *EMU@10: Successes and Challenges after Ten Years of Economic and Monetary Union*, European Economy 2/2008, Luxembourg, 2008.

[42] See Regulation (EU) No 1176/2011of the European Parliament and of the Council of 16 November 2011 on the prevention and correction of macroeconomic imbalances

Regulation defines imbalance as: 'any trend giving rise to macroeconomic developments which are adversely affecting, or have the potential adversely to affect, the proper functioning of the economy of a Member State or of the economic and monetary union, or of the Union as a whole'. It is therefore beyond doubt that Germany's policies created imbalances and fuelled the credit boom in the South. While it was not inevitable that such imbalances would be created, there was no mechanism inside the Eurozone for controlling Germany's policies. As a result, when the financial crisis struck, the states of the periphery were in a position of great weakness. Their banking systems in particular were hugely vulnerable.

I need here to add a note on Greece, since its problems were significantly different. The Greek government engaged in a very risky strategy of fiscal expansion in the period 2004 to 2009, making use of the very low interest rates at which Greece could borrow after having joined the Euro in 2002. The policy achieved high growth for a while, but it was unsustainable in the long run and created great risks. Fiscal expansion was increasing both the debt and the deficit. Eventually, the government lost control of public finances in 2007–2008 as the financial crisis reached Europe. At that point the government sought to cover up part of the relevant statistical data, especially as they affected health spending. In the end, in the summer of 2009, rather than taking drastic measures with spending cuts and tax rises, the Prime Minister Costas Karamanlis called an early election, which he lost heavily. When the new government took over, it discovered the true state of the public finances and the statistical inaccuracies. The new Prime Minister George Papandreou announced this to the world a few days after the election. Within a few months Greece was frozen out of the markets and sought help from the European Union and the IMF.

The problems of Ireland were different still. Although the problems in Ireland (as everywhere else) were related to the Eurozone's architecture, they also had a strong domestic political component.[43] Ireland had respected all its obligations under the fiscal compact. Both its debt and its deficit figures were within the targets. As in Spain, its public finances were in surplus at the start of the crisis. But the safeguards in place in the Eurozone looked only at public finances. The architecture did not consider the underlying liabilities of the banking sector, which had grown exponentially during the boom years. When the credit crunch happened the Irish government issued a blanket guarantee to cover deposits and bondholders in order to rescue its oversized banking system. Irish public finances became unsustainable overnight—the guarantee cost the Irish taxpayer approximately 40% of GDP, so that at the end of 2012 the Irish debt had risen to 118% of GDP.[44] The banking crisis transformed Ireland from solvent to insolvent overnight.

[43] See Fintan O'Toole, *The Ship of Fools: How Stupidity and Corruption Sank the Celtic Tiger* (London: Faber and Faber, 2009).

[44] Pisani-Ferry, *The Euro Crisis and its Aftermath* (n. 23) 54–6, 100–1.

If we pause here to summarize our account of the early years of the Eurozone from the point of view of the symmetry principle, we could note the following:

- The Euro created a common financial space, where risk travels instantly from one country to the next and from one financial institution to another. The Euro became effectively a union of financial risk.
- Inflation in the member states of the Eurozone diverged persistently, even though all states were subject to similar nominal interest rates. The cumulative effect of small, but persistent inflation differentials and converging nominal interest rates was a loss of competitiveness for the high inflation states (Ireland, Portugal, Greece, Spain), which hampered real economic convergence.[45]
- Once the member states were within the currency union, their policy options and their room for manoeuvre was limited, since it was impossible for them to adjust the exchange rate in any way or to have their own monetary policy.
- Germany's fiscal policies transferred risk to the states of the periphery, who had lost the policy tools to respond quickly to Germany's fall in demand.
- Greece, Portugal, Ireland, Cyprus, and Spain made serious policy errors. The Greek government violated the explicit terms of the Eurozone agreements in 2007–2008. Greece and Portugal increased their debt in an unsustainable way. Spain and Ireland fuelled a real estate bubble. Cyprus, Ireland, and Spain developed an unsustainable banking system.
- The consequences of these mistakes, however, were magnified by the Eurozone structures, since these states lacked the policy tools to address them effectively. Once they became highly indebted, these states could not devalue their currency in order to recover. If, as happened in the European Monetary System crisis in 1992–1993, the governments of the periphery had been able to devalue, recovery would almost certainly have been more rapid.[46]
- Whatever the structural effects of the Eurozone architecture on them, at the end of the Euro's first decade several states founds themselves in a very disadvantaged position: Greece, Italy, Portugal, Ireland, Cyprus, and Spain. On account of the level of their sovereign debt or the exposure of their financial system, these states found themselves open to disproportionate risks—and were duly hit very hard by the 2008 crisis.

[45] See also Jeffrey Franks, Bergljot Barkbu, Rodolphe Blavy, William Oman, and Hanni Schoelermann, 'Economic Convergence in the Euro Area: Coming Together or Drifting Apart?' *IMF Working Paper—WP/18/10* (Washington DC, IMF, 2018) 10–11. The paper concludes: 'While there was nominal convergence of inflation and interest rates, real convergence of per capita income levels has not occurred among the original euro area members since the advent of the common currency.'

[46] See Mark Copelovitch, Jeffry Frieden, and Stefanie Walter, 'The Political Economy of the Euro Crisis' 49 *Comparative Political Studies* (2016) 811–40, at 823.

In short, the structural defects of the Eurozone resulted in great losses for Greece, Ireland, Portugal, and Cyprus. These burdened member states were also culpable, however, for this outcome due to their own policy errors and excessive risk-taking. At this moment, however, the other member states did not sit idly by, even though the treaties implied that this is what they should do. The no-bailout clause was set aside and a huge programme of financial assistance was set up.

9.3 Fairness in Practice: The Response to the Crisis

We now turn to the period 2010 to the present. There are many detailed and thorough accounts of the Eurozone's response to the crisis written by economists and lawyers.[47] The broad outlines are well known. The European leaders agreed a 80 billion Euro package of bilateral loans for Greece in May 2010, offered similar assistance to Ireland in November 2010, to Portugal in May 2011, and to Cyprus in June 2012, as well as offering to dedicate up to 100 billion euros to Spain for the recapitalization of its banking system. In 2012 the Greek programme was adjusted in order to reduce interest rests on assistance loans to a non-punitive level and coordinated a programme of quasi-voluntary debt relief by way of the Private Sector Involvement (PSI), which saw a reduction of about 100 billion euros in the nominal value of the Greek debt. Each offer of assistance came with strict conditionality and the requirement to proceed to fiscal adjustment and structural reforms and supported by a system of close oversight by a 'troika' of officials from the European Commission, the ECB, and the IMF. The most important intervention in the crisis was, however, the intervention of the ECB, when Mario Draghi said in July 2012 that the Bank would do 'whatever it takes' to save the Euro.

The member states also acted to rewrite the rules of the Eurozone. They introduced more detailed rules regarding fiscal discipline in the Fiscal Compact of 2012 and then created the European Stability Mechanism (ESM) for the members of the Eurozone, again by way of an international treaty, which was concluded outside the formal mechanisms of the European Union. They also legislated to move the financial assistance programmes fully within the scope of EU law, which they did by way of Regulation (EU) 472/2013. When Greece required a new programme in 2015, after the new populist government allowed the programme to expire, the third Greek bailout was provided by the ESM on the basis of the new regulatory framework of EU law.

[47] See Markus K. Brunnermeier, Harold James, and Jean-Pierre Landau, *The Euro and the Battle of Ideas* (Princeton: Princeton University Press, 2018) 97–209, Pisani-Ferry, *The Euro Crisis and its Aftermath* (n. 23) 77–128. See also the extensive and thorough internal review of the IMF: Internal Evaluation Office of the IMF, *The IMF and the Crises in Greece, Ireland, and Portugal: Evaluation Report* (Washington, DC: International Monetary Fund, 2016).

These changes took place in an atmosphere of extreme urgency, which was partly generated by the Eurozone structures themselves.[48] Studies have shown that during the Euro-area financial crisis, interactions among sovereign spreads, sovereign credit ratings, and bank credit ratings appeared to have been characterized by self-generating feedback loops.[49] A large empirical literature has shown that the various fundamental variables that have been used in attempts to explain spreads have not been able to account for either the very low spreads (measured relative to German sovereigns) that prevailed in the years preceding the outbreak of the Euro-area crisis in 2009 or the very sharp rise in spreads that took place following the onset of the crisis. The general finding that spreads overshot (relative to the fundamentals) in a downward direction *before* the crisis and in an upward direction *after* the crisis holds regardless of: (a) the mix of fundamental variables used to explain spreads; and (b) whether the fundamentals are supplemented with additional variables.[50]

The member states and especially Germany have been criticized for three things in relation to their response to the crisis: first, they acted slowly, allowing the crisis to drag on needlessly; second, they did only what was minimally necessary to sustain the Euro at each step, without acting decisively to restore trust in the financial system as a whole;[51] third, by not giving Greece a debt restructuring in 2010 (but only in 2012), they effectively bailed out the private lenders that were co-responsible for Greece's colossal debt while transferring the burden to Greece's taxpayers.[52]

From the point of view of the symmetry principle we can summarize the response to the crisis with the following observations:

- The disadvantaged member states did not have a realistic option of leaving the Euro—since any exit would pose enormous risks for them. They therefore

[48] Throughout this period the IMF and the Commission made very optimistic assumptions of the effects of the crisis, which almost always proved wrong. See Rogoff, 'Crash Time' (n. 6).

[49] George Soros has written as follows: 'For about a year after the Lehman bankruptcy, interest rate differentials remained unrealistically low because the European Central Bank was still discounting government bonds on equal terms, so that markets erred on the side of optimism. Then came the Greek shock, when the markets realized that Greece could actually default. Suddenly, the markets imposed very severe risk premiums on all heavily indebted countries, which therefore no longer had the fiscal strength to support their banks—and that was really the onset of the euro crisis. So markets first failed to identify the flaws in the euro structure, and once they became aware of them, they overreacted.' See George Soros with Gregor Peter Schmitz, *The Tragedy of the European Union: Disintegration or Revival?* (New York: Public Affairs, 2014) 67–8.

[50] See Heather D. Gibson, Stephen G. Hall, and George S. Tavlas, 'Self-fulfilling Dynamics: The Interactions of Sovereign Spreads, Sovereign Ratings and Bank Ratings during the Euro Financial Crisis' 73 *Journal of International Money and* Finance (2017) 118–33.

[51] See Mody, *Eurotragedy* (n. 29) 232 ff.

[52] Just before Greece's debt restructuring Kenneth Rogoff wrote: 'Why should the Greek people (not to mention the Irish and the Portuguese) accept years of austerity and slow growth for the sake of propping up the French and German banking systems, unless they are given huge bribes to do so?'; see Kenneth S. Rogoff, 'The Euro's PIG Headed Masters' *Project Syndicate*, 3 June 2011.

had no realistic option of turning down any offers of help from the rest of the Eurozone.

- The response to the crisis was effectively a new beginning for the Eurozone: the rules were rewritten. Yet the states agreed to the changes under extreme pressure.[53]
- The response to the crisis was almost entirely intergovernmental. The most important decisions were taken by government leaders in meetings of the European Council, or in the informal meeting of the Eurozone finance ministers, the Eurogroup, where the ordinary rules of EU decision-making did not apply. The discrepancy in power between the larger creditor states over the indebted smaller states was overwhelming.
- The stronger states responded to the crisis by providing assistance to the weaker countries by way of loans, not grants. In effect the stronger members of the Eurozone took over some of the risks of default of the highly indebted countries from the private sector.
- The IMF—and many economists—favoured debt relief for Greece from the start of the crisis but was overruled by the ECB.[54] In the end the 2012 debt restructuring for Greece concerned private not official debt (so the EU taxpayers did not suffer any direct losses).
- The European Union as a whole proceeded to rewrite the rules of the Eurozone, making first steps towards a banking union and creating a formal mechanism for programmes of financial assistance.
- The indebted countries did not have a real choice whether to accept the financial assistance programme or not, since without assistance they faced almost certain disorderly default and exit from the Eurozone with catastrophic social and economic consequences. The bailout negotiations were therefore one-sided since the indebted countries had no option but to accept the rescue package offered by the EU and the IMF.
- The apparent imposition of economic terms by the Eurogroup on member states and the continuing monitoring of state budgets by the European Commission generated widespread criticism of the European institutions as undemocratic and authoritarian.
- In the spring/summer of 2015 Greece was offered the option of leaving the Eurozone. When the prospect of leaving became real after the Greek referendum

[53] For a detailed account see Jeffry Frieden and Stefanie Walter, 'Understanding the Political Economy of the Eurozone Crisis' 20 *Annual Review of Political Science* (2017) 371–90.

[54] Kenneth Rogoff writes: 'From 2010 onward, I and others suggested that the eurozone needed to write down sharply the debts of Portugal, Ireland, Greece, and probably Spain. Yet, at the same time, the IMF and the European Commission were offering rosy forecasts for Greece, which, as we all know, went on to suffer a massive and sustained output collapse. Policymakers failed to take radical steps when they had the chance because they were being told to stay the course by economic forecasters who simply could not accept that financial crises can significantly amplify the depth and length of recessions.' See Rogoff, 'Crash Time' (n. 6).

of July 2015, the Greek government changed course and opted into the austerity programme prescribed by its EU partners and the IMF. The crisis has left Greece (at 180% to GDP in 2017) and Italy (at 132% of GDP in 2017) with extremely high levels of debt and few policy options as to how to reduce it. The post-crisis Eurozone finds them in a worse position than they had been in 1999 before they entered.

In short, the European Union reacted to the crisis by both assisting the states in need and by changing the background rules for the future. The principle of 'no-bailout' gave way to a manifestation of solidarity. All the disadvantaged member states that faced problems were provided with emergency loans that helped them avoid sovereign default, at an interest that was reduced in all cases well below the market rate. The austerity measures imposed on them by the rescue packages by way of 'conditionality' were less drastic than the austerity that they would have had to go through had they defaulted.

The changes brought into the Eurozone's general architecture, however, were not sufficient to address some of the systemic and structural problems initially addressed by Kaldor and Feldstein. The disadvantaged states were protected from the worst outcomes of the crisis, but they remain disadvantaged into the future on account of their high levels of debt. A future crisis may create even more problems for them. Writing at the very end of the crisis Kenneth Rogoff said that in his view 'it is not obvious that the eurozone can survive another deep systemic crisis'.[55] He summarized the point by saying that: 'the eurozone is not going to survive in the long run without a system of EU-wide shared fiscal responsibility and, yes, transfers on a much larger scale than what currently exists'.[56] He was pessimistic about that because of the lack of political leadership. He noted: 'Anyone raising the issue of transfers with the Germans will run up against the fact that Germany's elites sold the eurozone to their voters by promising that it would never become a "transfer union"'.[57]

9.4 Loss and Redress

I now turn to the general assessment of the institutions of the Eurozone from the point of view of the symmetry principle, under the point of view of corrective justice. I ask three questions regarding fairness over the whole course of the Eurozone's lifetime. First, was there an act or acts that *wronged* another party? Second, did any parties incur any *losses* as a result of the unfair actions of their partners? And, third, what could be the appropriate and proportionate *redress* from

[55] ibid.
[56] See ibid.
[57] ibid.

wrongdoers to the victims? The story, even as simplified above in this chapter, is very complex. There was some wrongdoing on all sides. All the parties have behaved unfairly towards other parties in some way. I start with the collective responsibility that all states have as co-authors of the Eurozone's overall design. I will then turn to matters of individual responsibility.

The architecture of the Euro was flawed from the start. It created asymmetrical risks for several disadvantaged states either through sovereign debt or through the banking system. There is a clear case of 'structural responsibility' burdening all the original members of the Eurozone. They are responsible for creating an economic practice with potentially disastrous consequences for some of them. The general architecture of the Eurozone was flawed because it created a monetary union without a commensurate fiscal union, in exactly the ways observed by Kenneth Rogoff, Nicholas Kaldor, and Martin Feldstein, as we saw at the start of this chapter. The EMU provided that monetary policy would be conducted by the ECB, but that economic policy would remain in the hands of the member states. It is now common ground that the flawed design—for which all the founding members of the Eurozone must be held jointly responsible—contributed to the length and depth of the crisis.

Individual member states were responsible in other ways. The government of Greece pursued unwise fiscal policies in the period immediately after joining the Euro. When the financial crisis hit in 2008 it violated the terms of the Eurozone agreements by covering up the true state of its finances. Portugal and Italy allowed their debt to grow against the explicit commitments they made under the Maastricht Treaty. Interestingly, Ireland and Spain kept their side of the Stability and Growth Pact and kept well within the targets for fiscal deficits. But they are at fault—as indeed are the ECB and the Commission—for failing to properly regulate the financial sector and for fuelling a credit bubble that almost destroyed their banking systems and for failing to take precautionary measures when they had to. Germany, too, behaved with little regard for the effects of its policies for the rest of the Eurozone. Its own austerity policies harmed the economies of the periphery. It may not have anticipated this at the start, but by the end of 2010 the mechanism of imbalances was well understood.

Finally, France and Germany failed to enforce the Stability and Growth Pact at its infancy and allowed themselves to break the fiscal discipline required by the Maastricht Treaty. After they avoided sanction by the Commission, it was extremely hard to impose any sanctions on any other states in the future.

To complete this picture we must also say that the banking system failed to understand the risks of the Eurozone and mispriced debt throughout the pre-crisis period. Banks were to blame for the chaos of the crisis, even though many of them were protected from any losses by the delayed response to the crisis (and many of them were effectively bailed out during 2010–2012, when their losses were passed on to the Greek taxpayer).

What does this mean for solidarity, understood as a manifestation of corrective justice? Corrective justice is not punitive, it is restorative. Although, for example, Greece violated the terms of fiscal responsibility, it is not clear that its violation caused anyone else any appreciable loss at all. There was no higher inflation as a result, for example, given Greece's small size. Of course, the Greek crisis set off a world-wide financial tremor. But the fear of contagion was not created merely because of what Greece did, but also because of the weakness elsewhere in the financial system and the public finances of other Eurozone countries, such as Ireland, Italy, and Spain. The problems that the Greek crisis unearthed were systemic.

The bailout programmes, moreover, did not cost any other member states any money. All the financial assistance from the member states (as opposed to the 'haircut' that private investors accepted in 2012) took the form of loans, at an—admittedly discounted—interest. But while Germany had to increase its borrowing in order to lend to the indebted states, its costs of borrowing did not go up, since Germany became a safe haven during the crisis and the interest rate at which it borrowed dropped significantly for all its loans. Its bonds remained a highly sought-after asset throughout the duration of the crisis. Germany was exposed to the risk, of course, that Greece, Ireland, Cyprus, and Portugal may have ended up defaulting. Nevertheless, it was always extremely unlikely that there would be such a default, since the Eurozone controlled all the cards over the member states—as the Greek populist government discovered in the summer of 2015.

In addition, Germany benefitted greatly through the ordinary channels of trade, because of the fixed exchange rate vis-à-vis the other states of the Eurozone. According to Andrew Moravcsik's calculations, Germany benefits every year from the current structure of the Eurozone as follows:

> Because Germany is in the eurozone, its external competitiveness was not offset by a rising currency. Germany's real exchange rate today, under the single currency, is roughly 40 percent below where it would be if the deutsche mark still existed. The result: Germany's trade surplus, at $200 billion a year, is the world's largest, even greater than China's. Forty percent of the surplus comes from Germany's trade within the eurozone—a total roughly equal to the combined deficits of the crisis countries.[58]

Similar benefits applied to the other states of the core, Netherlands, Finland, and Austria. Although they could have incurred losses through the crisis, had the Euro disintegrated, they emerged without loss. The rescue operations cost them very little in real terms, if anything at all. So even though Greece and to some extent Portugal, Spain, and Ireland are to blame for their own woes, they did not cause any

[58] Andrew Moravcsik, 'Europe After the Crisis: How to Sustain a Common Currency' *Foreign Affairs*, 2012.

loss to others. The issue of reparation to Germany and the other creditors does not arise. But how about the other way round?

Remember that corrective justice provides redress for wrongful loss. It is not hard to find the real losers of the crisis. The distinction is clear between the prosperous North and the struggling South. Ten years after the Euro came to being, the economies of Greece, Italy, and Spain are now caught in a vicious circle of low growth, high indebtedness, and high unemployment.[59] In the highly indebted states of the South millions of people remain unemployed, or only partly employed, or trapped in low-skilled and low-paid jobs. The political climate in these countries is toxic and hospitable to demagogues of all descriptions and not conducive to radical reform. It is now beyond doubt that their economic prospects and their political cultures would have been better had they never joined the Euro in the first place. At the same time, however, these states cannot leave the Euro without running even more serious risks of economic collapse, which would set back their own economic recovery even further. Joining the EMU created real losses for them.

It follows that the rescue operations were not just manifestations of charity. Given that the crisis had systemic roots and caused loss directly, the rescue operations were morally obligatory for the Eurozone. Although the treaties provided for a 'no-bailout' rule, and a unilateral default would technically have been within the rules, the programmes of financial assistance permitted the disadvantaged states to remain within the Eurozone agreement without suffering the worst consequences of defaulting.

The programmes may well be seen as expressions of solidarity under the symmetry principle: they compensated the member states for the loss caused by the structural flaws of the Eurozone's design, although they also took into account those member states' culpability in not doing enough to avoid the worst aspects of the crisis during the boom years.

Corrective justice gives us an ethical account of the financial assistance programmes. Because there was a wrong that caused loss, there had to be some redress. Redress under corrective justice aims at remedying the wrongful losses caused to the disadvantaged members by the mistakes committed by all of them as they set up the first architecture and as they applied it in the years 1999 to the present. The burden of redress was borne by the winners, but it had to be proportionate, given that the highly indebted states were also to blame for their fate, due to their own errors. Corrective justice does not work in a punitive way, but seeks to remedy wrongful loss where it finds it. It is important to note here that corrective redress does not entail *permanent* fiscal transfers from the core states. It

[59] How the Eurozone contributed to this disparity was explained by Moravcsik and Feldstein, as we saw above. For a telling summary of the Eurozone's division between North and South see Deborah Ball, 'Aftereffects of Eurozone Crisis Plague Europe's South' *Wall Street Journal*, 1 June 2018.

only justifies redress for the losses caused in fact by the flawed architecture and individual actions, if such a loss can be sufficiently quantified.

This argument suggests that the programmes of assistance were expressions of solidarity under the symmetry principle for the period up until the crisis. There is an argument, however, that such programmes have not gone far enough. Although the assistance programmes alleviated the losses of the crisis in a proportionate way, they have not ensured that the lack of symmetry has disappeared for the future. Many leading economists have taken the view that without serious reform, the Eurozone will continue to create the same disparities. In a thorough study of the institutional structure of the Eurozone, Maurice Obstfeld, the IMF's chief economist, argues that the increased risks imposed by the Eurozone structure upon the highly indebted countries requires some form of fiscal union whereby some fiscal transfers will be made from the successful states to the less successful (through a mechanism that should eliminate moral hazard).[60] Similarly, a proposal for Eurozone reform by some senior French and German economists suggests that the Euro area continues to be financially vulnerable and is likely to underperform with respect to long-term growth, partly because of a 'poorly designed fiscal and financial architecture'.[61] The stagnation of the periphery is—partly—the result of the flawed architecture of the Eurozone, for which all member state are responsible.

We have arrived at a link between an important *wrong* and a corresponding and identifiable *loss*. The mistaken architecture of the Eurozone, for which all the parties are responsible, has caused the current economic stagnation in the periphery. What form can redress, realistically, take? One possibility is to create a temporary and one-off 'Growth Fund', possibly funded by the ESM, which would support investment in the disadvantaged states, i.e. those with a legacy of high debt, low unemployment, and low productivity. It can do so on the basis of strict conditionality, similar to that applying to the programmes of financial assistance. The fact that this will be a one-off programme, justified on the basis of the damage already caused to the burdened states because of the flawed architecture of the Eurozone, rules out moral hazard. The temporary nature of the fund also would reassure taxpayers in the core states that the logic of this Fund is not one of permanent transfers, such as they occur in a social welfare state. The transfers would be time-limited and have the clear aim of assisting the periphery to break the vicious circle of stagnation which was caused by the asymmetries of the Eurozone and the mistakes already made. The Fund would aim to return the periphery to a position of symmetrical

[60] Helge Berger, Giovanni Dell'Ariccia, and Maurice Obstfeld, *Revisiting the Economic Case for Fiscal Union in the Euro Area* (Washington, DC: International Monetary Fund, 2018).

[61] Agnes Benassy-Quere, Markus K. Brunnermeier, Henrik Enderlein, Emmanuel Farhi, Marcel Fratzscher, Clemens Fuest, Pierre-Olivier Gourinchas, Philippe Martin, Jean Pisani-Ferry, Helene Rey, Isabel Schnabel, Nicolas Veron, Beatrice Weder di Mauro, and Jeromin Zettelmeyer, *Reconciling Risk Sharing with Market Discipline, A Constructive Approach to Euro Area Reform: Policy Insight No 91* (CEPR, London, 2018) 2.

opportunity, which fairness requires that they should have had at the start of the common adventure.

The funding for such a 'Growth Fund' need not burden Germany and the other winners of the Euro. If the member states permit the states of the periphery—as a one off measure—to borrow by way of 'Eurobonds', so that they exceed the deficit and debt targets undertaken under the Stability and Growth Fund but under the joint guarantee of the ESM, again as a one-off mechanism in order to ensure the lowest possible interest, then the states of the periphery will be able to invest in infrastructure and retraining programmes that, it is hoped, may bring down unemployment more quickly. If these loans have the long maturities and low interest rates offered to Greece in the summer of 2018, then the borrowing states will be able to pay them off over a long period of time, absorbing the additional cost without negative effects in growth today. By guaranteeing those loans—and sanctioning the potentially inflation-increasing fiscal expansion in the highly indebted states—the core states will not be spending any money themselves. They will only be running additional risks. The greatest risk is that the borrowing states will default. Yet the risk is small given that the loans will be accompanied by strict conditionality backed by EU mechanisms for ensuring compliance. In any event, even if some loss does occur in the future, the core states will continue to benefit from the Eurozone's architecture and will receive great economic benefits through the single market. So this one-off 'Growth Fund' would act as a fairness-restoring remedy for the Eurozone's early mistakes, without much cost to the core states.

There is also a more ambitious argument, however. It has been made by Andrew Moravcsik, who wants the transfers from the core to the periphery to be permanent in order to bring about real economic convergence. He says: 'For as long as the Eurozone countries continue to take such radically different trajectories regarding labor costs, government spending, private-sector behavior, and competitiveness, Europe will remain no more of an optimal currency area than it was when the euro entered circulation.'[62] Moravcsik may be right about convergence. But the aim of our proposal is not convergence, which requires a certain outcome in the distribution of resources, but merely the symmetry of opportunities and risks, irrespective of distributive outcomes. Restoring fairness according to the symmetry principle demands redress for wrongs actually committed, if they cause loss. This is how corrective justice works. It does not involve a permanent distributive scheme with a view to converging prosperity.

Yet, Moravcsik's argument can be restated in line with the framework of corrective justice. We can say that if the parties make again *the same mistakes* and cause the same or similar loss to some disadvantaged parties in the future, they will then generate new claims of redress. The appropriate response to such an event

[62] Moravcsik, 'Europe After the Crisis: How to Sustain a Common Currency' (n. 20).

will not be distributive but restorative. The redress will have to follow every event of wrongdoing. Inevitably, thus, we now enter the domain of institutional reform for the future in a way that may appear permanent. This would perhaps be the balancing mechanism for a permanent failure to restore symmetry and fairness in the Eurozone.

This proposal for a permanent transfer mechanism is, however, a distinct theoretical question. It asks if the members states should aim to restore symmetry well into the future, and if for that purpose they should amend the rules in order to share fiscal risk (as argued, for example by Berger, Dell'Ariccia, and Obstfeld).[63] The ground for such a permanent mechanism set up by the parties by way of treaty amendment will not be, strictly speaking, the requirements of redress under corrective justice but the aim of redressing unfairness in a permanent way. Moreover, in case of treaty reform the basis of the relevant obligations will not just be the principle of corrective justice, but also the consent of the member states, assuming that a new treaty can be agreed (and assuming that the new treaty itself passes the symmetry test—because the risk of asymmetry may run the other way, with the formerly disadvantaged states becoming permanent recipients of disproportionate largesse).

The idea of a fiscal union has, therefore, two different manifestations: the first is a one-off attempt at redress for past injustice; the second is a permanent transfer union aiming at restoring fairness into the future.

9.5 Conclusion

We can now answer the questions we asked at the start. Was the financial assistance from some member states to those in need morally required as a manifestation of solidarity? The answer I have given is an affirmative one. Assistance was ethically required. This is so even though it was not required by distributive obligations of social justice, such as those that apply within a federation. Social justice on the basis of distributive justice only applies to a single state. But solidarity is not exhausted by distributive justice. Solidarity is also shown when we respond to wrongdoing and offer redress to someone whom we have harmed. The responsibility of providing redress is a matter of binding legal obligation in private law, but it may not be enforceable in international trade. Still, however, it is a moral obligation that arises in practical reasoning. The financial assistance programme can thus be seen to have been not only justified, but also required in the light of corrective principles of fairness in circumstances of interdependence created by the institutions of monetary union.

[63] Berger, Dell'Ariccia, Obstfeld, *Revisiting Fiscal Union in the Euro Area* (n. 60).

Our guiding framework has been that of corrective or cooperative justice. Since the member states jointly created a structurally flawed Eurozone, they remain jointly responsible for the asymmetric risks they created for the disadvantaged members. When the crisis caused important economic and social losses to the disadvantaged states, all the other states as a whole had a moral obligation of redress. Although the precise application of the principle to the historical facts requires careful factual argument about the extent of the damage caused—and of the contributory responsibility of policy-makers in the disadvantaged states—a tentative conclusion can be drawn based on the evidence already available. The financial assistance programmes can be reasonably seen as the expression of a new form of solidarity generated by European integration. This kind of solidarity, however, is transnational, not constitutional. It is the result of states cooperating, not of citizens setting up common political institutions.

10
Democracy and Reform

I have outlined a progressive internationalist theory according to which the European Union (EU) is a Union of Peoples that answers to three distinct tests: a principle of accountability, a principle of freedom, and a principle of fairness. These are political and legal principles appropriate to relations among states under the law of nations. My general conclusion has been that the European Union satisfies these three tests of legitimacy, at least for the most part. The argument, however, has not dealt with the most common challenge to the EU. Does the EU undermine democracy? This criticism is widespread and it is also complex.

One aspect of the criticism is that the European Union is itself 'undemocratic'. I have rejected this argument for reasons of principle. Democracy does not apply to the European Union because it is not the kind of thing that answers to a test of democracy. The EU is an international organization bringing together independent, self-governing states that wish to create common institutions with limited powers. I accept Stephen Weatherill's view that the European Union is 'a place to manage the interdependence of States in Europe'.[1] In Weatherill's analysis the EU is a process whereby 'States give up power to act unilaterally so that they may participate in the exercise of a collective problem-solving capacity that is a great deal more effective'.[2]

I accept also Andrew Moravcsik's analysis of the present political reality of the Union and his conclusion that in its present form the European Union does not come anywhere close to replicating the political functions of a state. Moravcsik observes that 'the issues handled by the EU—and even more so second-order institutional choices about how to manage them—lack salience in the minds of European voters' so that: 'of the five most salient issues in most west European democracies—health care provision, education, law and order, pension and social security policy and taxation—none is primarily an EU competence'.[3] Moravcsik concludes that for the European Union the question of democracy does not arise.[4] Even if this list is now to be amended in light of changes in migration flows from third states over the

[1] Stephen Weatherill, *Law and Values in the European Union* (Oxford: Oxford University Press, 2016) 20.

[2] ibid 398.

[3] Andrew Moravcsik, 'In Defence of the "Democratic Deficit": Reassessing the Legitimacy of the European Union' 40 *Journal of Common Market Studies* (2002) 603, at 615.

[4] See also Andrew Moravcsik, *The Choice for Europe: Social Purpose and State Power from Messina to Maastricht* (London: Routledge, 1998).

A Union of Peoples. Pavlos Eleftheriadis. Oxford University Press (2020). © Oxford University Press.
DOI: 10.1093/oso/9780198854173.001.0001

past five years, the point remains true. As a matter of fact the political role of the European Union has been greatly exaggerated.[5]

Many scholars agree with the general point that the processes of democracy cannot be adopted, or replicated, by an international union. Joshua Cohen and Charles Sabel, for example, argue in some detail for the position that the international domain is not to be assessed with the conventional tools of democracy but can instead be seen as a 'deliberative polyarchy'.[6] Ruth Grant and Robert Keohane take the view that 'there is no simple analogy that can be made between domestic democratic politics and global politics'.[7] Even those who argue for the creation of a supranational democracy in Europe agree, at least implicitly, with the premise that the EU cannot be a democracy in its present form. Jürgen Habermas proposes supranational democracy only after we manage to create a 'cosmopolitan community' that brings together the various European peoples.[8] In a joint book, the distinguished politicians Daniel Cohn Bendit and Guy Verhofstadt argue for a post-national, 'genuinely united', federal European Union at some time in the future.[9] They accept, albeit implicitly, that such a united people does not yet exist.

There is a second version of the criticism, however, which is much harder to respond to. Even if one agrees with Weatherill's analysis of the EU, democracy does not become irrelevant. There is a related pressing question of legitimacy. Does the European Union undermine domestic democracy? It is clear that the EU takes some powers away from domestic institutions. It changes the way they work. It is possible that the EU may undermine democracy, even if it does not undermine sovereignty.

Robert Dahl reminds us, for example, that democracy exists when a political association provides equal participation in public decisions by way of a number of qualitative standards. He lists them as: 'effective participation', 'voting equality', 'enlightened understanding', 'control of the agenda', and 'inclusion of adults'.[10] One could put these in different ways or use different terminology. But if none of these things work, democracy fails. The operation of the European Union could undermine all of them. For example, if decisions are taken by a bureaucracy in Brussels, there may be no effective participation in them. Participation in domestic politics would become meaningless and so would voting. Centralization in Brussels

[5] For a different—but ultimately non persuasive—view, see Andreas Follesdal and Simon Hix, 'Why There Is a Democratic Deficit in the EU: A Response to Majone and Moravcsik' 44 *Journal of Common Market Studies* (2006) 533–62.

[6] Joshua Cohen and Charles Sabel, 'Global Democracy?' 37 *New York University Journal of International Law and Policy* (2006), 763–97, 779 ff.

[7] Ruth W. Grant and Robert O. Keohane, 'Accountability and Abuses in World Politics' 99 *American Political Science Review* (2005) 29–43, at 34.

[8] For example Jürgen Habermas, *The Crisis of the European Union: A Response* (Cambridge: Polity, 2012).

[9] Daniel Cohn Bendit and Guy Verhofstadt, *For Europe! Manifesto for a Postnational Revolution in Europe* (Munich: Carl Hanser Verlag, 2012).

[10] Robert A. Dahl, *On Democracy* (New Haven and London: Yale University Press, 2000) 37–8.

among a technocratic elite would undermine 'enlightened understanding', since few would understand what was going on. It would also undermine 'control of the agenda', since the bureaucracy would set the pace of policy-making.

In all these ways the concentration of power in the institutions of the EU will be undermining the effectiveness of domestic democracy, without formally changing the shape of domestic institutions. Here is then the democratic risk. By taking away decision-making power from constitutional to international procedures, the EU renders the domestic process ineffective. Is this argument correct? Is the European Union an impediment to democracy? This is the difficult question we now need to address.

10.1 The EU as an Impediment to Democracy

This argument has been made with great clarity by the Oxford political theorist Larry Siedentop. In *Democracy in Europe* Siedentop writes that 'democratic legitimacy is at risk' because the European Union weakens democratic institutions within the states without replacing them with anything better.[11] If some of the most important decisions are taken in Brussels then the domestic democratic processes are pointless. This argument has been invigorated by the financial crisis of 2008–2010 and its aftermath. As we saw in Chapter 9, the programmes of fiscal adjustment were practically impossible to negotiate by the burdened states. The circumstances required that the states took urgent action. Observers now say that the European Union's rigid rules and processes around monetary union end up oppressing and dominating the member states. One author has argued, for example, that the financial assistance programmes were 'undemocratic' since they imposed an outcome on the electorates of the member states.[12]

Some of the more polemical arguments can be easily dismissed. For example, no 'technocratic' Prime Ministers were 'imposed' on Italy and Greece, as some critics have said. The allegation is simply false and misunderstands the parliamentary system.[13] In all cases these Prime Ministers won the approval of their domestic

[11] Larry Siedentop, *Democracy in Europe* (London: Penguin, 2001) 1.

[12] See e.g. Matthias Matthijs, 'Integration at What Price? The Erosion of National Democracy in the Euro Periphery' 52 *Government and Opposition* (2017) 266–94, where the author says: 'For a country like Greece, and others in the periphery, there would be no choice in economic policy, as fiscal austerity and structural reform were directly imposed on those countries by the Troika, with their national governments unable to design the programme, let alone define any of its content' (ibid 279). The IMF/EU programmes were all approved by parliament in the appropriate way. Matthijs forgets to take into account that the alternative to the IMF/EU programmes was the worse austerity that would have been caused by sovereign default and a disorderly exit from the Euro. The programme in fact provided extra funding for Greece and reduced the need for austerity.

[13] Matthijs considers the appointment of 'technocratic Prime Ministers in Italy and Greece, 'directly imposed' (ibid 281). The same mistake is made by Juri Viehoff, 'Eurozone Justice' 26 *The Journal of Political Philosophy* (2018) 388–414, at 402.

parliament in the ordinary way of parliamentary democracy. There was nothing undemocratic in their choice as a compromise solution between several unpalatable options which states faced at a moment of grave national crisis.

But the general point is an important one. What kinds of powers can a democracy *share* with international bodies, without running the risk of weakening its own legitimacy? Siedentop's argument suggests that there is a minimum of self-government, which a democracy cannot abandon, while remaining true to its principles. But what is that minimum?

Democracy requires that a range of choices must remain within the scope of our choice, otherwise equal citizenship cannot work. But where do we draw the line? What is that necessary content of democracy? The European Union throws up some obvious questions. Does monetary union with other states compromise or even undermine democracy? Does the law of the single market undermine domestic decision-making? Do the fixed laws of competition and state aid eliminate substantial democratic choices that should in principle be open to a fully democratic society? We need a more detailed argument about the nature of democracy in order to be able to identify the point where democratically legitimate internationalism ends and illegitimate imposition begins.

I start this chapter with the sophisticated arguments offered by the German Federal Constitutional Court. In a series of complex and influential judgments the court has spoken of the required 'identity' of a state, which should not be compromised by the process of European integration if the German constitutional order is to be respected. In its judgment on the Lisbon Treaty, for example, the German Constitutional Court started by outlining a very general view of the European Union as an international union of self-governing states.[14] The court said that 'the citizens' right to determine, in equality and freedom, the exercise of public authority with regard to persons and subject-matters through elections and other votes is the fundamental element of the principle of democracy'.[15] The argument is based on an article of the German Constitution, which states that 'all state authority is derived from the people' and 'shall be exercised by the people through elections and other votes and through specific legislative, executive, and judicial bodies'.[16]

In effect the German court distinguishes between two kinds of potential transfers. The first transfer is that of 'statehood' and it is allowed under one strict condition. The court said: 'The Basic Law does not grant the bodies acting on behalf of

[14] *Re the Lisbon Treaty*, 2 BvE 2/08 et al., Federal Constitutional Court, 30 June 2009, available at http://www.bverfg.de. For commentaries see D. Halberstam and C. Möllers, 'The German Constitutional Court says: "Ja zu Deutschland"' 10 *German Law Journal* (2009) 1241; C. Tomuschat, 'The Ruling of the German Constitutional Court on the Treaty of Lisbon' 10 *German Law Journal* (2009) 1259.

[15] *Re the Lisbon Treaty* (n. 13) 2 BvE 2/08 et al., par. 211.

[16] Article 20(2) of the German Basic Law.

Germany powers to abandon the right to self-determination of the German people in the form of Germany's sovereignty under international law by joining a federal state.'[17] However, the Court did not say that such a transfer would be entirely impossible. It said that such a step would be 'reserved to the directly declared will of the German people alone'.[18] An expression of the direct will of the German people could do it, presumably by way of a referendum. This is how Germany could decide to join in a new federal union.

But the Court also said that there is a second transfer that falls short of a transfer of statehood. This second transfer is constitutionally *impossible*. The Court said that there is a natural limit to how many powers could potentially be transferred to the EU, while Germany remains a self-governing democracy. The limit is constitutional and not merely procedural. The Court said that the principle of democracy, which is protected by the 'eternity' clause of Article 79 of the German Constitution, requires that an infringement of the 'constitutional identity codified in Article 79.3 of the Basic Law is at the same time an infringement of the constituent power of the people'.[19] Identity and 'constituent' power are the same problem, it suggests. In effect, the Court says, there is no institution in Germany, not even the 'direct' will of the people, which could legally amend the constitutional identity of Germany, as long as Germany remains a self-governing democracy. Technically, any such attempt would be unconstitutional, even if taken by unanimity in parliament or by a referendum. The Court relies on a principle of collective self-government or 'constitutional identity' as the highest principle of the German constitution. Germany can, under its constitution, move its entire self-government to a new federation, but it cannot fragment it by breaking up its 'constitutional identity'.

But what does 'constitutional identity' mean? Where are the relevant limits? The Court has offered greater detail in its *Maastricht* judgment, where the Court said that democracy requires a strong and cohesive people, so as to be able to successfully express itself. The motivating idea was that democracy is the *self-expression of a people*. When such self-expression is impeded, then democracy suffers. The court explained this relationship as follows: 'if the peoples of the individual States provide democratic legitimation through the agency of their national parliaments (as at present) limits are then set by virtue of the democratic principle to the extension of the European Communities' functions and powers'.[20] The logic here appears to be that if the source of legitimacy is a distinct self-governing people, then a condition for continuing legitimacy is that such a people must continue to exist. So the Court went on to argue:

[17] *Re the Lisbon Treaty* (n. 12) 2 BvE 2/08 et al., par. 228.
[18] ibid par. 228.
[19] ibid par. 218.
[20] *Manfred Brunner and Others v The European Union Treaty*, 2 BvR 2134/92 & 2159/92, Federal Constitutional Court, 12 October 1993, [1994] 1 CMLR 57, at 88.

> Each of the peoples of the individual States is the starting point for a state power relating to that people. The States need sufficiently important spheres of activity of their own in which the people of each can develop and articulate itself in a process of political will-formation which it legitimates and controls, in order thus to give legal expression to what binds the people together (to a greater or lesser degree of homogeneity) spiritually, socially and politically.[21]

The identity of each state depends therefore on a collective 'will-formation' which gives expression to 'what binds the people together' and which requires a degree of homogeneity. The German Constitutional Court sees democracy as a process of *collective* self-determination, not merely a process of the aggregation of individual civil and political rights. It relies on a metaphor: seeing a people in the way of a person. Just as a person has a claim to autonomy, so a people has a claim to the widest possible range of choices as a collective self-governing entity. This analogy lies at the core of the 'collective self-determination' theory.

It follows from this argument, however, that every international commitment is a democratic impediment of collective self-government. This is so because all international commitments limit the range of options available to a self-governing people. It follows too that the European Union is one such democratic impediment, since it limits each member state's policy options. Under this 'collective autonomy' theory, democracy can only be achieved through the most extensive power of domestic institutions. Only these institutions express the legitimate will of a people conceived as a collective person, for: 'If such a community power is to rest on the political will-formation which is supplied by the people of each individual State, and is to that extent democratic, that presupposes that the power is exercised by a body made up of representatives sent by the member-States' governments, which in their turn are subject to democratic control.'[22] In effect, democratic institutions transfer the collective will of the people to the mechanisms of the official state.

The collective self-government theory has some very unattractive features however. As J.H.H. Weiler noted at the time of the *Maastricht* decision, the intellectual origins of this view are in the thought of the constitutional theorist Carl Schmitt, an apologist for the most extreme forms of authoritarianism.[23] Schmitt offered the clearest argument for a conception of democracy as the collective empowerment of a people. For Schmitt democracy was the method for giving voice to the people as a fundamental source of political legitimacy. He said that 'the people are *anterior* to and *above* the constitution. Under democracy, the people are the subject of the

[21] ibid.

[22] ibid, paras 46, p. 88.

[23] J.H.H. Weiler, 'Does Europe Need a Constitution? Demos, Telos and the German Maastricht Decision' 1 *European Law Journal* (1995) 219–58. For Schmitt's legacy in legal theory see David Dyzanhaus, *Legality and Legitimacy: Carl Schmitt, Hans Kelsen and Hermann Heller in Weimar* (Oxford: Oxford University Press, 1997).

constitution-making power. The democratic understanding sees every constitution, even the *Rechtstaat* component, as resting on the concrete political decision of the people capable of political action.'[24] Schmitt went on to argue for the unusual position that democracy is beyond constitutionalism. He said: 'under the democratic theory of the people's constitution-making power, the people stand as the bearer of the constitution-making power outside of and above any constitutional norm.'[25]

Nevertheless, the most important problem with the 'collective self-determination' theory is not its authoritarian pedigree, but its ultimately paradoxical relationship to democracy. Once we think through the consequences of this view, it quickly becomes obvious that the idea of the most extensive empowerment of the collective will undermines democracy as an ideal of self-determination. For it is possible that the collective will may turn against the institutions that set up the processes of self-determination.[26] A majority may well turn out to attack the rights that constitute democratic decision-making. We can imagine a decision that limits the rights of a despised minority. Yet creating a category of second-class citizens rather obviously undermines the ideal of self-determination. The approval of such a decision by a temporary majority does not render it democratic. Collective capriciousness is not self-determination. Yet, this distinction is impossible to sustain under the collective self government theory, because democracy is seen there as identical to the collective will succeeding in becoming official will. It is highly questionable if this is a cogent view of democracy or of constitutional law.[27]

The collective self-determination theory comes in less radical forms. Jürgen Habermas has written that 'the source of all legitimacy lies in the democratic law-making process, and this in turn calls on the principle of popular sovereignty'.[28] Habermas seeks to address precisely the problem of the relationship of popular sovereignty to institutions, by emphasizing the need for the 'deliberative' character of a democracy through appropriate procedures. He explains, for example, that 'deliberative politics acquires its legitimating force from the discursive structure of an opinion—and will-formation that can fulfil its socially integrative function only because citizens expect its results to have a reasonable quality'.[29] Nevertheless,

24 Carl Schmitt, *Constitutional Theory*, trans. by Jeffrey Seitzer (Durham, NC: Duke University Press, 2008) 268. For constitutional theory that is influenced by Schmitt's view of 'popular sovereignty' see for example Martin Loughlin and Neil Walker, 'Introduction' in Loughlin and Walker (eds), *The Paradox of Constitutionalism* (Oxford: Oxford University Press, 2007) 1. I discuss some of the problems of this view in Pavlos Eleftheriadis, 'Law and Sovereignty' 29 *Law and Philosophy* (2010) 535.

25 Schmitt, *Constitutional Theory* (n. 23) 271.

26 For this argument in more detail see David Dyzenhaus, 'The Politics of the Question of Constituent Power' in Martin Loughlin and Neil Walker (eds), *The Paradox of Constitutionalism* (Oxford: Oxford University Press, 2007) 129–45.

27 I discuss this point, rejecting Schmitt's view, in Eleftheriadis, 'Law and Sovereignty' (n. 23) 535.

28 Jürgen Habermas, *Between Facts and Norms*, trans. by William Rehg (Cambridge: Polity Press, 1996) 89.

29 ibid 304.

these qualifications to popular sovereignty merely incorporate the paradox within constitutional theory: for at some point we must draw a distinction between manifestations of collective 'will' that are democratic and those that are not. Ultimately, however, the collective theory asserts the will of the majority empirically, not institutionally.

Since all institutional commitments, such as the separation of powers, or the rule of law, or the recognition of human rights, create potential obstacles to the instructions of a collective will—or the 'popular' will understood as the will of the majority—then all institutional commitments are also impediments to democracy. This simple point was seen quite clearly and accepted by Carl Schmitt. This is why he said that the empirically verifiable collective will prevails over any contrary institution. Such a theory is not democratic, however, at least not in any useful sense of the term. It is hostile to both international cooperation and domestic constitutionalism. For example, if we are willing to say that democracy is diminished by a policy of European monetary union, whereby national governments lose the power to set interest rates for the benefit of a supranational body such as the European Central Bank (ECB), the same problem arises for any domestic institution that is entrusted with monetary policy, such as a domestic central bank. If we say that international competition rules or environmental rules diminish domestic democracy, then we must also say that any constitutional commitment that reduces the powers of the majority is also 'undemocratic' in that sense. Of course constitutional protections of human rights would also, in this analysis, become obstacles to democracy. Any independent public body will be an 'obstacle' to democracy and of course so will be the courts.

This theory leads us to a paradox of constitutionalism. If we say that the ground of the democratic constitution is the collective will, or 'popular sovereignty', then the very institutions of the democratic constitution become supposedly hostile to 'democracy', since they create limits to this collective will. The theory of collective self-government is in this sense self-defeating. Democratic institutions turn out to be 'undemocratic'. The power of the collective will sweeps all in its wake.[30]

The most common response to this paradox is to say that one is to draw the line at some point in the quantity of collective power that a community sacrifices. If the amount of power it has surrendered is relatively small, then democracy, supposedly, survives. Such a response is implicit in some of the conclusions of the German Constitutional Court. In its discussion of the Greek bailout, for example, the German Constitutional Court said that Germany's commitments to the European Union were lawful because they were not excessive.[31] The Court said that

[30] I develop this point further in Pavlos Eleftheriadis, 'Power and Principle in Constitutional Law' 45 *Netherlands Journal of Legal Philosophy* (2016) 37–56.

[31] BVerfG, 2 BvR 987/10, 2 BvR 1485/10, 2 BvR 1099/10, Judgment of 9 September 2011, available on the court's website. I discuss the case in detail in Pavlos Eleftheriadis, 'The Euro and the German Courts' 128 *Law Quarterly Review* (2012) 216.

the amount of the guarantees given, namely 170 billion Euros in total, 'did not exceed' the limit of budget capacity in such a way as to threaten 'budgetary autonomy' or to render it empty of content. This was because 'there is no reason to assume an irreversible process with consequences for the *Bundestag's* autonomy'.[32] In effect, the Court finds that the European Union does not undermine German democratic 'autonomy'—or 'budgetary autonomy'—because it does not have much power.

This is not a principled distinction, however. Under the 'collective person' theory, *any* amount of sharing of power with foreign states must be an impediment to democracy. If sovereignty takes its value from the collective will formation of a people, why share even a small part of a state's powers? The objection to giving up control applies not only at the extreme end of essentially abandoning independence altogether, but also at the moderate end. Limiting collective self-government must be a bad thing for democracy whether it is large or small. For example, the delegation of decision-making on the labelling of food products must be a betrayal of self-government, since it puts the labelling of food products beyond the reach of the collective will. It therefore follows that every international agreement undermines democracy. The theory gives us no means by which to vindicate international cooperation as democratically legitimate. If we wish to identify some international cooperation as democratically legitimate, we shall need to do it with some different argument.

10.2 Egalitarian Internationalism

Jürgen Habermas' criticized the German Constitutional Court without, however, challenging the 'collective self-government' view of democracy. Habermas only said that the presupposition of the stability of the current 'demos' is false. In his view, a new identification is possible sometime in the future. A multinational community, such as the European Union, can form a new 'demos' if suitably focused on political and not communal values. He argued that the crisis of legitimacy of the EU could be answered by promoting transnational democracy by way of creating a 'cosmopolitan community' of European citizens, which would soon become the appropriate domain of self-government.[33] But this argument in effect accepts the identification of democracy with the collective will formation by a 'demos'.

Habermas argues that we can set up a common democratic procedure. He says: 'a transfer of sovereign rights does not diminish the scope of civic autonomy only on the condition that the citizens of the one affected state cooperate with the citizens of the other affected states in making supranational law in accordance with a democratic procedure'.[34] In other words, the institutions of democracy can be

[32] BVerfG, 2 BvR 987/10, 2 BvR 1485/10, 2 BvR 1099/10, par. 136.
[33] Jürgen Habermas, *The Crisis of the European Union: A Response* (Cambridge: Polity, 2012) 53.
[34] ibid 19.

replicated at the EU level once the mutual understanding and solidarity among European citizens reaches a required degree of completeness. Habermas seems to share the German Constitutional Court's analysis that democracy requires a strong and cohesive people, although he optimistically suggests that there is a real prospect of bringing about such a people in Europe. He accepts the kernel of the court's theory: one needs a 'demos' before we have a 'democracy'. But by doing that, he will eventually create the same paradox reversed: if such a demos were to be created at a European level, why should we have domestic democratic institutions at all? Wouldn't that be an impediment to *European* democracy and collective self-government?

How do we address these paradoxes? How can we reconcile democracy with shared power? I believe that we must begin by rejecting entirely the idea that democracy requires the *collective* empowerment of a self-governing people. The analogy between the individual person and a collective person is entirely misleading. Identification with certain traditions and histories, or widespread mutual trust are important ingredients of a successful democracy, but they are not its essence. The relationship between the person and political power is entirely different to that suggested by the collective theory.

What makes democracy valuable is not the fact that it gives effect to the views of the majority, but in the fact that it recognizes the equal standing of all members of a political community. The majority rule is one element of a democratic constitution, not its only one.

This point is not a radical departure for the theory of democracy. Indeed, most political philosophers consider collective identification as only a means to other ends. The best known defender of the ethical dimensions of nationality, the Oxford philosopher David Miller, argues that national self-determination is not an end in itself, the best means for achieving equality and social justice for every individual member of a political community. For Miller, nations provide the trust and deliberative context that can make democracy succeed.[35] He writes that deliberation requires trust among those doing the deliberating so that any compromise does not seem just 'a sign of weakness'.[36] Henry Richardson also writes that 'civic integrity and civic magnanimity are virtues that are practically necessary for [policy] discussion to progress towards a mutual acceptance of conclusions about what we ought to do and hence are necessary to motivate involvement in public discussion'.[37] But nothing more follows from these requirements of a deliberative basis for democracy. These and similar approaches show us that identification with a group are not

[35] David Miller, *On Nationality* (Oxford: Oxford University Press, 1995) 81–118.

[36] ibid 97.

[37] Henry S. Richardson, *Democratic Autonomy: Public Reasoning about the Ends of Policy* (Oxford: Oxford University Press, 2002) 188.

the same thing as collective self-government. Collective entities do not have the features of persons.

When we turn our attention back to the European Union, we find that the collective person view is not widely held by most legal and political theorists. If anything, most theorists are guided by the precisely opposite theoretical view. They seek to explain how pluralistic European and domestic democracies can be. These views articulate what we could provisionally call an 'egalitarian internationalism'. A response along those lines, which rejects the Schmittian theory of a 'collective will' in its entirety is being offered by the theorists of 'demoicracy', which we encountered in Chapter 5. As put forward by Francis Cheneval and Kalypso Nicolaïdis, the theory of 'demoicracy' argues for the radical breaking up of the connection between a single 'demos' and democratic political authority.[38]

Cheneval and Nicolaidis argue that popular understandings of a 'demos' are far more flexible than we think, so that it is possible to imagine a 'social construction of demoicracy',[39] whereby the people's self-consciousness contains both national and European dimensions. They consider that such a shift in public attitude could make 'demoicracy' stable: 'If citizens internalized the intentions that correspond to their status as joint sovereigns, they would identify horizontally as connected somehow with other European peoples, which may 'feel' different than to identify vertically as connected to a different realm called 'European'.[40] They therefore criticize Habermas for focusing only on the idea of a 'composite' demos, which is governed in a conventional unified way. One has to come up, they argue, with a novel composite set of institutions, whereby the exercise of democratic power will be broken up in a variety of ways. They argue that the 'multifaceted status of a citizen in a demoicracy' needs to be reflected in procedures that recognize the relevance of the various separate entities and not—as Habermas' position ultimately entails—in rules that 'split the status of citizen into two opposing personalities.'[41]

It is an interesting and compelling argument. Cheneval and Nicolaïdis offer a categorical rejection of the German constitutional court's argument. Whereas Habermas accepts that full democracy in the European Union will be inappropriate or in any sense unwarranted while the 'demos' is fragmented, Cheneval and Nicolaïdis argue that a fragmented 'demos' can indeed give rise to original democratic institutions, as long as they respect the complexity of a 'multilateral' political

[38] Francis Cheneval and Kalypso Nicolaïdis, 'The Social Construction of Demoicracy in the European Union' 15 *European Journal of Political Theory* (2016) 235–60. See also Kalypso Nicolaïdis, 'The Idea of European Demoicracy' in J. Dickson and Pavlos Eleftheriadis (eds), *Philosophical Foundations of European Union Law* (Oxford: Oxford University Press, 2012); F. Cheneval and F. Schimmelfennig, 'The Case for Demoicracy in the European Union' 51 *Journal of Common Market Studies* (2013) 334–50; Kalypso Nicolaïdis, 'European Demoicracy and its Crisis' 51 *Journal of Common Market Studies* (2013) 351–69; F. Cheneval, S. Lavenex, and F. Schimmelfennig, 'Demoi-cracy in the European Union: Principles, Institutions, Policies' 22 *Journal of European Public Policy* (2015) 1–18.

[39] Cheneval and Nicolaïdis, 'The Social Construction of Demoicracy in the European Union' 240–2.

[40] ibid 244.

[41] ibid.

community. Cheneval uses the term 'multilateral' democracy to capture this new institutional setting.[42]

The contrast between the arguments offered by Habermas, Cheneval, and Nicolaïdis helps us see the core point about the collective theory. Democracy, the German Constitutional Court says, requires a certain correspondence between the demos' collective will and political decisions. For this view democracy can only be a zero sum game. The will of a people will be threatened by the conflicting will of other states or of multilateral institutions. Either we have self-government for a national people, or self-government for the European people. This was also a concern of Noel Malcolm, which I discussed in Chapter 1. There appears to be no middle ground: the more powers are transferred to the European Union, the fewer powers remain at the disposal of a self-governing people. If one understands the problem of democracy in the EU in these terms, then the conclusion of the German constitutional court is inevitable: the EU is a democratic impediment. Any power that the EU accumulates deprives peoples of their own self-government. It destroys the correspondence, between collective will and the decisions of the state.

Cheneval and Nicolaïdis strike at the heart of this argument. They show that our institutions do not seek to correspond to some kind of pre-existing collective will. They *constitute* our collective will. There is no prior will to be contrasted to the political will that was established through our democratic institutions. Indeed, the only sense in which we have a collective will is that produced through democratic *institutions*. Cheneval and Nicolaïdis show that the whole idea of a correspondence between the will of a collective agent and democracy is misleading.

We must reflect on this larger point: democracy is not about reflecting a collective will but about constituting it. Cheneval and Nicolaïdis imply this when they say that the frustration of the will of the majority may be a virtue of our institutional system: 'A fully fledged demoicracy involves peoples checking peoples, through checks and balances among parliaments, the supreme-courts, the executives and direct democratic voting' and that 'the institutional design of demoicracy holds that all peoples involved are institutionally interconnected in various modes of co-decision making'.[43] This outlook leaves no room for a Schmittian theory. Our institutions do not give expression to an empirically verifiable 'popular will'. In my view, this premise has more far-reaching consequences than Cheneval and Nicolaïdis give it credit for. This view of democracy is based on an entirely different argument, which I outlined in Chapter 2 and which I have called the 'egalitarian' argument. Democracy has value as an ethical project, not as the facilitation of our collective will.

[42] See Francis Cheneval, *The Government of the Peoples: On the Idea and Principles of Multilateral Democracy* (New York: Palgrave Macmillan, 2011).

[43] Cheneval and Nicolaïdis, 'The Social Construction of Demoicracy in the European Union' (n. 37) 249.

It is important to return to this argument. As I argued in chapter 2, democracy embodies the ethical relationship of *equal citizenship*. The reason we value democracy is not a supposed 'transfer' of a 'collective will' of a demos from the social world to the state but a moral principle of equal citizenship. This is the reason we value the institutions of democracy: they create equal citizenship. Homogeneity or cohesion has nothing to do with this moral project. Collective self-expression is thus irrelevant to democracy. It follows that international cooperation is also harmless for the same reason. What matters is not the *amount* of power shared and exercised through democratic institutions, but whether the constitutional fundamentals of equal citizenship are being protected in the right way. The sharing of power between members states and the EU is not, therefore, an impediment to democracy, if it is done according to the constitutional fundamentals of equal citizenship. Only transfers that compromise equal citizenship will be an impediment to democracy.

The egalitarian view that lies at the heart of this argument is a familiar one and has eloquent defenders in the theory of democracy. Jeremy Waldron has argued that the individual right of participation in politics entails that majoritarian procedures of deliberation and decision-making should be available in all important political decisions, including matters of constitutional significance. For Waldron, successful self-government requires first of all justice about resolving our disagreements. We must offer grounds to each other for tolerating the fact that our views may lose out in the process. Belief in equal rights requires that we adopt procedures for settling political disagreements, which do not themselves specify what the outcome is going to be.[44]

A parallel interpretation of the egalitarian view is offered by Ronald Dworkin. For Dworkin democracy is continuous with our deeper moral duties to treat each other with equal concern and respect. Democracy entails the protection of rights even when this goes against the wishes of the majority. Dworkin contrasts this view to the 'majoritarian' conception of democracy, a term by which he seems to include both the collective conception I attributed to Schmitt and the more procedural view of Waldron I set out above. Democracy, writes Dworkin, 'confirms in the most dramatic way the equal concern and respect that the community together, as the custodian of coercive power, has for each of its members'.[45]

For this view political equality is not a matter of the share of political power that each one of us has, because that depends on contingent matters of how we divide on particular issues. If some of us are few in number and have no share in power, we cannot complain that the system is 'undemocratic'. If we have equal say and

[44] Jeremy Waldron, *Law and Disagreement* (Oxford: Oxford University Press, 1999). See also Richard Bellamy, *Political Constitutionalism: A Republican Defence of the Constitutionality of Democracy* (Cambridge: Cambridge University Press, 2007).

[45] Ronald Dworkin, *Justice for Hedgehogs* (Cambridge, Mass.: Harvard University Press, 2011) 390.

equal voting and other rights, then we can have no complaint against the system. Dworkin notes that this defence of democracy is far more consistent with the practice of institutions of representative government in the world today, which does not guarantee the results required by the majoritarian conception of democracy. Our practice does not follow the open-ended procedural theories, he argues, but secures outcomes that respect equal rights for all.[46]

Cheneval and Nicolaïdis in effect deploy a similar egalitarian view to show how the 'no demos' thesis is irrelevant to democracy. The Schmittian view sees democracy as a mechanism of transfer: a people's will must be transferred to a political decision. The egalitarian view rejects the image of a direct transfer of a collective will—since no such 'will' exists. The egalitarian view describes the problem differently: from the multiple, varied, and plural wills of equal citizens we produce the single will of the state through just procedures of representation and accountability. Elections are one of the necessary conditions of democracy, but not a sufficient one. Democracies also need mechanisms of accountability, that provide for techniques of retrospective evaluation after a decision has been reached.

It is obvious, that under the egalitarian theory, the idea of a 'constitutional identity' test, offers us no way of distinguishing between democratic and undemocratic international commitments. As we saw above, for the German Constitutional Court no power can be transferred to the EU if it entails an infringement of the 'constitutional identity codified in Article 79.3 of the Basic Law' which is 'at the same time an infringement of the constituent power of the people'.[47] The idea of a constitutional 'identity' in the Court's reasoning follows from the idea of the constitution representing the will of a 'demos' whose identity must be preserved. If we follow the egalitarian theory, however, democracy is not about representing an underlying collective will, but about giving every individual person *equal standing*. This can be done both in a state with a single 'demos' or in a state with multiple 'demoi' as shown by Cheneval and Nicolaïdis. Egalitarianism opens up a new argument that replaces the empty idea of identity.

The egalitarian approach suggests that the requirement for the equal standing of persons applies not just domestically but also internationally.[48] International institutions can come to the aid of domestic democracies, if they are to assist in defending equal citizenship. This is an argument made with great clarity by Robert O. Keohane, Stephen Macedo, and Andrew Moravcsik.[49] They contrast

[46] A powerful argument for the same view is also made by Elizabeth Anderson, for whom: 'democratic equality regards two people as equal when each accepts the obligation to justify their actions by principles acceptable to the other, and in which they take mutual consultation, reciprocation, and recognition for granted'. See Elizabeth Anderson, 'What is the Point of Equality' 109 *Ethics* (1999) 287–337, at 313.

[47] *Re The Lisbon Treaty* (n. 13) par 218.

[48] See in particular Cheneval *The Government of the Peoples* (n. 41) 113–30.

[49] Robert O. Koehane, Stephen Macedo, and Andrew Moravcsik, 'Democracy-Enhancing Multilateralism' 63 *International Organization* (2009) 1–31.

'majoritarian' to 'constitutional' democracy and emphasize that modern democracies are mostly already insulated against direct majoritarian control. Constitutional constraints are aimed to prevent majority rule form turning into faction or majority tyranny.

Keohane, Macedo, and Moravcsik argue that government becomes more democratic when nations ensure that minority or unpopular interests are fairly attended to and the equal rights of everyone protected.[50] Multilateralism enhances democracy when, for example, it assists domestic institutions in the protection of human rights (as in the case of the European Convention of Human Rights), whenever it contributes to the better understanding of policy issues (as in the case of the OECD), or whenever it directs the public interest towards the public good and not toward the benefit of special interests that are well organized domestically but powerless internationally (as in the case of the EU).

While they recognize that it would be undemocratic for an 'elite multilateral institution ... to override repeated demonstrations of informed rights-regarding, fairly represented popular will', they argue that the EU does not constitute such 'benign technocracy'.[51] They argue instead that 'properly authorized multilateral institutions, such as other commonplace constitutional institutions, may be justified in imposing checks, constraints and corrections on majorities that are not well-informed, rights-regarding, or fairly represented'.[52] They argue that the institutions of the European Union pass those tests.

This is, then, a second conclusion of our analysis. The collective will theory of democracy restricts the application of criteria of democracy to a single, cohesive people or public. The EU cannot be democratic under such a theory, until it becomes a new such bearer of a new 'collective will'. This is the view defended by the German Constitutional Court. We rejected this view. The egalitarian view, by contrast, takes democracy to be a matter of the protection of equal citizenship, which can be done both domestically and internationally. For the egalitarian theories of democracy, it follows that democracy can be enhanced by participation in appropriate supranational organizations.

Unlike the 'collective' theory, the egalitarian theory does not look at the EU as a zero sum game. It is indeed possible to arrive at a legitimate sharing of power between a self-governing state and a transnational organization, as long as the constitutional fundamentals of the self-governing state are not in any way diminished.

But where do we draw the line between a democratic union of peoples and illegitimate paternalism? The egalitarian argument does not say that such a line does not exist. It only says that it is not just a matter of the *sharing* of power. In the concluding section of this chapter, I offer some first thoughts towards a sketch of a

[50] ibid 5–6.
[51] ibid 15.
[52] ibid 15.

theory of the internationalist constitution. This section aims to complete the ideal of Europe as a democratic union of peoples. [53]

10.3 The Internationalist Constitution

In his magisterial account of democracy Ross Harrison explains that Kant's commitment to the equality of human beings leads to democracy with what appears to be a formal argument.[54] Democracy is based on the premise that 'law-making' members must have an equal involvement in collective law-making, irrespective of their disagreements. Harrison says that if we are to treat ourselves as 'ends in ourselves' then we must 'show an equality of respect to all other moral agents'.[55] And if this is the case then 'I must give weight (or moral consideration) to everyone expressing their moral views'.[56] It follows that I ought to give to all others equal respect in the process of voting, whatever their views.

The same argument can be extended outwards.[57] If we recognize the ethical value of jurisdiction for our fellow citizens, we must equally recognize the similar value of other jurisdictions outside our borders for other peoples. Respect for my fellow citizens as equal stakeholders in a democracy is no different from respect for the citizens of other states who set up democracies elsewhere. Constitutional law and international law have, thus, the same grounding in the equal moral standing of persons. This is the argument I set out in detail in Chapter 2.

This argument about the mutually supportive role of jurisdiction and the law of nations must also be our guide in defending democracy-enhancing internationalism. The argument for the limits of international law must follow the argument for the value of equal citizenship. If states are to remain democratic, they must ensure that their international commitments do not undermine equal citizenship.

How can this work in practice? In what follows I discuss four dimensions of domestic democracy in relation to international cooperation. I will examine, first, the powers of the executive, second, the role of the judiciary, and third, the reach of the legislature. I will, fourth, refer to the constitutional edifice as a whole and outline how constitutional powers may be exposed to international commitments.

[53] I summarize here the argument I made about egalitarian constitutionalism in Pavlos Eleftheriadis, 'Power and Principle in Constitutional Law' 45 *Netherlands Journal of Legal Philosophy* (2016) 37–56; Pavlos Eleftheriadis, 'Constitutional Change Through Deliberation' in Ron Levy, Hoi Kong, Graeme Orr, and Jeff King (eds), *The Cambridge Handbook of Deliberative Constitutionalism* (Cambridge: Cambridge University Press 2018) 191–202. I hope to be able to offer a more detailed account of this argument in the future in my book in progress 'The Deliberative Constitution'.

[54] Ross Harrison, *Democracy* (London: Routledge, 1993).

[55] ibid 228.

[56] ibid 228.

[57] Kant did just that. For an excellent analysis on Kant's argument for an 'internationalist' state see B. Sharon Byrd and Joachim Hruschka, *Kant's Doctrine of Right: A Commentary* (Cambridge: Cambridge University Press, 2010) 188–214.

a) Executive Power

The egalitarian constitution requires that executive decisions are taken by a democratically elected government, which is continuously accountable to a democratically elected Parliament. Nevertheless, much executive decision-making is transferred to independent bodies on the basis of clear rules of delegation and on the basis that such bodies will be held to account in different ways. This is true even in the United Kingdom, where the lack of a written constitution gives the impression of an all-powerful government. In fact, the UK has created some very important independent institutions with executive powers. Just like in the EU, monetary policy is exercised by an almost entirely independent central bank.[58] Similarly, tax collection is delegated to an independent body, which is not overseen by politicians. This is a 'non-departmental executive body', which is called 'Her Majesty's Revenue and Customs' (or HMRC).[59] The Bank of England and HMRC have very significant powers, but their existence does not upset the formal principle of equal citizenship. Everything they do is carefully circumscribed by detailed legal rules and their decisions are always subject to the control of independent courts. Moreover, the institutional framework is itself up for review, if parliament decides to change things. So the existence of powerful independent bodies does not undermine the democratic balance.

The same must apply to international delegations, i.e. delegations of executive power from a state to an international body. First, any such delegation must be carefully circumscribed in detailed legal rules. This is precisely the function of the European Union Treaties and the secondary law. The powers of the European Central Bank or the European Commission are carefully set out in detailed such rules. Second, the enforcement of these rules must be subject to the supervision of independent judicial authority. The institutional balance of equality would be undermined if these two tests failed, namely if such executive power was transferred without explicit authority or if its operation were not subject to effective judicial oversight. But this is not the case in the European Union.

All of the powers entrusted to European Union institutions are exercised according to the Treaties, under the constant supervision of the Commission, the member states, the citizens and, ultimately, the Court of Justice of the European

[58] See the Bank of England Act 1998. Of course, the independence of the Bank of England is at the mercy of the current majority in Parliament, which can amend any law under the current doctrine of the sovereignty of parliament. In a place where there is no written constitution, nothing is independent, unless the current majority wishes it to be so. Incidentally, the first law on the Bank was the Bank of England Act 1694.

[59] That body was established by the Commissioners for Revenue and Customs Act (CRCA) 2005. The Act gives legal powers and responsibilities in relation to taxation to independent 'Commissioners' appointed by the Queen on the advice of the government. HMRC is 'a non-ministerial department'. It is intended to ensure that the administration of the tax system is not subject to political interference.

Union. Indeed, this is one of the unique contributions of the design of the European Union to the law of nations. A strong supranational court, which is open in principle to all European Institutions creates mutual trust among all the parties. The member states, the European institutions, and in some cases the citizens can have access to the CJEU in order to ensure the lawful conduct of all parties.

I draw the conclusion that since the European Union replicates the two safeguards that apply to domestic bodies, there is nothing undemocratic in delegating some important executive powers to the institutions of the European Union. Is there any particular further executive power whose delegation might be upsetting the democratic balance? I do not believe that there is. As long as the executive powers given to the European Union are controlled by the law and monitored by the Court of Justice, there is no objection in principle to what could be delegated to the EU. I do not believe that police powers (as in Frontex) or tax-raising power, or even a joint military power could upset the *democratic* balance, if the above tests are met. Delegating executive powers to the European Union under these effective legal safeguards does not undermine domestic democracy.

b) Judicial Power

I have just said that the continuing effectiveness of the Court of Justice is essential to the democratic legitimacy of transfers of executive power. How much power, however, can be given to the European Union courts before democracy itself is compromised? I think the answer is included in the very idea of jurisdiction. For a state to remain independent and self-governing, it must control not only the making but also the authoritative interpretation and enforcement of its fundamental laws. The interpretation of laws is a moral project, which depends on the powers of reasoning, the judgment, and independence of those citizens who are appointed to serve as judges. Their selection is itself a major political act and a test of moral judgment. These processes cannot be left to the operation of an international body. It follows that the dualist relationship between EU law and domestic law must in all cases be monitored by the domestic superior courts. So the ultimate control of the judicial power must remain domestic and the ultimate constitutional jurisdiction must remain with the state courts. This is not surprising. This is, in fact, what all domestic courts have already said and done about the relationship of constitutional law to EU law. By doing so, they have protected their domestic democracies from undue erosion.

Within such a framework, however, there is no democratic objection to the creation of common European remedies and procedures. The delegation of power to European courts is in this sense not that different from the delegation of executive power. In any event, as long as a court is properly independent and has the skill and experience to offer authoritative interpretations of the law, it makes little difference if its operation is purely domestic or shared between domestic and transnational processes.

What happens, however, if the Court of Justice of the EU makes a flagrant mistake about the division of labour between the treaties and the member states? Some scholars have in fact already argued that the court has failed in this way.[60] The argument here must begin with the admission that any court can make a mistake. The authority of courts is not based on the supposition that they are infallible. The only possible democratic criticism against the Court of Justice must be that it favours the wrong theory of the EU in a way that goes beyond a good faith interpretation of the treaties. Yet, this criticism has been very hard to substantiate. There is little evidence of a federalist or monist or other bias in the most important cases. As I explained in the early chapters, the Court of Justice interprets the treaties closely and respects the division of labour between the EU and the member states through a theory of dualism. And after all, all judges of the court are appointed by the states for a six-year term. The states are responsible for appointing well qualified and independent persons to these positions. It is up to them to appoint those with the required impartial attitude or the appropriate temperament.

There is nothing, in my view, to substantiate the argument that the Court of Justice has undermined democracy by failing to respect the legal orders of the member states. It is an independent supranational court, giving effect to the Treaties as they have been agreed. If anything, democracy has been enhanced by the continuing operation of the Court. The good functioning of the Court of Justice helps us maintain the rule of law throughout the union and the member states.

c) Legislative Power

We now turn to the most sensitive power of the EU, its legislative power. Perhaps the most distinctive legal feature of the EU as a transnational institution is the fact that its own bodies have the power to make secondary law, in the form of regulations and directives. There is an element of competition here between domestic and European processes. Even when EU laws need to be incorporated into the law of a member state, as in the case of Directives, EU law has remarkably broad effect on a

[60] See for example Trevor C. Hartley, *Constitutional Problems of the European Union* (Oxford: Hart, 1999); Hjalte Rasmussen, *On Law and Policy in the European Court of Justice* (Dordrecht: Martinus Nijhoff, 1986). See also the response to Rasmussen by J.H.H. Weiler, 'The Court of Justice on Trial' 24 *Common Market Law Review* (1987) 555.

domestic legal system. Critics of the European Union often say that this process has gone too far. I explained in Chapter I that Noel Malcolm worried that this process might end up transferring sovereignty from the states to the Union. Nevertheless, just like the executive powers we examined above, the legislative powers delegated to the EU are set out in detail in the Treaties. Legislative competences are carefully outlined and are divided into exclusive competences, shared competences, and 'supporting' competences. Their operation is carefully monitored by the Court of Justice. It is hard to see how this process threatens democracy, as long as it operates in the way it was originally conceived.

Nevertheless, the problem here is that the lines are moveable. The EU keeps legislating in the areas of shared competences. But any legislation by the European Union has the effect of precluding further action by the states. In effect, EU secondary legislation gradually creates new areas of 'exclusive' EU competence. It is possible, therefore, that a member state legislature will find itself unable to change a rule that affects its constituents because at some time in the past that rule was legislated by an EU directive or regulation. Legislative action by the EU legislature moves the allocation of competences, because it renders exclusive an area of competence that in theory is shared. No treaty change is required for such a shift.

The problem here is structural. There is no other way of achieving the single market without producing such direct and exclusionary effects. Nevertheless, as a result domestic law-makers can suddenly discover that they are powerless to act in an area that affects them significantly. Of course, all member states have agreed in advance to create these shared competences by entering into the Treaties. They also had a chance to participate fully in the process whereby all secondary law was made. Still, however, the process may have the result that a subsequent domestic legislation will be powerless to address an issue of significance, without ever having agreed to give that power to the EU, since that decision will have been taken by the Executive in the council of ministers. Existing European Union law appears 'immoveable' from the point of view of the domestic lawmaker.

This structural problem is made worse by the rule that the European Commission has the exclusive 'right of initiative' in legislation. The Commission alone can propose legislative changes. A member state cannot formally propose that a directive or regulation be amended or repealed. It has to persuade the Commission first. This is a serious problem for domestic democracy, which becomes worse as time goes by and as the origins of EU laws become less known.

It is reasonable in my view to consider a new legislative process whereby a member state or a group of them may have the power to table a proposal for a legislative amendment. The same power, in my view, would have to be given to a number of members of the European Parliament, which currently does not have the right to propose legislation at all. In this way we can protect better the equal standing of all citizens, since we open up areas of existing EU legislation to further scrutiny, revision, and amendment, if a majority can be found. Here is an area where democracy has been compromised by the development of the single market laws. Reform must in my view touch on these legislative processes at a European level.

d) Constitution-Making

I now turn to a fourth but crucial question for democratic legitimacy. Does the European Union affect domestic constitutions? This is very important because the constitution is the epicentre of self-government. Moreover, the fundamental rules of the relations between the EU and the member states, the process of incorporation that I discussed in an earlier chapter, are included in the domestic constitution. If the EU could determine the content of that relationship, then the member states would have lost their power to effectively govern themselves.

Nothing in the operation of the European Union affects, in principle, domestic constitution-making. Under the doctrine of dualism, the law of the European Union is ultimately subject to the constitutional rules of the member states. The very membership in the European Union, given its deep institutional consequences, is a decision of constitutional significance. All members willingly adapted their constitutions to accept EU membership. The member states were and remain free to choose whether to accept membership by deciding to join or to leave the Union. The case of the United Kingdom proves that member states are free to leave. Those who choose to remain, choose also to bind themselves to the European framework. Membership, with all its associated bonds and obligations, is a democratic decision.

It could only be otherwise if the dominant theory of European Union law was monism or pluralism. Under monism, the domestic constitution would be the subject of open-ended transformation through EU law. This is entailed for example by Robert Schütze's conjecture that the EU treaties are the 'Grundnorm' of the legal systems of the member states. Anything like that would have seriously compromised domestic democracy, since the domestic constitution would have been made elsewhere. The citizens of any member states that might have accepted monism would not have power over those sections of the constitution that were subject to EU law. Their equal citizenship would to that extent be undermined—although the precise shape of inequality in power among them would depend on the particular political circumstances.

The same uncertainty would affect them under pluralism. If the domestic constitution stops enjoying unconditional primacy in a member state, even for some ill-defined cases, then the terms of equal citizenship under the rule of law are undermined. Again, one would not be able to point to any particular inequality before one knew of the particular constitutional effects of EU law. For example, one section of the economy may benefit from the constitutional status of state aid rules, whereas another one would be disadvantaged. Both groups would be losing their equal citizenship though, if they had no say over the legal changes that affected their lives. The winners and losers would only be known once the law was clear. But under the terms of ordinary constitutional justice, this kind of constitutional uncertainty would be unacceptable. One cannot leave equal citizenship to chance.

Nevertheless, internationalism does not solve all the problems of democratic legitimacy of the EU. The problem of legislation that appears immoveable occurs also at a constitutional level. Much of the single market law is included in detailed provisions of the Treaty on the Functioning of the European Union (TFEU). Such provisions have a constitutional role in the member states that give EU law a status equal to the constitution—the United Kingdom being one of them. For example, the free movement of persons is now fixed in the treaty. For these rules to be amended, there has to be a Treaty change, which in the normal case is time consuming and politically difficult.

Dieter Grimm has, therefore, proposed that a future intergovernmental conference will simplify the treaties by removing much of TFEU, which could be demoted to the status of secondary law.[61] It could in all likelihood become a more or less a simple regulation, which we may call 'Regulation on the Functioning of the EU'. By becoming part of such a regulation, the rules on the policies of the single market would be open to further amendment and refinement by the Institutions of the European Union presumably on the basis of unanimity, providing EU law with flexibility that it lacks at present. Their reform would not require treaty change but a simple legislative change. This is an interesting and practical proposal that maintains the integrity of the domestic constitutions. All member states would benefit from the additional clarity the EU could achieve if it selected the really fundamental elements of the European Union and placed them in a new 'Treaty on the European Union'. A result of this reform would be that the single market would become open to the deliberations of European Institutions. The states would retain the power to amend the rules of the single market, but they would so in a much less cumbersome way.

10.4 On Reform

The above paragraphs offer only preliminary reflections on what is a very difficult problem: how to reform the European Union in order to strengthen democracy in

[61] Dieter Grimm, *The Constitution of European Democracy* (Oxford: Oxford University Press, 2017) 81–104.

the member states. But this book is not offering a blueprint for reform. In the pages above I offered only a new systematic way of interpreting the European Union as an international political project, under a legal doctrine of dualism. I have argued that supporting further integration, which I do, is not the same thing as proposing a European federal state. I looked both to the past, discussing the law as it is, but also to the future, suggesting some avenues for fruitful and democracy-promoting reform.

I happily accept that I do not know how the European Union will manage to overcome the existential challenges posed to it by the nationalist revival of the past ten years. While I recognize that some grievances against the present political and social order are real and justified, I find the rejection of the European Union in the name of 'sovereignty', 'democracy', or 'fairness' a great error. The European Union does not undermine sovereignty, it does not impede democracy, and does not crush social justice. If anything, the European Union promotes justice within and among states. But the lure of populism is not down to arguments. Politicians everywhere exploit the electorate's emotions and fears for their own self-advancement. They cannot be defeated by arguments alone. Nevertheless, those of us who admire and support the European project and wish to see it succeed, do have a responsibility to respond to the populist arguments, such as they are. A proper defence of the European Union must deal with the most general questions of its nature and fundamental aims.

In order to convince, we must understand the European Union in the best possible way. And we cannot properly defend the European Union's achievements, unless we are clear about what these achievements are. I hope that some policy makers will take note of the abstract arguments made here. I have argued that from the point of view of the theory of law, the European Union does not threaten sovereignty; that it has been unfair at times, but that it has also responded to unfairness with appropriate redress. I also argued that the European Union is an institutional arrangement of progressive internationalism that promotes freedom, equality, and democracy. We can improve it further, strengthening the ways it exhibits accountability, freedom, fairness. We can improve it, but we should not criticize it for failing to be what it cannot be.

We do need further development of the political philosophy of transnational institutions. We should not leave the terrain of justice, sovereignty, and democracy to the populists and the nationalists. We must address their arguments and show that the European Union is an ethical achievement with great, indeed global, significance. What John Maynard Keynes said commenting on the international economic landscape as he saw it towards the end of his life, seems to me still true today:

> Practical men, who believe themselves to be quite exempt from any intellectual influences, are usually the slaves of some defunct economist. Madmen in

> authority, who hear voices in the air, are distilling their frenzy from some academic scribbler of a few years back. I am sure that the power of vested interests is vastly exaggerated compared with the gradual encroachment of ideas.[62]

Today, as much as when these words were first written, Europe needs better abstract ideas.

[62] John Maynard Keynes, *The General Theory of Employment, Interest and Money* (Cambridge: Macmillan & Cambridge University Press for the Royal Economic Society, 1936) 239.

Bibliography

Acemoglu, Daron, and Robinson, James A., *Why Nations Fail: The Origins of Power, Prosperity and* Poverty (London: Profile Books, 2012)

Adamski, Dariusz, 'Economic Constitution of the Euro Area after the *Gauweiler* Preliminary Ruling' 52 *Common Market Law Review* (2015) 1451–90

Alexy, Robert, *The Argument from Injustice: A Reply to Legal Positivism* (Oxford: Oxford University Press, 2009)

Anderson, Elizabeth, 'What is the Point of Equality?' 109 *Ethics* (1999) 287–337

Applbaum, Arthur Isak, 'Forcing a People to Be Free' 35 *Philosophy and Public Affairs* (2007) 359

Arangio-Ruiz, Gaetano, 'Dualism Revisited: International Law and Interindividual Law' 86 *Rivista Di Diritto Internazionale* (2003) 909–99.

Aristotle, *The Nicomachean Ethics*, trans. H. Rackham (Cambridge, Mass.: Harvard University Press, 1989)

Arnull, A., 'Me and My Shadow: The European Court of Justice and the Disintegration of European Union Law' 31 *Fordham International Law Journal* (2008) 1134–1211.

Avbelj, Matej, and Komárek, Jan, (eds), *Constitutional Pluralism in the European Union and Beyond* (Oxford: Hart, 2012)

Avbelj, Matej, and Davies, Gareth, (eds) *Research Handbook on Legal Pluralism and EU Law* (London: Edward Elgar, 2018)

Bantekas, Ilias, and Renaud Vivien, 'On the Odiousness of Greek Debt' 22 *European Law Journal* (2016) 539–65

Barber, Nicholas W., 'Legal Pluralism and the European Union' 12 *European Law Journal* (2006) 306

Barber, Nicholas W., *The Constitutional State* (Oxford: Oxford University Press, 2010)

Barents, R. *The Autonomy of Community Law* (The Hague: Kluwer Law International, 2004)

Barents, R. 'The Precedence of EU Law from the Perspective of Constitutional Pluralism' 5 *European Constitutional Law Review* (2009) 421

Barnard, Catherine, *EC Employment Law*, 3rd edn (Oxford: Oxford University Press, 2006)

Barry, Brian, 'Statism and Nationalism: a Cosmopolitan Critique' in Ian Shapiro and Lea Brilmayer (eds), *Global Justice* (New York: New York University Press, 1999) 12–66

Beitz, Charles, *Political Theory and International Relations*, rev edn (Princeton: Princeton University Press, 1999)

Bellamy, Richard, 'Sovereignty, Post-Sovereignty and Pre-Sovereignty: Three Models of the State, Democracy and Rights within the EU' in Neil Walker (ed.), *Sovereignty in Transition: Essays in European Law* (Oxford: Hart, 2003) 167

Bellamy, Richard, *Political Constitutionalism: A Republican Defence of the Constitutionality of Democracy* (Cambridge: Cambridge University Press, 2007)

Benvenisti, Eyal, 'Sovereigns as Trustees of Humanity: On the Accountability of States to Foreign Stakeholders' 107 *American Journal of International Law* (2013) 295–333

Besselink, L.F.M. 'The Proliferation of Constitutional Law and Constitutional Adjudication, or How American Judicial Review Came to Europe After All' 9 *Utrecht Law Review* (2013) 19–35

Berger, Helge, Dell'Ariccia, Giovanni, and Obstfeld, Maurice, *Revisiting the Economic Case for Fiscal Union in the Euro Area* (Washington, DC: International Monetary Fund, 2018)
Bergsten, C. Fred, 'Why the Euro Will Survive' *Foreign Affairs*, September/Ocrober 2012, 216
Berman, Harold J., *Law and Revolution: The Formation of the Western Legal Tradition* (Cambridge, Mass.: Harvard University Press, 1983)
Besson, Samantha, 'From European Integration to European Integrity: Should European Law Speak with Just One Voice?' 10 *European Law Journal* (2004) 257
Besson, Samantha, 'The Authority of International Law—Lifting the State Veil' 31 *Sydney Law Review* (2009) 343
Bingham, Tom, *The Rule of Law* (London: Penguin, 2010)
Bjorge, Eirik, 'The Vienna Rules, Evolutionary Interpretation, and the Intentions of the Parties' in Andrea Bianchi, Daniel Peat, and Matthew Windsor (eds), *Interpretation in International Law* (Oxford: Oxford University Press, 2015) 189
Blake, Michael, 'Distributive Justice, State Coercion, and Autonomy,' 30 *Philosophy and Public Affairs* (2001) 257–96
Bobak, Michal, 'The Effects of EU Law in the National Legal Systems' in Catherine Barnard and Steve Peers (eds), *European Union Law* (Oxford: Oxford University Press, 2014) 140–73
Browne, James, Johnson, Paul, and Phillips, David, *The Budget of the European Union: A Guide: IFS Briefing Note BN181* (London: Institute of Fiscal Studies, 2016)
Brunnermeier, Markus K., James, Harold, and Landau, Jean-Pierre, *The Euro and the Battle of Ideas* (Princeton: Princeton University Press, 2016)
Buchanan, Allen, 'Political Legitimacy and Democracy' 112 *Ethics* (2002) 689–719
Buchanan, Allen, *Justice, Legitimacy and Self-Determination: Moral Foundations for International Law* (Oxford: Oxford University Press, 2004)
Buchanan, Allen, 'The Legitimacy of International Law' in Samantha Besson and John Tasioulas (eds), *The Philosophy of International Law* (Oxford: Oxford University Press, 2010) 79–96
Buchanan, Allen, and Keohane, Robert O., 'The Legitimacy of Global Governance Institutions' 20 *Ethics and International Affairs* (2006) 405–37
Bullough, Oliver, *Moneyland: Why Thieves and Crooks Now Rule the World and How to Take it Back* (London: Profile Book, 2018)
Byrd, B. Sharon, and Hruschka, Joachim, *Kant's Doctrine of Right: A Commentary* (Cambridge: Cambridge University Press, 2010)
Campos, Thana, *The Global Health Crisis: Ethical Responsibilities* (Cambridge: Cambridge University Press, 2017)
Caney, Simon, *Justice Beyond Borders: Global Political Theory* (Oxford: Oxford University Press, 2005)
Caney, Simon, 'Global Poverty and Human Rights: The Case for Positive Duties' in Pogge (ed.), *Freedom from Poverty as a Human Right: Who Owes What to the Very Poor?* (Oxford: Oxford University Press, 2007) 275
Cheneval, Francis, *The Government of the Peoples: On the Idea and Principles of Multilateral Democracy* (New York: Palgrave Macmillan, 2011)
Cheneval, Francis, and Nicolaïdis, Kalypso, 'The Social Construction of Demoicracy in the European Union' 16 *European Journal of Political Theory* (2017) 235–60
Cheneval, Francis, and Schimmelfenning, Frank, 'The Case for Demoicracy in the European Union' 51 *Journal of Common Market Studies* (2013) 334–50
Cheneval, F., Lavenex S., and Schimmelfennig, F., 'Demoi-cracy in the European Union: Principles, institutions, policies' 22 *Journal of European Public Policy* (2015) 1–18

Cloots, Elke, *National Identity in European Union Law* (Oxford: Oxford University Press, 2015)

Cohen, Jean, 'Changing Paradigms of Citizenship and the Exclusiveness of the Demos' 14 *International Sociology* (1999) 245–68

Cohen, Joshua, and Sabel, Charles, '*Extra Rempublicam Nulla Justitia*?' 34 *Philosophy and Public Affairs* (2006) 147

Cohen, Joshua, and Sabel, Charles, 'Global Democracy?' 37 *New York University Journal of International Law and Policy* (2006) 763–97

Cohler, Ann M., Miller, Basia Carolyn, and Stone, Harold Samuel (eds and trans), *Montesquieu: The Spirit of the Laws*(Cambridge: Cambridge University Press, 1989)

Cohn-Bendit, Daniel, and Verhofstadt, Guy, *For Europe! Manifesto for a Postnational Revolution in Europe* (Munich: Carl Hanser Verlag, 2012)

Collier, J. G., 'Is International Law Really Part of the Law of England?' 38 *International and Comparative Law Quarterly* (1989) 924–35

Copelovitch, Mark, Frieden, Jeffry, and Walter, Stefanie, 'The Political Economy of the Euro Crisis' 49 *Comparative Political Studies* (2016) 811–40

Craig, Paul, 'The Legal Effect of Directives: Policy, Rules and Exceptions' 34 *European Law Review* (2009) 349

Craig, Paul, 'Constitutionalizing Constitutional Law: *HS2*' (2014) *Public Law* 373

Culver, Keith, and Giudice, Michael, *Legality's Borders: An Essay in General Jurisprudence* (Oxford: Oxford University Press, 2010)

Culver, Keith, and Giudice, Michael, 'Not a System but an Order: An Inter-Institutional View of European Union Law' in Julie Dickson and Pavlos Eleftheriadis (eds), *Philosophical Foundations of European Union Law* (Oxford: Oxford University Press, 2012) 54–76

Dahl, Robert A., *On Democracy* (New Haven and London: Yale University Press, 2000)

Dashwood, Alan, 'States in the European Union' 23 *European Law Review* (1998) 201

De Búrca, Gráinne 'Sovereignty and the Supremacy Doctrine of the European Court for Justice' in Neil Walker (ed.), *Sovereignty in Transition: Essays in European Law* (Oxford: Hart, 2003) 449

De Búrca, Gráinne, 'Towards European Welfare?' in Gráinne de Búrca (ed.), *EU Law, and the Welfare State: In Search of Solidarity* (Oxford: Oxford University Press, 2005)

De Witte, Bruno, 'The Nature of the Legal Order' in Paul Craig and Gráinne de Búrca (eds), *The Evolution of EU Law* (Oxford, Oxford University Press, 1999) 177

De Witte, Bruno, 'Do Not Mention the Word: Sovereignty in Two Europhile Countries: Belgium and the Netherlands', in Neil Walker (ed.), *Sovereignty in Transition* (Oxford: Hart, 2003) 351

De Witte, Bruno, 'European Union Law: How Autonomous is its Order?' 65 *Zeittschrift für Öffentliches Recht* (2010) 141

De Witte, Bruno, 'Direct Effect, Primacy and the Nature of the Legal Order' in Paul Craig and Gráinne de Búrca (eds), *The Evolution of EU Law*, 2nd edn (Oxford: Oxford University Press, 2011) 323

De Witte, Bruno, 'The European Union as an International Legal Experiment' in Gráinne de Búrca and J.H.H. Weiler (eds), *The Worlds of European Constitutionalism* (Cambridge: Cambridge University Press, 2012) 19–56

De Witte, Floris, *Justice in the EU: The Emergence of Transnational Solidarity* (Oxford: Oxford University Press, 2015)

De Schutter, Helder, 'The Solidarity Argument for the European Union' in Frank Vandenbroucke, Catherine Barnard, and Geert de Baere (eds), *A European Social Union After the Crisis* (Cambridge: Cambridge University Press, 2017) 68–91

Di Fabio, Udo, 'Karlsruhe makes a Referral' 15 *German Law Journal* (2014) 107–10
Dicey, Albert Venn, *Introduction to the Study of the Law of the Constitution* (Indianapolis: Liberty Fund, 1982)
Dickson, Julie, 'Towards a Theory of European Union Legal Systems' in Julie Dickson and Pavlos Eleftheriadis (eds), *Philosophical Foundations of European Union Law* (Oxford: Oxford University Press, 2012) 25–53
Dörr, Oliver, 'Article 26: *Pacta Sunt Servanda*' in Oliver Dörr and Kirsten Schmalenbach (eds), *Vienna Convention on the Law of Treaties* (Berlin: Springer, 2011) 427–51
Drake, Sara, 'Twenty Years after *Von Colson*: the impact of "Indirect Effect" on the Protection of the Individual's Community Rights' 30 *European Law Review* (2005) 329
Dyzenhaus, David, *Legality and Legitimacy: Carl Schmitt, Hans Kelsen and Hermann Heller in Weimar* (Oxford: Oxford University Press, 1997)
Dyzenhaus, David, 'The Politics of the Question of Constituent Power' in Martin Loughlin and Neil Walker (eds), *The Paradox of Constitutionalism* (Oxford: Oxford University Press, 2007) 129–45.
Dworkin, Ronald, *Law's Empire* (London: Fontana, 1986)
Dworkin, Ronald, *Justice in Robes* (Cambridge, Mass.: Harvard University Press, 2007)
Dworkin, Ronald, *Justice for Hedgehogs* (Cambridge, Mass.: Harvard University Press, 2011)
Dworkin, Ronald, 'A New Philosophy of International Law' 41 *Philosophy and Public Affairs* (2013) 1
Easterly, William, *The White Man's Burden: Why the West's Efforts to Aid the Rest Have Done So Much Ill and So Little Good* (Oxford: Oxford University Press, 2006)
Eeckhout, Piet, 'Human Rights and the Autonomy of EU Law—Pluralism or Integration?' 66 *Current Legal Problems* (2013) 169–202
Eleftheriadis, Pavlos, 'Aspects of European Constitutionalism' 21 *European Law Review* (1996) 32–42
Eleftheriadis, Pavlos, 'The Direct Effect of Community Law: Conceptual Issues' 16 *Yearbook of European Law* (1996) 205
Eleftheriadis, Pavlos, 'Begging the Constitutional Question' 36 *Journal of Common Market Studies* (1998) 255–72
Eleftheriadis, Pavlos, 'The European Constitution and Cosmopolitan Ideals' 7 *The Columbia Journal of European Law* (2001) 21–39
Eleftheriadis, Pavlos, 'Cosmopolitan Law' 9 *European Law Journal* (2003) 241–63
Eleftheriadis, Pavlos, 'The Idea of a European Constitution' 27 *Oxford Journal of Legal Studies* (2007) 1–21
Eleftheriadis, Pavlos, 'The Standing of States in the European Union' in Nicholas Tsagourias (ed.), *Transnational Constitutionalism: International and European Perspectives* (Cambridge: Cambridge University Press 2007)
Eleftheriadis, Pavlos, *Legal Rights* (Oxford: Oxford University Press, 2008)
Eleftheriadis, Pavlos, 'Human Rights as Legal Rights' 1 *Transnational Legal Theory* (2010) 371–92
Eleftheriadis, Pavlos, 'Human Rights for Liberals' 3 *Global Justice* (2010) 42–8
Eleftheriadis, Pavlos, 'Law and Sovereignty' 29 *Law and Philosophy* (2010) 535
Eleftheriadis, Pavlos, 'Pluralism and Integrity' 23 *Ratio Juris* (2010) 365
Eleftheriadis, Pavlos, 'The Structure of European Law'12 *Cambridge Yearbook of European Legal Studies* (2010) 121–50.
Eleftheriadis, Pavlos, 'The Law of Laws' 1 *Transnational Legal Theory* (2010) 597
Eleftheriadis, Pavlos, 'The Moral Distinctiveness of the European Union' 9 *International Journal of Constitutional Law* (2011) 695

Eleftheriadis, Pavlos, 'Citizenship and Obligation' in Julie Dickson and Pavlos Eleftheriadis (eds), *Philosophical Foundations of European Union Law* (Oxford: Oxford University Press, 2012) 159–88

Eleftheriadis, Pavlos, 'The Euro and the German Courts' 128 *Law Quarterly Review* (2012) 216

Eleftheriadis, Pavlos, 'Hart on Sovereignty' in Andrea Dolcetti, Luís Duarte d'Almeida, and James Edwards (eds), *Reading HLA Hart's* 'The Concept of Law' (Oxford: Hart Publishing 2013) 59–80

Eleftheriadis, Pavlos, 'Legality and Reciprocity' 10 *Jerusalem Review of Legal Studies* (2014) 1–17

Eleftheriadis, Pavlos, 'The Content of European Citizenship' (2014) 15 *German Law Journal* 777

Eleftheriadis, Pavlos, 'The Misrule of the Few: How the Oligarchs Ruined Greece' *Foreign Affairs*, November/December, 2014

Eleftheriadis, Pavlos, 'Power and Principle in Constitutional Law' 45 *Netherlands Journal of Legal Philosophy* (2016) 37

Eleftheriadis, Pavlos, 'Constitutional Illegitimacy over Brexit' 88 *Political Quarterly* (2017) 182–88.

Eleftheriadis, Pavlos, 'Two Doctrines of the Unwritten Constitution' 13 *European Constitutional Law Review* (2017) 525

Eleftheriadis, Pavlos, 'Constitutional Change Through Deliberation' in Ron Levy, Hoi Kong, Graeme Orr, and Jeff King (eds), *The Cambridge Handbook of Deliberative Constitutionalism* (Cambridge: Cambridge University Press 2018)

Eleftheriadis, Pavlos, 'In Defence of Constitutional Law' 81 *Modern Law Review* (2018) 154–178

Englard, Izhak, *Corrective and Distributive Justice: From Aristotle to Modern Times* (Oxford: Oxford University Press, 2009)

European Commission, *One Market: One Money; An Evaluation of the Potential Benefits and Costs of Forming an Economic and Monetary Union* (Brussels, 1990)

European Commission, EMU@10: Successes and Challenges after Ten Years of Economic and Monetary Union, European Economy 2/2008, (Luxembourg, 2008)

Fabbrini, Federico, 'After the OMT Case: The Supremacy of EU Law as the Guarantee of the Equality of the Member States' 16 *German Law Journal* (2015) 1003

Fabbrini, Federico, *Economic Governance in Europe: Comparative Paradoxes and Constitutional Challenges* (Oxford: Oxford University Press, 2016)

Fabbrini, Sergio, (ed.), *Democracy and Federalism in the European Union and the United States: Exploring Post-National Governance* (London: Routledge, 2005)

Feldstein, Martin, 'The Political Economy of the European Economic and Monetary Union: Political Sources of an Economic Liability' 11 *Journal of Economic Perspectives* (1997) 23–42

Feldstein, Martin, 'EMU and International Conflict' *Foreign Affairs*, November/December 1997

Feldstein, Martin, 'The Failure of the Euro: The Little Currency that Couldn't' *Foreign Affairs*, January/February 2012

Fernández-Villaverde, Jesus, Garicano Luis, and Santos, Tano, 'Political Credit Cycles: The Case of the Eurozone' 27 *Journal of Economic Perspectives* (2013) 145–166

Franks, Jeffrey, Barkbu, Bergljot, Blavy, Rodolphe, Oman, William, and Schoelerman, Hanni, 'Economic Convergence in the Euro Area: Coming Together or Drifting Apart?' *IMF Working Paper*, 18/10 (January 2018) (Washington, DC: International Monetary Fund, 2018)

Freeman, Samuel, 'The Law of Peoples, Social Cooperation, Human Rights, and Distributive Justice' 23 *Social Philosophy and Policy* (2006) 29–68
Frieden, Jeffrey, and Walter, Stefanie, 'Understanding the Political Economy of the Eurozone Crisis' 20 *Annual Review of Political Science* (2017) 371–90
Fossum, John Erik, and Menendez, Agustin Jose, *The Constitution's Gift: A Constitutional Theory for a Democratic European Union* (Lanham: Rowman & Littlefield, 2011)
Forst, Rainer, 'Justice, Democracy and the Right to Justification: Reflections on Jürgen Neyer's Normative Theory of the European Union' in Dimitry Kochenov, Gráinne de Búrca, and Andrew Williams (eds) *Europe's Justice Deficit?* (London: Hart Publishing, 2015) 227–34
Gay, Peter, *The Cultivation of Hatred* (New York: Norton, 1994)
Gibson, Heather D., Hall, Stephen G., and Tavlas, George S., 'Self-fulfilling Dynamics: The Interactions of Sovereign Spreads, Sovereign Ratings and Bank Ratings during the Euro Financial Crisis' 73 *Journal of International Money and* Finance (2017) 118–33
Gragl, Paul, *Legal Monism* (Oxford: Oxford University Press, 2018)
Grant, Ruth W., and Keohane, Robert O., 'Accountability and Abuses of Power in World Politics' 99 *American Political Science Review* (2005) 29–43
Grimm, Dieter, *The Constitution of European Democracy* (Oxford: Oxford University Press, 2017)
Habermas, Jürgen, *Between Facts and Norms*, trans. by William Rehg (Cambridge: Polity Press, 1996)
Habermas, Jürgen, *The Inclusion of the Other: Studies in Political Theory*, edited by Pablo de Greiff and Ciaran Cronin (Cambridge, Mass.: MIT Press, 1998)
Habermas, Jürgen, 'Why Europe Needs a Constitution' 11 *New Left Review* (2001) 5–26
Habermas, Jürgen, *The Crisis of the European Union: A Response*, trans. by Ciaran Cronin (Cambridge: Polity Press, 2012)
Habermas, Jürgen, 'Democracy, Solidarity, and the European Crisis' in Luuk van Middelaar and Philippe van Parijs (eds), *After the Storm: How to Save Democracy in Europe* (Tielt: Lannoo, 2015) 95–107
Habermas, Jürgen, *The Lure of Technocracy* (Cambridge: Polity Press, 2015)
Halberstam, Daniel, 'Of Power and Responsibility: The Political Morality of Federal Systems' 90 *Virginia Law* Review (2004) 731–834
Halberstam Daniel, and Möllers, Cristoph, 'The German Constitutional Court says: "Ja zu Deutschland"' 10 *German Law Journal* (2009) 1241
Harlow, Carol, *Accountability in the European Union* (Oxford: Oxford University Press, 2002)
Hart, H.L.A., 'Are There any Natural Rights?' 64 *Philosophical Review* (1955) 185
Hart, H.L.A., *The Concept of Law*, 2nd edn (Oxford: Oxford University Press, 1993)
Hartley, Trevor C., *Constitutional Problems of the European Union* (Oxford: Hart, 1999)
Harrison, Ross, *Democracy* (London: Routledge, 1993)
Hartwig Lojsch, Dagmar, Rodríguez-Vives, Marta, and Slavík, Michal, 'The Size and Composition of Government Debt in the Euro Area' *ECB Occasional Paper Series*, No 132, October 2011
Herman, Barbara, 'Mutual Aid and Respect for Persons' 94 *Ethics* (1984) 577–602
Herman, Barbara, 'Being Helped and Being Grateful: Imperfect Duties, the Ethics of Possession, and the Unity of Morality' 109 *Journal of Philosophy* (2012) 391–411
Hershovitz Scott, 'Integrity and *Stare Decisis*' in Scott Hershovitz (ed.), *Exploring Law's Empire: The Jurisprudence of Ronald Dworkin* (Oxford: Oxford University Press, 2008) 103–18

Hill, Steven, *Europe's Promise: Why the European Way is the Best Hope in an Insecure Age* (Berkeley: University of California Press, 2010)

Hinarejos, Alicia, *The Euro Area Crisis in Constitutional Perspective* (Oxford: Oxford University Press, 2015)

Holdgaard, Rass, Elkan, Daniella and Schaldemose, Gustav Krohn, 'From cooperation to collision: The ECJ's *Ajos* ruling and the Danish Supreme Court's refusal to comply' 55 *Common Market Law Review*, (2018) 17–53

Howse, Robert, *The Concept of Odious Debt in Public International Law: UNCTAD Discussion Papers, No. 185* (New York: United Nations, 2007)

James, Harold, *Making the European Monetary Union* (Cambridge, Mass.: Harvard University Press, 2014)

James, Aaron, *Fairness in Practice: A Social Contract for a Global Economy* (Oxford: Oxford University Press, 2012)

Joerges, Christian, 'Social Justice in an Ever More Diverse Union' in Frank Vandenbroucke, Catherine Barnard, and Geert de Baere (eds), *A European Social Union after the Crisis* (Cambridge: Cambridge University Press, 2017) 92–119

Judt, Tony, *A Grand Illusion? An Essay on Europe* (London: Penguin, 1997)

Julius, Anthony, 'Nagel's Atlas' 34 *Philosophy and Public Affairs* (2006) 176–92

Internal Evaluation Office of the IMF, *The IMF and the Crises in Greece, Ireland, and Portugal: Evaluation Report* (Washington, DC: International Monetary Fund, 2016)

Isiksel, Turkuler, 'European Exceptionalism and the EU's Accession to the ECHR' 27 *European Journal of International Law* (2016) 565–89

Isiksel, Turkuler, *Europe's Functional Constitution: A theory of Constitutionalism Beyond the State* (Oxford: Oxford University Press, 2016)

Kadelbach, Stefan, 'Union Citizenship' in Armin von Bogdandy and Jürgen Bast (eds), *Principles of European Constitutional Law* (Oxford: Hart Publishing, 2009) 443–78

Kaldor, Nicholas, 'The Dynamic Effects of the Common Market' in Nicholas Kaldor, *Further Essays On Applied Economics* (New York: Holmes and Meier, 1978)

Kant, Immanuel, *Practical Philosophy*, trans. and edited by Mary J. Gregor (Cambridge: Cambridge University Press, 1996)

Kelsen, Hans, *Pure Theory of Law*, trans. by Max Knight (Berkeley: University of California Press, 1967)

Keohane, Robert O., *After Hegemony: Cooperation and Discord in the World Political Economy* (Princeton: Princeton University Press, 1984) 214

Keohane, Robert O., 'Reciprocity in International Relations' 40 *International Organization* (1986) 1–27

Keohane, Robert O., Macedo, Stephen, and Moravcsik, Andrew, 'Democracy-Enhancing Multilateralism' 63 *International Organisation* (2009) 1–31

Keynes, John Maynard, *The General Theory of Employment, Interest and Money* (Cambridge: Macmillan & Cambridge University Press for the Royal Economic Society, 1936)

King, Jeff, *The Doctrine of Odious Debt in International Law: A Restatement* (Cambridge: Cambridge University Press, 2016)

Kingsbury, Benedict, 'Sovereignty and Inequality' 8 *European Journal of International Law* (1998) 599–625

Klosko, George, *Political Obligations* (Oxford: Oxford University Press, 2005)

Koh, Harold, 'Why Do Nations Obey International Law?' 106 *Yale Law Journal* (1997) 2599–659

Kolm, Serge Cristophe, *Reciprocity: An Economics of Social Relations* (Cambridge: Cambridge University Press, 2008)

Kolodny, Nico, 'Rule Over None II: Social Equality and the Justification of Democracy' 42 *Philosophy and Public Affairs* (2014) 287–336

Krastev, Ivan, *After Europe* (Philadelphia: University of Pennsylvania Press, 2017)

Krisch, Nico, *Beyond Constitutionalism: The Pluralist Structure of Postnational Law* (Oxford: Oxford University Press, 2010)

Krugman, Paul, Obstfeld, Maurice, and Melitz, Marc, *International Economics: Theory and Policy*, 9th edn (London: Pearson, 2011)

Küçük, Esin, 'Solidarity in EU Law: An Elusive Political Statement or a Legal Principle with Substance?' 23 *Maastricht Journal of European and Comparative Law* (2016) 965–83

Kumm, Mattias, 'Who is the Final Arbiter of Constitutionality in Europe?: Three Conceptions of the Relationship Between the German Federal Constitutional Court and the European Court of Justice' 36 *Common Market Law Review* (1999) 351

Kumm, Mattias, 'The Legitimacy of International Law: A Constitutionalist Framework of Analysis' 15 *European Journal of International Law* (2004) 907

Kumm, Mattias, 'The Jurisprudence of Constitutional Conflict: Constitutional Supremacy in Europe before and after the Constitutional Treaty' 11 *European Law Journal* (2005) 262–307

Kumm, Mattias, 'Beyond Golf Clubs and the Judicialization of Politics: Why Europe Has a Constitution Properly so Called' 54 *The American Journal of Comparative Law* (2006) 505

Kumm, Mattias, 'The Moral Point of Constitutional Pluralism: Defining the Domain of Legitimate Institutional Civil Disobedience and Conscientious Objection' in Julie Dickson and Pavlos Eleftheriadis (eds), *Philosophical Foundations of European Union Law* (Oxford: Oxford University Press, 2012) 216–46

Kumm, Mattias, 'The Cosmopolitan Turn in Constitutionalism: An Integrative Conception of Public Law' 20 *Indiana Journal of Global Legal Studies* (2013) 605–28

La Torre, Massimo, 'Legal Pluralism as an Evolutionary Achievement of Community Law' 12 *Ratio Juris* (1999) 182–95

Lacroix, Justine, 'Is Transnational Citizenship (Still) Enough?' in Dimitry Kochenov, Gráinne de Búrca, and Andrew Williams (eds), *Europe's Justice Deficit?* (London: Hart Publishing, 2015) 177–90

Laws, John, *The Common Law Constitution* (Cambridge: Cambridge University Press, 2014)

Lenaerts, Koen, 'Constitutionalism and the Many Faces of Federalism' 38 *American Journal of Comparative Law* (1990) 205

Lenaerts, Koen, and Gerard, Damien, 'The Structure of the Union According to the Constitution for Europe: The Emperor is Getting Dressed' 29 *European Law Review* (2004) 289

Lenaerts, Koen, 'Federalism and the Rule of Law: Perspectives from the European Court of Justice' 33 *Fordham International Law Review* (2011) 1338–87

Lenaerts, Koen, 'Exploring the Limits of the EU Charter of Fundamental Rights', 8 *European Constitutional Law Review* (2012) 375–403

Lenaerts, Koen, 'Demoicracy, Constitutional Pluralism, and the Court of Justice of the European Union' in Luuk van Middelaar and Philippe van Parijs (eds), *After the Storm: How to Save Democracy in Europe* (Tielt: Lannoo, 2015) 123–38

Lenaerts, Koen, and Corthaut, Tim, 'Of Birds and Hedges: the Role of Primacy in Invoking Norms of EU Law' 31 *European Law Review* (2006) 287–315

Lenaerts, Koen, and Desomer, Marlies, 'Bricks for a Constitutional Treaty of the European Union: Values, Objectives and Means' 27 *European Law Review* (2002) 377–407

Lenaerts, Koen, and Van Nuffel, Piet, *Constitutional Law of the European Union*, 2nd edn (London: Sweet & Maxwell, 2005)

Letsas, George, 'Harmonic Law: The Case Against Pluralism' in Julie Dickson and Pavlos Eleftheriadis (eds), *Philosophical Foundations of European Union Law* (Oxford: Oxford University Press, 2012) 77

Locke, John, *Two Treatises of Government*, edited by Peter Laslett (Cambridge: Cambridge University Press, 1988)

Loughlin, Martin, and Walker, Neil, 'Introduction' in Loughlin and Walker (eds), *The Paradox of Constitutionalism* (Oxford: Oxford University Press, 2007) 1

Ludwig, Bernd, 'Whence Public Right? The Role of Theoretical and Practical Reasoning in Kant's Doctrine of Right' in Mark Timmons (ed.), *Kant's Metaphysics of Morals: Interpretive Essays* (Oxford: Oxford University Press, 2002) 159–84

MacCormick, Neil, *Questioning Sovereignty: Law, State and Nation in the European Commonwealth* (Oxford: Oxford University Press, 1999)

Madsen, Mikael Rask, Olsen, Henrik Palmer, and Šadl, Urška, 'Competing Supremacies and Clashing Institutional Rationalities: the Danish Supreme Court's Decision in the *Ajos* Case and the National Limits of Judicial Cooperation' 23 *European Law Journal* (2017) 140–50

Malcolm, Noel, *Sense on Sovereignty* (London: Centre for Policy Studies, 1991), reprinted in Martin Holmes (ed.), *The Eurosceptical Reader* (London: Palgrave, 1996) 342–67

Malcolm, Noel, 'The Case Against "Europe"' *Foreign Affairs* (1995) March/April

Mancini, G. Federico, 'The Making of a Constitution for Europe' (1989) 26 *CMLRev* 595.

Mandle, Jon, *Global Justice* (Cambridge: Polity Press, 2006)

Marshall, T.H., *Citizenship and Social Class and Other* Essays (Cambridge: Cambridge University Press, 1950)

Martinez, Jenny, 'Towards an International Judicial System' 56 *Stanford Law Review* (2003) 430

Masuch, Klaus, Moshammer, Edmund, and Pierluigi, Beatrice, 'Institutions, Public Debt and Growth in Europe' *ECB Working Papers Series*, No 1963, September 2016

Matthijs, Matthias, 'Integration at What Price? The Erosion of National Democracy in the Euro Periphery' 52 *Government and Opposition* (2017) 266–94

McMahan, Jeff, 'Laws of War' in Samantha Besson and John Tasioulas (eds), *The Philosophy of International Law* (Oxford: Oxford University Press, 2010) 493

Mendez, Mario, *The Legal Effects of EU Agreements: Maximalist Treaty Enforcement and Judicial Avoidance Techniques* (Oxford: Oxford University Press, 2013)

Menon, Anand, *Europe: The State of the Union* (London: Atlantic Books, 2008)

Miller, David, *On Nationality* (Oxford: Oxford University Press, 1995)

Miller, David, 'Republicanism, National Identity and Europe' in Cecile Laborde and John Maynor (eds), *Republicanism and Political Theory* (Oxford: Blackwell, 2008)

Miller, David, 'A Plea for Pluralism' in Luuk van Middelaar and Philippe van Parijs (eds), *After the Storm: How to Save Democracy in Europe* (Tielt: Lannoo, 2015) 179–88

Mody, Ashoka, *Eurotragedy: A Drama in Nine Acts* (Oxford: Oxford University Press, 2018)

Moravcsik, Andrew, *The Choice for Europe: Social Purpose and State Power from Messina to Maastricht* (Ithaca: Cornell University Press, 1998)

Moravcsik, Andrew, 'In Defence of the "Democratic Deficit": Reassessing Legitimacy in the European Union' 40 *Journal of Common Market Studies* (2002) 603–24

Moravcsik, Andrew, 'The European Constitutional Compromise and the Neofunctionalist Legacy' 12 *Journal of European Public Policy* (2005) 349–86

Moravcsik, Andrew, 'Europe After the Crisis: How to Sustain a Common Currency' *Foreign Affairs*, May/June 2012

Morgan, Glyn, *The Idea of a European Superstate: Public Justification and European Integration* (Princeton: Princeton University Press, 2015)

Mundell, Robert, 'A Theory of Optimum Currency Areas' 51 *American Economic Review* (1961) 509–17

Murphy, Liam, 'International Responsibility' in Samantha Besson and John Tasioulas (eds), *The Philosophy of International Law* (Oxford: Oxford University Press, 2010) 299

Murphy, Liam, 'Law Beyond the State: Some Philosophical Questions' 28 *European Journal of International Law* (2017) 203–32

Nagel, Thomas, 'Moral Conflict and Political Legitimacy' 16 *Philosophy and Public Affairs* (1987) 215–40

Nagel, Thomas, 'The Problem of Global Justice' 33 *Philosophy and Public Affairs* (2005) 113–47

Nebbia, Paolisa, 'The Double Life of Effectiveness' 10 *Cambridge Yearbook of European Legal Studies* (2007–2008) 287

Neyer, Jürgen, *The Justification of Europe: A Political Theory of Supranational Integration* (Oxford: Oxford University Press, 2012)

Neyer, Jürgen, 'Justice and the Right to Justification: Conceptual Reflections' in Dimitry Kochenov, Gráinne de Búrca, and Andrew Williams (eds), *Europe's Justice Deficit?* (Oxford: Hart, 2015) 211–26

Nicolaïdis, Kalypso, 'We the Peoples of Europe' 83 *Foreign Affairs* (2004) November/December Issue, 97–110

Nicolaïdis, Kalypso, 'The Idea of European Demoicracy' in Julie Dickson and Pavlos Eleftheriadis (eds), *Philosophical Foundations of European Union Law* (Oxford: Oxford University Press, 2012) 247–74

Nicolaïdis, Kalypso, 'European Demoicracy and its Crisis' 51 *Journal or Common Market Studies* (2013) 351–69

Nicolaïdis, Kalypso and Howse, Robert (eds), *The Federal Vision: Legitimacy and Levels of Governance in the United States and the European Union* (Oxford: Oxford University Press, 2001)

Nicolaïdis Kalypso, and Pelabay, Janie, 'One Union, One Story? In Praise of Europe's Narrative Diversity' in Alex Warleigh-Lack (ed.), *Reflections on European Integration* (London: Palgrave 2008)

O'Leary, Síofra, 'Solidarity and Citizenship Rights in the Charter of Fundamental Rights of the European Union' in Gráinne De Búrca (ed.), *EU Law, and the Welfare State: In Search of Solidarity* (Oxford: Oxford University Press, 2005) 39–87

O'Neill, Onora, *Bounds of Justice* (Cambridge: Cambridge University Press, 2000)

O'Neill, Onora, *Constructing Authorities: Reason, Politics and Interpretation in Kant's Philosophy* (Cambridge: Cambridge University Press, 2015)

O'Toole, Fintan, *The Ship of Fools: How Stupidity and Corruption Sank the Celtic Tiger* (London: Faber and Faber, 2009)

Olson, Mancur, *The Rise and Decline of Nations: Economic Growth, Stagflation and Social Rigidities* (New Haven: Yale University Press, 1982)

Payandeh, Mehrdad, 'The OMT Judgment of the German Federal Constitutional Court: Repositioning the Court within the European Constitutional Architecture' 13 *European Constitutional Law Review* (2017) 400–16

Pernice, Ingolf, 'The Autonomy of the EU Legal Order–Fifty Years After Van Gend' in A. Tizzano, J. Kokott, and S. Prechal (eds), *50ème Anniversaire de l'arrêt Van Gend en Loos, 1963–2013* (Luxembourg: Office des publications de l' Union européenne, 2013) 55–80

Perreau-Saussine, Amanda, 'Immanuel Kant on International Law' in Samantha Besson and John Tasioulas (eds), *The Philosophy of International Law* (Oxford: Oxford University Press, 2010) 53–78

Pettit, Philip, 'Legitimacy and Justice in Republican Perspective' 65 *Current Legal Problems* (2012) 59–82

Pisani-Ferry, Jean, *The Euro-Crisis and Its Aftermath* (Oxford: Oxford University Press, 2014)

Pocock, J.G.A., 'The Idea of Citizenship since Classical Times' in Ronald Beiner (ed.), *Theorizing Citizenship* (New York: State University of New York Press, 1995) 29–52

Pogge, Thomas, 'Severe Poverty as a Human Rights Violation' in Pogge (ed.), *Freedom from Poverty as a Human Right: Who Owes What to the Very Poor?* (Oxford: Oxford University Press, 2007) 11–53

Pogge, Thomas, *World Poverty and Human Rights: Cosmopolitan Responsibilities and Reforms*, 2nd edn (Cambridge: Polity Press, 2008)

Pogge, Thomas, *Politics as Usual: What Lies behind the Pro-Poor Rhetoric* (Cambridge: Polity Press, 2010)

Poiares Maduro, Miguel, 'Contrapunctual Law: Europe's Constitutional Pluralism in Action' in Neil Walker (ed.), *Sovereignty in Transition: Essays in European Law* (Oxford: Hart, 2003) 501

Poiares Maduro, Miguel, 'Europe and the Constitution: What if this is as Good as it Gets?' in J.H.H. Weiler and Marlene Wind (eds), *European Constitutionalism Beyond the State* (Cambridge: Cambridge University Press, 2003) 74–102

Rasmussen, Hjalte, *On Law and Policy in the European Court of Justice* (Dordrecht: Martinus Nijhoff, 1986)

Rawls, John, *Political Liberalism* (New York: Columbia University Press, 1993)

Rawls, John, *A Theory of Justice*, rev edn (Oxford: Oxford University Press, 1999)

Rawls, John, 'Justice as Reciprocity' in Rawls, *Collected Papers*, edited by Samuel Freeman (Cambridge, Mass.: Harvard University Press, 1999) 190

Rawls, John, *The Law of Peoples* (Cambridge, Mass.: Harvard University Press, 1999)

Rawls, John, and van Parijs, Philippe, 'Three Letters on the Law of Peoples and the European Union' (2003) 7 *Revue de philosophie économique* 7–20

Raz, Joseph, *The Authority of Law* (Oxford: Clarendon Press, 1979)

Raz, Joseph, 'Human Rights Without Foundations' in John Tasioulas and Samantha Besson (eds), *The Philosophy of International Law* (Oxford: Oxford University Press, 2010) 321

Reinhart, Carmen M., and Rogoff, Kenneth S., *This Time Is Different: Eight Centuries of Financial Folly* (Princeton: Princeton University Press, 2009)

Richardson, Henry S., *Democratic Autonomy: Public Reasoning about the Ends of Policy* (Oxford: Oxford University Press, 2002)

Ripstein, Arthur, *Equality, Responsibility, and the Law* (Cambridge: Cambridge University Press, 1999)

Ripstein, Arthur, 'Authority and Coercion' (2004) 32 *Philosophy and Public Affairs* 2

Ripstein, Arthur, *Force and Freedom* (Cambridge, Mass.: Harvard University Press, 2009)

Rodrik, Dani, *The Globalization Paradox* (Oxford: Oxford University Press, 2011)

Rodrik, Dani, 'The Future of European Democracy' in Luuk van Middelaar and Philippe van Parijs (eds), *After the Storm: How to Save Democracy in Europe* (Tielt: Lannoo, 2015) 55–65

Rogoff, Kenneth S., 'Crash Time' *Project Syndicate*, 8 September 2018

Rosanvallon, Pierre, *Democratic Legitimacy: Impartiality, Reflexivity, Proximity*, trans. by Arthur Goldhammer (Princeton: Princeton University Press, 2011)

Rosas, Allan, and Armati, Lorna, *EU Constitutional Law*, 2nd edn (Oxford: Hart, 2012)

Ross, Malcolm, 'Solidarity—A New Constitutional Paradigm for the EU?' in M. Ross and Y. Borgmann-Prebil (eds), *Promoting Solidarity in the European Union* (Oxford University Press, 2010) 23–45

Roughan, Nicole, *Authorities: Conflict, Cooperation and Transnational Legal Theory* (Oxford: Oxford University Press, 2013)

Sabel, Charles, and Gerstenberg, Oliver, 'Constitutionalising an Overlapping Consensus: The ECJ and the Emergence of a Coordinate Constitutional Order' 16 *European Law Journal* (2010) 511

Sales, Philip, and Clement, Joanne, 'International Law in Domestic Courts: The Developing Framework' 124 *Law Quarterly Review* (2008) 388

Sangiovanni, Andrea, 'The Irrelevance of Coercion, Imposition, and Framing to Distributive Justice' 40 *Philosophy and Public Affairs* (2012) 79–110

Sangiovanni, Andrea, 'Solidarity in the EU' 33 *Oxford Journal of Legal Studies* (2013) 1–29

Scharpf, Fritz W., *Governing in Europe. Effective and Democratic?* (Oxford: Oxford University Press, 1999)

Scharpf, Fritz W., 'The European Social Model: Coping with the Challenges of Diversity' 40 *Journal of Common Market Studies* (2002) 645–70

Shaw, Jo, 'Citizenship: Contrasting Dynamics' in Paul Craig and Gráinne de Búrca (eds), *The Evolution of EU Law*, 2nd edn (Oxford: Oxford University Press, 2011) 575

Schilling, Theodore, 'The Autonomy of the Community Legal Order: An Analysis of Possible Foundations' 37 *Harvard International Law Journal* (1996) 389

Schmitt, Carl, *Constitutional Theory*, trans. by Jeffrey Seitzer (Durham, NC: Duke University Press, 2008)

Schimmelfennig, Frank, and Winzen, Thomas, 'Instrumental and Constitutional Differentiation in the European Union' 52 *Journal of Common Market Studies* (2014) 354

Schütze, Robert, *From Dual to Cooperative Federalism: The Changing Structure of EU Law* (Oxford: Oxford University Press, 2009)

Schütze, Robert, *European Constitutional Law*, 2nd edn (Cambridge: Cambridge University Press, 2016)

Siedentop, Larry, *Democracy in Europe* (London: Penguin, 2000)

Simmonds, Nigel, *Law as a Moral Idea* (Oxford: Oxford University Press, 2007)

Simmons, A. John, *Justification and Legitimacy: Essays on Rights and Obligations* (Cambridge: Cambridge University Press, 2001)

Singer, Peter, 'Famine, Affluence and Morality' 1 *Philosophy and Public Affairs* (1972) 229–43

Singer, Peter, *The Life you Can Save: How to Do your Part to End World Poverty* (New York: Random House, 2010)

Sinn, Hans Werner, *The Euro Trap: On Bursting Bubbles, Budgets, and Beliefs* (Oxford: Oxford University Press, 2014)

Shany, Yuval, *Regulating Jurisdictional Relations Between National and International Courts* (Oxford: Oxford University Press, 2009)

Shklar, Judith N., *American Citizenship: The Search for Inclusion* (Cambridge, Mass.: Harvard University Press, 1991)

Shklar, Judith N., 'The Bonds of Exile' in J. Shklar, *Political Thought and Political Thinkers*, edited by Stanley Hoffmann (Chicago: The University of Chicago Press, 1998) 56–72

Slaughter, Anne Marie, 'A Global Community of Courts' 44 *Harvard International Law Journal* (2003) 191

Smith, Anthony D., 'National Identity and the Idea of European Unity' 68 *International Affairs* (1991) 55–76

Somek, Alexander, 'The Preoccupation with Rights and the Embrace of Inclusion: A Critique' in Dimitry Kochenov, Gráinne de Búrca, and Andrew Williams (eds), *Europe's Justice Deficit?* (Oxford: Hart, 2015) 295–310

Somek, Alexander, *The Cosmopolitan Constitution* (Oxford: Oxford University Press, 2016)

Soros, George, with Gregor Peter Schmitz, *The Tragedy of the European Union: Disintegration or Revival?* (New York: Public Affairs, 2014)

Spaventa, Eleanor, 'A Very Fearful Court? The Protection of Fundamental Rights in the European Union after Opinion 2/13' 22 *Maastricht journal of European and Comparative Law* (2015) 35–56

Stephens, John D., 'The Social Rights of Citizenship' in Francis G. Castles, Stephan Leibfried, Jane Lewis, Herbert Obinger, and Christopher Pierson (eds), *The Oxford Handbook of the Welfare State* (Oxford: Oxford University Press, 2010) 511

Stiglitz, Joseph E., *Globalization and its Discontents* (London: Penguin, 2002)

Stiglitz, Joseph E., *The Euro: How a Common Currency Threatens the Future of Europe* (New York: Norton, 2016)

Stilz, Anna, 'Why Does the State Matter Morally? Political Obligation and Particularity' in Sigal R. Ben-Porath and Rogers M. Smith (eds), *Varieties of Sovereignty and Citizenship* (Philadelphia: University of Pennsylvania Press, 2012) 244–64

Summers, Robert S., 'The Conceptualisation of Good Faith in American Contract Law: A General Account' in Zimmermann and Whittaker (eds), *Good Faith in European Contract Law* (Cambridge: Cambridge University Press, 2000) 118–44

Tamanaha, Brian, *A General Jurisprudence of Law and Society* (Oxford: Oxford University Press, 2001)

Tasioulas, John, 'The Legitimacy of International Law', in Samantha Besson and John Tasioulas (eds), *The Philosophy of International Law* (Oxford: Oxford University Press, 2010) 97–116

Tomuschat, C., 'The Ruling of the German Constitutional Court on the Treaty of Lisbon' 10 *German Law Journal* (2009) 1259

Torres Pérez, Aida, *Conflicts of Rights in the European Union: A Theory of Supranational Adjudication* (Oxford: Oxford University Press, 2009) 76–84

Tridimas, Takis, *The General Principles of EC Law*, 2nd edn (Oxford: Oxford University Press, 2006)

Tsoukalis, Loukas, *In Defence of Europe: Can the European Project be Saved?* (Oxford: Oxford University Press, 2016)

Tuck, Richard, 'The Left Case for Brexit' *Dissent*, 6 June 2016

Tuori, Kaarlo, and Tuori, Klaus, *The Eurozone Crisis: A Constitutional Analysis* (Cambridge: Cambridge University Press, 2014)

van der Mei, A. Pieter., 'Freedom of Movement for Indigents: A Comparative Analysis of American Constitutional Law and European Community Law' 19 *Arizona Journal of International & Comparative Law* (2002) 803

Van Gerven, Walter, *The European Union: A Polity of States and Peoples* (Oxford: Hart, 2005)

Van Parijs, Philippe, 'Should the EU Become More Democratic?' in Andreas Follesdal and Peter Koslowski (eds), *Democracy and the European Union* (Berlin: Springer, 1997)

Van Parijs, Philippe, 'Justifying Europe' in Luuk van Middelaar and Philippe van Parijs (eds), *After the Storm: How to Save Democracy in Europe* (Tielt: Lannoo, 2015) 247–62

Vandenbroucke Frank, 'The Idea of a European Social Union: A Normative Introduction' in Vandenbroucke Frank, Catherine Barnard, and Geert de Baere (eds), *A European Social Union after the Crisis* (Cambridge: Cambridge University Press, 2017) 3–46

Verhofstadt, Guy, *Europe's Last Chance: Why the European States Must Form a More Perfect Union* (New York: Basic Books, 2017)

Viehoff, Juri, 'Eurozone Justice' 26 *The Journal of Political Philosophy* (2018) 388–414

Vinx, Lars, *Hans Kelsen's Pure Theory of Law: Legality and Legitimacy* (Oxford, Oxford University Press, 2007)

Von Bogdandy, Armin, 'Constitutional Principles' in Armin von Bogdandy and Jürgen Bast (eds), *Principles of European Constitutional Law* (Oxford: Hart Publishing, 2007) 14

Von Bogdandy, Armin, 'Founding Principles' in Armin von Bogdandy and Jürgen Bast (eds), *Principles of European Constitutional Law* (Oxford: Hart Publishing, 2009) 11–54

Von Bogdandy, Armin, 'Founding Principles of EU Law: A Theoretical and Doctrinal Sketch' 16 *European Law Journal* (2010) 95

Wade, H.W.R., 'Sovereignty—Revolution or Evolution?' 112 *Law Quarterly Review* (1996) 568–75

Waldron, Jeremy, *Law and Disagreement* (Oxford: Oxford University Press, 1999)

Walker, Neil, 'The Idea of Constitutional Pluralism' 65 *Modern Law Review* (2002) 317

Walker, Neil, 'Justice in and of the European Union' in Dimitry Kochenov, Gráinne de Búrca, and Andrew Williams (eds) *Europe's Justice Deficit?* (London: Hart Publishing, 2015) 247–58

Walker, Neil, *Intimations of Global Law* (Cambridge: Cambridge University Press, 2017)

Walzer, Michael, 'The Moral Standing of States: A Response to Four Critics' 9 *Philosophy & Public Affairs* (1980) 209–29

Watts, Ronald L., 'Federalism, Federal Political Systems, and Federation' 1 *Annual Review of Political Science* (1998) 117–37

Weatherill, Stephen, *Law and Values in the European Union* (Oxford: Oxford University Press, 2016)

Weiler, Joseph H.H., 'The Court of Justice on Trial' 24 *Common Market Law Review* (1987) 555.

Weiler, Joseph H.H., 'Does Europe Need a Constitution? Demos, Telos and the German Maastricht Decision' 1 *European Law Journal* (1995) 219–58

Weiler, Joseph H.H., and Haltern, Ulrich R, 'Autonomy of the Community Legal Order–Through the Looking Glass' 37 *Harvard International Law Journal* (1996) 411

Weiler, Joseph H.H., *The Constitution for Europe: 'Do the New Clothes Have an Emperor' and other Essays on European Integration* (Cambridge: Cambridge University Press, 1999)

Weiler, Joseph H.H., 'In Defence of the *Status Quo*: Europe's Constitutional *Sonderweg*' in J.H.H. Weiler and Marlene Wind (eds), *European Constitutionalism Beyond the State* (Cambridge: Cambridge University Press, 2003) 7

Weiler, Joseph H.H., 'Deciphering the Political and Legal DNA of European Integration: An Exploratory Essay' in Julie Dickson and Pavlos Eleftheriadis (eds), *Philosophical Foundations of European Union Law* (Oxford: Oxford University Press, 2012) 137

Weinrib, Ernest J., *Corrective Justice* (Oxford: Oxford University Press, 2012)

Wesseland Ramses A., and Blockmans Steven (eds), *Between Autonomy and Dependence: The EU Legal Order Under The Influence of International Organisations* (The Hague: T.M.C. Asser Press/Springer, 2013)

Williams, Andrew, *The Ethos of Europe: Values, Law and Justice in the EU* (Cambridge: Cambridge University Press, 2010)

Winter, J. A., 'Direct Applicability and Direct Effect: Two Distinct and Different Concepts in Community Law' 9 *CMLRev* (1972) 425

Wyatt, Derrick, 'New Legal Order, or Old?' 7 *European Law Review* (1982) 147

Zuckerman, Adrian, *Zuckerman on Civil Procedure: Principles of Practice*, 3rd edn (London: Sweet & Maxwell, 2013)

Index

Note: *For the benefit of digital users, indexed terms that span two pages (e.g., 52–53) may, on occasion, appear on only one of those pages.*